LOUIS AND VICTORIA

RICHARD HOUGH

Louis & Victoria

THE FIRST MOUNTBATTENS

HUTCHINSON OF LONDON

Hutchinson & Co (Publishers) Ltd
3 Fitzroy Square, London W1

London Melbourne Sydney Auckland
Wellington Johannesburg Cape Town
and agencies throughout the world

First published 1974
© Richard Hough 1974

Set in Monotype Baskerville

Printed and bound in Great Britain by
R. J. Acford Ltd., Industrial Estate, Chichester, Sussex

ISBN 0 09 121160 3

Acknowledgements

I WISH to acknowledge the gracious permission of the Queen for unhindered access to the Royal Archives at Windsor Castle. Her Majesty also found time to talk to me about her memories of Prince Philip's grandmother, Victoria, Dowager Marchioness of Milford Haven, Prince Philip's mother, Princess Andrew of Greece, and other of her relations, and to answer my questions. Her contribution was of special value in forming a picture of Victoria's last years and I am most grateful.

In addition I wish to acknowledge gratefully the contribution of Prince Philip, Duke of Edinburgh, for his colourful recollections of his grandmother and his own mother, and for allowing me to quote from some of the letters his grandmother wrote to His Royal Highness when he was a boy and young man.

Queen Elizabeth the Queen Mother graciously submitted to my prolonged questioning, and for this privilege I am very grateful to Her Majesty.

The late King of Sweden, Gustaf VI Adolf, was kind enough to talk of his wife, Louise Mountbatten, Queen of Sweden, and of his family.

Princess Alice, Countess of Athlone, and the last of Queen Victoria's grandchildren, freely offered me the riches of Her Royal Highness's marvellous memory which extends back to the time when monarchs long since dead were children or young men.

I am most grateful for the hospitality of Princess Margaret of Hesse and the Rhine, and for her recollections of Victoria Milford Haven and other Hessians, and for making available to me certain papers in the Darmstadt Archives.

Prince Philip's sisters, and Victoria Milford Haven's granddaughters, Princess Margarita of Hohenlohe-Langenburg and Princess George of Hanover, very kindly offered me their vivid recollections of a number of people who figure in this book.

v

Lord Mountbatten's daughters Lady Brabourne and Lady Pamela Hicks remember their grandmother mainly through the perceptive eyes of intelligent children, and the contribution of their recollections was especially fresh and alive. I am most grateful to them both.

It is difficult to know what to write of the contribution of Admiral of the Fleet Lord Mountbatten of Burma. The importance of his role has really been incalculable. First he granted me complete access to the Broadlands Archives, a privilege enjoyed by no other historian or biographer. Then, while I experienced total lack of interference, I also had the immense benefit of unlimited time with him and of introductions to others inside and outside his family.

The writing of this book demanded an intimate knowledge of two people, of 19th and 20th century naval history, and an understanding of the royal families of Europe and their genealogy. It was therefore an extraordinary experience for a writer to have, freely available for consultation and embodied in one person, a man who is the last surviving child of Louis and Victoria, a Naval Officer who became First Sea Lord after being Supreme Allied Commander and Viceroy of India and thus the best known figure the Navy has produced since Nelson, *and* the President of the Society of Genealogists!

This book could not have been written without him. When I first discussed it with him I was somewhat anxious about his health. It was with immense relief and satisfaction that I found him looking younger and fitter as my work progressed, and by the time I had finished there appeared every likelihood that he would comfortably outlive me!

The most encouraging and gratifying aspect of working on this book has been the kindness, frankness and trust in me which all the family have shown throughout.

Lord Mountbatten's Archivist, Mrs Mollie Travis, and his personal secretary, John Barratt, have been patient and helpful during all the time I have spent at Broadlands.

A number of Naval Officers, including Vice-Admiral H. T. Baillie-Grohman, Captain Andrew Yates, Commander Harry Pursey, Rear-Admiral Frank Elliott and the Late Commander David Joel, were generous in their time and contribution and I am very grateful to them.

Professor Arthur J. Marder of the University of California, Irvine, found the time both on his own campus and in London for long and valuable discussions on the work of Prince Louis as a Naval Officer.

Acknowledgements

Others who were generous with their advice and knowledge include Commander William Willett, Lieutenant-Commander P. K. Kemp and Ruddock Mackay, Senior Lecturer in Modern History at the University of St Andrews.

Among those who were especially helpful in my documentary research were Robert Mackworth-Young, Librarian at Windsor Castle, and the Registrar and Assistant Registrar, Miss Jane Langton, and Miss Elizabeth Cuthbert; D. S. Porter the Assistant Librarian in the Department of Western MSS at the Bodleian Library; Dr. Noble Frankland, Director of the Imperial War Museum, and his Head of the Department of Documents, Roderick Suddaby; and A. W. H. Pearsall, the Custodian of Documents at the National Maritime Museum.

List of Illustrations

Queen Victoria's funeral procession in Windsor.
Victoria with her infant son ' Dickie '.
' Dickie ' with his fancy animals and his elder brother ' Georgie '.
Family group, 1903.
Prince Louis with his sons in 1906.
' Dickie ' Battenberg with his nieces.
Prince Louis at Toronto City Hall, 1905.
Prince Louis landing at Annapolis U.S. Naval Academy, 1905.
Portrait of Princess Alice by De Laszlo.
The Russian Grand Duchesses Marie, Olga, Anastasia and Tatiana
    with ' Dickie ' Battenberg.
A day ashore on the Baltic coast in 1909.
The Emperor and Empress of Russia on board the Imperial Yacht.
Princess Victoria with her young widowed sister ' Ella '.
The Russian Imperial Yacht steams through Kiel Canal in 1909.
The Russian children.
Tha haemophilic Tsarevitch Alexei with his sailor, Dirivinko.
The present Lord Mountbatten as a Naval Cadet.
Prince Philip's parents, Prince and Princess Andrew of Greece, 1912.
Prince Louis as First Sea Lord, with Winston Churchill, 1913. [*Hulton
    Picture Library*]
Louis and Victoria in 1919 at Kent House.
The Greek family in 1922.
Lord Louis Mountbatten marries the Hon. Edwina Ashley, 1922.
    [*Hulton Picture Library*]
Victoria, Dowager Marchioness of Milford Haven.
Prince Philip at Gordonstoun School. [*Black Star*]
Prince Philip with his fiancée, Princess Elizabeth, 1947. [*Hulton
    Picture Library*]

Genealogical Note

(Genealogical tables appear on pages xx and xxi, and as endpapers)

THE subtitle of this book requires an explanation. In 1884 Prince Louis of Battenberg married his first cousin, once removed, Victoria, the eldest daughter of the Grand Duke Louis of Hesse and the Grand Duchess, Alice, Queen Victoria's second daughter.

In 1917 when foreign names were considered unsuitable and the British royal family took the name of Windsor for their House and family, on King George V's decision British royalty with names such as Teck and Battenberg were asked to take names with a more Anglo-Saxon ring.

Prince Louis renounced the name Battenberg and his title, took the name Mountbatten and was granted the title Marquess of Milford Haven. At the same time Victoria voluntarily renounced her royal title.

Thus Louis and Victoria became 'the first Mountbattens'.

It is also genealogically relevant, although the events are much more recent, that at the suggestion of the Home Secretary and on his naturalization in 1947, Prince Philip took the new English name of his mother's English family, Mountbatten. (He was already, as it turned out, a British subject under an Act of 1704, but no one at the time realized that!)

On marriage the present Queen became Elizabeth Mountbatten. For the first two months of her reign she ruled as a Mountbatten and not as a Windsor, and Prince Charles and Princess Anne also had the surname Mountbatten.

Thus the Family of Mountbatten ruled Britain for two months.

Then in April 1952 the Queen announced by order in council that she had taken Windsor as the name of her house and family for herself and her children.

In 1960 the Queen decided on a compromise solution and Prince Charles and Princess Anne and the Queen's yet-to-be-born children were given the family surname Mountbatten-Windsor of the House of Windsor.

But the legal position was so ambiguous that the Queen's wishes were not finally clarified until Princess Anne married on 14 November 1973. In the marriage register she was described as Anne Mountbatten-Windsor, thus establishing the fact that this is also Prince Charles's surname.

Chronology

(excludes short periods on half-pay)

24 May 1854	Prince Louis (PL) born
5 April 1863	Princess Victoria of Hesse born
3 October 1868	PL joined British Navy, appointed *Victory*
15 January 1869	PL appointed *Ariadne*
9 June 1869	PL appointed *Royal Alfred*
2 October 1869	PL rated Midshipman
5 January 1874	PL appointed *Duke of Wellington*
7 April 1874	PL promoted Sub-Lieutenant
12 April 1874	PL appointed *Excellent*
22 July 1875	PL appointed *Serapis* (Prince of Wales's tour of India)
18 May 1876	PL promoted Lieutenant
19 May 1876	PL appointed *Sultan*
26 April 1878	PL appointed *Duke of Wellington*
8 May 1878	PL appointed *Agincourt*
25 April 1879	PL appointed *Osborne*
24 August 1880	PL appointed *Inconstant* (Flying Squadron)
17 November 1882	PL appointed *Duke of Wellington*
14 September 1883	PL appointed *Victoria and Albert*
30 April 1884	Victoria and Louis married
25 February 1885	Princess Alice born
30 August 1885	PL promoted Commander
1 September 1885	PL on half-pay
29 July 1887	PL appointed *Dreadnought*
13 July 1889	Princess Louise born
3 October 1889	PL appointed *Scout*, in command
30 December 1891	PL promoted Captain
21 July 1892	PL appointed *Andromache*
6 November 1892	Prince George born
23 November 1892	PL appointed Naval Adviser to Inspector General of Fortifications
16 October 1894	PL appointed *Cambrian*, in command

7 June 1897	PL appointed *Majestic*, in command
28 June 1899	PL appointed Assistant Director of Naval Intelligence
25 June 1900	Prince Louis (Earl Mountbatten of Burma) born
10 September 1901	PL appointed *Implacable*, in command.
September 1902	Commodore in command of 'X' Fleet Argostoli Manoeuvres
15 November 1902	PL appointed Director of Naval Intelligence
7 October 1903	Princess Alice married Prince Andrew of Greece
1 July 1904	PL promoted Rear-Admiral
1 February 1905	PL appointed Rear-Admiral commanding Second Cruiser Squadron, *Drake*
24 February 1907	PL appointed Acting Vice-Admiral Second-in-Command Mediterranean Station, *Venerable*
12 August 1907	Same appointment, *Prince of Wales*
30 June 1908	PL promoted Vice-Admiral
12 November 1908	PL appointed Commander-in-Chief Atlantic Fleet, *Prince of Wales*
24 March 1911	PL appointed Command 3rd and 4th Divisions, Home Fleet, based on Sheerness
6 December 1911	PL appointed Second Sea Lord
9 December 1912	PL appointed First Sea Lord
29 October 1914	PL resigns as First Sea Lord and is appointed a Privy Counsellor
1 January 1919	PL retired from the Royal Navy
10 June 1921	Prince Philip of Greece born (their grandson)
4 August 1921	PL promoted Admiral of the Fleet (retd.)
11 September 1921	PL died
18 July 1922	Lord Louis married Edwina Ashley
3 November 1923	Lady Louise married Crown Prince Gustaf Adolf of Sweden
14 February 1924	Lady Patricia Mountbatten born
21 April 1926	Princess Elizabeth (Queen Elizabeth II) born
19 April 1929	Lady Pamela Mountbatten born
8 April 1938	George Milford Haven (Second Marquess) died
26 October 1946	Lady Patricia married Lord Brabourne
8 October 1947	The Hon. Norton Knatchbull (Second Heir to the Mountbatten Earldom) born
20 November 1947	Prince Philip and Princess Elizabeth married
14 November 1948	Prince Charles (Heir to the British throne) born (their great grandson)
24 September 1950	Victoria (Dowager Marchioness of Milford Haven) died

Chief Characters

'AFFIE' see Alfred, Prince of Gt Britain and Ireland

ALBERT Victor, Prince of Gt Britain and Ireland ('Eddy' or 'Eddie') (1864–92) Duke of Clarence 1890

ALBERT, Prince of Gt Britain and Ireland ('Bertie') (1895–1952) Duke of York 1920. King George VI 1936

ALEXANDER, Prince of Battenberg ('Sandro') (1857–93). Prince of Bulgaria 1879. Count Hartenau 1889. Married Johanna Loisinger 1889

ALEXANDER, Prince of Hesse (1823–88) Father of Louis

ALEXANDRA, Princess of Denmark (1844–1925) ('Alix' or 'Alex'). Married Albert Edward, Prince of Wales 1863

ALFRED, Prince of Gt Britain and Ireland (1844–1900) ('Affie') Duke of Edinburgh 1866. Married Marie Alexandrovna, Grand Duchess of Russia 1874. Duke of Saxe-Coburg-Gotha 1893

ALICE, Princess of Albany, Countess of Athlone (1883–   ). Married Alexander, Prince of Teck ('Alge') 1904, who in 1917 took surname Cambridge and was created Earl of Athlone

ALICE, Princess of Battenberg (1885–1969) Daughter of Louis and Victoria. Married Andrew, Prince of Greece and Denmark 1903

ALICE, Princess of Gt Britain and Ireland (1843–78) Mother of Victoria. Married Ludwig, Prince of Hesse 1862 who became Grand Duke of Hesse 1877

'ALICKY' see Alix, Princess of Hesse

'ALIX' or 'ALEX' see Alexandra, Princess of Denmark

ALIX, Princess of Hesse (1872–1918) ('Alicky'). Sister to Victoria. Married Nicholas II Emperor of Russia 1894

'ANDREA' see Andrew, Prince of Greece and Denmark

ANDREW, Prince of Greece and Denmark ('Andrea') (1882–1944). Married Alice, Princess of Battenberg 1903

ASHLEY, Hon. Edwina (1901–60). Married Lord Louis Mountbatten 1922

BEATRICE, Princess of Gt Britain and Ireland (1857–1944). Married Prince Henry of Battenberg 1885

'BERTIE' see (Albert) Edward, Prince of Wales

'DAVID' see Edward, Prince of Wales 1911

'DICKIE' see Louis, Prince of Battenberg

'DUCKY' see Victoria Melita, Princess of Edinburgh

'EDDIE' or 'EDDY' see Albert Victor, Prince of Gt Britain and Ireland

(ALBERT) EDWARD, Prince of Wales ('Bertie') (1841–1910) Uncle of Victoria. Married Alexandra, Princess of Denmark 1863. King Edward VII 1901

EDWARD, Prince of Gt Britain and Ireland ('David') (1894–1972). Prince of Wales 1911. King Edward VIII 1936. Abdicated and Duke of Windsor 1936. Married Wallis Warfield Simpson 1937

ELEONORE, Princess of Solms-Hohensölms-Lich (1871–1937) ('Onor'). Married Ernst-Ludwig, Grand Duke of Hesse 1905

ELIZABETH, Princess of Hesse (1864–1918) ('Ella') Sister of Victoria. Married Sergius, Grand Duke of Russia 1884

'ELLA' see Elizabeth, Princess of Hesse

'ERNIE' see Ernst-Ludwig, Prince of Hesse

ERNST-LUDWIG, Prince of Hesse ('Ernie') (1868–1937) Younger brother of Victoria. Grand Duke of Hesse 1892. Married Victoria Melita, daughter of Alfred, 1894. Divorced 1901. Married (2) Eleonore, Princess of Solms-Hohensölms-Lich

FRANCIS JOSEPH, Prince of Battenberg ('Franzjos') (1861–1924) Younger brother of Louis. Married Anna, Princess of Montenegro 1897

'FRANZJOS' see Francis Joseph, Prince of Battenberg

FREDERICK, Prince of Hesse (1870–73) ('Frittie') Brother of Victoria

FREDERICK, Crown Prince of Prussia ('Fritz') (1831–88). Married Victoria, Princess Royal of Gt Britain and Ireland 1858. German Emperor 1888

'FRITTIE' see Frederick, Prince of Hesse

'FRITZ' see Frederick, Crown Prince of Prussia

GEORGE, Prince of Battenberg ('Georgie') (1892–1938) Son of Louis and Victoria. Married Nada, Countess de Torby, daughter of Grand Duke Michael of Russia 1916. Marquess of Milford Haven 1921

GEORGE, Prince of Gt Britain and Ireland ('Georgie') (1865–1936) Cousin of Victoria. Duke of York 1892. Married Mary, Princess of Teck 1893. Prince of Wales 1901. King George V 1910

'GEORGIE' see (1) George, Prince of Battenberg; (2) George, Prince of Gt Britain and Ireland

GUSTAFUS Adolf, Prince of Sweden (1882–1973). Married Margaret, Princess of Connaught 1905. Crown Prince of Sweden 1907. Married (2) Lady Louise Mountbatten 1923. King Gustafus VI Adolf 1950

HENRY, Prince of Battenberg ('Liko') (1858–96) Younger brother of Louis. Married Beatrice, Princess of Gt Britain and Ireland 1885

HENRY, Prince of Prussia (1862–1929). Married Irène, Princess of Hesse 1888

IRÈNE, Princess of Hesse (1866–1953) Sister of Victoria. Married Henry, Prince of Prussia 1888

JULIE, Countess of Hauke (1825–95) Mother of Louis. Married Prince Alexander of Hesse 1851. Countess of Battenberg 1851. Princess of Battenberg 1858

LEOPOLD, Prince of Gt Britain and Ireland (1853–84) Duke of Albany 1881. Married Helen, Princess of Waldeck 1882

'LIKO' see Henry, Prince of Battenberg

LOUIS, Prince of Battenberg ('Dickie') (1900–   ) Son of Louis and Victoria. Lord Louis Mountbatten 1917. Married Hon. Edwina Ashley 1922. Earl Mountbatten of Burma 1947. Viceroy and Governor-General of India 1947, 1st Sea Lord 1955.

LOUIS, Prince of Hesse ('Lu') (1908–1960) nephew of Victoria. Married Hon. Margaret Geddes 1937

LOUISE, Princess of Battenberg (1889–1965) Daughter of Louis and Victoria. Lady Louise Mountbatten 1917. Married Gustafus Adolf Crown Prince of Sweden 1923. Queen of Sweden 1950

'LU' see Louis, Prince of Hesse

LUDWIG, Prince of Hesse (1837–92) Father of Victoria. Married Alice, Princess of Gt Britain and Ireland 1862. Grand Duke Ludwig IV of Hesse 1877

MARIE, Princess of Battenberg (1852–1923) Elder sister of Louis. Married Gustaf, Count of Erbach-Schönberg 1871

MARIE, Princess of Hesse ('May') (1874–78) Sister of Victoria

MARIE, Princess of Hesse (1824–80) Tsarevna of Russia 1841 on marriage to Tsarevitch Alexander. Empress of Russia 1855

MARIE Alexandrovna, Grand Duchess of Russia (1853–1920). Married Alfred, Prince of Gt Britain and Ireland, Duke of Edinburgh 1874

'MAY' see Marie, Princess of Hesse

MOUNTBATTEN, Lady Patricia (1924–   ) Granddaughter of Victoria. Married Lord Brabourne 1946

NICHOLAS I, Emperor of Russia (1796–1855)

NICHOLAS, Tsarevitch of Russia ('Nicky') (1868–1918) Emperor of Russia 1894. Married Alix, Princess of Hesse 1894

'NICKY' see Nicholas, Tsarevitch of Russia

'ONOR' see Eleonore, Princess of Solms-Hohensölms-Lich

PHILIP, Prince of Greece and Denmark (1921–   ) Grandson of Louis and Victoria. Duke of Edinburgh 1947. Married Princess Elizabeth, Heir Presumptive to the British throne 1947

'SANDRO' see Prince Alexander of Battenberg

SERGIUS ('Serge'), Grand Duke of Russia (1857–1905). Married Princess Elizabeth of Hesse 1884

'VICKY' see Victoria, Princess Royal of Gt Britain and Ireland

VICTORIA, Princess Royal of Gt Britain and Ireland ('Vicky') (1840–1901). Married Frederick, Crown Prince of Prussia 1858. Empress Frederick 1888

VICTORIA MELITA, Princess of Edinburgh ('Ducky') (1876–1936). Married Ernst-Ludwig, Grand Duke of Hesse 1892. Divorced 1901. Married (2) Kyril Vladimirovitch, Grand Duke of Russia

WILHELM, Crown Prince of Prussia ('Willie' or 'Willy') (1859–1941). Married Augusta Victoria, Princess of Schleswig-Holstein 1881. German Emperor 1888. Abdicated 1918. Married (2) Hermine, Princess of Reuss

'WILLY' see Wilhelm, Crown Prince of Prussia

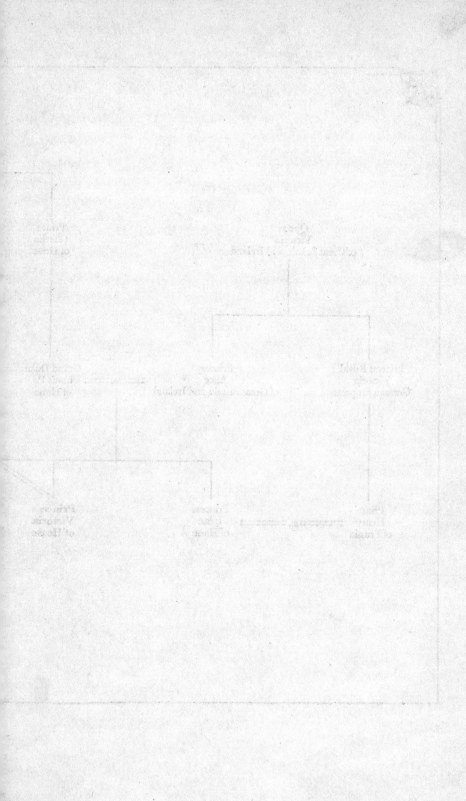

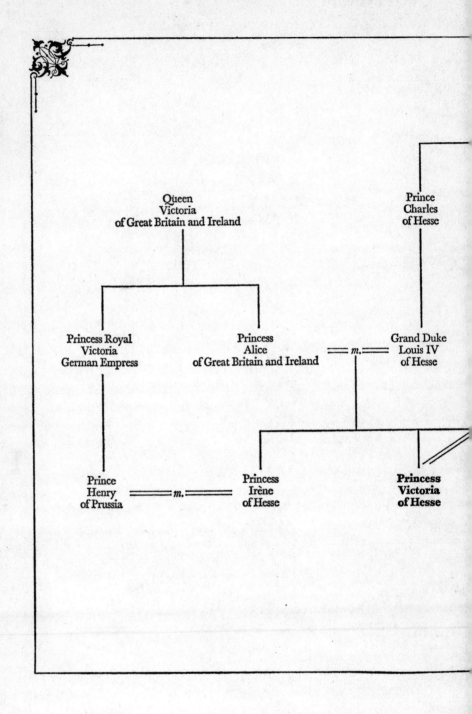

Queen
Victoria
of Great Britain and Ireland

Prince
Charles
of Hesse

Princess Royal
Victoria
German Empress

Princess
Alice
of Great Britain and Ireland

= *m.* =

Grand Duke
Louis IV
of Hesse

Prince
Henry
of Prussia

= *m.* =

Princess
Irène
of Hesse

**Princess
Victoria
of Hesse**

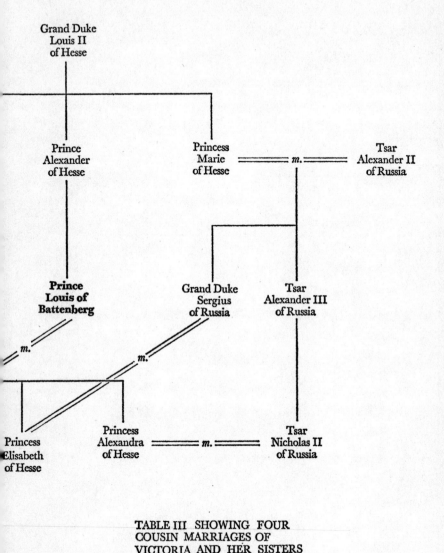

Grand Duke
Louis II
of Hesse

Prince
Alexander
of Hesse

Princess
Marie ══════ m. ══════ Tsar
of Hesse   Alexander II
                                      of Russia

Prince
Louis of
Battenberg

Grand Duke
Sergius
of Russia

Tsar
Alexander III
of Russia

m.

m.

Princess
Elisabeth
of Hesse

Princess
Alexandra ══════ m. ══════ Tsar
of Hesse   Nicholas II
                                      of Russia

TABLE III SHOWING FOUR
COUSIN MARRIAGES OF
VICTORIA AND HER SISTERS

Note: Only some children shown
and not in order of ages.

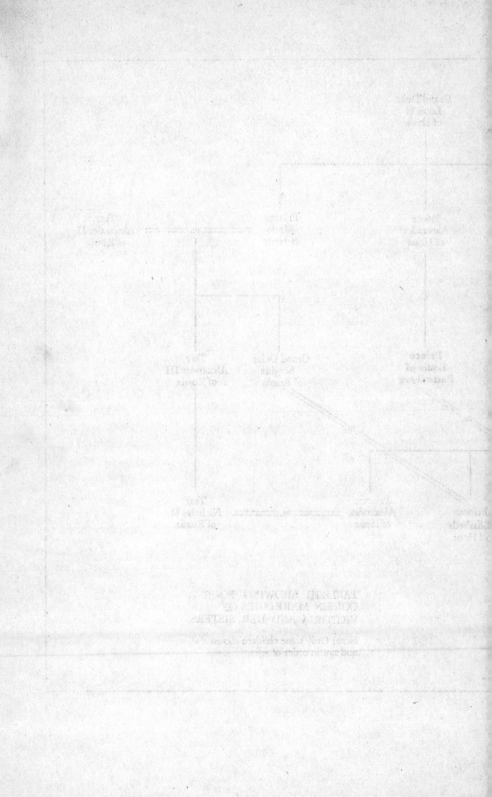

I

'It is worth a great deal to a soldier to have
looked death in the face so often . . .'

PRINCE ALEXANDER OF HESSE

PRINCE ALEXANDER of Hesse, Prince Louis of Battenberg's father,
enjoyed a fiery youth, living for love and combat. These in turn
brought him trouble and pain, and finally fulfilment in an intrepid
and passionate marriage. It was a marvellously romantic inaugura-
tion of an ancestral line which has witnessed the end of most of the
great dynasties, yet has preserved to this day its own strength and
influence under another name.

The Hessians go back into that dark world of ancestral doubt, but
certainly to Henry I of Hesse in the thirteenth century, and through
the Dukes of Brabant and Lorraine another five hundred years to
Aubris, to Ydulfs and Brunulfs. More than 1,100 years ago Count
Giselbert abducted the daughter of the Emperor Lothair to Aqui-
taine, and married her. Her great-grandfather was Charlemagne.

Our Prince Alexander (1823–88) was in the thirtieth generation of
father to son descent from Giselbert. So for well over a thousand
years the Hessians have provided Europe with kings and queens,
princes and princesses, grand dukes and grand duchesses; and, moreover, of an ever enriching quality. From the late eighteenth century
Hesse gave to the Romanoffs several tsarinas, to the Danish, Spanish,
Greek and Russian royal families innumerable injections of their
good blood. Two of Queen Victoria's daughters married Hessian
princes. Greece and Denmark with Hesse gave a consort to Queen
Elizabeth II, and the blood of the British royal family is richer in
Hessian than any other strain.

The Grand Duchy of Hesse has never been especially powerful, nor rich, nor strategically important. There is little grandeur in its landscape, even the Rhine is not at its best here, though the wine is. But, viewed regally, the Grand Duchy is situated in a geographically advantageous position with direct lines of communication with the royal seats of Europe.

For centuries the horses, and the carriages, and later the trains, carried away the dynasty-strengthening young brides and grooms, the future princesses and queens, the princes and kings, from Hessian palaces. Royal demand for the fine figures and the outstanding brains of the Hessians has been insatiable. The Grand Dukes and Grand Duchesses of Hesse and the Rhine and later the Princes and Princesses of Battenberg, have been punctilious in meeting these demands.

Prince Alexander was the third son of Grand Duke Louis II, and Wilhelmina, born Princess of Baden. His parents were cousins, and both were exceptionally well endowed with good looks and intelligence, and both had been brought up to be cultivated and progressive in their beliefs. (Progressive liberalism is one of the survival qualities of the Hessians.) Here, once again for the Hessians, was a match made in heaven. Their first child, Louis, was ravishingly handsome and grew to be a giant of 6 feet 10 inches – as magnificent a prince as one could ever hope to see enthroned. Then there was Charles, and fourteen years later, in 1823, Alexander.

Alexander grew to be as handsome and muscular as his brothers, who had married while he was still a boy. His constant companion was his sister Marie, a lovely child with her mother's soft complexion, who had been born only thirteen months after him. They shared the enclosed and rarefied life of the Darmstadt court at palaces, castles, *schlosses*, *fürstenlagers* and shooting lodges throughout the Grand Duchy.

The cult of militarism and enlightened authoritarianism toughened the boy's fibre. It began early in his life. He was given his first military appointment on the day of his christening to ensure that the lust for battle would be strongly planted in his little heart. His godfather, the future Tsar and Emperor Nicholas I of All the Russias, appointed him a lieutenant in the Imperial Russian Army. His second appointment was made in 1833 when he had reached the mature age of ten, as second lieutenant of the Life Company of the 1st Hessian Infantry.

Hessian ties with the Romanoffs were especially close. Wilhelmina's sister Elizabeth had married Tsar Alexander I, who died a year after Alexander's sister Marie was born. As the Dowager Tsarina, with a strong penchant for match-making, Elizabeth kept her eyes on Marie, seeing her always as a future Tsarina. Wilhelmina died of consumption before the match could be concluded. At her funeral Elizabeth mentioned her ambition to the widowed Grand Duke, and three years later the Tsarevitch came to stay at Darmstadt.

Princess Marie was 15, the Tsarevitch 20, at the time of this informal visit in April 1840. It was more successful than the Dowager Tsarina could have hoped for. The delicate fair-haired artlessly charming Princess succumbed to the masculine attractions of the tall, virile Tsarevitch. It was a real love match.

Eight days after his arrival an official announcement of their betrothal was issued at Darmstadt. Before returning to St Petersburg, the Tsarevitch presented his Princess with a priceless engagement diamond bracelet. Both were in tears when the parting took place.

There was nothing leisurely about the pace of events now. The Tsarevitch left with a portrait of his future bride painted by her brother, and in turn left with Alexander an invitation to accompany his sister to the court at St Petersburg in case she was at first lonely and homesick.

Prince Alexander thought this a splendid idea. He got on well with the Tsarevitch – they enjoyed one another's company and used to let off steam by wrestling together. Moreover, the Tsar would confer upon him a captain's commission in the Chevalier Gardes, and for a Hessian this was a sufficient lure by itself.

In accordance with dynastic protocol, the Emperor of All the Russias and the Tsarina themselves accompanied their son to Darmstadt to collect the Princess. The road between the two courts was well worn by betrothal missions, and so it continued to be for another seventy years.

Life at the court of Tsar Nicholas I in the 1840s was glittering, elaborate, corrupt, self-indulgent and wearisomely tedious. Ritual and protocol alternated with intrigue and gossip. For hot-blooded young princes, the round of balls and banquets, receptions and investitures, picnics and parties, was made tolerable by the military activities that from time to time broke this routine.

The tone was set by the Tsar. Militarism was Nicholas's whole life – the weapons, the exercises, the multitudinous uniforms and regiments, the mystique of military history, life and tradition, the ordering of great bodies of men, mounted or on foot, through their

3

evolutions, all culminating in the glory and the heady sound of the clash of arms. The beat of drums and boots was the very beat of life to this soldierly Tsar. Fortunately, so vast, multi-racial and restless was his empire that he could be sure of finding trouble somewhere most of the time. Later he bit off more than he could chew when he took on Turkey, France and Britain at the same time. But he loved every minute of the Crimean War.

Alexander revelled in his new and exciting military life. In 1845 there was a particularly nasty war going on down in the Caucasus. Some mountain tribes, led by the Muslim zealot Shamyl, refused to be tamed and fought with fanatical enthusiasm against the large forces sent to suppress them. On both sides if prisoners were taken it was only for the purpose of subjecting them to torture before despatching them. Alexander volunteered for this campaign.

For a while the Army Alexander had joined was in retreat and in danger of annihilation. 'It is an uncomfortable feeling,' wrote Alexander in his diary at one critical moment, 'and this has been the longest day of my life. If relief does not come soon, the whole detachment will be wiped out. The enemy grows ever more numerous, and I am writing under shellfire.'[1]

In accordance with Hessian tradition, Alexander performed many valiant deeds. He led charges with sword and pistol, saw men at his side blown to pieces. This was the real thing, remote from the ostentatious parade ground evolutions so beloved of the Tsar. When they finally had the tribes on the run and casting away their arms and possessions for greater speed, it was Alexander's good fortune to pick up a copy of the Koran. It turned out to belong to Shamyl himself. Today it is in the possession of his grandson, Lord Mountbatten.

With the worst of the danger past, Alexander wrote to his sister that he had never expected to see her again. 'It is worth a great deal to a soldier to have looked death in the face so often. You feel that you have more right to wear the uniform.' His satisfaction was complete when the Tsar appointed him Colonel-in-Chief of the Borissoglebosky 17th Lancers, now renamed in his honour 'Prince Alexander of Hesse's Lancers', and presented him with the highest honour for gallantry, the Cross of St George. Both the medal and his war record were later to stand him in good stead.

It is clear that Alexander was a handful at court. At the age of 23 he began a period of extravagance and dissipation. There was a lot of drinking, and a lot of womanizing and gambling in his young life. His influence on the young A.D.C.s gave the Tsar and Tsarina, and even his sister and brother-in-law, much worry. He was sent off to Darmstadt to cool off. When he returned he was given such a serious and fierce lecture that he was forced to take himself in hand. At the beginning of 1848 he set his heart on one woman, instead of half a dozen, and reduced his gambling and drinking.

This woman, who was to be innocently and indirectly responsible for Alexander's downfall in Russia, and the creation of the Battenberg line, was Countess Sophie Shuvaloff. She responded warmly to Alexander's advances and fell head over heels in love with him. Her shrewd and observant mother, however, believed that this was a one-sided affair, and who could blame her on Alexander's past record? She determined to put an end to it before her daughter's heart was broken.

At a ball in early January 1848, the Countess's mother sent a message between dances to her daughter's suitor. The messenger was one of Marie's ladies-in-waiting, Countess Julie of Hauke. And so it came about that the first words spoken to Alexander by his future wife were stern words of warning: if the Prince danced the next mazurka with the Countess Sophie, she would be taken home by her mother. Alexander responded saucily by taking Julie in his arms and sweeping her on to the floor instead when the music began.

Julie Hauke's love grew more quickly and abundantly than Alexander's. For a time he was scarcely aware of her existence, except as someone who was sometimes seen about his sister's suite. Then, when Sophie and Alexander determined to continue their affair secretly in the teeth of her parents' disapproval, Julie was used as a go-between, taking passionate love letters from one to the other and arranging secret assignations.

Inevitably, word of this clandestine affair reached the ears of her parents. Now it was to be temporary banishment for her, the last resort of harassed parents. But before Sophie was sent away, Alexander was asked by his sister to make clear to his mistress that all was over between them in the hope that she would not pine too much for him in her absence.

Alexander did not doubt that this suggestion came from the Tsar himself and he did as he was told. 'It was the saddest evening of my life,' he wrote in his diary after finally breaking with the Countess. But the Tsar also made it clear that he would like Alexander to settle down now, and that his choice of wife should be the Grand Duchess Catherine Michailovna, the Tsar's niece.

Alexander did not respond gladly to this suggestion. In fact a profound change of outlook was taking place in him – as changes of more dramatic import were occurring all over Europe. After the whirlwind years of love-making and fighting – non-stop now for almost a decade – this Hessian Prince was at last beginning to take life more seriously. (Most Hessians were the same: their wild oats period was usually long and intense.)

European politics hastened if they did not cause this sobering up of Alexander, for the year was 1848, when a new revolution burst over France and the royal family were driven out, their palaces plundered; when Metternich was overthrown in Vienna; when rioting broke out in Berlin; and even in Darmstadt the progressives temporarily seized power. It seemed that soon all Europe would be in flames.

'What I wish with all my heart,' exclaimed the autocratic but alarmed Tsar Nicholas I, 'is that we could build a real Chinese Wall against the rest of Europe.'

With this growing awareness of a troubled and dangerous world beyond the Russian frontiers, Alexander's mood matched the more serious temperament of the little Countess who had fallen so ardently in love with him. Now he had begun to take notice of her. She was not pretentiously beautiful, not at all like the flashy 'French' ladies of the court, who could be picked up two at a time. Her face was intriguing and intelligent rather than beautiful, with a long strong straight nose – the 'Mountbatten nose' of today. She was 5 feet 2 inches tall, with dark hair and clever, kindly, brown eyes. 'Julie Hauke is lovely,' wrote Alexander in his diary, which also revealed that he was falling in love. They began to exchange passionate love letters and to meet in secret – it had to be in secret for if word ever reached the Tsar that his godson, the future Tsarina's brother, was consorting with Marie's lady-in-waiting, Nicholas's rage would be fearful indeed.

For a time all went well. Then the couple were unlucky. The Tsar himself, missing a turn somewhere in the rabbit warren of the Winter Palace, surprised the lovers together. It was said that his fury did not abate for several days. They were ordered never to see one another again. Julie disappeared quietly to nurse her broken heart. Alexander, furious and humiliated, asked for a long leave of absence from his military duties. The Tsar granted it, readily but testily. Again Prince Alexander rode off on the long journey back to his native Hesse.

6

Julie Hauke was of Polish birth and of mixed German, French and Hungarian stock. About her there always hung the aura of the dark tragedy of Poland, a nation which has for so long suffered intermittent bloody dismemberment. Many of her ancestors had met violent ends, by furtive assassination or sword or bullet on the battlefield. Julie's German blood came through her father and it was strongly tinged with military endeavour. Maurice Hauke fought for and against Poland, served in Napoleon's *Grande Armée* in Austria, Italy, Germany and in the Peninsular War, switched sides again to fight for Russia and did such good service for Tsar Nicholas that he was granted the title of Count and appointed Minister of War in the Warsaw puppet government after Russia had reconquered that unfortunate country.

In 1830 there occurred a ferocious patriotic uprising. It was led by revolutionary army cadets, and their first targets were the Governor-General, Tsar Nicholas's brother the Grand Duke Constantine, and the Minister of War. Hauke died while successfully defending the life of the Grand Duke. He was cut to pieces by sabres before the horrified eyes of his wife and children. She died of shock – or a broken heart – shortly after the assassination of her husband.

In recognition of their father's loyal service, Tsar Nicholas had the three children brought to St Petersburg and made his wards. Julie, as the youngest (she was only five when she was orphaned) was instructed in the proper Russian aristocratic manner, and when she was old enough received her appointment as Tsarevna Marie's lady-in-waiting.

For Alexander the summer of 1850 revealed a new and wonderful world that was to revolutionize his own life amidst a world of revolutions. Darmstadt did not delay him for long. His father had died and his oldest brother, now the huge Grand Duke Louis III, had grown dull and eccentric and Alexander left Darmstadt for Paris and then for London.

The first experiences of these liberal and cultivated cities made a deep impression on him. He had not believed that there could ever be such freedom of thought and expression. 'It is utterly amazing,' he wrote to his sister from London after a visit to *The Times* offices and machine rooms, 'how the journalists can write quite freely about the Royal Family, even about the private lives of Queen Victoria and her Consort in a newspaper which is being read by everybody.'

Alexander saw much of English life and his admiration for all that he learned was boundless. The visit was to have an important influence on his marriage and on his own children's lives.

Alexander returned to St Petersburg early in 1851, his mind broadened, his will strengthened. What was there here for a professional soldier discredited in the country of his adoption, deeply in love with a woman beneath his social station? The future was all black, with the shining golden exception of his love for the little Countess, and his determination to make her his own. He confided in her his plan to escape from the restrictive stuffiness of the Russian court – perhaps to the freedom of England. Queen Victoria would surely grant him a commission in her army? 'Take me with you – please,' begged Julie, Alexander recorded in his diary.

Alexander confided in his sister and brother-in-law his plan to elope with little Julie. Neither took him very seriously, perhaps because they had heard this wild talk before.

Alexander's social status sank lower as it became evident that he was going to commit the supreme indiscretion of becoming engaged formally to Julie. Today it is hard to conceive the enormity of the offence of a prince of royal blood marrying a commoner – and poor Julie was little better than that. It was regarded by the closely-linked royal families of Europe as an act not just of disloyalty but of sedition. It threatened the whole delicately balanced and mutually inter-dependent dynastic structure built up over the centuries with the family-tree-like complexity of tall scaffolding.

It was not only the act itself; it was the precedent it set as a dangerous example to the young princesses and princes from Tsarkoe Selo to the Palazzo Reale, from Balmoral to Darmstadt, who would be more than ever inclined now to follow their fancy rather than their stern course of duty.

Steadily the opposition to the match increased. Under pressure from the Tsar, the slothful Grand Duke of Hesse was driven to writing a letter of warning to his young brother. But the pressure of gallant duty was more powerful still. Alexander had promised himself to Julie, and Julie – in her joy and pride and excitement – had let this promise be known about the gossip-loving court. Both honour, and the deepest love he had ever known, were therefore at stake, and were driving him towards the inevitable confrontation with the Tsar. There was no escape from this meeting, for legal as well as protocol reasons, because Alexander had to make a request for the hand of His Majesty's charge.

For many uncomfortable and miserable weeks, the Tsar kept Alexander on tenterhooks. When he at last granted a formal audience and Alexander made his request, the consequence was all that he had feared it would be. The Emperor did not spare his protégé. After all that he, and the Russian court, had done for him, promoting him at the age of 20 to the rank of Major General, granting him countless privileges! No, it was impossible. Alexander bravely pressed his case. The Tsar responded by threatening to strip him of his military ranks and Russian decorations, and of course banishing him for ever from the Russian court. And what would he do then, a penurious soldier of fortune? No royal army in Europe would engage him after this . . .

Alexander bowed himself out of the Tsar's presence. It was the end. He could do no more. There were no good-byes. Silently and separately and secretly, the 28-year-old Prince and his 26-year-old fiancée left the Winter Palace at St. Petersburg and headed west.

Some reports say that they did not meet again until they reached Warsaw and continued their elopement together from that city. Others say that Alexander acquired a droshky outside the palace, and that they travelled together, wrapped in furs, across the snow-covered steppes, beneath a new moon. Whichever happens to be true, the romance and the daring of the occasion make the disparity unimportant, although in fact the moon was almost new on the night of 4 October when the couple made their escape. Perhaps the more romantic story is true.

No doubt the Tsar did not trouble to send his cavalry in pursuit, nor issue orders to hold the eloping couple at the frontier. No doubt in his anger he reasoned that they would pay the price, and that was an end to the matter.

It is 700 miles to Warsaw. But they scarcely paused there. By 27 October they were in Breslau, another 200 miles on, and there – without ceremony, without the presence or even the knowledge of their closest relatives – this tall, soldierly Prince of Hesse was married to the clever, determined and passionate 'poor little Polish orphan girl', as she was so often called behind her back at the Russian court. What she would be called in the future neither she nor her husband knew, though they could surmise. For the present she was without title or friends, even without roots or a home; and, for the present, no doubt, she did not care.

The enormity of what they had done was brought home to Alexander and Julie by slow, cruel stages. They learned first that the Tsar had carried out all his threats. Both of them had been banished from their country of adoption; Alexander had been discharged dishonourably from the army and been deprived of his rank and decorations. They were, in effect, *persona non grata* at every court in Europe.

The Grand Duke of Hesse refused to see them and stirred himself into an outburst of threats and recrimination. By marrying this commoner, he accused his young brother, he had brought the Hessian name into disrepute. He and his bride were a shame and an embarrassment. They were informed of a letter from Queen Victoria, who always disapproved of everything Russian anyway. It was couched in uncompromising terms of anger and dismay. So there was no question of applying for a commission in the British army. There were similar messages of outrage and commiseration from other courts, other relatives.

Within a few days of marriage they were without a home, without a job, and almost without any money. Nor could they know what Julie should call herself. The price of breaking Europe's dynastic laws was as heavy as that.

Wearily and crossly, the Grand Duke at length realized that he would have to do something about them. At least he had to find her a name for no one else but he could do that. Wily in the art of compromise, after a lot of discussion with the Grand Ducal First Minister and Chief of Protocol, a suitable name and rank were decided upon.

In the north of the Grand Duchy, on the River Eder, there was a large village called Battenberg – a pretty place of a few houses and many cottages, a narrow street, a grand ducal hunting lodge, and an impressive ruin of a castle strategically placed above the river – or so it was then. This castle was once the seat of a knightly family who had fought in the Crusades, and whose title was long since extinct. A Grand Ducal edict was all that was needed to revive the title. This was done forthwith. The marriage would be recognized – morganatically only of course – Alexander would retain his present title of His Royal Highness the Prince Alexander Ludwig Georg Emil of Hesse and by the Rhine, and Countess Julie of Hauke would be known as the Countess of Battenberg. Their children would be known only as counts or countesses, and they would have no right to the succession to the throne of Hesse in any circumstances.

For a short time the couple lived in a modest little hotel in Geneva, then they moved to a rented villa. On 18 July 1852 Julie gave birth to a girl. She was christened Marie after her Russian aunt. 'I have a daughter, given me as a birthday present,'[2] exclaimed Alexander joyously.

After a while the royal anger throughout Europe abated. Alexander's record of gallantry was remembered. It was also recalled that they were not the first couple to break the rules and cast shame upon their family name. What about the Emperor of Austria's uncle, Archduke Johann? He had gone off with the daughter of the local postmistress. At least Alexander had chosen a minor Countess.

And so it came about that in October 1853, Battenberg affairs were regularized with the appointment of the Prince as a brigade colonel in the Austrian army: it was demotion, but Alexander was thankful for anything. It was tactful, too. For the Emperor posted his new officer to the Styrian town of Graz, far from any society embarrassments in Vienna where the family would certainly have been ostracized.

The only other grand person in Graz was Archduke Johann, so the Prince and the Archduke became a pair of black sheep in the Austrian hills. Alexander enjoyed the company of the Archduke. Of his wife he noted in his diary: 'A very pleasant woman, but rather common.'

At this quiet and healthy town Julie gave birth to a second child on 24 May 1854, Queen Victoria's 35th birthday. This time it was a boy, and the parents were proud and overjoyed. He was christened Louis Alexander.

But these were troubled and confusing times for this infant's mother and father. Alexander was not popular with his fellow officers. This should have been no surprise to him. He was, after all, depriving a regular Austrian officer of a command, and no foreign favourite of the Emperor was likely to be warmly welcomed. Britain, France and Turkey were now at war with Russia, and Austria was under heavy pressure to join in the conflict against that other Empire which had so recently been Alexander's and Julie's adopted homeland and where they had met.

It was appropriate, if cruelly ironic, that the little Count Louis of Battenberg, who was to suffer from the storms of divided loyalties and of divided dynasties for all his life, should be born into such a sea of cross currents and threatening gales.

The first years of the Battenberg dynasty were turbulent and unpromising for the future. Alexander fought the good fight for Austria in the Empire's wars. His timely arrival with his division at the Battle of Solferino prevented the rout of the Austrian army. He was granted the highest awards for courage; and on the diplomatic front, after his brother-in-law became Tsar Alexander II, carried out delicate diplomatic negotiations between his two adopted Empires.

But as a foreigner holding high rank, the presence of Prince Alexander was increasingly resented by the Austrian military. Even after he was posted to Italy jealousy led to attacks in the newspapers. One incensed general published a serious military essay seeking to prove that Alexander was responsible for the defeat at the Battle of Solferino by arriving on the battlefield too late with his division, when in fact he was already widely known as 'the hero of Solferino'. It was, to these small-minded people, too much that Alexander should be the Emperor's favourite, a superb general carrying the highest decorations for valour two Empires could offer and a successful diplomat with the ear of Europe's elite.

By the autumn of 1861, Alexander had had enough of Austria. The personal attacks against him continued unabated, he was weary in mind and body, and above all weary of living without a settled home or roots. Just at this moment, the new Tsar Alexander II offered him a substantial pension. This became the deciding factor. Moreover, the climate had long since changed in Darmstadt and he would be welcomed back permanently in the Grand Duchy.

Alexander made up his mind at once, and with a face-saving medical document purporting to show that he suffered from an internal complaint, he obtained an audience with Emperor Francis Joseph to request his retirement. In May 1862 he and his family, with their *entourage* of nursemaids and servants and all their possessions, left for Darmstadt.

It was the second time in twelve years that Alexander and Julie had turned their back on an adopted land. But this parting was a great deal less painful, and much less hazardous, than that earlier moonlight dash across the steppes for the frontier. This time Alexander was a settled 39-year-old family man with a notable record behind him – whatever these gossipy, jealous Austrians might say.

The Battenberg family had grown to five. After Louis Julie had given birth to three more boys, Alexander in 1857, Henry a year later, and then in 1861, Francis Joseph, named after his godfather the Austrian Emperor. (To minimize the confusion caused by duplicated and even triplicated names among the royal families, nicknames were almost *de rigeur*. Alexander and Henry, born in Italy, had Italian nurses who called them Alessandro and Enrico. The first became Sandro, the second – R's being slow to come in the nursery – Liko, pronounced 'Leekoh'. More prosaically, Francis Joseph was called Franzjos.)

They came, these newly rehabilitated Battenbergs, to a palace Alexander had built in the centre of Darmstadt – the Alexander Palace no less – for winter residence, the season of balls and theatres, and to the castle of Heiligenberg, ten miles south of the Hessian capital, their summer place.

The family is complete. There will be no more children. After a turbulent decade, their future is assured and seemingly tranquil, at least for the time being. Domestic bliss, in mid-century peace and plenty, seems to lie ahead for them. Four years before, in 1858, the Grand Duke of Hesse, after one of Alexander's major diplomatic coups, had created Julie a Princess, to the grave displeasure of all those in society – especially Viennese society – who had so much enjoyed snubbing her; and her children are Princes instead of Counts.

Socially and financially secure, with two palaces and an appropriate quota of servants to meet the family's needs, little Julie Hauke, now Her Serene Highness the Princess of Battenberg, begins to enjoy the good life. She has filled out, in the fashionable style of a middle-aged woman after her years of childbearing; but even more evident is the strength and character in her face. Experience of a wicked and ruthless world has hardened her resolve; success has brought her new self-confidence. She shows little affection and softness towards her children, and is rarely with them. 'It was not her habit to be tender,' wrote Marie many years later, 'and I remember how we elder ones would sometimes comment upon this among ourselves.'[3]

But Julie has all the attributes of a successful dynastic co-founder. She is an enthusiastic intriguer and loves the to-ing and fro-ing of great people going about great affairs. She has witnessed plenty of this, and hopes to see more.

There are no surprises in Alexander to uncover. In middle years he is a typical Hessian. We have witnessed his courage, his determination to get what he wants, his fortitude in the face of grave and embarrassing difficulties, and the skill with which he contrives to resolve them. Now, in his fortieth year, he has kept his figure, his hair has receded, he wears full trimmed whiskers and moustache. His bearing is soldierly and princely.

13

Yet Alexander also possesses the Hessian interest in the arts. He enjoys the theatre and the ballet and opera; he reads widely; enjoys painting. Like his brother the Grand Duke (though it is all they have in common) he is a collector, especially of coins. He is affectionate towards his children and more sentimental with them than we would be today – but that is German, not Hessian. But he is also much stricter with them than we would dare to be today.

These children are being brought up properly as royalty, even though they are only serene highnesses, upright in their moral principles, firm but also kind and considerate towards servants and those less privileged than themselves, able to stand up to responsibilities when others might yield under their weight.

Heiligenberg was their favourite home, just as it was to be forever associated in the minds of every Battenberg with the warm and relaxed happiness of family summers, the comings and goings of cousins and nephews, the romance of balls and concerts far into the night. It stands proud on a mountain bluff above the village of Jugenheim and the flat farming land that flanks the Rhine. On clear days you can see far into France.

It was no more than a substantial farmhouse when Alexander's mother Wilhelmine bought it. She greatly enlarged it, but sensibly retained the old arrangement of a *Forder Haus* or 'front house' for adults, and across a courtyard a *Hinter Haus* quite separate for the children and their nursemaids. The Grand Duchess passed it on to her son, and it remained empty and unvisited for years while Alexander was away at the courts and wars of Europe. Then it was greatly enlarged, the two wings joined by domestic offices and a ballroom, stables befitting this *schloss* added. There were now two towers and accommodation, in regal style, for sixty and more people, a small palace really. It has to be, for at one time or another most of the crowned heads of Europe, and the princes and princesses, the grand dukes and duchesses, will come to stay here – and stay in style.

Prince Louis was eight years old when he and his family settled at last in their real homeland. He was a clever, kind, polite little boy, tall for his age, and good looking. He was a proper little prince, especially on formal occasions, which already in his life were frequent, when he dressed in Russian national costume, with a collarless crimson or bright blue silk shirt with long loose sleeves, voluminous knickerbockers, black velvet breeches and red-topped boots. The shirt was gathered in by a Caucasian silver laced belt and buckle at the waist, and on his head he wore a soft round velvet hat, decorated with the eyes of peacocks' feathers, and with the brim turned up all round. Out of doors or in the carriage he would wear over this a rich black velvet kaftan.

Louis took his responsibility for his three younger brothers seriously. He was especially close to Sandro, who was only five at this time. Louis loved to explain things to him. 'It was lovely on the steamship,' he wrote to his father of a trip on the Rhine. 'Sandro liked the big waves made by the paddle-wheel best of all.'⁴ The children normally talked German amongst themselves. But they were already bilingual for their mother invariably spoke to them in French. One of the first requirements of a Hessian was to be a linguist.

A few of Louis's early letters have survived. They reveal that he drew skilfully almost as soon as he could hold a pencil. The subject of the drawings he enclosed with his letters to his mother or father are the usual ones, his favourite dog Jeni, a *schloss* in which he has been staying with the family. They also show his pride in his father's military fame and prowess. In the first letter he wrote to his father after the Battle of Solferino he enclosed a picture of him with his charger and holding aloft the Austrian flag. Louis was five years old.

The tempo of life in Hesse seemed tumultuous after the rented villas of the past years in Italy. During that first winter of 1862–3 there was a constant coming and going of relations and friends, and ministers of many countries. Within a few weeks of the Battenbergs' arrival, there had been great celebrations of the marriage of Alexander's nephew and young Louis's first cousin, Prince Ludwig* of Hesse, to Queen Victoria's second daughter, Princess Alice on 1 July 1862 at Osborne, Isle of Wight.

As the Grand Duke had been recently widowed and had no children, his brother Charles's eldest son, Prince Ludwig, was heir to the throne of Hesse next after Charles. This marriage, therefore, was a powerful dynastic Hessian coup, and the people of the Grand Duchy were delighted to welcome this pretty English Princess. The marriage had been warmly blessed in England too, at a time when

* The German rendering is used to distinguish the subsequent Grand Duke Louis IV of Hesse and Prince Louis of Battenberg, although he was usually referred to as Louis in the family.

the royal family had been cast into paroxysms of grief over the recent death of the Prince Consort.

The fact that the Prince Consort himself, before succumbing to his fatal illness, had approved of the match was to mark it in the Queen's eyes as a wedding made in heaven. Before the bride and groom left for Darmstadt, an anonymous poet had written for *Punch* (and this was only the last stanza):

> Too full of love to own a thought of pride
> Is now thy gentle bosom; so 'tis best:
> Yet noble is thy choice, O English bride!
> And England hails the bridegroom and the guest
> A friend – a friend well loved by him who died.
> He blessed your troth: your wedlock shall be blessed.

The summer of 1862 was as colourful and exciting as any in the memory of the people of Hesse, with the arrival home of the glamorous and faintly naughty Battenbergs followed so swiftly by Prince Ludwig of Hesse and his bride. There seemed to be no end to the balls and parades, the theatres, operas and receptions.

It was not only about the wide streets of Darmstadt that the carriages rattled to and fro, from mansion to mansion, from opera house to museum, from the new railway station to the Grand Palace and the new Alexander Palace. There were hunts and expeditions to the Grand Duke's country palaces, lodges and shooting boxes, the Pavillion, the Prinz Emil's Garten, Braunshart, Mayence, Friedberg, Konradsdorf or the *Fürstenlagers* at Seeheim and Auerbach.

The newly married Prince and Princess of Hesse began an exhausting round of visits about the hot countryside, to Ludwig's ruined castle at Stauffenberg, to Giessen for a Musical Festival, to Auerbach, to Heidelberg and Baden and back to Darmstadt, greeted everywhere by the local dignitaries and cheering people. 'Our visit to Baden was charming,' Princess Alice wrote home to her mother, 'and dear Fritz and Louise [Grand Duke and Grand Duchess of Baden] so kind! Louis [Ludwig] and I were both delighted by our visit. The Queen, the Duchess of Hamilton, and Grand Duchess Hélène were there, besides dear Aunt [Princess Hohenlohe], and Countess Blücher. The two latter, dear and precious as ever . . .'5 And on another day: 'At the station we were again received: the whole town so prettily decked out; the Bürger rode near our carriage; countless young ladies in white, and all so kind, so loyal . . . I believe the people never gave so hearty a welcome . . .'

The Battenbergs were caught up joyfully in these celebrations, and if they took second place behind the newly-weds at all the functions, they were observed just as keenly. The two Princesses – the one from such humble stock, the other a daughter of the most imperial, the most imperious of all sovereigns – met for the first time at Jugenheim on an 'extremely hot' day in July. Tea together at Heiligenberg was a great success. 'The whole family are very amiable towards me,' wrote Princess Alice, 'and Prince Alexander is most amusing.'

Queen Victoria noted this with interest, and the crowning moment of the Battenbergs' rehabilitation occurred in the spring of 1863 when the Queen invited Alexander to Windsor Castle.

At the Queen's insistence, Alice had returned home to her mother at Windsor Castle for the birth of her first child, and 'dear Alexander', his young brother Henry, and Prince Ludwig of Hesse together were to represent the Hessian Grand Ducal family at the christening.

On this his second visit to England, Prince Alexander wrote endearingly indiscreet letters about the English royal family to his relations in Russia and elsewhere. To his sister Marie in Russia he wrote of Princess Alexandra: 'This Danish princess, whom all call Alix, is perfectly lovely, very natural and charming, as beautiful as her husband is plain. Bertie [Prince of Wales, later King Edward VII] is a funny little man. His features are not bad, he is a male edition of his sister Alice, but he is so broad for his height that he looks shorter than his wife. He is exceedingly friendly and cordial to me. The younger sisters, Helena and Louise, are pretty and intelligent, especially the former. The Queen's youngest child, Beatrice, is a dear little girl with flying golden curls down to her waist, but she seems to be thoroughly spoiled by everyone. The boys are nice: Alfred, the Duke of Edinburgh, frank and jovial, is a typical naval officer; Arthur is 13 and rather shy, so is 10-year-old Leopold; they are strictly brought up – two little Scots in kilts, with blue knees, but they look intelligent . . .'[6]

A few words in a later letter to his sister hint at the wonderful ability of the Hessians to adapt themselves to foreign ways, another aptitude developed by generations of dynasty-building. Prince Alexander is writing of Ludwig of Hesse, who while awaiting his wife's confinement, spent some of his time studying industrial Britain. But in between he was carefully observing the ways of the English country gentleman – and emulating him. 'He wears a Norfolk jacket,' Alexander wrote admiringly of his nephew, 'short breeches and multi-coloured garters, is very fond of sherry and horses, reads as little as possible, and never writes at all . . .'[7] So very English, so *very* un-German!

Three weeks after the birth of Alice's baby, the Hessian Princes dined with Queen Victoria. That night she wrote in her Journal:

Pce. Alexander is very clever & agreeable & after dinner, when we were sitting in Alice's room, he talked of the Polish Revolution, etc., & of the Italian campaign of the Peace of Villafranca. He gave me some very interesting details about it. I felt as if old times had returned & dearest Albert were there listening or that I was treasuring it all up to tell him. For the first time since my great loss (excepting Uncle Leopold) I heard someone of our own rank speak at his ease, & someone who had some experience of the world, & could impart the knowledge he had gained in such an interesting way. I feel the lack of that so much now, I only wish I had been surer of my facts to have been able to talk more myself . . .[8]

Prince Alexander returned to Darmstadt soon after the christening of his great niece. He faced a busy summer. The Russian royal family had invited themselves to stay at Heiligenberg. This was the first of numerous visits, which continued almost to the outbreak of the First World War, each one sealing more closely the relationship between the two families, until the assassinations which both families suffered in the Bolshevik revolutions of the twentieth century.

Prince Alexander and his young Battenberg family and the young Romanoffs had remained close even during the difficult years after the elopement of the young couple from the Russian court thirteen years earlier. The affectionate brother–sister relationship formed in the nursery at Darmstadt between Marie and Alexander had withstood all the batterings inflicted by the royal establishments. Now that the Battenbergs were not only *persona grata* but actually sought after by the best royal families, now that they had established themselves in suitable palaces, it was only natural that they should see more of each other than ever. Besides, the ages of the Tsar's younger children were nearly complementary with those of Alexander's boys.

This first 'Russian invasion', as it was affectionately termed by the Battenbergs and their servants, occurred in 1863. The Tsar's family consisted of Alexander, the oldest boy of 18 years, Vladimir, two years younger, Alexis aged 13, and the two boys of six and three years, Sergius ('Serge') and Paul.

Each invasion caused a huge upset at Heiligenberg. Alexander and Julie and all five children, nursemaids, tutor and the rest moved out of their rooms and crammed themselves into the *Hinter Haus*, while the sub,tantial Russian entourage, the Emperor and Empress, their children, maids and valets, occupied the whole of the front of the castle, the lesser servants spilling out into villas and hotels in Jugenheim.

To house, feed, entertain and transport the royal suite required the co-ordinated powers of a military operation; as well, the food and wine had to be of the finest and the protocol and precedence punctiliously observed without giving the visit an air of formality. For these were days of relaxation for the families. The corridors and halls of the castle rang with laughter and voices calling out in Russian and French, German and English, the grounds were filled with young running, laughing figures, and the dancing and games went on far into the night.

Sharp at one o'clock dinner (as it was called) was served, the men in evening tail coats and waistcoats, pearl grey trousers and black bow ties, and wearing the stars and sashes of their orders. The children, by Russian custom, were allowed in for the dessert course but were not permitted in any way to be intrusive. Then the women retired to talk and drink more coffee while the men attempted to work off some of the vast intake of food with strenuous games of bowls – 'a very heating amusement' as the young Prince Louis described it – before the families all retired for a siesta.

If there was no shooting party, at four o'clock the carriages came round to the front of Heiligenberg and the party travelled along the hot dusty roads to the New Palace at Darmstadt, or perhaps to Wolfsgarten, the Grand Duke's summer palace, or to one of the numerous shooting lodges within easy reach of Darmstadt.

The procession was led by the Battenbergs' open *Korbwagen* with Alexander and Julie, the Emperor and Empress, and the Emperor's indulged black retriever on the floor between the facing seats. At the sight of water the dog would leap out, submerge and wallow briefly before racing to catch up his master. He jumped back in and began once again to dry himself against the skirts of the Empress and the Princess, who were expected not to notice, let alone to protest.

Tea and coffee and cake were served at the destination of the day, and the party returned to change – the men into frockcoats – for eight o'clock supper in the *Terassen Saal*. When that meal was at last over, the long table running the length of the room was removed and replaced by a number of card tables. Meanwhile, young Prince Louis and the other children had been served a lighter supper in their own quarters and been put to bed by their nursemaids to the distant sound of music from the orchestra.

Among those who were invited to Heiligenberg, or were visited by the Romanoffs and Battenbergs on one of their daily excursions, were Alice and Ludwig. The Battenbergs were especially fond of the English Princess, who seemed so lost in the foreign Hessian environment.

Alexander wrote to his sister in St Petersburg, 'I think you would like Alice. She is a funny little woman, full of charm . . . very cultured and very talented.'9

But these were hard days for Alice and she was thankful for the sympathy and comfort she received from Alexander and Julie. Though hundreds of miles distant, Queen Victoria was a great trial to her daughter, pouring out in every letter her grief in tones of boundless self-pity at a time when Alice herself was in sore need of support and encouragement in her new life.

Alice did her gentle best to ease her mother's burden of pain and grief. At the same time the practical improving streak in her nature, which was to make her into such a good nurse, can be seen in her letters of sympathy.

'Try and gather in the few bright things you have remaining and cherish them . . .' she will write one day. Or, 'Can you give me no ray of hope that you in some way, bodily or mentally, feel better?'10

Queen Victoria wanted no such implied strictures from her second daughter, and made it clear that what she did want was unadulterated sympathy, or better still her company. But Alice could not come as frequently or for as long as her mother wished. Her husband had duties in Darmstadt, they had a home to make, they were short of money and these visits were expensive.

The penury was something the little Princess had not bargained for. Brought up among the comforts of Windsor, Balmoral, Osborne and Buckingham Palace, she had not had to consider things like domestic economy. And now, here she was, married to a foreigner at the innocent age of nineteen, with a child, a home to build and arrange and then run on a royal shoe-string budget, all the while conforming to local ways – or, sometimes, rebelling against them.

Prince Alexander's daughter Marie saw her in those early days through the eyes of a twelve-year-old child: 'She was a foreigner, come from distant England, and, as I soon remarked, did not fit in at all with the Darmstadt connections. I often felt sorry for her, she was so kind and so congenial to us, more so than our Hessian relations, and in a different way . . . [she] was a most attractive and arresting personality; her voice particularly, and her pretty mouth with its even teeth, aroused my admiration . . .'[11]

Among Alice's many trials was her uncle the Grand Duke. The tall, handsome figure who had succeeded to the throne (at first as co-regent) fifteen years earlier had become gross, eccentric and alarming, a figure fit only for a Hans Sachs farce. His wife, the Grand Duchess Mathilda, Princess of Bavaria, had recently died, and his ways had now become even more curious.

Revolving about him, satellites by day and night, were the three brothers Fleck, one his valet, one his major domo and pipe boy and the third his hairdresser. His sparse hair on each side of his bald pate had to be curled with hot irons so frequently that it required the full-time services of one of the Flecks. As to the pipes, it was one of the Grand Duke's obsessions that they should be smoked in strict rotation. There were many of them, and they were more than pipes; they were large Meerschaum cigar holders, elaborately carved and, together, forming an unique and ever-increasing collection. Fleck the pipe boy mellowed them for the Grand Duke's use by smoking them himself until they assumed the right colour.

Fleck the valet seems to have been the busiest of the three. A bell called him when the Grand Duke wished to blow his nose, and the handkerchief, as big as a small tablecloth, was brought in on a silver salver.

Every day the gargantuan Grand Duke was helped out of his palace and into his barouche-and-four in which he was taken to one or other of his small country houses or shooting lodges, with postillions and outriders. Before him drove his chefs and assistants with the food, and in a smaller carriage the three Flecks. In every lodge there was an identical apartment reserved for his exclusive, if infrequent, occupation: dark green wallpaper, mahogany furniture upholstered in green rep; a cigar stand; a bookcase containing a collection of memoirs and novels bound in black leather.

This Grand Duke had a wide repertoire of grimaces which used to terrify his great nieces and nephews out of their wits. Princess Alice might have laughed at this ludicrous figure. Instead, she was at first very frightened, and later rather disgusted by him and avoided him whenever possible.

If Grand Duke Ludwig III was a disappointing Hessian, Princess

Alice's young husband, who would succeed to the throne, was an authentic and splendid example of the breed. 'My dear Louis', as Alice always referred to him: 'unselfish, loving, good and industrious'. To her mother she would even compare him to the late Prince Consort in his qualities – a brave thing indeed to do.

In her domestic life Princess Alice was blissfully happy. Her baby was a model baby, and she nursed her herself, a practice which deeply upset Queen Victoria, who considered it indelicate. One should have a wet nurse. The old Grand Duke had given Ludwig and her the nearby old castle of Kranichstein, where they lived during the summer, and in September of 1863 Queen Victoria, her younger children, and her entire retinue came to stay.

The Queen had not made the journey for her own amusement or pleasure. On the contrary, it was a great effort for her, as she made amply clear. She came dutifully and anxiously about a family situation of great complexity and with possibly calamitous consequences.

The cause of all the trouble was Bismarck, whose dreams of a greater Germany to be created by power diplomacy and the Prussian armies, were causing alarm all over Europe, and therefore among many of the British Queen's closest and most cherished relatives. For instance, her eldest son's recent marriage to the lovely Princess Alexandra of Denmark was a great coup for Queen Victoria over King Wilhelm I of Prussia, who did not fancy this dynastic link between the two families. Moreover the Tsar of Russia had had his eye on the Princess for one of his sons.

Now on the death of the King of Denmark, weak King Wilhelm had been persuaded by Bismarck to demand from Denmark the province of Schleswig-Holstein. Bertie and Alex never forgave the Prussians for the war and seizure that followed. Alice, however, thought Bismarck's cause a just one, that the province really belonged to Prussia. So did the Queen. On the other hand, the Queen's first daughter, Victoria ('Vicky') and her husband Frederick ('Fritz'), the Crown Prince of Prussia, were at loggerheads with Bismarck and the King of Prussia.

There were many other ramifications of enormous complexity and of a dynastically conflicting nature. Of the Schleswig-Holstein issue alone, it was said by the British Prime Minister Lord Palmerston that the only people who understood it were the Prince Consort who was dead, a German professor who had gone mad, and himself – and he had forgotten. Anyway, he was dead within two years.

22

The Queen could do nothing to reduce the antagonism, and when she returned she heard over the following months and with increasing dismay of Prussia's continued intransigence. Bismarck had determined on war with Austria and the simultaneous absorption of the independent German states.

On the Prussian side, of course, would be Vicky and Fritz, and Prince Henry of Hesse who was making a career in the Prussian Army.

Against them would be lined up the Grand Duke, his brother Alexander, and among others of the Hessian family, Alice's beloved Ludwig. 'War would be too fearful a thing to contemplate,' wrote Alice to her mother in despair. 'Brother against brother, friend against friend. May the Almighty avert so fearful a calamity!'[12]

In June 1866 the Prussian armies crossed the Hessian frontier. Alice sent her children to her mother in England. Victoria had been followed by a baby sister Elizabeth, always called Ella, and she was expecting a third child.

Ludwig went off to the war on a horse given to him by Queen Victoria, and on 11 July Alice was delivered of this third child – Irène – in a heatwave and with all the confusion and frightfulness of war about her.

The Hessian armies were rapidly crushed. They had no chance of survival against the Prussians, who were well drilled, had planned the campaign meticulously, were lavishly equipped and possessed an experienced staff. Hesse-Cassel was quickly over-run. As the Prussians advanced into Hesse-Darmstadt the Tsar became alarmed for his relations and sent a telegram to the King of Prussia to say that if they attempted to seize his brother-in-law's land he would declare war on Prussia. Thus was the Grand Duchy saved to become an independent state within the German Empire.

Ludwig came back safely from the war, unwounded and with his horse unharmed, having experienced great dangers.

Alice had already received word of his gallantry. Early in August Julie Battenberg had managed to get a letter through to her. She had heard from Ludwig's uncle and commander that Ludwig had gained an excellent reputation and had been admired by all his men, and that he had been nominated for promotion.

Alexander's son Louis was twelve years old when the Prussian war ended, his father came home again, and the North German

Confederacy – the beginning of modern Germany – was created by Bismarck. Louis was tall for his age, and already notably handsome. 'It was as if Nature, in addition to outward beauty, had showered her gifts in profusion on this, her favourite. He looked like a Velasquez when he was older, like a Raphael when he was a little boy,'[13] wrote his admiring sister Marie.

By his eighth birthday his pencil was so skilful and confident that – if there was likely to be the need – he could have looked forward to a career as a professional artist. He was reading and writing German at four. At eight he was fluent in German, Russian and Italian and knew some French.

Marie was especially close to Louis and told of 'the inseparable character of our mutual relations'. But all five children played together well, and there were only nine years between them. The coach house at Heiligenberg was one of their favourite places. Among the coaches parked in the exciting darkness was the one Prince Alexander once used to travel to St Petersburg, before the train cut the travelling time to hours. The girls would be packed into this, and then a combined highwaymen force of all the boys would attack it.

'Louis is full of mischief and often fails to attend his lessons,' wrote Alexander in his diary. 'He is leading his younger brothers to mischief and disobedience.'

Prince Alexander wanted no more of war. He determined now to give his time to his family, and to help Julie guide them into their careers and marriages. Yet, as far as his oldest boy was concerned, the matter soon appeared to have been taken out of his hands. Even before the war with Prussia, Princess Alice had taken a special interest in the oldest Battenberg boy, and 'little' Louis was often in Darmstadt, or she would see him at the Alexander Palace or at Heiligenberg.

Alice recounted the delights of life in Hesse to her brothers and sisters in the many letters she wrote home, and begged them to visit her whenever they could. The New Palace in Darmstadt was now finished, a vast and opulent place on the site of the old botanical gardens.

At this time, and for many years to come, the English court offered little joy or pleasure to Queen Victoria's children. The mourning for their father seemed endless and the grey twilight gloom seemed to these spirited children as if it would never end and give way to the gaiety and sunlight they had known while he was still alive. In their eyes, the Hessian palaces, *schlosses*, castles and shooting lodges

24

became havens of joy and relaxation. Everyone was such fun (that old bogey of a Grand Duke excepted, but they did not see much of him), there was so much to do, and the informality was as good a tonic as the newly-acquired English middle-class practice of visiting the seaside. Above all else, was the delight of being with their sister again.

The Prince of Wales especially loved the Hessian court. While for the younger of Queen Victoria's children life at home was merely gloomy, for him it was cruelly oppressive. His mother believed that he had, by his errant ways, contributed to his father's breakdown and death, and she refused to allow him to take any part in state responsibilities, nor even to know about them. She seemed to disapprove of everything he did, harassed him, rebuked him, regardless of the fact that he was now, in 1867, a married man of twenty-six years.

His younger brother Alfred loved Darmstadt, too, ever since his first visit with the Queen two years before. Affie was now twenty-three, an absurdly young post-captain in the Royal Navy. In 1867 it was arranged that he should take a University course at Bonn. Whenever time allowed he took the train up the Rhine valley to Darmstadt to stay with his sister.

How they both loved these visits! The Battenberg children were often there, too, enchanting, lively, intelligent – 'Those four handsome sons'. Affie played with them and told them tales of his life in the Royal Navy, the greatest Navy in the world, which had defeated Napoleon at sea and helped to create the greatest empire the world had ever known.

Prince Louis, thirteen years old, listened enraptured to this wonderful looking officer in his naval uniform with the orders across his chest. Louis had seen the sea only occasionally, in his early childhood, when they were living in Italy. Now, touched by the magic brush of this gallant officer, it took on a texture of glittering romance. Its distance from land-locked Hesse, its mystery, only added to its enchantment in his eyes.

'Would it ever be possible for a foreign prince to serve in your Navy?' he once asked Prince Alfred.

Affie was at first amused by the boy's questioning and interest. When he recognized how genuine and enthusiastic this interest was, he encouraged him. Princess Alice, who favoured anything that would secure more tightly the bonds between England and her adopted country, added her encouragement.

Alexander and Julie were at first appalled at the prospect. He was the oldest son, the Battenberg heir, and the military tradition was strong in Hesse. It did not extend to the navy, a remote and, in Continental eyes, a rather rough and alien service.

Louis showed his mettle for the first time on an important issue. Pushed on by Queen Victoria's children, Princess Alice and Prince Alfred, Louis continued to press his demand on his parents. It was all he wanted to do with his life – to serve as an officer in the British Navy.

Louis had passed his 14th birthday when his parents at last yielded. They might have argued for longer and more persistently if it had been possible to serve the Fatherland. But the German Navy did not exist and was not to be formed for another two years, and no Hessian could have brought himself to serve in the Navy of the hated Prussians. The Austrian Navy was briefly put forward as an alternative in view of Papa's long and honourable service for the empire. But if you were going to sea at all, Louis argued, it would be only with the *best* Navy and the *biggest* Navy – the British Royal Navy.

When Princess Alice and Prince Alfred heard the news they were delighted. 'Soon I am going to commission the frigate *Galatea*,' Affie pronounced proudly. 'We are going all round the world. I shall be the captain, and you must come with me.'

2

'Look on me as on a Mother . . .'
QUEEN VICTORIA *to Princess Victoria*
4 November 1879

THE birth of Princess Alice's baby at Windsor in 1863 had been
an important occasion for Queen Victoria, and she had recorded
it in loving detail in her Journal. The baby was to be her first
grandchild to be born in her own home; and it was only appropriate that 'dear Alexander' as well as the baby's father should be
invited to Windsor in order to represent the Grand Ducal family at
the christening.

Alice was given the room alongside the Tapestry Room for her
lying-in. It had a marvellous view from its windows, looking straight
on to the Long Walk. It was an early and beautiful spring. The
daffodils were at their best, the willows already touched with green.

But the Queen hated the room because of an unhappy childhood
memory. 'In it she had been terribly scolded by her mother [the
Duchess of Kent], who had accused her of making up to King
William IV at the dinner he had given for her birthday, when he had
drunk her health and had insulted the Duchess . . .'[1]

The Queen herself, with dark satisfaction, prepared things down
to the last detail, including laying out the shift she had worn at the
birth of all her children – lamenting that she would have no more
herself, though she heartily detested childbirth and all that accompanied it and had frequently (even despairingly) complained when
she had found herself 'expecting again'.

Princess Alice's labour began on Easter Saturday. That night the
Queen slept little. 'The brightest moon shone in at the windows and

27

continued till the sun rose,'[2] she wrote. Those who are born on Easter Sunday are supposed to be lucky and to be able to see fairies and find hidden treasure. The Queen prayed that Alice's ordeal would soon be over. Her labour continued through most of that day. At 2 o'clock the Queen went to Alice's room again. The 'poor dear Child' was terribly tired and worn out. Complaining of equal weariness, the Queen retired and lay fully clothed on her bed and sipped some tea. Almost at once there was a knock on the door and 'I hurried off as fast as I could. I stood close to the bed, stroking darling Alice's shoulder and feeling terribly agitated, but I was able to control myself completely, thank God!'

The child was born at a quarter to five on the afternoon of 5 April 1863, and, according to the Queen, at once 'cried vehemently'. It was a fine bouncing girl.

Later, Alice wrote to her mother, 'I shall never forget that day – your kindness to us, and the tender nurse you were.'[3]

For the Queen the joy was fleeting and soon her mind was again playing on her bereavement. 'Oh, could . . . my adored one have only seen her, lying so happily with her little Baby in her arms! [He] would have rejoiced so tenderly and quietly at his child's happiness.'

The baby was given the names Victoria (after her grandmother), Alberta (after the Prince Consort), Elizabeth (after her German grandmother), Mathilda in memory of the old Grand Duchess of Hesse, and Marie in honour of one of her godmothers, King Louis Philippe's widow, Queen Marie Amelie. The christening took place at Windsor on 27 April; and in the teeth of the Queen's disapproval, it had to be conducted in the manner of the Lutheran Church. In fact a German pastor had to officiate, Hof Prediger Bender. The Queen reluctantly approved of him as 'a kind, good little man'; but thought that in his address he 'made too many allusions' – to what we shall now never know.

Baby Victoria 'was christened in my arms,' wrote the Queen in her Journal, 'her cap being removed, and the Clergyman sprinkling her head 3 times . . . It was a trying ceremony for me, for I always kept thinking *how* different it would have been, had *I* not been *alone*, without our beloved one to rejoice in his grandchild, and the blank and sorrow left by his loss, overshadowing everything!'[4]

After her return to Darmstadt, Alice's letters to her mother were punctuated by lovingly phrased references to 'Baby', to her exceptional beauty, to her exceptional accomplishments. The little

Princess remembered only scrappy fragments of the first four years of her life – very dimly the upheaval of the war against Prussia and of Irène's christening at Darmstadt.

She remembered nothing of being sent back to England to escape the dangers of the Prussian invasion, and the cholera and smallpox which raged in Hesse as a result of the war. A stronger childhood recollection was of the arrival of 'Orchie' as nurse in 1867 – Mrs Mary Anne Orchard from England who remained with the family until Alicky, Victoria's youngest sister, was grown-up; then she went with Alicky to Russia when she became Tsarina. 'Such order she keeps,' Alice once wrote, 'and is so industrious and tidy, beside understanding so much about the management of the children's health and characters.'5 Under her there was a German nurserymaid ('Little Katrinchen') Katherine, and Miss Emma Bailie also from England.

The governesses were of more varied quality. The first, Fräulein von Eckenstein, arrived just before the Franco-Prussian war, lustily singing patriotic songs like *Die Wacht am Rhein* which she made the children recite. She was from a noble Prussian family, and wore the family crest on her signet ring – just the person to see the family through the celebrations for the victory over France.

Next there was Fräulein Kitz, who suffered from sick headaches. Victoria remembered her tolerantly playing the part of King Arthur in one of the noisier imaginative games the children played, sitting on a bench with a wreath round her neck, holding her aching head in her hand.

'She was succeeded by a gushing woman called Hasters,' Victoria recounted, 'whom my mother found to be a fibber, so that her reign came to a premature close. She was followed by a Miss Graves, the daughter and sister of retired naval officers, and whom we were fond of, but who took too great a fancy to me for my comfort. She must have suffered from persecution mania, and ended in an asylum.'6

Last and best by far was Miss Margaret ('Madgie') Hardcastle Jackson. She had left her previous post with Lady Maud Herbert on her employer's sudden conversion to the Catholic faith. Miss Jackson did not approve of change, nor of Romans. She was very much the Protestant Conservative. She instilled qualities of probity and responsibility in all the children, and her influence lasted all their lives. She hated gossip, malicious or otherwise, and this, too, was something she passed on to her charges. She remained until all the children were grown up, becoming increasingly cantankerous, and was eventually given a grace-and-favour establishment by Queen Victoria. She mercifully died before the worst of the family tragedies occurred.

Alice's elder sister Vicky was experienced in the ways of foreign courts and German mores after four years of marriage to Fritz. Vicky was a great comfort and source of advice on the bringing up of little Princes and Princesses. When Victoria was four-and-a-half her uncle and aunt came to stay. She remembered little of this visit, at which, according to her mother, 'Vicky and I spoke much together about education and taking a governess.'[7]

Fräulein von Eckenstein did not arrive for another year ('for financial reasons', as Alice explained to her mother); but in the meanwhile Victoria had 'a little lesson every other day' from a Mr Geyer. She was reading within a few weeks, first in German, then in English, before she was seven. Thus began a lifetime with books during which as girl, young woman, during her married life and her long widowhood, her appetite for knowledge from books was never satisfied. At six years old she remembered 'reading every book I could lay my hands on, only understanding a quarter of it some-times'.[8] Her mother encouraged her enthusiasm, which she had passed on to her daughter.

It is a measure of this enthusiasm for the printed word that she read part of a book lying on a table while she and the family were being photographed – admittedly a tiresome business in those days, with iron supports to keep your head and waist still for the long exposure. At the time she did not discover its title and author, but many years later she read Theodor Storm's *Immensee* and recognized a passage which she had first read when she was a six-year-old impatiently awaiting the reappearance of the photographer from beneath his black shroud.

Victoria and Ella were loving and intimate friends from the earliest days they could remember in the nursery. They shared a bedroom until Victoria's marriage, and shared, too, one another's joys and sorrows and secrets. They looked pretty little things together, Ella prettier, more feminine (Victoria did not share her passion for dolls), but less thoughtful, practical and clever. Victoria had more of the tomboy in her, seemingly fearless in trees and on roofs. She always longed to climb everything, even the full-sized ship's mast erected for her young cousin Henry of Prussia, who was to join the new German Navy.

Alice watched lovingly over her children's infancy and wrote frequently to her mother about them. 'I am proud of my two girls [then seven and five], for they are warm-hearted and gifted, too, in appearance. Victoria's facility in learning is wonderful, and her lessons are her delight.'[9]

Victoria's travelling life began at the same time as her reading life, and she was to continue to travel, just as she was to live with books, until she was a very old woman. Not that she especially enjoyed travelling. The interest in new places, it is true, was always present, but she was often to tire of the packing and unpacking, the preparations and the embarking and arrivals, which she had to endure, especially during her married life. The first visit to England that she was to remember was in 1867, when she crossed from Calais to Dover with her mother and father on 10 June. Her first view of the British navy was appropriately grand and auspicious – a review at Spithead of forty-nine of the most powerful men-o'-war drawn up in two columns, the sailors manning the yards, the Royal Salute being fired – all in freezing, wet and choppy weather. The review was in honour of the Sultan of Turkey, who steamed up the line with the Queen on board the Royal Yacht *Osborne*.

Travelling within Germany and Austria occupied much of Victoria's childhood. The widespread scattering about Europe of her relations caused all this moving around. Unlike other people whose friends and relations tended in those days to be within a short carriage drive, royalty by their very nature tended to live at least a Grand Duchy if not a nation distant from one another. And so the mechanics, the sounds and smells and discomforts of travel – the packing of the trunks and guncases and pet animals, the arrival of the carriages, the smell of coal smoke and leather seats in the trains – all these were to evoke memories which Victoria could recall all her life.

Let us take a brief glimpse at the early summer of 1869 when, as Victoria later wrote, 'all my recollections are much clearer';[10] a damp and cool summer in Prussia. Her parents are visiting Potsdam to stay with Vicky and Fritz. The children travel with them, with the entourage of nurserymaids. Now there are four children. Victoria, Ella and Irène have a baby brother upon whom they lavish an abundance of love. A few months earlier they were playing in their nursery when they were startled by the boom of cannon. Together they counted. Twenty-five guns for a sister – another Hessian princess. But this time the salute continued. 'That is for a brother,' the nurserymaid told them: Ernst-Ludwig, or 'Ernie', future Grand Duke of Hesse and by the Rhine.

So a little baby, with all its accoutrements, is beside them in the railway carriage as the train makes its way across Germany via Frankfurt and Leipzig and at last to Berlin, and the Crown Prince and Princess's palace at Potsdam. 'Life with dear Vicky – so quiet and pleasant – reminds me in many things of our life in England in former happy days,' writes Alice to Queen Victoria, the mother who has 'given' these two loving sisters to Germany, and now misses them so much. At Potsdam the children play together, mainly indoors as it is so cold and wet this June. Vicky's children are of course older than her younger sister's. Wilhelm, the future Kaiser, is eleven, Charlotte nine and Henry, the future naval officer, seven-and-a-half. As in Darmstadt, militarism is the preoccupation. Victoria and Ella attend a military parade that is typical of the times, of the place and of the duties, even of young children, in this land of soldiers. It is of the First Guards Regiment. Little Wilhelm takes part, dressed in a lieutenant's uniform tailored to conceal his withered arm. He cannot keep pace with the marching so his good hand is held by a tall sergeant and he is thus forced along in step.

Wilhelm has a tutor, a Dr Hinzpeter, a fearsome man of whom Victoria and Ella stand in awe. Everything is very cold and formal. A footman in livery follows each of them wherever they go about the palace or the grounds – and there, at the back of the palace among the trees, is Prince Henry's beloved ship's mast. Victoria looks at it longingly. Dare she try? Henry runs up the ratlings, watched carefully by a sailor.

Victoria and Vicky's Charlotte are being gently introduced to the grand ways and occasions they must soon accept as a natural part of their lives. The Khedive of Egypt is on a state visit to Berlin. He has a little son of nine who speaks only Arabic but must be looked after, solicitously and dutifully, by the young German princesses. There is a special state ballet in honour of the Khedive. The young heir, dressed in a frock coat with grand cross and star and a fez on his head, sits between the two girls, looking very solemn and very bored. 'To show our goodwill,' Victoria told her family, 'we took turns in kissing his little yellow cheeks.'[11]

Almost as soon as they returned home to their summer palace, Kranichstein, the Prince and Princess of Wales arrived with their five children, Eddy, Georgie, Louise, Toria and Maud*, ranging from five to a few months old. ('My boy is as tall as little Louise,'[12] Alice told her mother proudly. There was plenty of healthy rivalry between the Queen's children.) Queen Victoria had sent Alice a pony for her children, and this gave them all a great deal of noisy fun. But indoors it was very cramped. 'No gentlemen or ladies [court officials-in-waiting] are in the house,'[13] noted Alice in some dismay, who had given up her bedroom and dressing room to her brother and sister-in-law. But everybody seemed to enjoy the informality of the occasion – it was, after all, for the Prince of Wales one of the main reasons for coming to Hesse. As for Alice, 'I am so delighted to see them all again,' she wrote to England; though she deplored Bertie's shaving off of his beard. 'It does not suit him.' She was right. It was not a good chin, and the beard was later grown again.

Later in the summer Vicky returned the visit they had made to Potsdam, with all her children and a suite of twenty-five people, every one of them fully qualified masters of Prussian protocol. Then they all went on together to Baden, the Hesse suite a characteristically modest, informal and happy one. After this Ludwig went off on a diplomatic visit to Constantinople, Alice to Geneva and Brindisi . . .

These restless progressions prohibited anyone – adult or child – from becoming bored in one place. It was happening all over Europe, with all the royalty, from mighty emperors and empresses to minor princes and princesses. All were infected with the nomadic urge, forever, it sometimes seemed, in and out of carriages and palaces, railway trains and shooting lodges, opera houses and parade grounds.

Only one thing could call a halt to these to-ings and fro-ings, and that was a war. A year after Victoria had watched her cousin Wilhelm marching past beside the tall sergeant, the Guards Regiment and all Germany's soldiers marched off to fight the French. Victoria's memories as a seven-year-old of the Franco-Prussian War were concerned with the small, tender and sometimes melancholy events that all wars throw up to sadden the minds of compassionate children.

* Prince Albert Victor, later Duke of Clarence, 'Eddy', b 1864, d 1892. Prince George, later Duke of York and King George V, 'Georgie', b 1865, d 1936. Princess Louise, later Princess Royal, b 1867, d 1931. Princess Victoria, 'Toria', b 1868, d 1935. Princess Maud, who became Queen of Norway, b 1869, d 1938. Another child, Prince Alexander, died in infancy 1871.

The winter set in early in 1870 and the swallows were caught by the frost before they could migrate. The children brought them in and Orchie warmed them by the fire before they let them fly away again. The cold had other victims, the poor of Darmstadt, made poorer by the disruptions of war. There were soup kitchens for the relief of their sufferings, and Victoria often visited them with her mother to help with the distribution. At the station, too, there was work to be done among the wounded in the ambulance trains, and in the troop trains that were constantly passing through to the fighting front.

Victoria remembered the sufferings of the wounded in the emergency hospital huts set up in the palace grounds, and the cold of the French prisoners in their compounds in the city. She remembered, too, her own first chilblains – poor circulation was to be the bane of her life – and the burn on her arms when she collided with another helper at the soup kitchens.

For a time they were so near to the fighting that Queen Victoria felt real anxiety for all of them, and not only for the father who was commanding the Hessian division. The war attracted the camp-followers, the battlefield looters and other riff-raff. An armed guard accompanied their carriage when they went out. Prisoners on parole wandered about the streets of Darmstadt. There were wounded even in the New Palace. One officer showed Victoria the bits of his shattered leg bone which he kept in a pillbox.

The war brought to a new height all Victoria's mother's urge for self-sacrifice and devotion to the cause of easing pain and suffering. Alice put everything into her hospital work. Her little dark figure was seen scuttling about from ward to ward, organizing and giving comfort. Nothing was too much trouble, no pain, no wound, too frightful for her attention, and the nervous and physical endurance of the English Princess was a wonder to all who witnessed it.

At Osborne Queen Victoria continued to worry dreadfully for her two eldest daughters, and most especially for Alice and her children. But even at the worst times letters managed to get through from them. On 25 August 1870 Alice wrote:

'I see daily, in all classes, so much grief and suffering; so many acquaintances and friends have fallen! It is heartrending! I ought to be *very proud*, and I am so, to hear from the mouths of so many wounded officers the loud praise of [Ludwig's] great bravery on the 16th and 18th [the battles at Vionville, Mars-le-Tour and Gravelotte]. Always in front, encouraging his men where the battle raged

34

the fiercest and the balls fell thickest. He was near our troops, speaking to them, directing them, and right and left of him they fell in masses. This lasted eight hours!

'. . . Hourly almost the trains bring in fresh wounded, and many and shocking are the sights one sees. I only returned here by one, having gone to town at half-past eight this morning, and have still three hospitals for this afternoon.'[14]

Queen Victoria understood the physical and mental strain this crisis must be imposing on her volatile daughter, and dreaded the consequences. Sure enough, by November Alice had reached the limit even of her endurance. She complained of pain in the nerves of her forehead and eyes, a total breakdown was feared, and at last she was persuaded by her doctor to leave Darmstadt to stay with Vicky in Berlin. She returned to Darmstadt with the children for Christmas. The biggest of her hospitals – the one named after her – was still full of wounded. But by now French resistance had almost ceased, except in Paris itself which was under siege, and the end of the war was in sight.

Victoria had just passed her eighth birthday when peace was declared. She remembered the celebrations well. Darmstadt was illuminated. At the New Palace the window ledges were covered with saucers of grease, and the children watched anxiously when the nurserymaid climbed out on her knees to light the wicks.

There was a great military march-past with the bands playing, and the soldiers' helmets were decorated with oak leaves. The women rushed out to kiss them, the children of the city, many of them wearing *kepis* given to them by French prisoners, running and cheering beside them.

The horses drew captured cannon and quick-firing *mitrailleuses*, the forerunner of the machine-gun.

Proudest moment of all came when the Hessian division arrived in the centre of the city and marched through the packed crowds – the pouring rain proved no discouragement – with their own father at the head. He had been awarded the *Pour le Mèrite*, the highest German honour for bravery in battle, and the blue and gold medal shone on his chest. A wonderful day!

On 11 February 1871 Victoria's younger brother was christened. He had been born as long before as 7 October 1870 but his father's family had insisted that the ceremony should wait for his return from the war. He was named Frederick William, and as was customary amongst all royalty, he had as sponsors a glittering array of names ranging from the Empress of Russia to Alice's young brother Prince Leopold. Inevitably he was given a nickname and was always known as 'Frittie' in the family. This second son, born in time of such trouble and anxiety, became the apple of his mother's eye and was deeply loved by his brother and sisters for his liveliness and winning ways.

When Frittie was nearly three months old, Alice wrote to her mother that he 'sits up, and, though not very fat, is round and firm, with rosy cheeks and the brightest eyes possible. He is very healthy and strong, and in fact the prettiest of all my babies.'[15]

It made the tragedy that was soon to strike the family all the more unbearable. For some time there was no suspicion that there was a fatal flaw in the little boy's health. Very little was known about haemophilia, the inherited disease of very slow-clotting blood, and the royal families of Europe liked to comfort themselves with the belief that it was neither serious nor widespread amongst them.

Nearly twenty years had passed since Queen Victoria had given birth to a haemophilic baby. Prince Leopold had been sickly from infancy and the Queen had almost despaired for his life. It therefore seemed impossible that little Frittie, so bouncy and jolly, could be suffering from the dread disease – soon to be known as 'the royal disease'.

Then, early in 1872, when he was still only eighteen months old, bruises with lumps were noticed on his body for the first time. Alice remembered the same thing happening at this age to Leopold, who, ironically, was one of the baby's godfathers. Desperately she wrote to Queen Victoria telling her of the discovery, and that on Sir William Jenner's advice she was giving him iron. 'I trust he may outgrow this,' she ended plaintively.

There could no longer be any doubt that Frittie was a haemophilic. With the advantage of experience and example, we can see today a certain pattern in this disease, although little enough is still known. First, it strikes only at males, and can be transmitted only by females. Queen Victoria herself was an agent, a fact which she at first refused to believe, then resented. She was deeply shocked by the idea. But, pathetically, she had later to admit, 'Our poor family seems persecuted by this awful disease.'

It will never be known for sure from which of her parents Queen Victoria inherited the disease as a carrier. She always denied that it could be from the Hanovers, and there is no ready record of it amongst the Saxe-Coburgs. But that means little. Haemophilia can skip a generation, or even two generations. Royal families above all families have every reason for covering up the disease for dynastic reasons. Besides, with infant mortality at such a high rate, there was the possibility that, say, the one male victim of a family might die before the disease manifested itself. (Leopold was the only one of Queen Victoria's boys to have it.)

It is said that Lord Melbourne attempted to discourage young Victoria from marrying Albert because he believed that there was a haemophilic strain in his family. That, too, may be apocryphal, for the whole subject is historically obscure.

Queen Victoria learned that Prince Leopold was a haemophilic soon after his birth in 1853. Many more years passed before she was forced to accept the fact that her first and second and last (Vicky, Alice and Beatrice) daughters were all carriers. Altogether these Princesses had fourteen children, and spread haemophilics and carriers throughout Europe and, most fatally, to Russia. Of Alice's eight children, two of her girls were carriers – Irène and Alicky*, and possibly the last daughter, Mary ('May' born 1874).

The origin and course of Frittie's haemophilia are now reasonably clear. His grandmother, Queen Victoria, was the victim of a spontaneous mutation in the genes she inherited from her mother and/or her father. Alice in turn inherited these, and transmitted the disease to her second male child.

Frittie's sufferings were fearful, and tender-hearted, loving Alice shared every spasm of pain experienced by her winsome little son. One of the tragedies of the disease is that many sufferers are especially lively in mind and body. Frittie was irrepressibly energetic, and the most attentive mother and nursemaids could not entirely prevent him from bruising and cutting himself. Early in 1872 he cut his ear. For three days efforts to staunch the flow of blood were ineffective. The use of caustic, tight bandages and iron finally succeeded. But this treatment led to painful side-effects. 'He could not remain in bed or anywhere quiet for the first two days and nights,'[16] Alice wrote to her mother in anguish.

In March Alice, ever keen on self-improvement, left the children for a short holiday in Italy to study the cathedrals and art galleries of Rome, Florence and Naples. She arrived home in early May,

* Princess Alix was called Alicky by the Queen and others, but more often Alix. To avoid confusion with the Princess of Wales, I use the former.

exhausted but overjoyed at the reunion with Ludwig and the children. While she was recovering from the rigours of her travels she remained late in bed in the mornings, reading or sometimes playing the piano in the adjoining sitting-room – she was an accomplished pianist, and especially loved Chopin preludes. It was the time in the day when she liked her children to visit and chat and play before they went to the nursery or began their lessons.

On the morning of 29 May – a beautiful sunny spring morning, Victoria remembered – Alice had got up and played the piano for a while, choosing this morning 'that splendid, touching funeral march of Chopin's'. Then she returned to her bedroom as Frittie and his elder brother Ernie came running, chasing one another from window to window. Ernie, it seems, disappeared into the sitting-room and did not answer when his mother called to him. She got up, one imagines in some anxiety, and followed him there. When she returned, satisfied about his safety, there was now no sign of Frittie. The Princess ran to the window and looked down onto the stone steps that led out into the garden from the room below.

Perhaps she had had a presentiment of what was to happen that morning, even while she was playing that funeral march. It was an unlikely accident for the stone windowsill was high enough off the ground for even a grown-up to look out safely.

Now what she saw was the ultimate horror scene for any mother – her child lying still and spreadeagled on the stone steps. She ran down the stairs in her nightgown. When she arrived at the steps there was no sign of the little boy again. For several more minutes she was left bewildered and distraught. Was this all part of some nightmare? Would she soon wake up?

Then one of the servants broke the truth to her. An elderly housemaid had discovered the unconscious boy immediately after his mother had seen him and had picked him up and carried him indoors. There was little the doctor could do for him. He was suffering from a fractured skull and effusion of blood on the brain. He might have died anyway. But his haemophilic condition deprived him of any chance of survival. How the accident had happened would now never be known.

By the evening the news had spread from the New Palace to all the Hessian royal family and all over Hesse. Ludwig, who had left that morning to inspect some of his troops in Upper Hesse, was summoned home. Telegrams were dispatched to Windsor, to Tsarkoe-Selo, Potsdam and other royal palaces.

Princess Alice was struck with a fearful grief from which she never fully recovered. On 1 June 1873 Frittie's little body was taken to the Grand Ducal Mausoleum – the Rosenhöhe – in Darmstadt.

'The horror of my Darling's sudden death at times torments me too much,' Alice wrote to her mother, 'particularly waking of a morning . . . He was such a bright child. It seems so quiet next door. I miss the little feet, the coming to me, for we lived so much together.'[17]

Victoria was ten years old at this time, and she remembered that fatal May day for all her life, too, It was the first of her many experiences of domestic tragedy. But the shock was worst and longest lasting for the elder of the two brothers. 'Ernie feels so lost, poor love,' observed Alice.

It is difficult to imagine today the effect on the mind of a young and sensitive boy of the prolonged and passionate grief in which Queen Victoria's family indulged themselves. Although Princess Alice had earlier gently and implicitly rebuked her mother for her continuous harping on her grief and loss, now that she herself was bereaved she was just as unrestrained. Nor did she discourage her children from remembering those happy days when 'Frittie was still with us'. Victoria, already well-controlled and self-disciplined for a ten-year-old – though as deep-feeling as any of them – was probably least wounded by the family loss. Ernie, aged four, was still harping on death eighteen months later – and long after that, too. When he heard that his mother was planting chestnut trees, he exclaimed to Orchie, 'Oh, I shall be dead and gone before they are big; what a pity we had none sooner!' Then he burst out crying. 'No you must not die alone – I don't like people to die alone; we must all die together!'[18] Alice, who should have known better, thought it beautiful and touching and told her mother so, recounting proudly to her what he had told her about a dream he had had.

'Mama, I had a beautiful dream; shall I tell you? I dreamt that I was dead and was gone up to Heaven, and there I asked God to let me have Frittie again; and he came to me and took my hand. You were in bed, and saw a great light, and were so frightened, and I said, "It is Ernie and Frittie'. You were so astonished! The next night Frittie and I went with a great light to sister.'[19] Ernie grew into a brilliantly clever but highly-strung young man.

We have a clear picture of Victoria three years after this accident, and when she was thirteen, from her own memories and the recollections of those who knew her. She was tall for her age, with firmly set but not especially beautiful features, though with a nice mouth and clever-looking blue-grey eyes, a strong, straight nose, and pretty ears. Her best feature was her hair which was curly and a lovely golden red colour. Her mother wrote of her at this time, that she 'is immensely grown, and her figure is forming. She is changing so much – beginning to leave the child and grow into the girl. I hear she has been good and desirous of doing what is right; and she has more to contend with than Ella, therefore double merit in any little thing she overcomes, and any self-sacrifice she makes.'[20]

Victoria's mind was forming fast, too. She was learning the art of debate and loving it. She thrived on controversy, sought out the unorthodox with joy, and embraced causes. She espoused the cause of the underdog, suddenly became a progressive and proclaimed to all who would listen that the end of monarchy was nigh. To the dismay of her family her radicalism proved more than a passing fad – and in fact she remained a progressive all her life, and always believed royalty was anachronistic.

In spite of this, and in spite of what her mother said, Victoria was still the lively tomboy, revelling in wild physical games, in competition of all kinds, and in leadership. 'I ruled all the younger with a rod of iron,' she recalled, 'though my sister Ella being nearest my age, would rebel sometimes against too much ruling. So we ended by dividing the authority over the younger ones between us.'[21]

Some of the wildest horseplay took place in a private park, the Prince Emil's Garten, where there was a sham ruin in a shrubbery. Victoria would lead her family and her friends – the children of the family doctors, of her mother's secretary and so on – and there devise war games defending and attacking the ruin.

One year they were joined by the seventeen-year-old Lord Charles Montagu, the son of Alice's friend the Duchess of Manchester (later Devonshire), who was in Darmstadt ostensibly to learn German. Victoria perceived that he was madly in love with Ella and always fought protectively and fiercely at her side. 'The sedately brought up Darmstadt girls would become almost as wild as we were,' Victoria remembered, 'but had a tendency to cry when they got hurt, for which I cordially despised them.'[22]

Victoria and her brother and sisters became notorious around the European palaces as they grew into adolescence and travelled widely every summer. They were always up to some boisterous play – but observing, too, the people and the world into which they were growing up, indulging in what Victoria liked to describe as her 'many philosophical conversations'. At Laeken, one of the Belgian royal family's palaces, they stopped with 'Cousin Leopold', as Alice called him – King Leopold II and 'Aunt' Marie.

The King's brother, the Comte de Flandres, and the Comtesse had a bevy of children who were 'great romps' according to Victoria. Both their father and their grandmother, the Princess of Hohenzollern, were very deaf, and the poor Comtesse had to shout everything, even the merest triviality, into each ear in turn.

Victoria, more sensitive than she liked to imagine herself, worried about things like this. She was also very much in awe of the King – 'A tall thin man,' she described him, 'with a nose nearly as long as Cyrano de Bergerac's, and his slow, drawling voice seemed to proceed from it. His big, square-cut dark beard, the monocle he kept dropping from his eye, his limping walk, gave him a singular appearance.'[23]

The long rail journey from Darmstadt to Brussels was also broken at Koblenz where Queen Augusta of Prussia lived in a vast palace for part of the year and expected everyone who passed near her to come to see her – an unenjoyable experience at the best of times. King Leopold was once rebuked for not doing so, and from that time he referred to her as 'The Dragon of the Rhine'.

All these journeys about Europe were very expensive for the penurious Alice and Ludwig. Queen Victoria therefore tactfully sent one of her Yachts for the passage to England. Balmoral was usually the first destination. In London there were 'improving' visits to the national institutions.

Professor Richard Owen took Victoria and Ella round the Natural History Museum, Professor Joseph Hooker round Kew Gardens, the Usher of the Black Rod round the House of Lords. Black Rod at that time – 1878 – was Sir Augustus Clifford, the illegitimate son of the Duke of Devonshire, who had fought at Trafalgar as a midshipman.

The Prince and Princess of Wales always provided lighter entertainment. Their children made splendid sparring partners, and for some time the Queen's last daughter Beatrice was young enough to join in, too. Eddy, the Duke of Clarence, was between Victoria and Ella in age; and Georgie between Ella and Irène.

The Hesses had nearly five months in England one year – 1871–2 – and got to know all the Wales children better than ever, as well as many other lively families. This was the time when the Prince of

Wales almost died of typhoid, the disease that had killed his father ten years earlier, and the Queen was in a torture of anxiety for weeks on end. All the Wales children, and Victoria and all her younger sisters and brother, succumbed to whooping cough at the same time. They were packed off, lock, stock and barrel to Buckingham Palace, and to confinement in the top floor at that.

It was November, and very bleak outside. Victoria read whatever she could lay her hands on, including one book about the subjugation of the natives of Tasmania – anything would do. Then when the worst of the coughing was over, games and exploration occupied their time over the long days of convalescence. Here they discovered on the same floor the old nurseries, dusty with age, where their mother and Aunt Vicky and Uncle Bertie and the rest of Queen Victoria's children had played. Some of their old toys were still there, including a full-size toy lion with a crank attached to its body – turn the crank and the lion swallowed the figure of a Russian soldier or an Indian Sepoy: so this was how you trained to rule the Empire. As well, there were rusty old bicycles for playing horses; indeed, they were already adorned with horses' heads and tails.

When they were fit to travel, this group of children – nine of them in all – were despatched to Windsor Castle, where Queen Victoria was (and understandably) still worrying about 'poor Bertie'. The towers, staircases and the long corridors offered a warren-like paradise for games. 'There were lovely corners and curtains behind which one could hide and leap,' Victoria remembered. 'Our wild romps in the great corridor . . . were often interrupted by one of the pages bringing a message from the Queen that she would not have so much noise.'[24] There were endless opportunities for 'dare' games – pilfering from the Queen's refreshment tray on the table outside her room. The lemonade and biscuits tasted especially delicious like this. Pilfering lumps of sugar from the nursery store. These they would melt in lighted candles in the hope of making caramel; instead they made an awful smell and burnt their fingers.

It was with profound relief that the servants learned that the Prince of Wales was out of danger at last, that his children could go back to Marlborough House, that the whooping coughs had finished and the fiendish little Hessians could go back to Germany with Princess Alice – who had been helping to nurse her brother all this time.

Victoria's passion for boisterous games and dare-devilry was matched by her deep feeling for the pet animals in her life – and there were many of them. Among the larger was Alice's brave bull terrier, Boxer, which loved pursuing wild boar. Inevitably, he was worsted in a fight with one, and there had to be a major operation. 'I can still see him,' Victoria remembered, 'lying on a wooden table in the nursery held down by a footman while his whole flank was stitched up.'

Victoria remembered, too, a fatal collision between three race horses at Chantilly; and she never again saw a horse race, even when, in later life, it was almost *de rigeur* to go to the Derby or to Ascot. But this did not affect her love for horses, which began with the little Shetland ponies Queen Victoria gave the family while the first children were still toddlers. Her own first pony, inherited from Princess Beatrice when she became too big for it, she named Dread after the character in *Uncle Tom's Cabin*. She remembered all her life the steady old horse at Windsor which the Queen had had schooled to carry small children from the castle to Frogmore. With harness and bridle all in red Morocco, the children sat in panniers, their weight equalized by little sandbags like early balloonists.

The pets at Kranichstein were innumerable, widely varied, orthodox and unorthodox. There was the fox that became intolerably smelly, the baby wild boar that became highly dangerous before Victoria could be persuaded to let it go free, white rabbits and guineapigs in ever increasing numbers, a lamb that of course grew into a sheep which she dragged about with a string round its neck to the sound of strangled coughs. She remembered conceiving the idea of tying the string to the sheep's leg instead and the laughter that followed when the animal still continued to cough pathetically when dragged against its will.

We see, then, a happy, active, full-blooded childhood with a healthy and invigorating routine. The time spent at lessons inevitably increased, but this did not bother her. On the contrary she seems to have enjoyed them all and welcomed the stimulus of examinations. Besides holidays in England and Scotland, the Hessian children shared holidays with their German relatives, most often with Aunt Vicky and her children. (The fathers tended to be conveniently away on manoeuvres or shooting boar during family holidays.) These visits were rather less pleasurable than some others – was it because the Crown Prince of Prussia's children had already begun their training for the stiff ceremony of the German Court? Perhaps they were just duller. Victoria recalled the strong competition between herself and the other Princess Victoria, the fourth of the Crown Princess's children, sometimes called 'Cousin Vicky' even by those not so related to her in order to avoid confusion. On the beach close to where they stayed with the Grand Duke and Grand Duchess of Baden there were pebbles of many colours – enough to set in the sand replicas of their family's standards – yellow and red for Cousin Vicky, white and red for the Hessian flag. This was good training for family loyalty, even in a unified Germany, but there were fierce battles for the rare red pebbles.

The belief in the curative properties of sea air and sea water had been strongly supported by the Prince Regent, Victoria's great-uncle. This was a complete reversal of the eighteenth-century idea, when the world was being opened up so dramatically by sea exploration, that sea air was unhealthy and a contributory cause of scurvy, boils and heaven knows what else. By the middle of the nineteenth century it was believed to be both highly fashionable and healthy to stay by the sea, and swim in it – but no longer, thank goodness, to drink it.

Every other year, therefore, the family went *en masse* to the Belgian coast so that Alice could recuperate from her childbearing and the nervous strain imposed on her by her hospital and charity work, in which she never seemed able to restrain herself. Cannes or Venice were considered too hot and 'soft' and therefore less curative. Blankenberge was bracing and healthy. It also had the additional advantage of being cheap. As anyone who has endured seaside holidays in northern Europe will know, the wind can blow bitterly for days on end in August, and it is often necessary and nearly always desirable to find protection against both wind and driving rain. However, this was considered an attraction rather than a deterrent to the spartan Alice.

At this *petit-bourgeois* resort Victoria spent hours on the wind-whipped sands, organizing games and creating castles for attacking and defending, and eventual destruction. Her memories were happy ones: of racing round the fish market, buying little men made of lobster claws, noisy games of croquet with the three Comtes d'Assche (boys, older than her), excursions on donkeys to the next village, bumping and rocking down to the sea in the horse-drawn bathing machine while the driver shouted 'Hué!' Then there was the day when, in very rough weather, a woman who was supposed to be a very strong swimmer got into difficulties – she had in fact been seized with cramp in the bitterly cold water. No boat was in sight. Without hesitation, Ludwig plunged into the boiling breakers and made his way out to her. It was a long struggle to get her back, and both were completely exhausted when they emerged from the ordeal. Brave Papa! How they all admired him – in war and peace!

When Ludwig succeeded to the Grand Dukedom in 1877 there was much more money available, and they went to a fashionable French resort. Many children of the French nobility were staying there with their nurses. One day, Victoria recalled, 'we saw a stoutish old lady being driven past in a pony carriage by a small dark-moustached gentleman, and we were told that she was ex-Queen Christina of Spain, the mother of Queen Isabella. I cannot say that she looked particularly queenlike.'25 The French nurses called their charges by their Christian names, which sounded very curious to Victoria's ears. But, 'being somewhat of a snob', she was more outraged than amused when Orchie, for the first time in her life, dropped the 'Princess' before *their* names.

Back home in Darmstadt, Victoria's tastes and more intellectual enthusiasms were being developed by her education and her inclinations. She was strong in mathematics and the sciences, and showed evidence of a practical mind, a 'wanting-to-know-why' mind. Her mother remained the dominant influence, and Victoria loved her deeply. She inherited Alice's love of music and the opera but not her talent as a pianist. Culture was traditionally strong in Darmstadt, and under Alice's influence, flourished even more richly. The opera and the theatre were both well-supported. Alice was a close friend of Ruskin and knew Carlyle and Tennyson, and many of the great figures of European literature and music stayed at Darmstadt. Victoria told of seeing her mother playing the piano with Brahms, 'an uncouth, shy man'; and of rehearsal for big concerts on Sunday mornings which the older children always attended. True to his fascination for the mystical, Ernie was especially thrilled by a performance of Schumann's *Paradise and the Peri*.

Julie Battenberg was an amateur dramatics enthusiast, and this often brought her children and Alice's children together – though the two families of cousins saw much of one another anyway. But even little Liko was five years older than Victoria, in whose eyes they all seemed rather grand – especially the oldest boy Louis, who went away to sea when she was only five, and thereafter reappeared only intermittently – a tall, glamorous figure in his smart British Navy uniform. But the Battenbergs were not in the least patronising to their younger Hessian cousins, in amateur dramatics or anything else, and the two families made a marvellous joint acting team.

Victorian Anglo-Germanic virtues and austerities applied as strongly at the New Palace, Darmstadt, as in mid-century Windsor: plain food, strict regularity, early-to-bed and early-to-rise. Victoria remembered especially the rising soon after six, in winter in freezing cold, with lessons starting at seven o'clock. Two hours later she and Ella had breakfast with their mother, and with their father too when he was not with his army: porridge, sausage, cold meats. Then there was an hour out of doors, winter and summer, riding or walking about the gardens and parks, followed by mid-morning 'little-lunch' of milk, fruit and biscuits. More lessons until 2 o'clock, then luncheon with Mama and Papa for Victoria and the older children. Simplicity was the dietical order of the day, and every day. Nothing spiced, nothing rich. Real Lutheran food without a trace of the Catholic. Never a chocolate or sweet. But good, sensible lumps of sugar were always there to assuage the natural needs of adolescence.

The children accepted all this with a good grace in Hesse – and why not, for they had never known anything else? But in England austerity walked hand in hand with incompetence through the royal kitchens. There the food was not just plain; it was awful – 'awful bread and butter pudding without a raisin', as Victoria described it. Or 'stodgy tapioca pudding full of lumps'.[26] Anything would do so long as it nipped in the taste buds the hopeful young appetites of the children.

The second domestic crisis which did so much to shape Victoria's childhood occurred in 1878, a year after her father had succeeded his uncle as Grand Duke of Hesse. Early in November she was reading aloud *Alice in Wonderland* to the younger children. Her throat was sore, but it was not like her to give up for such a small reason. By the evening it was obvious that she was running a fever. The doctor was called and he immediately diagnosed diphtheria.

Ella was moved to another bedroom – to Irène's – and then out of the palace altogether and to her grandmother's when Irène succumbed too. Ella was the only member of the Grand Ducal family to escape the disease which swept through the palace like a plague.

Beautiful little six-year-old Alicky was the next to go down, followed by Ernie and May – Alice's precious 'Sunshine' who was only four. For several nights in succession the anxious, attentive

Orchie aroused Alice with reports that she had discovered another of the children with a white membrane on both sides of the throat, an early and certain sign of the disease. Then mother and nursemaid together got out the inhaler and the chlorate of potash, the only known treatment which alleviated the sufferings.

Diphtheria that year was especially virulent. The telegrams flashed between Darmstadt and Balmoral. Six days after Victoria was stricken, her father fell with the fever. Alice never slept. For day after day she nursed her entire family, supported by no fewer than eight doctors and nurses. 'My precious May no better,' she telegraphed to Queen Victoria on 15 November. 'Suffers so much. I am in such horrible fear. Irène and Ernie fever less. Ernie's throat very swelled.'

By this time Victoria, always physically resilient, had ridden out the storm and had almost completely recovered. But for the others the crisis had not yet passed. The Queen, in great alarm, had despatched Sir William Jenner to Darmstadt. There was little he could do. On 16 November, two days after Ludwig took to his bed, little May died. Alice wrote to her mother: 'Our sweet little one is taken. Broke it to my poor [Ludwig] this morning; he is better; Ernie very, very ill. In great anguish.'

Fate played her most cruel tricks on poor Alice. Just as Ernie seemed really better, and the others were recovering, he had a relapse. Half delirious, he asked for a book to be sent to his baby sister May to cheer her, for Alice had not told him of her death. It was almost too much for her to bear. She leant over his pillow and kissed her son's forehead. It will never be known whether she caught the disease at this moment, or perhaps when in equal agony of mind she rested her head on her husband's pillow. It seemed to everyone that the virus had run its course. Prayers of grief for Princess May, and of gratitude for the recovery of the rest of the family, had been said all over Hesse. On 7 December Alice went to the railway station to greet Marie of Russia, the Tsar's daughter who had married her brother Affie. It was perhaps as well for the Duchess that they met only in the draughty chill of Darmstadt station, or perhaps she, too, might have received what the British Prime Minister later described as the Darmstadt 'kiss of death'.

That evening, Alice experienced the dread symptoms. She knew that her chances of survival were slim, and she made every preparation for death, tidying up her family affairs, speaking while she still had a voice, then writing little notes which became briefer and less legible as the effects of the disease sank more deeply into her frail constitution.

It was not only that she was physically and spiritually exhausted after a month of sleepless anxiety. She had complained frequently to her mother that she had not felt well for the past two years. As if she knew that her time was running out, she had worked feverishly at her duties both as the new Grand Duchess and at her charity work, piling on more and more responsibilities as if to suffocate herself in them. The effects of Frittie's death six years earlier had been deep and profound.

Before 1872 she had a for a while been unorthodox and even experimental in her religious thoughts and beliefs. After this blow, she had reverted to the simple religion of her childhood. There was much less joy in her life. It is significant that she called the daughter born two years later 'Sunshine' – as if all else in her life was in darkness.

Queen Victoria, shrewd and knowing in family matters, understood Alice better than Ludwig or anyone else. She knew what Alice had been through, ever since those dreadful weeks when she had nursed Albert through his last fatal illness seventeen years earlier. Alice just did not possess a strong enough constitution to withstand a dangerous illness in the midst of her grief and worry. On hearing that she had diphtheria, the Queen wrote with terrible truth, 'She will never have the strength to get through it.'

Poor Alice suffered dreadfully. She seemed to recover a little around 12 December, saw a number of her close relatives, suddenly, miraculously, could talk again, and then fell asleep. At half past eight on the morning of 14 December she awoke briefly and was heard to say, 'From Friday to Saturday – four weeks – May – dear Papa . . .' Then she died.

It was indeed exactly four weeks to the day since little Sunshine had died; and seventeen years to the day since her father had died. For Queen Victoria and all her family, anniversaries held a special significance. Few of the happy ones, and none of the tragic ones, were ever forgotten. 'The terrible day' for the Queen was 14 December, and for years she retired, prostrated with grief when this day came round, breaking off only to go to the mausoleum or to pray in the Blue Room at Windsor. Year by year the calendar appeared to lend credence to the superstitions of the Queen and her family.

'14 Dec. – this terrible day come round again!' On her way to breakfast the Queen met John Brown, her good, stalwart Scottish gillie – and, oh how she needed him on this of all days! He had two telegrams from Darmstadt, one from Jenner, the other from her son-in-law. Neither held out much hope for the life of her daughter. A third telegram arrived shortly afterwards. It told of Alice's death early that morning. 'That this dear, talented, distinguished, tender-hearted, nobleminded, sweet child, who behaved so admirably during her dear father's illness, and afterwards, in supporting me and helping me in every possible way, should be called back to her father on this very anniversary of his death, seems almost incredible and most mysterious.'[27] Then she took a sheet of black-edged writing paper, always in demand at Windsor, and wrote to her favourite and bereaved grandchild,

WINDSOR CASTLE[28]
Dec 14 1878

Darling Victoria,

Poor dear children, for I write this for you all *– You have all had the most terrible blow which can befall Children – you have lost your precious, dear, devoted Mother who loved you – and devoted her life to you & your dear Papa! That horrible disease which carried off sweet little May & from which you & the others recovered has taken her away from you & poor old Grandmamma, who with your other kind Grandmamma will try & be a Mother to you! Oh! dear children, dearest beloved Mamma is gone to join dear Grandpapa & your other dear Grandpapa & Frittie & sweet little May where there is no more sorrow or tears or separation.*

I long to hear every detail! Poor dear Ernie, he will feel it so dreadfully! May he & dear Papa not suffer from this dreadful blow. Try & do everything to comfort & help poor dear Papa! God's will be done! May he support and help you all.

From your devoted & most unhappy Grandmamma

VRI

let Ella see this letter.

Before we pass on into the darkness left by Princess Alice's death, there are three little-considered characteristics of hers which a less shrewd and observant child than Victoria might not have recognized.

The first was her unreserved self-abnegation, which was a contributory cause of her death. The second was her ability to overcome triumphantly the deep differences in outlook, temperament and interest between herself and her husband. Ludwig was a military-minded outdoor man, reviewing soldiers and enjoying manoeuvres and shooting, rather than studying pictures or enjoying the opera in Darmstadt. Their affection was never disturbed by these disparate enthusiasms.

The third was Alice's talkativeness, which her eldest daughter inherited in full measure, by contrast with her father's strong silence. Their garrulity is what people remember most clearly about these eminent Victorians. Many people believe that Queen Victoria talked her head off at every opportunity. Queen Elizabeth II has no doubt of this, recalling from her own childhood how the Good Queen's surviving last daughters, Beatrice and Louise, talked, sometimes until their audience was stunned by the outpouring of words.

On the first day of the New Year, 1879, a day in her Journal always reserved for summary and philosophy, the Queen exclaimed, 'What misery in her [Alice's] once dear, bright, happy home!' In many ways the Queen's judgement was true: there was among the children a dreadful sense of deprivation, with some exquisite agonies, like the loss of all their toys, burned as a disinfecting precaution. Years later, Victoria wrote of the effects of this new double catastrophe, 'My mother's death was an irreparable loss to us all and left a great gap in our lives . . . My childhood ended with her death, for I became the eldest and most responsible.'[29]

Victoria was ideally equipped to carry this burden. All her life she enjoyed exercising her strength and command, and even at fifteen she possessed the wisdom and self-discipline to face confidently the new and uncertain future of the family. Of course, her father was there as background support, though his administrative duties since he had become Grand Duke, added to his military duties, filled almost all his life; and, in any case, he 'was somewhat lost as the head of a household of growing children',[30] as Victoria herself observed. As to the rest of the Hessians, they were mainly very old and preoccupied with their health or eccentric hobbies, and were not much help.

In some ways these Hessian children were insulated by their class and position from the worst consequences of their loss. All about them, for most of the day, were the old familiar and kindly faces – the servants and teachers, the gardeners and coachmen. The children had always seen more of them than of their mother, deeply devoted to her though they had all been.

The sheer numbers of relatives helped too. There were nearly always visitors at Darmstadt – that was the reward (or penalty) of their background and future – and all were loving and concerned.

Then, as before, there were the long travels in the summer, and the festivities shared with the local families in the winter and spring. Certainly, they were never lonely.

Queen Victoria ordered the whole family to Osborne immediately after the disaster to offer them comfort and spiritual guidance. The Queen's letter to Victoria did not give much promise of cheer.

OSBORNE *Jan 14 1879*[31]

Darling Victoria,

 ... It is today a month since that most dreadful day which shattered your happy home. It seems impossible *it can be so long. In a week, please God! you will be with us! What a meeting! I trust you will be comfortable ...*

 Poor dear Ernie I am so glad he is better. How sad he must feel! ...

 Love to dear Papa & Brother & Sisters. Have you been to Rosenhöhe lately?

Ever your devoted sorrowing Grandmama

VRI

The cheer which she could hardly be expected to offer to the children was provided by Uncle Leopold, who went through life gamely and cheerfully in spite of his haemophilia. He was adored by all the children and even came back with them to Darmstadt after the ordeal of sharing Grandmama's grief was over.

'He was a delightful uncle to us all,' wrote Victoria, 'only ten years older than myself – I, 16 and he, 26 – inventing games for us and firmly looking after our manners. He was the most cultivated of the Queen's sons and influenced our growing taste in art and literature, besides understanding my father very well.'[32]

Leopold had suffered perhaps less from his haemophilia (though that was bad enough) than from the assiduous over-protection of his mother, who showed as little imagination in her treatment of him as of his much older brother, the Prince of Wales.

His brothers and sisters conspired to find Leopold something to do but it was difficult as any sort of a military post was out of the question because of a permanently disabled knee – the result of climbing the high steps into Continental trains.

Resolute as ever, Prince Leopold found himself a wife – a woman of great strength of character and determination who pooh-pooed the haemophilic risks. She was Princess Helen of Waldeck, a sister of the Queen of the Netherlands. Now created Duke of Albany (though in Queen Victoria's presence still to be known as Prince – 'I always say no one can be a Prince, but anyone can be a Duke'),

Leopold had the joy of telling his mother early in 1883 that the Duchess was expecting a child. This child, Princess Alice, later Countess of Athlone, is, happily, still alive and well.

The joy of Prince Leopold's marriage was brief. Refusing to guard against the risks of his condition, he fell down some steps at a hotel in Cannes where he was staying with the Duchess who was expecting her second child. As with his nephew Frittie, an infusion of the blood set in and he was soon dead – 'the dearest of my dear sons' mourned the Queen, who also noted with morbid satisfaction that it was the first anniversary of the death of her beloved Brown. Victoria and her brother and younger sisters all greatly missed this happy uncle.

Prince Leopold was only one of a number of her relatives whom Queen Victoria ordered to lend a hand at Darmstadt. The Queen also despatched a succession of letters to Victoria to remind her of her new responsibilities. 'At your age kind advice is of the greatest importance,'[33] she wrote; and prayed 'that God may bless protect – keep and guide you ever in the right path & make you a good, loving straightforward and God fearing Child or rather more *Girl*, for you are fast growing out of a Child.'[34] Then again, 'Try & be like [your Mother] – unselfish & courageous, loving & good,'[35] and, 'Try to follow in her footsteps – modestly, unpresumingly, *not* putting yourself forward too much but being always ready to help . . . You must learn to be posée . . .'[36]

This well-meant advice was invariably interspersed with reminders of the sadness of Victoria's loss, and told her that, from her own experience, the pain and grief would increase with the years rather than diminish. 'As life goes on and you get older, and require the support & advice of a loving Mother you will more & more feel the terrible loss! Let *every* day bring you nearer to her & to her dear memory.'[37]

Victoria refused to be cast down in gloom for ever. She and Ella especially were cheerful young girls and Victoria's spiritual resilience was as strong as the physical resilience she had shown in her rapid recovery from diphtheria. And she was managing quite well at Darmstadt, thank you; even enjoying the new burdens placed on her young shoulders. Prince Leopold was not the only one of the 'helpers' the Queen sent to Darmstadt to notice the firm sense of responsibility demonstrated by the eldest of the Hessian children. Victoria was always politely pleased to see these helpers but made it amply clear that she could cope with everything herself. At fifteen she was already the 'good manager' she was to be all her life.

But Victoria, paradoxically, was not as self-assured as the outside world might believe. She worried about what people thought of her, and for a brief period of adolescence fussed about her clothes and appearance. Tomboy she may still have been, even at sixteen. But she also remembered all her life what she had worn at this opera, or that ball or reception. On one of her English visits she recalled that she and Ella were given white muslin dresses trimmed with acacia sprays by Aunt Alix when they stayed with her and Uncle Bertie at Marlborough House. They wore these at a ball, and Victoria remembered how waltzing in the heat and the scent of the gardenias and stephanotis after supper made her fell quite faint; and how the all-seeing Prince of Wales tactfully gathered her up and took her to the cooler supper room for champagne and supper. Kind Uncle Bertie! She remembered, too, her anxiety that she would be observed and thought greedy by those who had seen her eating earlier. So here we see momentarily a sensitive and vulnerable girl.

Exchange visits with the English royal family were now more frequent than ever. Most summers Uncle Leopold or his sisters Aunt Louise and Aunt Helena would reinforce family solidarity by staying for a few weeks at the Hessian summer palace, Schloss Wolfsgarten, just north of Darmstadt – an enchanted place set in the forest only some ten miles from the Rhine.

Aunt Louise especially reminded the children of their mother. Although five years younger, she had similar looks and a similar agile mind, lacking only the mysterious brooding melancholy that embraced their mother during her last years. They saw less of their eldest aunt, Aunt Vicky, who was now very Prussian and lived in such a military atmosphere. In the past there had been an annual get-together at Wiesbaden after the annual (and enormous) army manoeuvres, where the two families would take solemn walks together, headed by the parents and, taking up the rearguard, the inevitable liveried footmen carrying cloaks and umbrellas. These meetings had been arranged by the two sisters; with Alice's death the fathers showed little inclination to continue them. (The Prussians were *so very* military: they scarcely paid lip service to the arts.) They did, however, see something of Wilhelm, who was studying at Bonn University and used to come over to stay at Wolfsgarten in the summer. He was twenty and Victoria four years younger at this time. Willie already smoked heavily and used to offer his cigarettes to his cousin. She became a confirmed smoker at sixteen.

Smoking added a spice of danger to the visits to Balmoral in the autumn. Queen Victoria, of course, forbade anyone – and especially her own family – from smoking in her palaces. Tales of her eldest son's ruses to smoke his cigars in secret rooms when staying with her were widespread in England. The Queen seemed to have an uncannily well-developed sense of smell for tobacco.

Victoria, who never hid anything, smoked everywhere she pleased at Balmoral and elsewhere, except in the presence of the Queen, or where it might discomfort her. Perhaps only she could have broken this timeless and rigid rule. The Queen adored Victoria, and had done so since she was a little girl. The fact that she had been present at her birth, that the child was growing up with her mother's lively mind; the fact that she showed independence of spirit (admirable in girls, deplorable in her sons) and had lost her mother so young, created a special bond between them. Victoria returned her love, and the two were very close.

Queen Victoria knew perfectly well that her young granddaughter smoked. Once when Victoria was a young woman and the two were out together at Balmoral, she observed that the mosquitoes were exceptionally troublesome. 'I am told that you smoke, Victoria,' the Queen observed surprisingly. 'I wonder if you would mind lighting one now.' Victoria obliged, and the Queen, intrigued by the mechanics of finding one, inserting it in its holder and then lighting it, asked if she might try. Victoria lit one for her Grandmama who 'declared that she thought the taste horrible!' But the smoking ban was never again so rigid.

In the Spring of 1880, three weeks after her own seventeenth birthday, Victoria was confirmed in Darmstadt. Queen Victoria ('it will be a terrible trial for me')[38] announced that she would be present, her first visit to Darmstadt since Alice's death. The ceremony was followed by equally sacred but much more melancholy events.

First a visit to the Rosenhöhe. 'We saw on the floor, close to the door,' wrote the Queen in her journal that evening, 'my darling Alice's coffin, covered with a crimson velvet pall, on which were embroidered my darling child's initials . . . We knelt down and I felt terribly shaken. It seemed too dreadful! . . . the 2 small coffins of dear Frittie and May, also covered with crimson pall and flowers, are beside their dear Mother's.'[39] After that the Queen went alone to Alice's bedroom, which, like dear Albert's, had been left just as it had been at death.

But, for her family, grief at past tragedies was overwhelmed by joy at future marriages. The new decade was a time for a fresh start.

It was time for the last of Queen Victoria's children and the first of her grandchildren to find husbands and wives. Leopold's wedding had been a great relief to the Queen. Princess Beatrice, on the other hand and according to Queen Victoria, was *not* to marry. She was absolutely indispensable to the Queen in her ever pressing duties at home.

Bertie, who believed in the Queen's children getting away from home as soon as possible, thought otherwise. He thought a perfect husband for Beatrice would be (of all people) Alice's widower, the Grand Duke of Hesse. Not until much later did Victoria learn of her uncle's valiant efforts to marry her father off to her aunt – the same aunt who so recently had participated in the rumbustious goings-on in the corridors at Windsor Castle, her friend and near contemporary.

For the present, such a marriage was against the law which forbade a man marrying his deceased wife's sister. Then the law shall be changed, announced the Prince of Wales, and used every ounce of his political and social weight to bring this about through the Deceased Wife's Sister Bill. But the Church of England bishops would not have any part of it and the bill was thrown out of the House of Lords. For the present, then, Victoria's father had to look elsewhere for a new wife.

The next frustrated romance was that of Wilhelm. While teaching Victoria the art of smoking, Willie was falling deeper and deeper in love with her younger sister. But Ella felt nothing for this defiant, edgy young student cousin with the withered arm. Her eyes were already set on the endless horizons of Russia.

The Grand Duchess of Baden, too, had marriage plans for beautiful Ella. She and Alice had long before decided that she would make a good wife for their eldest son, Fritz. So did the Empress Augusta, the boy's grandmother. Ella thought otherwise, and her father, being of a more liberal school of thought that did not hold with arranged marriages, told her she need not.

The Empress was not accustomed to being denied her wishes and at a special ball which she had arranged for the announcement of the long anticipated engagement, cut both Ella and Victoria dead. It was a new experience for the girls.

Other royal matches made smoother progress. Ella's dreams of Russia were realized in the handsome person of the Grand Duke Serge, the Tsar's fifth child. 'Oh dear!' exclaimed Queen Victoria. 'How very unfortunate it is of Ella to refuse good Fritz of Baden so

good & steady, with such a safe, happy position, & FOR A RUS-
SIAN.'[40] The Battenberg boys were falling in love all over the place.
Victoria, not to be outdone by her pretty younger sisters, was having
what she described as 'a great flirtation'[41] with Micha, the son of
Grand Duke Michail Nicolaewitch, whose daughter Nada later
married her elder son Georgie.

But for Victoria something deeper and more enduring than a
flirtation was beginning to reveal itself. She had only caught
glimpses of her tall and exceptionally handsome cousin Louis of
Battenberg since he went off to sea. She remembered his homecoming
in 1870. He was almost sixteen and wore a Royal Navy midshipman's uniform. He had come back from the other side of the world
for his confirmation. Victoria remembered the excitement and the
pride in the Battenberg family.

A month later the war with France broke out and all was confusion. Later he told her how fascinated he was with the battles
taking place so near to Heiligenberg, and how he had seen through a
glass from the clock tower of the castle the German guns opening
fire on Strasbourg. The war had been at its height when Midshipman His Serene Highness the Prince Louis of Battenberg, Royal
Navy, was confirmed by his tutor, Herr Hager, in the little Lutheran
church above Jugenheim. Princess Alice took time off from her
nursing. Victoria recalled it all as one of the fund of memories, some
alarming, some exciting, some sad or horrifying, but all of them
strong memories of the war with France.

In the summer of 1878 Victoria and her brother and younger
sisters had spent some weeks at Eastbourne, a modest resort and
fishing village on the south coast of England. While Alice gave up
most of her holiday to studying social conditions and hospitals – in
spite of being in desperate need of a rest – the children rode donkeys
on the beach and played on the sands, or learnt to play tennis at
the Duke of Devonshire's Compton Place nearby.

It was their last summer together as a family, and this was one
reason why the picture of that time remained so vividly in Victoria's
memory. Another reason was that their holiday was broken by a
visit to Buckingham Palace, which led to a colourful social life at
the height of the London season, with parties and much going about.
Uncle Bertie gave a big garden party at Marlborough House, and
even persuaded the Queen to come up from Windsor for it. It was
altogether a more pleasant and eventful time than that miserable
whooping cough period six years earlier.

Lieutenant Louis Battenberg was on leave, and Victoria saw him frequently. He was very gallant, very gay and debonair in her eyes – and indeed in all eyes, in spite of the fierce competition among the young bloods and blades.

Victoria and Ella had for long wanted to row a boat on the Buckingham Palace lake but had always been frustrated by Orchie. 'Only if you have an experienced person to look after you,' she insisted. Who could be better than a strong, young sailor? And who could refuse such an enchanting pair of young cousins when they appealed to him? In his best morning clothes, the lieutenant R.N. launched the rowing boat and rowed them laughingly round the pretty little lake.

Now, four years later, in the winter of 1882, Louis and Victoria met again at Darmstadt. She was fresh and lively, provoking and clever. Louis was 28, had just been to the other side of the world and back, was bronzed and fit and full of charm and of tales of romantic foreign parts. Suddenly they were no longer childhood cousins, friendly and teasing. Everything was different that winter – the nights sharper, the moon brighter, happiness more complete than either had ever known it.

Victoria was a young woman in love for the first time. Louis, experienced in love and the ways of the world, found in this quick-witted girl a new contentment, a love like he had never known before – for here was a new and exciting transfiguration of the little tomboy he had seen as a boy, and from time to time since; until now, at just nineteen, he was helplessly in love with her.

They danced together at many balls that winter, and experienced old Hessians at court knew they were to be married before they knew it themselves. At the end of the winter season Queen Victoria sent her usual invitation to Balmoral. This time Victoria wanted to refuse – she had other things on her mind. Ella, the ever-watchful younger sister, observed to her father that 'If Victoria does not go with me to Scotland she will become engaged to Louis Battenberg.' By this time it was hardly a subtle prophecy. Louis and Victoria were engaged in June 1883 and the formal announcement was made on 1 July.

3

'I shall never feel quite at home in the
English Navy.'
PRINCE LOUIS *to his sister Marie*

'Stick it out!'
THE PRINCE OF WALES *to Prince Louis*

As soon as it became known that a young German prince wanted to
join the Royal Navy, the well-oiled cogs of privilege engaged
smoothly and speedily. The age limit for entering the training ship
Britannia was 14. Louis had just passed that birthday. Princess Alice
arranged through her mother that the limit was raised by six months
in this special case. Louis would have to pass a naval examination
at Portsmouth Naval College in December. A tutor, a Mr Everett,
was therefore despatched from Magdalen College, Oxford, to 'cram'
Louis in Algebra, Euclid, Latin and English Composition.

There was less fun than usual for Louis during that summer of
1868. It was very hot at Heiligenberg. The Russian invasion was in
full swing. Uncle Alexander and Aunt Marie of Russia, and for some
of the time all nine of their children, crammed the castle, their
servants crammed Jugenheim, their horses (many borrowed from
Darmstadt), crammed the stables. When the whole lot went over to
Wolfsgarten for parties and picnics (and that was like moving an
army corps), Louis was left behind with Mr Everett.

Luckily for Louis, Uncle Affie's grandiose plan to take him round
the world even before he began his training had been judged unwise
and was cancelled. So, on 25 September, with bags packed into a
carriage, the wide terrace in front of Heiligenberg was the scene of

a prolonged and moving farewell from his own family and the entire Russian imperial family. Julie was in tears, certain in her mind that her eldest boy would be drowned and that she would never see him again. Why England? Why the Navy? she continued to wonder. That far away island she had never seen, and that hostile, dangerous sea! If only it could have been the Army.

Mr Everett and Prince Alexander were to accompany Louis to England and get him settled in at a crammer school at Alverstoke, on the coast between Gosport and the naval town of Portsmouth, where he would be prepared for the December examination. The crossing from Calais to Dover was very rough, and it was with some satisfaction that Louis – in his newly-chosen element – thoroughly enjoyed himself while his tutor succumbed to seasickness.

Dr Burney, the headmaster of the school, collected Louis in London and took him down to Portsmouth by train. There was the reassuring promise of a visit from his father within a few days. Because of his rank, Louis was not expected to mix much with the other boys, and was to live with the Burney family and have his lessons in the house.

It was his first experience of being utterly cut off from his own family, his first experience of loneliness. He was very homesick and wrote sad letters to his mother telling how he would look at her portraits which he had brought with him and placed in his bedroom.

Meals with the Burneys were excessively dreary and prolonged, the men in dress coats, Louis in a little velvet jacket and breeches – course followed course in stodgy profusion. Louis had a fine hearty appetite, and also a discerning palate, and he asked his mother to pass the message to her cook that she was better than the English cook at Alverstoke. The good doctor's attempts to soften the blow of separation and grant Louis every privilege were well intended but unsuccessful. If only he could be treated like an ordinary boy! When Louis wrote to his mother that he could tell her little about the others, she gave instructions that he must at least eat and play football with them. Surely he would then soon make friends.

But Louis was kept too busy to remain sad for long. One day in early December he saw a big warship at close quarters for the first time. And what a mighty vessel, the mightiest in the world, flagship of the Channel Fleet – H.M.S. *Minotaur*! The twenty boys at Alverstoke who were preparing for the Navy were taken out to this battleship by Dr Burney and shown round. Louis wrote proudly home to his mother about her. No fewer than five masts, compared with the three masts of Nelson's *Victory* on the other side of the harbour; and, nestling among them, two tall funnels, for this great hermaphrodite of a fighting ship had a 7,000 horsepower engine and could steam at 14 knots or sail at a much slower speed. However quaint she looked later in Louis's naval career, neither sailing ship nor steamer, neither wooden wall nor ironclad, at the time the *Minotaur* was the cynosure of all eyes.

Besides the lessons, there were many other outings with the ever-assiduous Dr Burney to keep him busy – to a notary public at Gosport where as a newly-naturalized British subject, he took the oath of allegiance to the Queen (and kissed a very dirty Bible), to a tailor for clothes to visit the Queen, and for the elaborate kit required by a Naval Cadet. He was recommended to Uncle Affie's tailor: 'Mr Burney and my tailor say that I cannot go to the Queen in my short Cadet jacket,' he wrote to his mother, 'but must have what is called a Full Dress Coat . . . with anchor buttons and a few other gold trifles.'[1] The uniforms were soon made, and Louis went along to collect them, together with his sea chest and sextant, his dirk and hammock and pillow cases and all the other paraphernalia a fully kitted-out cadet required. Then he had himself photographed. It is easy to understand why the Queen took such a fancy to him – his soft brown eyes, sensitive full mouth and tender, vulnerable face. He was a handsome boy indeed. But she noticed that he was by no means without spirit and confidence, so perhaps any anxious thoughts of how he would stand up to the uninhibited life ahead of him in the gunroom of a British man-o'-war were allayed.

There are already signs of Louis's sharp observation and intelligence. He missed very little, as one can see from his letters. He was invited out to dine at the local barracks, and several times with the Commander-in-Chief, Portsmouth, Admiral Sir Thomas Pasley. He comments on one of his neighbours at dinner – she was, it seems, 'extraordinarily stupid and dreadfully dull. At table she doesn't open her mouth and sits there in a most affected attitude.' He watches the three elderly unmarried daughters of the Admiral who are served with champagne very sparingly by the steward. At the end, one of them, seeing that Louis has drunk only water through the meal, grabs his full champagne glass before leaving the room with the other ladies. 'If you won't drink it, I will.'

At any army dinner, too, his eyes are wide open all the time, observing with great interest the red mess jackets of the 67th Infantry Regiment, and listening spellbound to the cries of 'Hip Hip Hurrah' when a departing officer's health was drunk. How very foreign! But how very interesting!

When the examination took place on 14 December he passed through in all subjects without any trouble – a testimonial to Mr Everett and a reward for his busy summer. Well in time for Christmas and home leave, he was officially in the Royal Navy – Cadet His Serene Highness the Prince Louis of Battenberg. Everything seemed promising for the future. He was not, after all, to go to the *Britannia* – it had been decided that he would go straight to sea in the training ship *Bristol* in the New Year. Then, privilege struck the first of many sharp blows he was to suffer in his naval career. Having escaped the voyage round the world with Uncle Affie, Uncle Bertie – briefed by Princess Alice to look after his young nephew – took his instructions literally and demanded that he should join him in a Mediterranean cruise as an A.D.C.: which would mean all pomp and circumstance and special favours, and little naval instruction.

Louis felt highly honoured at the time – he, a boy of only 14! – but it was not long before he realized how damaging to him this voyage was to be.

Christmas at beloved Heiligenberg! Dear Mama, dear Papa! And all the loving cousins from Darmstadt, and the welcoming, smiling servants. And of course the admiring young brothers, Sandro Liko, and seven-year-old Franzjos. Louis was in transports of joy and relief to be back amongst the familiar scenes, the familiar objects, of a happy childhood. He wore his uniform on all possible occasions, often with his dirk – to the theatre in Darmstadt, to balls and dances. Aunt Alice was especially glad to see the pleasure and pride he was deriving from his new career.

Louis's first ship could hardly be called a man-o'-war, and was a very odd vessel indeed. For many weeks she had been in dockyard hands at Malta being prepared for her royal passengers. She was the *Ariadne*, a ten-year-old frigate from which all the guns had been removed, their ports being converted to windows for the royal suite. Louis first set eyes on her on 20 January 1869 in Trieste harbour. His father had brought him from Darmstadt by train, calling at a few family friends and relations on the way. This time the parting was less painful. Louis knew that he would be in kind and powerful hands. The Prince and Princess of Wales would look after him.

But the short trip out to the *Ariadne* in a hired boat was as cold as his reception on board. The gunroom, the midshipmen's living quarters, was 'a dark and stuffy hole'. The food, unchanged since Nelson's day, was almost uneatable. The officers appeared indifferent to him. Louis had only once trodden the decks of a warship, he did not know how to sling a hammock, how to climb the rigging, even how to distinguish port from starboard. His training was nil – but the moment he arrived on board he was told off to keep watch.

Miserable and lonely, Louis did his best to pick up the rudiments of the unfamiliar language and lore of the sailor; to accustom his stomach to the weevil-ridden biscuits and tough gristly salt beef; and to learn to sleep in a hammock slung in among twenty others in the stuffy depths of the gunroom. It was all a great contrast with the gentleness, kindness, privacy and luxury of the life he had known all through his childhood.

The royal party arrived late on the evening of 27 January, the Prince and Princess with a suite of aristocrats. The Prince was at this time twenty-seven years old, genial and fun-loving away from his mother, a great traveller partly for this reason, affectionate with his friends and misunderstood (or so he thought) by all his family, except by Alice who was always his favourite. Any favourite of Alice was his favourite, too.

The Prince was already showing the stoutness of good living, but his face did not yet carry the marks of self-indulgence which even his full beard later failed to conceal. The Princess was as lovely and statuesque as on the day of her wedding, when all England fell in love with her, nearly six years earlier. She was bearing children at the same relentless pace as her mother-in-law: they already had four, and she was expecting another.

When Louis was presented to the Prince and Princess of Wales in the royal quarters he was at once invited to dinner. From gunroom to palace! This was the beginning, for Louis, of many topsy-turvy weeks, during which he found himself alternately abused and forced to suffer the full rigours of a raw recruit's life in the toughest service in the world, and wined and dined and made much of by two of the most powerful and indulged people in the world. Often the contrast was experienced in one day. It was all very bewildering!

Over dinner in the royal quarters the Prince suggested that Louis might like to go for a cruise up the Nile with his party. It was, of course, a royal command rather than an invitation and there was no question of refusing. All this was done, Louis recognized, 'out of pure kindness'; but he also saw very soon that it was 'a great mistake'. He was missing the systematized training his contemporaries were receiving in the training ship *Bristol* and having to pick things up as well as he could. Nor did this favoured treatment endear him to his fellow (and much senior) midshipmen in the *Ariadne* whenever he returned from his elevated life above them in the royal quarters.

At Alexandria, where they arrived on 2 February, Louis disembarked from the *Ariadne* with some relief. The preparations for the Royal Nile Expedition had been going on for months, and on an impressive scale. The results certainly impressed the young Prince. The flotilla, which Louis first saw four days later at Cairo and described in admiring detail, consisted of a large paddle steamer equipped with a deckhouse which acted as dining saloon, and cabins for the entourage. This towed a houseboat – a *dahabieh* – on which had been built an enormous deckhouse for the Prince and Princess of Wales. The deck was deeply carpeted and the divans and chairs and stool for the grand piano were covered in blue silk. It was named *Skandria*, the nearest they could achieve to the Princess's name.

Then came the kitchen steamer which in turn towed floating stables with Arab horses for the men to ride and 'a splendid white donkey' for the Princess. Besides the rich range of exotic foodstuffs, the kitchen steamer stored 3,000 bottles of champagne, 4,000 of claret, 10,000 of beer and 20,000 of soda water. As a guide the party had the most notable Nile authority of all time, Sir Samuel Baker; there was an official artist; and no less a writer than Dr W. H. Russell of *The Times* who was soon to add to his laurels gained in the Crimean, American Civil and Austrian wars with his reports on the Franco-Prussian conflict.

This glittering flotilla, in company with numerous auxiliary craft and a parallel party sailing under almost as lavish conditions and headed by the Duke of Sutherland, set off on 6 February. The entertainment consisted of sightseeing at temples, tombs, statues and other ancient remains ('The enclosed piece of mummified material was given to me by the Prince of Wales,' wrote Louis to 'Dear, good Mama',)[2] and the destruction of animal and bird life which went on wherever the Prince travelled. Crocodiles proved too tough until the Prince used explosive bullets. Birds were easier, from a duckpunt usually. Flamingoes, Louis had to admit, 'were mere slaughter'. Hyenas were more difficult. Louis and the Prince spent the best part of a moonlit night crouched behind cover with a fresh-killed kid as bait. Nothing turned up.

The arduous and confusing duties on board the *Ariadne* seemed very remote to Louis under such majestic circumstances. Their host, the Khedive of Egypt, was there to greet them in Cairo when the flotilla returned. These were great days for Cairo. The Khedive had never been richer nor more powerful, and the Suez Canal was about to be opened. Verdi had already composed *Aïda* for the occasion, and every crowned head in Europe would soon be there for the festivities.

After a gilded banquet at the Khedive's palace, and the presentation of Orders – Louis got a Medjidieh, Fourth Class – they travelled to Suez to be entertained by Ferdinand de Lesseps, who lived in very considerable style close to his work, and then took them to inspect the wonder of the day. The Prince, as a prelude to the completion of the canal, opened a ceremonial sluice to release the waters of the Mediterranean.

On a different scale, but also described as 'a wonder of the day' by Louis, was the Khedive's yacht in which they embarked at Port Said for another banquet and passage to Alexandria. It was more like a floating palace than a yacht, with marble staircases and parquet floors, Sèvres china, silver candelabra, marble fittings and heavy gilt chairs. There were many more servants – powdered footmen, French *maîtres-d'hôtel* – than guests. The Prince and Princess and full entourage descended straight to dinner.

Louis called what followed 'indescribable', and then proceeded to do so very graphically. 'Suddenly, as we rounded the breakwater, the ship gave two or three very heavy rolls. The whole of the heavy gilt chairs on one side slid away to leeward with their occupants along the parquet floor to the ship's side, while the candelabra and fruit dishes fell over with a great clatter. At the next roll the chairs on the other side slid away, leaving the bare table deserted. At the same time piles of plates which stood on the marble consoles along each wall crashed down in two avalanches; most of the lights also went out. Needless to say, the Khedive's servants were sprawling on the floor, mixed up with the guests, and the general wreckage. A few minutes later the ship was once more as steady as a church . . .'

This idyllic, memorable existence continued for more weeks for Louis, and after the *Ariadne* left Egypt the pageantry, the sightseeing, the meetings, continued, all at the highest level. At the Dardanelles he helped the Prince fire some trial rounds from the huge stone-shot muzzle-loaders which defended the Straits, watching the 600-pound ball bouncing sixteen times on the glass-still water. There were banquets and entertainments at the British Embassy in Constantinople and at the Sultan of Turkey's palace, Saleh Bazar, which made the Khedive's palaces seem like slums. Across the Black Sea to Sebastopol, and there a less alien hierarchy received them – notable Russian generals who knew Louis's father from the old days when they had fought alongside him. Russell took them over the battlefields of the Crimean War, and with the Prince at his side, Louis galloped 'Into the Valley of Death' where 'rode the six hundred' in the Light Brigade's great charge a few years before.

On the way back the Sultan came out in his enormous oared *caique* and presented more honours, this time an Osmanieh 4th Class for Louis. Then on to Greece where they anchored in the Piraeus, and the Princess of Wales's brother, the King of Greece, came on board for lunch. At dinner ashore, which even Louis, after all he had seen, described as 'a very grand affair', the King made him smoke his first cigarette. At the island of Corfu, which was to figure so prominently in the life of his own family, he met Queen Olga of Greece at the beautiful Adams Brothers' villa of 'Mon Repos' and 'succumbed to her charms'. W. H. Russell wrote of 'her exquisite fairness . . . great warmth and grace'.[3] She had just given birth to a little boy who became King Constantine, brother of Prince Andrew of Greece and future uncle to Prince Philip. It was an idyllic week at 'Mon Repos' for Louis, surrounded by loving and charming friends and relations. They lived in the palace in the nearby town and rode about the island in the spring sunshine.

These experiences made the succeeding weeks all the harder to bear. At Brindisi he bade a grateful farewell to the Prince and Princess of Wales as they set off for England by train, and the *Ariadne* sailed for Malta. There were to be no further releases from the rigours of the gunroom. Gunroom cruelty was an old tradition in the Royal Navy. Like public school bullying, it was intended to 'knock rough edges' off a boy, to test his endurance, to make him conform, and to let off steam. After particularly nasty injuries, and even accidental deaths, there were attempts to reduce the hardships, but reform was still a long way away – it was still on a vicious scale in the Grand Fleet in the First World War, and it took Admiral David Beatty himself a great deal of time to stamp it out in his flagship. Louis was ripe game – the product of a soft, luxurious home life, a foreigner with a gutteral accent, the subject of endless favouritism over the past weeks while they had been working and eating ship's biscuit against Louis's caviare. His gentle demeanour did not help either.

From Malta Louis wrote a despairing letter to Heiligenberg, telling his parents of his sufferings and begging his father to use his influence to have him released from the Navy. He could stand it no longer. But, for the present, there could be no relief. And matters became worse on the long voyage home, through the Bay of Biscay under sail all the way. Still without any training, he was ordered aloft with the rest, working high up on the yards, uncertain that he could hold on as the frigate tossed and rolled through the grey seas. 'It was a constant terror for me,' he wrote of this passage. Back at Spithead at last, no one seemed to know or care about him. The Lords of the Admiralty had obeyed the Prince of Wales's instructions to appoint him to the *Ariadne* in the first place. They now seemed totally uncaring about what happened to him next.

Lonely, homesick and alarmed, Louis wrote to the only man who could help, the Prince of Wales, who invited him to Marlborough House to stay for a few days. Louis obtained leave and took the train to London. There he poured his heart out. The Prince of Wales had neither first- nor second-hand experience of a raw cadet's conditions on board H.M. ships. He may perhaps have been astonished and indignant at how bad they were, and angry that anyone should treat a young boy so cruelly. But Bertie was not the fool some people – including his own mother – believed him to be. He never rushed in with poor advice. It is very unlikely that he showed indignation if he felt it, he was far too sensible for that. What he did do was to advise against a hasty decision – 'stick it out for a bit longer'. They agreed between them that nothing should be done until Louis had talked things over with his parents; and meanwhile there is little doubt that the Prince took steps to see that in future a little more interest was taken in the boy by the Admiralty.

Back in Germany for a few weeks' leave, Louis's whole outlook and regard for the Navy was altered in the loving happiness – and the hero-worshipping – at Heiligenberg. It was mid-June 1869, a warm and glorious summer. Suddenly, he was ashamed of having written that letter from Malta and upsetting his mother. No, the Royal Navy was wonderful, he told everyone. And there followed stories of taking in a reef of the mains'l in an Atlantic gale. Still wearing his uniform, he spent all his spare time making a full-rigged

model of the *Ariadne* – the first of so many ships in which he was to
serve.

22 July 1869. Cadet Battenberg has been appointed to serve on the
North American Station in the flagship *Royal Alfred*, under the
Commander-in-Chief Vice-Admiral G. Wellesley. Princess Alice
and the Senior Naval Lord have seen to it that Louis is posted far
from the benign but crippling influence of the Prince and Princess
of Wales. On the other side of the Atlantic he will have to stand on
his own feet and will be free to follow the regular course of training of
which the *Ariadne*'s cruise had deprived him. With his enthusiasm for
his chosen career rekindled at Heiligenberg, Louis himself favours this
arrangement, which will take him far from home for many months.

He has stowed his sea chest outside the gunroom of the *Revenge*,
which is to transport the C.-in-C., his family and furniture and the
flagship's new crew. In his kit there are small comforts lovingly
prepared in the kitchens at Heiligenberg, including some beef
extract cleverly soldered into tins. It is crowded and dark down here,
but less cramped than in the *Ariadne*, right aft on the lower deck and
with big ports across the stern. There are familiar faces about him,
old shipmates from the Mediterranean cruise, all now more anxious
to be agreeable to one another – even those who had bullied Louis
mercilessly before – in view of the long voyage ahead. This is no time
to make enemies. There are also several who were friendly in the
Ariadne – young Francis Spring-Rice was one, and Charlie Cunninghame Graham, his only other fellow-cadet in the *Ariadne*.

The *Revenge* is a two-decker line-of-battleship, little different from
the wooden walls of England which had fought at Trafalgar,
although there is an apology of an engine, a single screw which can
be hoisted in, and a single funnel which can be lowered – an 'up-
funnel-and-down-screw' ship – simple auxiliary power, in fact, and
when a powerful westerly wind hits them outside the Channel, they
are blown far north of Ireland and there is nothing their little engine
can do about it. A few days later, Louis experiences his first gale.
It is his 'night in', but all hands are turned up and he is aloft with
the rest of them in no time, shifting topsails in the dark, with the wind
howling about him. This is the real thing, and he is excited, no
longer frightened at the experience. There is a great splitting sound
below. It is the cross jack yard being carried away, and they hear it
crashing down on the poop.

67

It is daylight, and the carpenter's crew are mending the hole in the deck, before they can get back to the gunroom for breakfast. It is half full of water and all their gear is floating about with the furniture. The old hands make light of it, and the new boys try to assume an indifference to this experience which they certainly do not feel. Louis is triumphant that he is numbered among the few who have not even felt seasick. He secures his gear, finds one of beloved Mama's tins of beef extract and sets about making soup for all.

Two days later, in blazing sunshine, they sight their first icebergs, gleaming magnificently green in the sunshine, and close one of them in order to fire a round at it from one of their aged 32-pounder cannon. On 24 August the *Revenge* docks at Halifax.

The North American Squadron was responsible for showing the flag, and when necessary exerting power and influence, along the eastern coast of Canada and throughout the West Indies. It also made the presence of the Royal Navy known along the eastern United States seaboard, with occasional calls at Annapolis, New York and other ports. It was only one of numerous squadrons and fleets all over the world which protected British interests and demonstrated British imperial power. For the greater convenience of the C.-in-C. the flagship normally lay at Halifax during the summer months, only occasionally going out for target practice and local cruises or up the St Lawrence River to Quebec. In November, when the cold really set in, the Admiral closed down his official residence ashore, and the flagship embarked his wife and child, house servants and grooms, horses and carriages and fodder, and all his livestock which included cows, one hundred sheep and poultry. The gun deck became a farm-yard, and Louis described with relish how the midshipmen of the middle watch would surreptitiously milk one of the cows for their cocoa brew. Goodness knows what would have happened if war had broken out with the U.S.A. while *en route* to Bermuda. But once there, everything was quickly disembarked and the Admiral set up residence at Admiralty House on the island for the winter.

The *Royal Alfred* was of the same vintage as the *Minotaur*, a product of compromise and uncertainty in naval architecture. She was begun as a wooden two-decker and was left half-completed when the French startled the world – and especially the Royal Navy – by laying down the first ironclad. Finally, rather than waste the hull and start all over again, it was decided to stick some 6-inch iron plates over her vital parts and equip her with a heavy battery of 9-inch and 7-inch guns. It says much for the effectiveness of the compromise that she could sail under a full spread of canvas at over twelve knots and steam at exactly the same speed with her 3,000 horsepower engine. At the end of her long commission Louis came to learn every inch of her rigging, and knew his way around her decks as well as he knew every corner of beloved Heiligenberg.

The routine of cruising, visiting, exercises and gunnery practice was as unchanging as the ships of the squadron and the officers and men. For year after year it was almost unknown to see a new face on this station. Amongst the few people who left were the flagship's Commander and the Admiral himself. Commander Charles H. Stirling, Louis recalled, had a wife who was something of a martinette and insisted on coming on board her husband's ship nearly every day in one of the gigs. She would call out the regular orders in a loud voice, perhaps pointing out that the flagship's fore royal yard was not square by the lifts, or some other irregularity, and seeing that the gig was brought alongside in a seamanlike manner.

This sort of thing did not endear her to the ship's company, and the Commander was finally asked to choose between his ship and his wife. He chose his wife, and shortly afterwards left Halifax with her and their little girl. Their ship, the *City of Boston,* was never heard of again.

Louis tells of another agonizing choice which had to be made at this time, by none other than the ship's new Commander, who went by the name of 'Buffles'. 'At any hour of the day,' Louis recounted, 'he could be seen through the skylights sitting at the ward room table drinking neat gin out of a square bottle ... Once when he returned very unsteadily over the brow and then turned forward towards the forecastle instead of aft to his cabin, I guided him to bed, for which he thanked me very profusely. In the end he was given the choice between the ship or the bottle, and he chose the bottle.'

Another officer to leave the station, to a lesser fate, was Admiral Wellesley. He departed in 1870 to take command of the much larger Channel Fleet. But he was soon back again with his wife and (very spoilt) daughter and the rest of his domestic entourage after his Channel flagship piled up on a rock outside Gibraltar in broad daylight.

Just as there were occasional changes among the faces on board the flagship, so there were also welcome breaks in the routine. And when there were entertainments ashore, Louis was among the first to be invited, for it was socially advantageous for the hostesses of St George's or St Kitts to let it be known among their guests that a Prince would also be present. Louis remembered being 'rather mobbed by families of black people who used to come on board and demand to see me. When I appeared and asked them whether they would like to go round the ship they generally declined, saying they had only come to see me. After a long and deliberate stare and final handshake they would climb back into their boats and go home.'[4]

At every island visited by the squadron there would be a grand ball, the social event of the year for the locals. At first Louis relished the iced lemonade and fresh fruit almost as much as the local girls. As he got older the balance of his taste changed, and with each season he danced and flirted more enthusiastically. The girls adored his looks, his gentle voice with its faint foreign intonation, his eager liveliness and enthusiasm for everything and especially for them. In the gunroom of the *Prince Alfred* he began to acquire the reputation of a Lothario. If it was not quite a girl in every port, it was, for Louis, a girl in every other anchorage, island and naval establishment. There was the one at Halifax, one of two lovely De Vebber sisters with whom he used to dance the night through. There was 'the prettiest girl by far' at Hamilton, whose father kept the dry-goods store at which she sometimes served. 'I used to buy my white kid gloves from her on the day of a dance,' Louis reminisced, 'and make my dance engagement with her at the same time.'[5] Then he fell madly in love with the beautiful Isabel Macpherson with whom he used to go riding and sing duets and dance. This was one of the happiest episodes of the whole long commission and they both wept and were inconsolable when they had to part. (She became Lady Kirkpatrick instead of Princess Louis but remained a life-long friend.) At Jamaica there was a Jewish girl called Julia Hart. In Louis's memory in later years, they were all perfectly lovely. Julia was just one of them – but this time 'I fell so hopelessly in love with her that I nearly gave up food and drink. Every spare moment was spent at her fat mother's house.'[6] But at last (as sailors do) Louis sailed away, his heart bleeding, and next time he returned the beautiful Julia had married a fat and wealthy globe-trotting English widower.

The next-most-ardent lover among the *Royal Alfred*'s young midshipmen may have been Louis's closest 'pal' Salis Schwabe. It was with Schwabe that he first visited New York, on the strength of an unexpected generous tip sent from Russia by kind Aunt Marie. Later these two young bloods made extended tours to Montreal, Detroit, Chicago, St Louis, and then through Cleveland and Buffalo back to Toronto and Halifax, travelling by train, coach and all sorts of river craft including three-storied American paddle steamers.

On these trips, and for that matter wherever the *Royal Alfred* sailed on her commission, Louis drew in pencil and pen and ink the people and places. It was an enthusiasm that was to last all his life, and he became increasingly proficient. His fellow midshipmen were not an artistic lot. Lord Mountbatten recalls his father talking of these days. 'They had no intellectual aspect to their lives at all – they were just boisterous lads from a "huntin'-'n-shootin'" background who did not just despise intellectualism, they did not know what it was.'

In fact Louis was the only one among them who could play the piano, and his services at dances and concerts were always much in demand. Another thing that singled him out from the others was his abstinence. The heavy drinking that took place among the officers had at first shocked him. Then he became used to it, and they became used to his sobriety, doing good trade for his rum ration and taking it for granted that 'the German lad' would cover up for them if they were totally unconscious when their watch came up. Louis remembered at the end of some squadron binge in the flagship's gunroom marking out the deck with the names of the other ships in chalk, and having the prostrate bodies of the visiting junior officers placed accordingly for the guidance of the crews of their ships' boats who came to collect them.

Only occasionally did the arrival of some distinguished figure forcibly remind him of his Princely rank. The first of these was Prince Arthur, Queen Victoria's third son, who was four years older than Louis and a youthful army subaltern. During his reception at Halifax, Louis dined with him and was invited to all the local ceremonies and entertainments. Later, in March 1872, he met his Russian cousin Alexei, who was serving on board the frigate *Svetlana* and formally visiting Havana. Again Louis was invited to all the festivities and a great ball in honour of Grand Duke Alexei Alexandrovitch of Russia, including a ball on board the Spanish guardship *Gerona*, which temporarily dispensed with its entire armament for the sake of providing more dancing space.

When any friend of the Prince of Wales arrived on the station, Louis was always called for and would be entertained with him. One of these was that remarkable high-living and gay society bachelor sailor 'Ocean Swell' – or Rear Admiral Sir Frederick Beauchamp Seymour, who was later to become a national hero. 'Ocean Swell' saw to it that not only Louis but any of his pals he chose should come for a vast dinner on board his flagship.

For Louis, the high point of this long commission was, of course, his period of leave. This occurred early on because his family wanted him to be confirmed in the summer of 1870. When he first heard that it had been arranged, he wrote to his father: 'Dearest beloved Papa, My mind is in a whirl and I can hardly think for joy. But I must pull myself together and try to express myself clearly . . .'7 It began well. In London, when the Prince of Wales heard that he was coming, he cancelled Louis's hotel and told him firmly that he must stay with him at Marlborough House – and in the future *always* to stay there and *never* at a hotel. But after that, it was another three years before he saw his family again, and there were times when he felt close to despair, starved of intellectual people, intellectual thoughts and ideas, and the intellectual stimulation as well as the merriment of life at home.

Louis's letters at this time reveal his mercurial and sensitive nature, and the contradictions point to a mind that was still not set in its form – he was, after all, still in his 'teens until shortly before the end of the commission. Sometimes he writes proudly of his friends, at other times he complains that he has none, and that everything is past bearing. He kept up a steady correspondence not only with his mother and father, but also with his brothers and sister.

Princess Marie had married Gustavus, later Prince of Erbach-Schönberg, a year after Louis's confirmation leave. Louis continued to write to her as lovingly as ever, always addressing her as 'My dearest beloved sister', and signing himself her 'devoted and affectionate old brother'. To her he revealed more than he was prepared to expose to his mother and father, whom he was anxious not to distress. No doubt it gave him some relief during his periods of black misery to express himself on paper.

In April 1873 it was nearly three years since he had last been on leave. 'What a blessed day it will be when I can telegraph to you from Halifax "Sailing for England today",' he exclaims, then continues to recount what has been happening in 'this desolate hole',8 Bermuda. His homesickness had been increased by the arrival of H.M.S. *Challenger*, which was beginning its epic round-the-world scientific voyage. On board was a notable German professor, Baron von Willemoes-Suhm, with whom Louis had long talks and walks.

They had many mutual friends back in Germany, and when he left, Louis told his sister, 'I felt very clearly why it is that I am beginning to find it so dull in the English Navy; it is because of the lack of anyone with whom I could have a good talk – in a word a friend. That's why I long to be with my own countrymen. I have not yet found a friend among the many comrades I have had in the 'R.A.' [*Royal Alfred*]; and senior officers will always be senior officers, particularly on board ship. So I am thrown entirely on my own resources, and although I have, in time, become accustomed to many things, I shall never feel quite at home in the English Navy . . .'[9]

Of course, by April 1873, this was rubbish, and no doubt Louis later regretted having written these words. In fact, in the same letter, he writes of having 'spent some of the best years of my life' in the *Royal Alfred* 'in which, so to speak, I have grown up'. And grown up he had! When he had first arrived at Halifax, he could easily stand up 'tween decks in the garrison ship *Irresistible*. By 1873 'I can't stand upright anywhere in her, it is quite disgraceful'. He had grown greatly in height and in strength. He was now 6 feet tall, and he had grown a moustache and a beautiful soft brown beard – soft because he had never shaved – so that his family scarcely recognized him when at last he returned to Darmstadt.

Louis's period on the North American Station, then, formed the outline of the great sailor who was to emerge and take high responsibility thirty years later. Out here he learned to accept manfully misfortunes and injustices, and to accept modestly and with concealed pleasure the successes that came to him. He passed his exams well, to be rated midshipman within a few months of arrival at Halifax, continued to do well at his studies, and pleased – and became friends with – his Naval Instructor, Littlejohns. In spite of what he had written, he did make friends in the gunroom – Francis Spring-Rice, Charlie Cunninghame Graham and Salis Schwabe remained friends all his life.

In Canadian and Caribbean waters, Louis became a real sailor, learning to go aloft in all weathers, to splice a rope, to handle small craft, to navigate and understand both the moods of the sea and the moods of the men who would one day serve under him.

The next two years marked a difficult time for Louis. Rank and privilege – their delights and dangers – were again the cause. With the most powerful and rich in the land tempting him with offers of every kind of entertainment and pastime, it is remarkable that he succumbed so rarely. Few of his temptors appeared to understand that anyone as attractive, personable, princely and marriageable should want to take his chosen career seriously. After all, in their eyes, one joined the Army or the Navy only as an excuse to wear the uniform and for the social advantages: one was not expected *seriously* to be a soldier or a sailor. It was a full-time and exhausting occupation to follow the social round of society in mid-Victorian England – the shooting, the hunting, the balls and receptions, the dinners, the entertainments of all kinds. Even if one limited one's society life quite seriously, there was little time for responsible attention to one's service duties.

Louis had already, but briefly, recognized the dangers of these temptations. Within hours of his return from leave at Heiligenberg, he was made to realize how great they would now become, and how safe from them he had been at Halifax. It would have been easier if he had not enjoyed the social scene so much. But he enjoyed every aspect of it – the beautiful, adoring women, the dancing, the riding, the shooting, the fun of meeting people. Nor had he by any means adjusted himself to the rigours of the gunroom, the taste of ship's biscuit, and the philistinism and long periods of boredom in the Royal Navy.

Louis's only ally in the struggle with his conscience was the Queen herself. Queen Victoria knew better than most people how to judge the calibre of a man's charms. Not only was she born with shrewdness, she had also watched with loving anxiety her own daughters succumbing to German charm. She needed Beatrice by her side, and was determined not to allow her last daughter to go to anyone, least of all to another German prince, even if he was now a newly naturalized Englishman. She recognized very clearly Prince Louis's attractions and had watched Beatrice dancing with him. Shortly afterwards, dining at Osborne House with the Queen, Louis found himself next to Beatrice again, but could not get one word out of her.

Many years later Louis learned that the Queen had forbidden her daughter from talking to him and had arranged the seating deliberately in order that the young Princess could indicate by her silence that she was not for him, although really she was very fond of him. To complete her plot, the Queen let it be known to the Admiralty that Prince Louis was to be employed exclusively on foreign stations for the foreseeable future.

Perhaps she had good reason for her anxieties. It was such an obvious match that later a gossip took a chance and announced to the press that they were secretly betrothed. Louis learned this when he was on the other side of the world and read the news in an obscure local newspaper with some dismay.

Louis returned to England from Germany at the beginning of March 1874 to cram for his sub-lieutenant's examinations. It was, unhappily for him, a more than usually intensive royal spring and summer, even by mid-Victorian standards. The Duke of Edinburgh had recently married Louis's Russian cousin, the Grand Duchess Marie Alexandrovna, in St Petersburg. There were great celebrations when the happy couple returned to the British court, and as the Duke's protégé and friend, Louis could hardly avoid them.

There was a week-end at Osborne when all the Queen's available sons foregathered, and later, when the bride's father arrived in London – the first time the Emperor of All the Russias had been in England for many years – there were seemingly endless festivities at Buckingham Palace.

Louis recalled many years later how he had proudly worn his new full dress uniform and, with the Queen's permission, all his Hessian Orders, at the State Banquet. He remembered, too, the shame of being taken quietly into a corner by Tsar Alexander II after dinner and being told that he was wearing the Ludwig's Order over the wrong shoulder. As the Emperor helped him to change it he comforted his young nephew by telling him that he had made just the same mistake the first time he had worn this order at Darmstadt many years before.

In the autumn, when the newly-weds moved to their country seat in Kent, and the Prince and Princess of Wales to Sandringham, there were pressing invitations to hunt and shoot. Louis was now at the Royal Naval College at Greenwich, and the President, the redoubtable Admiral Sir Astley Cooper Key, had to warn Louis that Royal duties were one thing and could not be avoided, but that week-end hunt balls were quite another thing – even if the invitation came on pasteboard a quarter inch thick embossed with the royal coat of arms.

Louis responded by refusing them all and working harder than ever, employing two special teachers and, on most days, working from early morning until late at night. But he still found invitations to dances in London irresistible, and there was a good deal of burning the candle at both ends, arriving on the milk train from Charing Cross station in London and going straight back to work.

The results were discouraging. Admiral Cooper Key told him gravely that he had got only a second, then attempted to console him by telling him that there were only three firsts that year.

But the examination results of the subs' courses which followed should have satisfied even Louis. He passed out first – and best student ever – at seamanship, and first – and joint best student ever – at gunnery. At French, in which he was completely bi-lingual and far ahead of all the others, he got only a second. A Frenchman took the examination and discovered – though he should not have been able to – that Louis was a German-born prince whose family, only three years earlier, had fought with such success in the Franco-Prussian war.

After this long period of intensive work, Louis was thankful to yield to all the delicious temptations that were offered to him. In April 1875 there were three heavenly weeks at Marlborough House. The Prince of Wales put Louis up for the Marlborough Club (Papa paid the £42 entrance and subscription), there were concerts at Buckingham Palace, Cousin Marie Edinburgh gave birth to her first child and her mother came over for the event and Louis stood as one of the godfathers. Alice and Ludwig arrived from Darmstadt with their little children and Louis proudly showed his pretty little cousins Victoria and Ella round London – besides giving them that longed-for row on Buckingham Palace's lake. Then it was back to Germany for them all, and the arrival of the Russians for the summer.

In the midst of these delights, the Prince of Wales divulged to Louis that he would be making a long state visit to India in the winter. Would Louis care to accompany him as an orderly officer?

Louis thought the invitation over very carefully. The last tour had been a great mistake. But now he had been in the service for six years, he was no longer a greenhorn, he was much more self-assured and much more accepted by his generation of naval officers. This, surely, could not damage him as the earlier tour had done? He accepted gratefully; and then went off to enjoy himself buying all the kit and uniforms he would require for the occasion. Second to wearing uniforms, Louis liked best to buy them.

Everything about the Prince of Wales's Royal Tour of India in 1875–6 was on the imperial scale. Today the mind tends to flinch back timorously from the grandiose. Our Victorian ancestors did not suffer from this self-consciousness. Except for a very small minority of intellectual radicals, the whole nation revelled in the magnificent details of this tour and all the delights of imperial splendour at its summit. Where the little figure in black shrank from public exposure and was living out her widowhood in privacy and austerity, her eldest son swaggered weightily through all the pomp and pageantry that his mother's subjects loved, and with which they identified themselves.

The start, however, was neither grand nor auspicious. The *Serapis*, an elaborately converted Indian troopship, suffered from boiler trouble, and her peppery, hard-drinking captain had to give orders for an Inspector of Machinery to rush out urgently to Malta to meet the ship as she steamed through the Mediterranean. He had such a knack with boilers that the captain dared not offend him, and this Geordie with his rich Northumberland accent dined with his Royal Highness and suite, dressed in a tailcoat and waistcoat – 'me yeller wais'coat' – with numerous buttons (upper half undone to show he was formal), a roll collar and tight sleeves. After the initial shock, the Prince of Wales was greatly entertained. He himself was making sartorial history by wearing for the first time 'a dark blue Dinner Jacket, with black silk facings' – the original of the semi-formal 'black tie' dress worn today; and his staff conformed to this fashion.

There was more trouble at Athens. The whole Greek Navy, the Greek Royal Yacht, the flagship of the Mediterranean Fleet and other ironclads, were all in the Piraeus to greet the *Serapis*. Perhaps Captain the Hon. H. Carr Glyn was suffering from too much port wine the previous evening, or was too eager to show off his prowess in front of such a glittering audience. Anyway, the *Serapis* came in towards her allotted billet at twice the speed she should have done, and after parting both her anchor cables went full astern in a desperate attempt to avoid catastrophe. The Royal vessel almost sank her own attendant, the little paddle Royal Yacht *Osborne*, collided with the Greek Royal Yacht, *Amphitrite*, taking away her bowsprit, and narrowly missed a number of other vessels before coming to.

The departure a few days later was nearly as inglorious. A French gunboat, the little commander in full dress uniform and saluting on the bridge, cut across the *Serapis*'s bows as she was passing out through the narrow harbour entrance. Captain Glyn raced to the end of his bridge and yelled in appalling French, '*Mossoo, vous êtes un cochon!*' The Frenchman bowed deeply several times at what he supposed was a typical British courtesy. It was the sort of situation the Prince adored, and Louis watched him 'in convulsions'.

Calcutta, which the royal party reached on Christmas Eve, was spectacular in its reception, and the exchange of gifts with ruling princes was on a heroic scale – priceless jewels to take home to the Princess, a fully-grown tiger complete with attendants for the Prince, among other dangerous livestock.

But nothing could surpass in grandeur the arrangements at Benares where a city of tents had been laid out. Louis's own tent had a large double bedroom, sitting room fully furnished with armchairs, writing table and a dressing room and bathroom – a fleet of servants ever at the ready with hot water, and grooms with a choice of Arab horses ever at the ready in case he felt like a ride.

Louis particularly liked the European touch – a brick fireplace, complete with fuel, built into the side of every tent. He also enjoyed visiting the Prince's spectacular suite of tents, all carpeted, luxuriously furnished and with the walls hung with shawls and embroideries. The most elaborate arrangements were made for the Prince's comfort and convenience – even to a young girl of noble birth being placed in his bed at nights. The rest of the suite were not forgotten either, and Louis wrote of one evening when they were wined and dined until they could manage no more. Each one of them was then guided to his own private 'enormous divan with many soft cushions. Refreshments and smoking material were laid out on a little table. On the divan reclined a native girl in transparent white garments.'[10]

Pig-sticking was a more robust sport offered to them, and Louis loved the excitement and the special skills and dangers. The spear was so sharp that it could go through a pig without the slightest effort. In fact, in the course of a high speed collision between two officers of the 10th Hussars, one had pushed his spear clean through the body of the other without realizing it. Lord Carrington's horse was charged by a particularly furious boar while the suite were standing having tiffin, and he was thrown off and broke his collar bone. The Prince sometimes took part, but not with much success. He was now too heavy to ride anything but the big English horses brought out specially for him, which were very un-handy compared with the Arabs.

The Prince of Wales preferred shooting tiger, and in Nepal especially no pains were spared to ensure his personal success. No fewer than eight hundred elephants were employed as beaters, and amongst these were the privileged few on specially trained elephants

– the guns. Louis was one of these. He hunted everything with the royal party from peacocks to fighting elephants, black buck to wild boar, and the execution was on the same impressive scale as the hunt organization.

In the Royal tour's 7,600 miles by land through the sub-continent, they travelled in grand style by train, in spectacular coach cavalcades, on fast elephants, on slower elephants, including one for the Prince which had carried Warren Hastings himself nearly a century earlier, sometimes on horseback, which Louis enjoyed the most. They met fabulously rich maharajahs and nawabs, penurious vice-consuls, Sikh chieftains, ferocious warriors – every sort of leader and celebrity from the frightening to the ridiculous.

The Maharajah of Patiala was already drunk when they arrived; he was wearing the Empress Eugenie's diamonds, which he had recently bought. He was very proud of them and wore them over his 'scarlet tunic with gold epaulettes which were literally paved with diamonds'. From Nepal Louis, who had recently suffered a broken collar bone from a riding accident while pig-sticking, wrote to his mother and father about the leader of that remote kingdom:

> PRINCE OF WALES'S CAMP[11]
> JAMOA
> NEPAL
> *22 February 1876*

My dearest parents,

Since my last, hurried note to you on the evening before I left Agra so much has happened that I really don't know how I can describe it all. My journey here was long, but thanks to the care of dear Wales everything was most comfortably arranged for me. I had been announced everywhere as Prince L. of B. and suite . . .

Nepal is an independent kingdom ruled by a puppet king, the real head being Maharaja Jung Bahadur, the Prime Minister, who has had a curious career. In 1846 he was a simple infantry captain in the Nepalese Army; then he conceived the grand idea of taking over the Government. To do this he invited about 30 of the highest of the land to a party at his house, had the house surrounded by his soldiers, and shot down the entire company with his own hands *with his hunting rifle. The King was thus frightened into making him Prime Minister . . .*

A thousand kisses and all my best wishes to everyone at home. Wales sends you his warmest regards.

> *Your devoted*
> *Louis*

Louis also sent many drawings back, and these were for a wider audience. The regular *Illustrated London News* artist, who accompanied the royal party on the tour, was sent on to China when they embarked for the homeward journey at Bombay, and Louis accepted the task of covering the final stages. His drawings almost filled one issue of the magazine. He had a marvellous time with his sketch book, especially among the extraordinary collection of livestock which were presented to the Prince and had to be transported back to England. This is how he described one incident which he illustrated:

Loading an ostrich, a Maharajah's gift to the Prince of Wales. (Sketch by Prince Louis of Battenberg, by courtesy *The Illustrated London News*)

'As soon as we had anchored, after dark, a lighter came alongside the ladder, containing three full grown ostriches ... Their legs were fortunately tied, so the petty officer of the quarterdeck took some of his hands down, one of whom seized the first head his lantern showed, walked up the ladder with it, and when the neck was "taut", the rest closed round the body, and somehow, legs kicking, and feathers flying, managed to drag it up. Being on watch, I had them locked up in the small wheel house right aft on the poop. They were able to put their heads out of the windows, and travelled home quite comfortably there . . .'[12]

It was an eventful passage home in other ways. Among Louis's fellow officers was Lieutenant Lord Charles Beresford, one of the Prince's more fiery and furious friends and a near-contemporary of Louis's. They saw a great deal of one another on the tour but did not become close friends. They never did. The wild Irish charm of this handsome, blue-eyed, dashing and eccentric marquess's son was not to Louis's taste, though their ways were to cross many times in the years ahead.

When they were in India Louis had been invited to go to sea again after he had returned home. The ship was the battleship *Sultan* of the Mediterranean Fleet, commanded by the Duke of Edinburgh. When the Prince of Wales heard this he made clear that he did not at all like the idea of his brother's invitation. 'You would do much better to get a little half-pay and spend the season with me at Marlborough House,' he said. He loved to have young Louis about wherever he went. But Louis wisely resisted this attractive alternative.

4

'I think you have done well . . .'

QUEEN VICTORIA *to Princess Victoria of
Hesse, 19 June 1883, on the announcement of her
engagement to Prince Louis*

ON 31 March 1878, amongst the multitude of papers that arrived on
Queen Victoria's desk, in files and folders and red boxes, there was a
memorandum from Sir Henry Ponsonby, her private secretary,
supporting the loyalty and integrity of Lieutenant Prince Louis of
Battenberg. 'General Ponsonby feels convinced that while serving
your Majesty,' a part of it ran, 'Prince Louis would never be guilty
of any conduct against Your Majesty and the giving of Secret
information to the Russians at this moment respecting the defences
of the fleet would be simply traitorous.'[1]

This document in the Royal Archives causes the reader to wonder
in dismay what could have happened to this admirable young man,
and Queen Victoria's favourite naval officer, to make such a defence
necessary. Her Majesty's interpolation beneath this paragraph,
written in her favourite blue pencil, is equally surprising. 'He may
not intend to do anything wrong but will not be trusted considering
his connections,' she writes.

The answer, as we shall soon see, is that Louis has landed himself
in one of those predicaments which had scarred the fortunes of his
father in his military-diplomatic career. It was a hazard the European royal families had had to face for centuries. While their
supposed function was to strengthen alliances, seal breaches and
create strength through harmony by their dynastic match-making,
the results were sometimes disastrous. The confusion of conflicting
loyalties could be too much for them.

82

Their first strength was their unity. This could be – and sometimes was – their undoing when family ties proved stouter than loyalty to their adopted nation. This is easy to understand. What proves more difficult to understand is that, with his father's mistakes as an example to him, Louis – like his father – failed all through his life to understand fully why wrong interpretations could be made about what he did and who he was.

For the present, however, all is well. It is 11 May 1876, a beautiful spring day down at Portsmouth. The Princess of Wales, looking as delectable as ever, comes on board the *Serapis* with her five children, Eddy, Georgie, Louise, Toria and Maud, to welcome home Papa. So do the Prince's younger brothers, Prince Arthur and Prince Alfred, and of course the venerable Duke of Cambridge, the Queen's cousin who has already been Commander-in-Chief of the Army for twenty years and is to continue in this post for another nineteen years.

Here is a real family gathering, and the Prince gives all officers medals and most officers (including Louis) promotion. Then everyone travels up to London in the Royal Train where vast crowds testify to the people's love for the most princely Prince of them all, and there are homecoming ceremonies and homecoming balls.

Louis hurls himself into the festivities, dances and, as usual, falls in love several times. After that, back once more to Heiligenberg, the heat of Hesse, picnics in the forest with his family and friends. Sandro, who has followed his father's example and is serving as an officer in the Russian Army, is home on leave too. The brothers fall into each other's arms and talk and laugh far into the nights. All seems to be enchantment and there is not a cloud in the summer sky.

Prince Alfred, Duke of Edinburgh, had already played an important part in Louis's life. Since he had first suggested the Royal Navy as a career for the young Prince, he had given him much avuncular advice about the singular dual role of royal prince and naval officer he would have to play. In addition Prince Alfred was expected to act as liaison officer and peacemaker between his mother and the Royal Navy. Queen Victoria had never quite forgiven the Navy for refusing to make her beloved Albert an Admiral of the Fleet.

Prince Alfred is a grey figure little noticed among the wicked and the good, the colourful and the black, of Victorian royalty. Like his older brother Bertie, he had a mainly miserable childhood, at first both loved and bullied by him, then forcibly separated from him when Albert decided that Bertie's influence on him was harmful. It was a savage parting that scarred them both for life. The Navy saved him. Affie adored sea life from the start, even though he had to drag his unfortunate tutor around with him wherever he went. His rate of promotion was swifter even than Horatio Nelson's, though less justified.

When he was only eighteen he had been offered the throne of Greece, one of those comfortable little sinecures for which royalty of respectable rank occasionally qualified. King Otho was a very unpopular King, so unpopular that he had been thrown off the throne and forced to flee the country. Everybody loved the idea of replacing him with this youthful and handsome English naval officer. But at the last minute, and to Affie's chagrin, it was re-membered that a treaty between Great Britain, France and Russia prohibited them from putting up their own candidates, and the throne was given instead to his Danish brother-in-law Willie, who became King George I. Many years later, in April 1886, and when Affie was an admiral, he commanded an international fleet that blockaded Greece because she was threatening war against Turkey – such were the ironies and hazards of royal naval life.

Prince Alfred developed into a good naval officer in his own right, and some said that he gained command of the Mediterranean Fleet on merit alone. He could certainly handle a big fleet as well as anyone, and loved doing so. Of course he longed for action as they all did in those days, but he never saw any. The only time he heard a shot fired in anger was when a would-be assassin fired a pistol and wounded him in the back at Port Jackson in New South Wales.

Prince Alfred had some odd ways about him, and because of his shyness, mistaken for aloofness, it was not easy to make friends with him. In an age of heavy drinking he was regarded as a heavy drinker. He was not one of Queen Victoria's favourite sons, though she adored his children, who were beautiful and charming. Nor was Affie good with John Brown, his mother's constant attendant and manservant who did so much to console her after Albert's death. They were always having rows.

There was the occasion when the Queen demanded a meeting and showdown between her Scottish gillie and her naval officer son. Affie called for a witness to the peace conference. 'If I see a man on board my ship on any subject,' he announced (and one discerns a pompous note in his voice), 'it is always in the presence of an officer.'

Later Queen Victoria was heard to comment tartly: 'This is not a ship, & I won't have naval discipline introduced here.'[2]

Affie's love life gave the Queen many anxious moments. At one time it was thought that the Prince favoured Princess Frederika, daughter of the blind King of Hanover; at another time, when he was at Darmstadt and recounting the glories of the Royal Navy to Louis, he was having affairs on all sides and giving the Queen great anxiety about the Hessian 'love of society'. When Affie seemed to favour the Tsar's daughter Marie, the Queen's dismay knew no bounds. She really could not put up with the Romanoffs at all. But Affie persisted in his suit, and as it turned out, it was not only a happy marriage but the Queen came to love her new daughter-in-law, who was lively and spirited and, by contrast with Affie, a cheerful influence about the place. Queen Victoria's flexibility of mind and her honesty were among her greatest virtues.

In 1893 Prince Alfred's uncle, the Duke of Saxe-Coburg, died and he succeeded to the Dukedom and had to resign from the Royal Navy, which had meant so much to him. There was little more pleasure in life for him after this. His only son Alfred was a sickly lad. He died, at the age of twenty-five, in 1899. His father was already mortally stricken with cancer, and Prince Alfred died, a year before his mother, in 1900 of cancer of the throat. He was, noted *The Times*, of 'a more reserved disposition than his Royal brothers, and he never attained to quite the same degree of universal popularity as they have done.'[3]

When Louis left Heiligenberg on 18 June 1876 he was filled with excitement and enthusiasm for the unfettered life at sea that seemed to open before him with his appointment to the battleship H.M.S. *Sultan*. He was at last to serve in the Mediterranean Fleet, the greatest single concentration of naval power in the world.

He went first to Naples, where the Russian cruiser *Svetlana* lay at anchor with his cousin Alexei still serving on board. A week later he proceeded to Messina and made his way across to Malta, and thence to the Dardanelles where, appropriately, considering her name, Uncle Affie's ship H.M.S. *Sultan* lay at anchor in Besika Bay.

Louis was dismayed to discover the state of decay into which this once mighty fleet had fallen. In his eight years of service he had never seen anything like it. On paper it was indeed formidable. In fact, it was a collection of heterogeneous men-o'-war with a high proportion of dissolute officers, a scant regard for the fighting fitness of their vessels and uncertainty even whether they were better at sailing or steaming.

On the rare occasions when gunnery was practised, the results were appalling. Tactics had changed little since Nelson's time, and if it had not been for the introduction of the high explosive shell, critics claimed Nelson's Trafalgar fleet could have defeated it before luncheon. The gunboat that brought Louis to the Dardanelles could do only seven knots, under power or sail, and it was full of cockroaches.

The Commander-in-Chief was Admiral the Hon. Sir James Drummond, whom Louis described as 'a dear old white haired gentleman'. He was also tone deaf and Louis recounted how, at the end of a concert when 'Rule Britannia' was unexpectedly played before the customary 'God Save the Queen', Drummond had risen in outrage at the first notes of 'Rule Britannia' and called out to his Flag Lieutenant, 'Tell them to stand up and take their caps off. Bless my soul, they don't seem to know "God Save the Queen" when they hear it.' He then sat firmly down, his hat replaced, in front of the whole embarrassed ship's company while the solemn notes of the anthem rang out.

The *Sultan* was full of rats; they even scampered about Louis's cabin at night and ran across his chest. On the other hand, the protocol on board was rigid, and the Duke of Edinburgh was forever seeking occasions for wearing the numerous orders and decorations to which he was entitled. Fortunately there were frequent opportunities. There were holidays in the Crimea, where they were joined by all the Russian royalty from the Emperor down. There were many exchange visits with the Greek royalty in the Pireaus, and banquets ashore and afloat.

But Malta was the richest centre for social life. Everything on the island was designed to entertain and relieve the boredom of the long peace. Louis bought himself polo ponies and took up this sport with characteristic enthusiasm and a skill he was to bequeath to his son Dickie. At Malta there were suitable facilities for families to join their officer husbands, and in winter when the fleet was in port for most of the time there were as many nursemaids on the front at Floriana just outside Valetta, as in Belgrave Square, London. Here the third Edinburgh child was born to Aunt Marie, and was given the names Victoria and Melita, this second name being Maltese for Malta.

Life with the fleet, Louis soon discovered, was arranged to conform as closely as possible with social activities at home. There was horse racing as well as polo at Malta, and hunting and shooting and fishing at most anchorages and ports of call.

An innovation in the Fleet at this time was the arrival from England, at considerable cost, of a pack of beagles. They were taken to Besika Bay off the Dardanelles where the fleet was wintering and provided with special kennels ashore. A proper hunt was set up, with huntsman and whips recruited from among the sailors, and most of the officers had their own ponies by this time.

One of the more serious exercises carried out by the fleet was 'Embark the Hunt', an emergency exercise in the unlikely event of any sort of disturbance in the tranquil round. Then kennels and stables had to be dismantled and embarked at speed along with the pack of beagles and all the ponies. One battleship, the *Agincourt*, had especially spacious accommodation for livestock below the main deck.

This, then, was the sort of un-warlike life led by the Royal Navy in the Mediterranean. The state of affairs was improved when Admiral Phipps Hornby took over command and began to order steaming manoeuvres, evolutions and gun drill. At gunnery practice one day a heavy gun in the battleship *Thunderer* was double-loaded and burst on firing, wrecking the turret and killing nine officers and men. This was part of the price of reform, but Hornby's heart was in the right place, and the state of readiness and fighting condition of the fleet were soon improving.

Besides his disappointment at the poor state of the fleet Louis soon became disillusioned in his own appointment. Prince Alfred had explained to Louis's father that he would regard Louis as an unofficial Flag-Lieutenant, a privilege to which, as a Captain, he was not yet entitled. Instead, Louis found that he was to act as a naval A.D.C. and equerry, the duties being mainly formal and as remote as ever from the real life of a junior officer afloat.

Louis was by now despairing of ever being treated normally and of getting on in his career like everyone else. Things became more and more miserable. He found that he was expected to mess with his captain, and the more meals he had with him the less he enjoyed them. He now discovered for the first time that the Duke of Edinburgh was touchy and quirky. It did not help that the Duke was scarcely on speaking terms with his Commander, Richard F. Britten, who evidently believed that H.R.H. was quite incapable of

managing the ship and had to be constantly drynursed. Louis
agreed with his captain that the man was rude, overbearing and a
(very rich) cad. But Louis also had to act as go-between and peacemaker. Luckily he had inherited his father's skill in negotiation and
diplomacy.

As if this was not bad enough, Louis later found himself at the
centre of a political storm. War in the Balkans had broken out.
Eastern politics and antagonisms were little understood at the time;
only scholars can sort them out today. But on one side stood Russia,
the cruel, predatory, relentless 'bear' in the eyes of Britain; on the
other side were Austria-Hungary and Turkey.

Russian policy was always expansionist in the Balkans, this time
especially at the expense of Turkey. The autonomy of Turkey, as a
barrier to Russia, was as essential to Britain then as it had been more
than twenty years earlier at the time of the Crimean War. Turkey,
'the sick man of Europe', was in frequent need of the support of
Imperial Britain, whose strength in the Mediterranean was manifested in her fleet.

On 24 April 1877, the Russian 'bear' was on the rampage again
against Turkey, and there was less beagling at Besika Bay. Back
home in England, the favourite music hall song, in which the
audiences lustily joined in the chorus, ran:

> We don't want to fight but by jingo if we do,
> We've got the ships, we've got the men, we've got the money too.
> We've fought the Bear before and while Britons shall be true
> The Russians shan't have Constantinople [oo!]

The Russian armies at first had a rough time of it and suffered
fearful casualties. Louis was desperately worried about his younger
brother. A curious situation arose in the Mediterranean Fleet. In
every ship the Turkish victories were acclaimed and glasses were
raised in the wardrooms to the gallant Turks. There was a great
thirst for battle, but there was one exception. On board the *Sultan* the
officers had to be more circumspect for their royal captain was
married to a Russian Grand Duchess, and both he and Lieutenant
Prince Louis of Battenberg, were known to be strongly pro-Russian.
It was all very embarrassing.

But orders were orders, and on 13 February 1878 the fleet,
including the *Sultan*, steamed up the Dardanelles cleared for action
and with the pack of beagles and officers' ponies safely stowed below
decks in the *Agincourt*. Word had been received of crushing Russian

victories, and Britain was indeed seeing to it that 'the Russians shan't have Constantinople'.

Meanwhile Sandro had crossed the Danube with General Skobeleff, had seen action at Shipka Pass, and was with an army commanded by the Grand Duke Nicholas, the Tsar's brother, which was known to be close to the Turkish capital.

Sandro had, incidentally, emulated his father and fought with great gallantry and been decorated in the field. He wrote home frequently to his parents, describing the joys of victory, and – with naïve innocence – the joy of marching ever closer to his beloved elder brother.

'My heart beats when I think how close we are together,' he told his mother and father. 'This morning I rode out with the Grand Duke (who looks after me like a father) up to the heights of San Stefano, and we saw Constantinople before us, with the Aya Sophia, all the minarets, Scutari, etc. Tears filled the Grand Duke's eyes. What a satisfaction it must be for him to be standing at the gates of Constantinople with his army!'[4]

That was all very well, but whose finger was on the trigger of the naval guns preparing to defend Constantinople?

Within a few days the Turks were forced to surrender and appeal for peace. A treaty was signed at San Stefano, but the British fleet remained in the Sea of Marmora as a reminder to the Russians that they were to go no farther. The peace would remain precarious until the great powers got together to put the situation on a more sturdy footing.

Into this delicate situation strode the tall, handsome Sandro, Captain Prince Alexander of Battenberg, intent on visiting his brother on board the British battleship anchored off shore.

When word reached Louis through the German ambassador that his brother had arrived in Constantinople, he hastened ashore with the Duke of Edinburgh's blessing. There was a deliriously happy reunion and Louis invited Sandro on board.

'A small boat very soon brought us to the *Sultan*, where I was received by Alfred and the whole ship's company with *extraordinary friendliness*.' Sandro continued this letter to his parents with astonishing naïveté, 'They all feel more Russian than the Russians, and make no secret of it.'[5]

Later, Louis took his brother to the flagship, and to the newest battleship of all, the *Temeraire*, which sported new secret devices. It was a difficult situation for Admiral Hornby. He could not very well refuse his royal officers from inviting their young relative to the fleet; and, once on board, he had to be given the honours due to him, even including a dinner in the flagship.

Later, to the relief of the Admiral and his staff, the two brothers disembarked together and went to the Russian army headquarters, were entertained by the Grand Duke, and rode round the huge camp to see with their own eyes the vast numbers of guns and Turkish soldiers Sandro had helped to make prisoner.

When he heard of these exchange visits, the British ambassador in Constantinople was furious and believed, with some reason, that the peace negotiations might now be at risk. His agitated cable to London quickly reached the ears of the Queen, and then the whole royal fury burst like a shrapnel shell above the heads of the young Battenberg princes and her son.

'[It] was *most injudicious* & *imprudent* and you will hear of it from the Admiralty,' she wrote to Prince Alfred. 'Alexander Battenberg may be very discreet & no doubt is very honourable, but *how* can *you* think that the *officers* & *men* of our Navy and in the Fleet of which you are a Captain will *ever believe* that the *important secrets* will not be divulged? Anyhow, will they ever trust you & Louis Battenberg? I own I should hardly believe you *capable* of such imprudence & want of (to say the least) *discretion*. I will give you credit for it's being an act of *extreme thoughtlessness*, but that for a Captain in command of a ship, that Captain the Sovereign's Son & at *such* a moment, when we don't know if we may not very soon be at war, is a very serious thing. And I fear the profession will not put so favourable a construction on your act, Louis Battenberg's prospects will be seriously injured by it & I don't see how he can or ought to continue to serve in the same ship with you . . .'[6]

Louis was at once ordered to transfer to another ship, and was shattered by the storm his innocently and affectionately intended meeting with his brother had aroused. Prince Alfred was greatly put out, and Sandro was as horrified as his brother.

'The poor boy is beside himself,' wrote his aunt the Tsarina, who was always as plain-spoken about Queen Victoria as the Queen was about her, and now wrote of her to the boys' father as a 'crazy old hag' who had made poor Sandro 'the pretext for persecuting Alfred, and more especially Louis. I was so indignant,' she continued, 'that at first my one idea was that he should leave the English service.'[7]

For a while it was Louis's 'one idea' too. The shock waves had already reached Darmstadt, where Alice's concern was sharpened because she had so warmly recommended Louis, through her mother, to the Admiralty just ten years earlier.

There were already some difficulties between the Battenbergs and the Grand Ducal household in Darmstadt. The Battenbergs in 1877 had, quite innocently, created a domestic crisis by being responsible for the introduction of the Grand Duke's brother Henry to an attractive commoner, Caroline Willich. They fell in love, and proposed to marry in the new year.

Louis had received this news, and of Alice's grave displeasure at it, when he was at Malta and before he joined the fleet at Besika Bay. On 8 January 1878 he wrote to his mother, 'It is such a bolt from the blue that I still cannot get over it. It is quite dreadful, especially for us. The only good thing is that Alice is so furious about it . . . If only they would go right away from Darmstadt after their wedding it would not be so bad, but sooner or later Henry is sure to come back. It would be quite dreadful of Alice if she changed her attitude towards us because of this; to judge by what she said to you recently, one might almost believe she had . . .'[8] In this same letter Louis told his mother that he had 'faith in Alice's friendship'; and his confidence proved justified.

Alice's passion at this morganatic marriage subsided long before her own more fearful family crisis and death later in the year. But relations were still delicate when Louis returned to Heiligenberg in a resentful and mutinous frame of mind in early April. Alice was saying that Affie could no longer show his face in England after his pro-Russian behaviour, and was quoting a letter from her sister Princess Helena saying she was ashamed of being Affie's sister.

Louis's father agreed with him that the dignity and *amour propre* of the Battenberg family had been affronted by the insinuations of the English Queen, and that he must resign his commission unless an apology was forthcoming. It might be a good thing to do anyway. As Louis's father had written to him as long before as 11 April 1877, 'I am afraid that England's animosity towards Russia is so great that she will not rest until Russia is forced to go to war.'[9] And in that event, his son could scarcely be expected to take up arms against his own brother and so many of his closest and most loved relations.

But already powerful forces were at work to calm Queen Victoria's anger. The Prince of Wales appealed to good sense on behalf of his brother.

Slowly the Queen was persuaded to believe that the early tele-gram from the British Ambassador had been exaggerated in its tone, and that not all the statements were even quite true. For instance, Sandro had *not* been shown the *Temeraire*'s confidential equipment.

On 19 April news came to Darmstadt in a telegram to Alice that the Queen's anger was at last dying down. 'No fault whatever has been found with Prince Louis of Battenberg by the Admiralty. He has simply been changed from one ship . . . to another ship in the Mediterranean. The change was made in the usual manner, and without haste.'

Well, not *quite* 'the usual manner', as the Queen by now knew full well. In fact, only a few days earlier, already aware that she had deeply upset her son as well as the Hessians and Battenbergs, she had instructed Ponsonby to write reprovingly to the First Lord of the Admiralty about the manner in which Louis's transfer from the *Sultan* had been carried out.

'The Duke of Edinburgh is surprised and annoyed,' Ponsonby protested. 'As His Royal Highness had no notice of it, the transfer has the semblance of being made for some secret reason. The Queen hopes you will be able to satisfy the Duke of Edinburgh that such was not the case . . .'[10]

While Affie was being placated at Malta, back at Heiligenberg father and son decided that there was just enough of an apology implicit in the telegram to Alice to allow Louis to proceed to London to sample the real climate of opinion.

When he arrived on 24 April there was at once no doubt that all royal breaches had been healed. The Prince of Wales welcomed him effusively to Marlborough House, the First Lord of the Admiralty (and notable bookseller) W. H. Smith invited him to his office and personally assured him that 'Sandro's visit and all connected with it was of no consequence whatever and that my position in the Navy, which was a high one, was in no way affected.'[11]

The Queen had Louis to luncheon – 'and I was received most graciously'. Louis was greatly relieved, and celebrated by throwing himself into the social round – garden parties, Sandringham, Goodwood, Cowes week – in the company of the ever gregarious, ever vigorous Prince of Wales.

The comment at this *volte face* by Louis's aunt, the Tsarina Marie, was however crisp and pointed. You had only to give 'the old fool' a 'good fright to make her draw in her horns'.[12]

Any lingering doubts about relations between the Battenbergs and Queen Victoria were dispelled in the following year when both Louis and his younger brother Sandro were invited to Balmoral. Sandro was now the provisional sovereign of Bulgaria. Under a treaty as tortuously complex as only a 19th century Balkan quarrel could produce, Bulgaria had been divided into two, and Sandro had been elected first Sovereign Prince of the northern half and 'entrusted with the mission of piloting Bulgaria towards a happier future'.[13]

One of the conditions of his election was that he must visit in turn the signatory nations to the treaty. And so it came about that in the summer of 1879 Louis's brother, who had so displeased the Queen only a year earlier, was commanded to Balmoral to be looked over and to recount how he had been offered this appointment. Louis accompanied him to learn at first hand how the two would get on together. He need not have worried: all was as sweet as Highland honey.

Louis and Sandro went up on the night train to Scotland, arriving at Ballater at half past two on 6 June, to be met at the station by Prince Leopold the Duke of Albany. The carriage took them to the great castle, and they went straight into the drawing room where the Queen awaited them. It was her first meeting with the younger of the two Princes since he was five years old. 'Sandro . . . is not very like his brother, much taller, 6 foot 2¾,' she wrote that evening in her journal, 'dark, more like his mother, broad, & with a very good figure, a very open, good-natured face, good looking, but hardly as much as his brother Louis, who is 3 years older . . . Both Sandro & Louis are so amiable intelligent, & nice, so well brought up.'[14]

With his talent for diplomacy, Louis hastened to reassure the Queen about Sandro's association with that ultimate earthly evil – Russia. By the end of their visit she seemed to have been quite satisfied. Sandro was 'clearly not Russian in his ideas,' the Queen commented. 'Not at all Russian and did not wish to be considered as such.'[15] (The Tsarina noted later that she would 'have liked to have seen the two boys while they were in her [the Queen's] toils!')[16]

Sandro also explained most carefully the Bulgarian situation, which was even more curious than what the Queen regarded as normal Balkan political carryings-on. Both Prince Alexander of Hesse and his wife had been against their son's nomination. Louis had been against it, too, believing that his brother would be putting his head into the 'boar's' mouth. It had been Bismarck's idea.

93

The Queen recorded Sandro's account of the meeting between the Iron Chancellor and the reluctant prince: 'Sandro went to him saying, he did not wish to accept the offer, & thought someone older would be better, upon which Pce Bismarck shut the door, & told him, he would not let him out, before he promised to accept. Sandro asked, what would happen, should be fail, as his whole future would be ruined & he answered, "you will at all events take away a pleasant recollection with you." This made us all laugh.'[17] Thus were crowns thrust upon unwilling heads.

The two young men returned to London, Sandro continued his political-social pilgrimage round Europe to Paris and Rome, while Louis rejoined the gay merry-go-round with the Prince of Wales.

Since his little upset in the Dardanelles Louis had served for a short time in the battleship *Agincourt* in the Mediterranean, but had soon been lured away, this time by Prince Arthur the Duke of Connaught who was using the Royal Yacht *Osborne* for his Mediterranean honeymoon and thought he needed another lieutenant on board. When the yacht returned she was sent into dock for an overhaul and Louis again found himself unemployed.

Nothing suited The Prince of Wales better than to have his favourite sister's cousin at a loose end. 'Theatres and balls were the daily fare,' wrote Louis of this time. There were weeks at Marlborough House, visits to Cowes, visits to Dunster Castle in Somerset for the hunting – 'we had a capital run of 1 hour and 40 minutes and killed a good stag in the Badgery Waters'[18] – and to Plymouth for the Prince of Wales to lay the foundation stone of the Eddystone lighthouse, one of the few serious duties of that summer of 1879.

With the yacht out of dock, they embarked for Cherbourg, and while the *Osborne* went on to Kiel, Louis took Bertie, who deeply mourned the death of Alice, to Wolfsgarten to share the sorrows of the recently bereaved Grand Duke and his children and then to Heiligenberg to meet his parents.

The Prince of Wales hated Germany and the Germans as much as ever but he excepted Hesse and the Hessians. His favourite foreign country, after France of course, was his wife's Denmark, where they next foregathered with Princess Alexandra and all the Wales children. At the country Palace the activities were very like those at Wolfsgarten, Heiligenberg or Sandringham: picnics, entertainments, dinners, hunting and shooting parties.

Louis recalled one enormous hunt dinner at a forester's house on the island of Hven between Denmark and Sweden at which he was the only non-king or crown-prince present. Among those sitting round the table were the King and Crown Prince of Sweden, the King and Crown Prince of Denmark, the Prince of Wales and the Tsarevitch of Russia. The enormous 6 ft 6 in King Oscar of Sweden was the host, and characteristically he made an interminable speech followed by long proposals of health of every royal guest in turn, shaking the hand continuously while doing so. At last there were three cheers, and a band of Hussars assembled below the window for the occasion and played appropriate music.

Louis was still awaiting an appointment. The months passed and he heard nothing. Had the First Lord, and the Queen, both been wrong? Perhaps his reputation had, as the Queen at first feared, been irretrievably damaged. Louis fretted – yet revelled in the pleasant life that was offered to him as the only alternative. It was certainly no use feeling guilty. The few duties he was expected to perform were scarcely taxing. For instance, the Tsarina was increasingly poorly and had been sent to Cannes for the winter. Louis, Sandro and their father went to stay there to keep her company.

Then it was off to Russia in February 1880. By contrast, this was an unhappy country with an anxious court, and everything seemed to bear out Queen Victoria's opinion of the place. Tsar Alexander II was the best-intentioned and yet most attacked nineteenth century monarch. His rule was absolute, but he was at least endeavouring to bring about some reforms to free the serfs and to relieve them of some of their worst sufferings – unlike his father, and the son that followed him.

But the country was seething with unrest, and the Nihilists were busy everywhere. Recently the Chief of Police had been stabbed to death in broad daylight in a public place, and his assassin had escaped. The Chief's successor was shot at soon afterwards and escaped only by a miracle. The Tsar himself was shot at four times at point blank range by another Nihilist. All the shots missed, but in the struggle that followed, with the guards beating the man down with their swords, another shot rang out and wounded the Tsar in the foot. A number of attempts were made to blow up his train, and the strain under which the old man was suffering was beginning to show.

Meanwhile plans for the most elaborate and destructive bomb attempt of them all were going ahead. Every morning a carpenter by the name of Stephen Chalturin arrived at the Winter Palace and gained access, supposedly to do his work, to the cellar under the great dining-room. His toolbox contained sticks of dynamite, and by the middle of February 1880 an enormous load of destructive power had been built up.

It was known to the conspirators that Prince Alexander and his son Prince Louis were to arrive in St Petersburg by train on 17 February, and that they would be dining with the Tsar and all the Grand Dukes at 7.30 p.m. A fuse was laid and timed to go off at 8 p.m. The Tsar and the Grand Dukes, and Sandro, went to the station, and to their intense annoyance were kept waiting for half an hour. When the train arrived they all went by carriage, carefully guarded, to the Palace, changed, and came down to dinner. They had regained only a few minutes on their timetable.

The two oldest and grandest men, the Tsar and his brother-in-law Prince Alexander of Hesse, led the way down the long corridor leading to the dining-room, with Louis and Sandro behind them, followed by the Grand Dukes. The charge went off exactly as planned, but the Tsar had not yet reached the dining-room.

The explosion was fearful, blowing out all but a few back windows of the enormous palace, and was followed by clouds of smoke and dust. The Tsar and Prince Alexander reeled back choking but uninjured. The gas lighting flared up brightly and then all but a few jets blew out.

'My brother and I found our way to the dining-room,' Louis recalled, 'which was filled with smoke and groans of wounded coming through.' An immense hole had been torn in the floor, and another in one wall. The guardroom below had been completely wrecked and many of the soldiers had been crushed to death.

In later life when some of his nearest and dearest relations were suffering at the hands of Russian revolutionaries, Louis recalled the shock wave that seemed to half crush his body and the ear-cracking sound and the screams of the wounded.

Louis was glad to be back in England in March 1880. He was madly in love again, this time with the most fascinating and (many said) most beautiful woman in London society, whose rouée Irish husband had long since disappeared from her life. Encouraged by her most famous admirer, the Prince of Wales himself, Lillie Langtry had brought all her charms to bear on this most handsome of all naval officers –

> Oh, never, never since we joined the human race
> Saw we so exquisitely fair a face

wrote Sir Arthur Sullivan of 'Jersey Lily'. And Oscar Wilde:

> '. . . Lily of love, pure and inviolate!
> Tower of ivory! Red rose of fire!'

Louis conducted the affair with such discretion that few people realized that it was going on, and quite wrongly supposed that the Prince of Wales was her paramour at this time – at least until the infamous party given by Lord and Lady Randolph Churchill at which Lillie Langtry, too full of champagne, dropped a piece of ice down Bertie's back, and herself was dropped instantly by society when he left the house in a silent rage.

Only Louis, and a number of writers and artists and actors who considered themselves above the petty goings-on of society, stuck by Mrs Langtry during this period. They both enjoyed the stimulus of the clever and amusing 'artistic set' as a relief from the stuffiness of the rich and aristocratic, and Louis got to know such famous characters as Sir Henry Irving, Sarah Bernhardt and Madame Patti.

Oscar Wilde and many more of her friends advised Mrs Langtry to go on the stage during this hiatus in her social life and she was offered a part in a new play Irving was going to put on in the autumn. The decision to refuse was made for her when she discovered that she was expecting a child.

Alexander and Julie acted promptly and resolutely when Louis sent them this serious news. An aide-de-camp was despatched from Jugenheim to arrange a financial settlement, and Louis was told that of course there could be no question of marriage.

Suddenly the Admiralty found him an appointment on board a man-o'-war, with the unfortunate name *Inconstant*, that was about to go very slowly round the world. This would please the Queen, too. She knew nothing about Lillie Langtry, but her worry about Beatrice falling in love with him continued unabated. Lillie Langtry's own good sense and absolute discretion saved the Battenbergs from any sort of a scandal, and the passionate affair had died before the child was born.

There is a curious postscript to this love affair. Many years after her own stage career was over – and indeed eleven years after her death in 1929 – a touching little play ran in London, only briefly because this was April 1940 and Hitler's European invasions were just beginning. The play was called simply 'The Jersey Lily', and it was written by Basil Bartlett, and starred Paul Hernried as Prince Louis and Leo Genn as the Prince of Wales. Hermione Hannen played the part of Mrs Langtry. It was put on at the Gate Theatre and was well received.

Paul Hernried's performance was praised by the *New Statesman* as 'moving and persuasive'. That splendid gossip and socialite, Sir Henry 'Chips' Channon, went to see it with Lady Cunard and reported in his diary: 'A pleasant trivial little play, interesting because it actually portrays King Edward VII on the stage; the theme is the love affair between Prince Louis of Battenberg and Mrs Langtry (the offspring of this romance is Lady —, who was only told who her father was, when she was 20, by the then Mrs Asquith) . . .'[19] When she complained bitterly of her illegitimacy, she was asked sharply, 'Who would you prefer to have as a father, a penniless drunken Irishman or a Royal Prince and the most handsome of all naval officers?'

Louis's longest voyage began on 16 October 1880. The chill waters of sub-Antarctica and the spume-laden winds of the Roaring Forties acted as a tonic after the troubles and indulgences of life on half-pay in the company of the Prince of Wales and the 'Marlborough Set'. It was also an experience he badly needed at this stage in his life and naval career.

Louis's ship was one of five men-of-war which were to sail round the world (only using their engines under dire necessity) as a 'Flying Squadron' by way of Cape Horn and the Cape of Good Hope. This was planned as a demonstration of the Royal Navy's continued attachment to sail, in defiance of the rest of the world's navies which had long since embraced steam with open arms. It would also be an experience for the service's new raw royal recruits, the Prince of Wales's young sons, Eddie and Georgie.

The two Princes were in the *Bacchante*, an under-masted tub by contrast with the *Inconstant*, which was the fastest sailer in the fleet, a beautiful frigate in which engines and coal seemed an offence against nature. The *Inconstant* was always having to shorten sail to prevent herself from running away from the rest, and, wrote Louis of these eventful and refreshing days:

'Occasionally we would tow the worst sailer, under sail. At daylight we would in that case shorten sail with the "Disregard"*

---

* A naval signal flag meaning 'Disregard the Admiral's motions', allowing the flagship to manoeuvre independently.

flying, and gradually drop down to the weather bow of the stern-most ship, veer a hawser with a breaker astern for her to pick up, and as soon as it was fast inboard, we would crack on every stitch of canvas, and by sunset cast her off miles ahead of the rest.'[20]

It was as if nothing had changed since the days of Hawkins and Frobisher, as if Fulton had never been born, the industrial revolution had never happened. It was a ten days' passage to Vigo against a south-west gale 'which shook us up with a vengeance', arriving at last in Montevideo just before Christmas.

A very odd thing happened here a few days later which was to change the course of the Flying Squadron and perhaps the course of history.

As a romantic and a young man who had been so often and so ardently in love, Louis enjoyed recounting this true story of the British ambassador in Montevideo who was in love with a beautiful woman. He was dancing with her at a ball given in honour of the Royal Princes and the Squadron when he was given an urgent telegram, just at the moment when he was about to propose to her. He put it in his pocket and, astonished and delighted at being accepted, forgot all about it until after the Squadron had sailed.

The Squadron had arrived in the Falkland Islands and was preparing for the passage round Cape Horn when a little breathless gunboat arrived with the delayed telegram telling of a rebellion that had broken out in South Africa. The Squadron was to proceed to Simon's Bay and land guns and a thousand men.

The Squadron crossed the South Atlantic at best speed, but arrived three weeks later than expected. During that time the British force under General Sir George Colley had been defeated at Majuba Hill and the General killed.

The naval reinforcements would certainly have altered the balance of power, the Boers could hardly have avoided defeat, the Transvaal would not have become independent and there would have been no Boer War at the turn of the century.

Louis never saw any action in South Africa for sufficient reinforcements had meanwhile arrived. But it was at this remote outpost that he heard the fatal echo of that murderous explosion a year earlier. The news reached him that the Nihilists had at last got his Uncle Alexander. A bomb had blown up his carriage in St Petersburg, close to the Winter Palace where Louis had so nearly been blown up with him. His horses and escort were wounded, his carriage shattered.

The Tsar stepped out unhurt from the wreckage as if to prove his invulnerability. He was, in fact, thanking God and enquiring after the welfare of the bomb-thrower, who had been arrested, and the wounded, when another assassin threw a bomb at him crying, 'It is too early to thank God.'

He was right. This time the old man was fatally wounded in the explosion, and died in his palace, surrounded by his relations. Violent death, evaded so often, had come to Louis's family for the first time.

Disaster in the Flying Squadron itself was averted only by a miracle shortly after this news arrived. Its plans had been changed. Instead they were to make for Australia, and then Japan, by the easterly route.

A month out of Simon's Bay the Squadron was hit by a storm. 'On the night of 11/12 May,' wrote Louis, 'I had the middle watch. Steering became extremely difficult. The seas were parallel hills and vales, stretching to right and left as far as the eye could reach. They were so far apart that this long ship could run down one side and up the other, just keeping ahead of the seas which were continuously breaking astern of us. The sky was perfectly clear, with full moon and all the stars out. The foam of the wave crests was continually being spread by the wind like snow on the surface of the water which shone white under the moon.

'We rolled so heavily that the quarter boats (cutters) were dipped repeatedly, whilst the whalers hoisted at the same long, straight davits inside the cutters, were flattened out like the cocked hat carried by diplomats at Court, under the arm. I spent the four hours clinging to the standard compass and watching it and the double-manned steering wheel just below.'[21]

Worse things were happening to the *Bacchante* with the young Princes onboard. And Louis knew that her captain, Lord Charles Scott, the younger brother of the Duke of Buccleuch was incapable of dealing with a crisis of these proportions. Luckily the commander took over at the worst moment of the storm when the ship would not pay off because of a smashed rudder and was liable to broach to at any moment and be swamped. The two Princes – one a future King – and the ship's company were saved when the commander ordered his men to spread themselves as a sort of indestructible human sail in the weather fore rigging. Very slowly the *Bacchante*'s bows came round and, while the seamen held on tenaciously, she was brought before the wind again.

Four of the Flying Squadron's ships found one another when the storm abated. But the *Bacchante* was nowhere to be seen, and there was great anxiety for her and her precious Princes.

'No colours were shown on approaching the land lest a panic should be caused in London by the reported arrival of four ships instead of five,' wrote an officer's steward in one of the ships. 'But as the afternoon approached a fire was lit ashore upon a mountain top, and . . . the Admiral stood as close in to the shore as he dared. A boat was lowered and sent in for news, and after some hours of waiting she was seen returning.

'She was watched with breathless anxiety as she alternately rose into view on the crests and disappeared in the troughs. Reaching the flagship she was hoisted in, and then came the joyful signal that the Princes were safe. The cheers were deafening . . . It would have been a weird sight for a landsman to see those heavily rolling ships with everyone on board, officers as well as men, shouting themselves hoarse in their relief.'[22]

After this it could be said that the Princes had had sufficient sea experience for the time being and they were transferred to the *Inconstant* for their own safety until they went home separately.

Louis already knew his future cousins well. But on the long voyage across the Pacific, and in Japan and China, he formed a friendship with the future George V that was to last for all his life.

Prince George had not been in the least frightened in that massive storm though he was very seasick. He adored the sea, he adored the Royal Navy with a deep passion and it nearly broke his heart when his soldier brother died prematurely and, as the new future heir to the throne, he had to give up active service.

When he was King 'he loved cruising in the Royal Yacht, and when she was in harbour often commanded the Captains of the escorting vessels to dine. After the ladies had left the men to their port, he would sometimes sit back and say, "Now let's have some real saucy sea stories."'[23] A sailor King indeed.

Louis made other lifelong friendships with young officers who were to rise up the promotion ladder close behind him. William May was one. He became an Admiral of the Fleet and a notable tactician, although he finished his service before the First World War. Percy Scott was another lieutenant who went far, his peppery nature notwithstanding. In fact he became the most able and farsighted gunnery officer in the service and made a lot of enemies on the way, though Louis supported him through all his trials. Then there was

Mark Kerr, grandson of the Marquess of Lothian, a short officer like Percy Scott and almost as great a reformer.

Louis learned many things about the Royal Navy and about seamanship on this long voyage. In this Flying Squadron, of all squadrons, he learned, too, the pains and pleasures of sailing rather than steaming, and the price the Royal Navy paid for its tenacious adherence to canvas. The *Inconstant*, like the *Revenge* in which he had crossed the Atlantic, was an 'up-funnel-and-down-screwer'.

While sailing across the Pacific the Flying Squadron was becalmed in the doldrums. The heat was appalling and the men's spirits were sagging. But the Admiral, the Earl of Clanwilliam, would not allow a screw to be lowered – he was determined that they should complete the voyage under sail.

Earlier in the voyage he had been taken ill, and had recovered. In this great heat, he suffered a relapse and had to retire to his cabin. He did so with a bad grace, and after giving firm orders that they must await God's wind.

His flag captain became more and more exasperated, knowing that the rattle of the screw being lowered and the beat of the reciprocating engines would bring the sick admiral raging onto deck – and probably killing him into the bargain. He finally decided to take the risk of ordering one of the other ships to tow the *Inconstant*.

For two days the squadron made excellent progress and in total silence as far as the flagship was concerned. Then the Admiral, momentarily convalescent, sat up and noticed through the porthole the glass-smooth sea slipping by at a fine pace. The shock and anger did not kill him. But Louis recalled that his language to his unfortunate captain was so frightful that even he apologized a few days later.

On the other hand there was nothing to equal the satisfaction of handling with success a ship under sail in difficult circumstances. A member of the crew of one of the other ships wrote in his diary of the *Inconstant*'s arrival in Hong Kong harbour from Japan. 'She appeared off the entrance very light and high out of the water, and consequently in bad trim for sailing. Nevertheless, in spite of the crowded anchorage, the Admiral made the signal: "Come in under sail."'

'Captain Fitzgerald was quite equal to the occasion, and it was a sight to see the ship make plain sail in full view of the foreign men-of-war and come in like some great bird. It was necessary for her to tack many times as she got among the shipping, and the narrow margin left on each occasion almost made our hair stand on end.

Ten or twelve times she had to go about with all the foreigners on deck staring at her in blank amazement. She finally got to her berth without turning a hair to receive a signal: "Well done, *Inconstant*" Signals of congratulation were all too rare . . .'[24]

Louis and 'the Wales boys' had met the Mikado in Japan, the self-styled Kings of various Pacific islands, and diplomatic and government officials by the score all over Australia and south-east Asia.

The *Inconstant* reached Gibraltar on 2 July 1882 and there the ship's company learned of another African crisis which was threatening the country – this time at the other end of the continent.

The extravagance of the Khedive of Egypt which Louis had witnessed and enjoyed with the Prince of Wales back in 1869 had since reached new heights of profligacy. The British Prime Minister, Lord Beaconsfield, had shrewdly bailed out the Khedive by buying his half portion of the Suez Canal shares. This had not stopped the Egyptian rot, however, and in the end the British and French governments had set up joint accountancy control over what was still nominally a Turkish possession.

The Khedive was at length forced out of office by the Sultan of Turkey, but the army and public servants, who had lived for so long on graft, could not tolerate its ending and, under the pretext of a nationalistic campaign, 'Egypt for the Egyptians', the army, under a ruthlessly ambitious brigadier, Arabi Pasha, took control of the country and its appalling finances.

The setting and the characters are all too familiar to those who remember the 1956 Suez crisis. There was much international procrastination and duplicity, and France backed out from supporting Britain at the last minute. The Royal Navy sent a fleet of eight battleships with minor warships to protect British nationals and British financial interests, including the Suez Canal itself.

The *Inconstant* was ordered to proceed with despatch through the Mediterranean. She was not the only man-of-war in which hearts were beating faster and expectantly. Could there be action at last after these decades of peace – even though there was no Egyptian Navy?

On 11 July, the day after the *Inconstant* arrived at Malta, an ultimatum to Arabi Pasha expired and the bombardment of the Alexandria forts began. It was a golden day for those officers who had been thirsting for combat for so long. The commander-in-chief, Admiral Sir Frederick 'Ocean Swell' Seymour himself, watched with relish the guns of his fleet making practice against the Egyptian earthworks and ancient smooth bore cannon.

Lord Charles Beresford fearlessly took his ship the *Condor* into point-blank range, even 'making play with his Gatlings', until the Admiral remarked admiringly, 'Good Lord, she'll be sunk.' She was not, and only five men in the whole fleet were killed under the erratic but brave Egyptian fire before the white flag was hoisted.

That day of concussive sound and drifting gun smoke lived long in the memory of the Mediterranean Fleet, and for decades legends were created from individual heroic deeds. It was not often that the Royal Navy got any live target practice, and the results, with 3,000 rounds fired and only four Egyptian guns put out of action, showed that more was needed.

'We were all terribly disappointed to miss the action,' wrote Louis. But there was still excitement to be had in Egypt. Armed parties were being sent ashore to clear up and protect the town against Arabi's army of 20,000 which was hiding threateningly somewhere out in the desert when the *Inconstant* arrived at Alexandria. Louis was placed in command of a Gatling-gun battery with six of these quick-firers and established himself in a ruined part of the city.

It was a priceless opportunity for individual initiative. 'Jacky' Fisher, captain of the *Inflexible*, fitted out a makeshift armoured train and went storming off into the desert with Charlie Beresford. Percy Scott got some guns ashore and exchanged shots every evening at sundown with one of Arabi's heavy guns. Louis got some serviceable Egyptian heavy guns from the battered forts and dragged them to an extemporized site first by brute man-power and then with the help of a railway locomotive.

For a while the rough and unhygienic living conditions and the heat were all gladly accepted in the cause of active service. But the weeks dragged by with no more action, nor much likelihood of any, and men died of typhoid and spirits began to sag. When at last it was learned that General Wolseley had met and soundly defeated Arabi's army at Tel-el-Kebir and all danger had disappeared, everyone wanted to get out of the smelly, fly-infested place, and back to sea or back home.

Louis was among those who longed for home. It was nearly two years since he had seen his family. He ached for a sight of Heiligenberg, of his father and mother, his younger brothers, and especially of Sandro whom he always greatly missed. He had never even visited him since he had become the Sovereign Prince of Bulgaria.

But things moved very slowly, as if the Royal Navy was stunned into paralysis after the orgy of the bombardment. And unfortunately for Louis, old 'Ocean Swell' had joined the ranks of those anti-foreigner senior officers in whose eyes Louis's German birth alone was sufficient to condemn him. Louis applied to him, asking if he 'had any objection to my going'. Later Louis told the Prince of Wales that 'my request was refused point blank, in, I may say, a very rude manner without giving any reason . . . it would seem that I am Admiral Seymour's bête noir – but why? I keep on asking myself that question.'[25]

But it was not long before Louis could tell more to the Prince of Wales at first hand, for two weeks later the *Inconstant* got away from Alexandria and reached Spithead on 16 October 1882. Soon he was at Marlborough House 'where Uncle Bertie and Aunt Alix received me like a lost son'.

The autumn balls were in full swing, and Louis danced with joy and vigour – so much vigour that he sprained an ankle and had to go into the Naval Hospital at Haslar, which was very different from his own bedroom at Marlborough House and was, as he described it, 'more like a prison'.

Before he left for Germany on leave, Queen Victoria pinned the Egypt War Medal onto his full dress coat, congratulated him on his safe return and thanked him for helping to look after her grandsons who had been so far from home and in such danger. Louis could never bear to turn down a decoration of any kind when it was offered to him, but in this case he did express doubts as to whether he really deserved it.

His cousin Ludwig IV, the Grand Duke of Hesse, was on a visit to Windsor at this time, so they returned to Germany together, chattering happily the whole way about their families and their travels. Then they parted, each to his own palace, and Louis was soon embracing in turn his family and greeting the joyfully tearful servants. Surely, they were saying, there was no more romantic, charming and handsome figure in the whole of the Grand Duchy than Louis of Battenberg?

Here was a young British naval officer who had survived the dangers of storm and war, who had travelled the world, had talked with the Mikado of Japan, ridden across the South American pampas, hunted in Africa, India and Australia, danced the night away in distant Melbourne and Marlborough House . . .

Marriage for Louis seemed almost ordained. Everything was right –
his age, his position, the point he had reached in his career. Any
more ephemeral love affairs now would seem unsuitable and inappropriate, and the passion, and the consequences, of the last affair,
now made more remote in time by Louis's long absence, all pointed
one way.

His parents watched with approval his growing attachment to his
cousin Victoria that winter and spring. It would be a most suitable
marriage, a cementing of relations between Heiligenberg and the
New Palace which had not always been as happy as they could have
been.

When he returned from a visit to his brother Sandro in the late
spring, he renewed his suit with fresh ardour – and what a handsome
couple they made together, everybody said so!

Victoria's family were much less pleased at the way things were
going. As the eldest daughter and so soon after the death of her
mother, they considered that her first duty was to her father and to
her younger brother and sisters. At nineteen she was, they considered,
too young and inexperienced for marriage.

This disapproval extended outside the family, and especially to
the Imperial families in Berlin and in St Petersburg. Uncle Fritz
and his eldest boy Willy (still smarting from the rebuff at Ella's
hands) and the new Tsar Alexander III and the Tsarina Marie
Feodorovna, and a whole multitude of Grand Dukes and Grand
Duchesses, Princes and Princesses, and other minor royals, all
thought it quite unsuitable that anyone as grand as Victoria should
marry into this morganatic sub-branch of the Hessian family.

Louis's adopted nationality was against him, too, for England
was popular neither with Prussia nor Russia; and on more human
grounds, a naval officer was considered unsuitable as a husband
because he was often away at sea for long periods.

A good deal of pressure was brought to bear on Victoria by this
weight of disfavour when an engagement seemed imminent, and she
was disconcerted by it for she was a dutiful young woman who
instinctively wished to do the right thing – but, oh! the pangs of
first love were very powerful. The fact that, in Darmstadt eyes,
Louis was not 'a Royal Prince', a mere Serene Highness, only
added to his desirability and to the egalitarian in Victoria. Better
still if he had been a commoner! The Hessian Parliament responded
by refusing to grant the couple any money if they married.

Ella and Irène were a great support at this time, for both of them were devotedly loyal sisters. But, in the final count, it was inevitably to Windsor that Victoria had to look for wise counsel. What would that small black figure, who had been the first to hold her in her arms after her own mother, who had been such a pillar of support during family crises – what would she have to say about her marriage to Louis?

Victoria's relationship with her grandmother had been on a very intimate and special basis for many years, and long before she had been told to 'look on me as on a Mother' after Alice's death. Their correspondence was regular and frequent, revealing the loving, but always firm and even severe guiding hand of the older woman, and the loving, dutiful but always lively response from Victoria.

The letters from the Queen became more frequent, the guidance even steadier, after Alice's death, and they are shot through and through with love for all her motherless grandchildren – '*You* are so doubly dear as the children of my *own* darling Child I have lost and loved so much,' she once wrote after they had returned to Germany from a holiday in England, adding beloved Brown's comment that 'It seemed all wrong without you & as if a Blight had come over us.[26]

After the Queen had left Darmstadt on her visit for Victoria's confirmation, she wrote a 17th birthday letter which is also typical in its strictures and evidence of her shrewdness and power of observation. Note that she is already concerned about Victoria's garrulousness, which she quite failed to cure!

VILLA HOHENLOHE[27]
Baden Baden
Ap 4 1880

Darling Victoria,

May EVERY EVERY *blessing be showered on you on your dear 17th birthday & may you have* strength *given you to be that support & help to your dear Papa wh he so gtly needs! Every, everywhere you see what your beloved Mama did – how she worked for your country, watched over & led everything & how she stood by & supported your dear Papa – & you must try to follow in her footsteps – Modestly, unpresumingly,* not *putting yourself forward too much but being* always *ready to help & ready to do at* Home *what Papa wishes & requires. You must learn to be* posée, *not talk too much or too loud – but take your place as your beloved Father's eldest daughter deprived of your beloved Mother!*

It is the greatest misfortune *wh cd befall you & your dear Sisters – but if you trust in God's help & keep fast to the* solemn *vows wh you took at your Confirmation, if you are humble minded & loving to all & occupy yourself with serious*

107

things, you will succeed. Be always ready to listen to the advice of those whom you know to be truly devoted to you – & not to those who will flatter you & wish to do what you may like, but wh often may be bad for you. My prayers for your good will be unceasing. Since I have been in your Home – I see better than ever what you have all lost! I was dreadfully upset by it all but so thankful to have been there!

My presents are 2 pearls – a box from here & a print you liked.
With many loves to dear Papa & all
Ever your most devoted Grandmama

VRI

I was so pleased to lead you to your confirmation.
Thank Miss Jackson for her letter.

Dearly though the Queen loved her favourite grand-daughter, she not only considered her a gasbag but very much deplored her voracious appetite for reading. '*Read some good & serious religious book,*' she appealed to her, '*not materialistic & controversial ones – for they are very bad for everyone – but especially for young people.*'[28] This was the sort of advice which Victoria never could take; indeed the more controversial the book the better she liked it.

Nor could the Queen quite succeed in stopping her from shooting. The tomboy in Victoria always came out again when she got the feel of a gun in her hands, and she loved going out with her father. '*I was, darling Child,*' (and that was always an ominous opening) '*rather shocked to hear of your shooting at a mark but far more so at your idea of going out shooting with dear Papa. To look on is harmless but it is not lady like to kill animals & go out shooting – & I hope you will never do that. It might do you gt harm if that was known as only fast ladies do such things.*'[29]

But Victoria listened with great attention to anything critical of her character and behaviour, and the Queen was so penetrating and so often right that only an arrogant and stupid person could ignore what she had to say.

'Don't, young as you are be too severe & critical of other girls or other people older than yourself,' advised the Queen. '*Quick & clever as you are, you might be tempted, standing so much alone, without your darling Mama to guide & advise you, to be sharp in your remarks – & it wld do you harm & not make people as fond of you as they otherwise wld and shld be . . .*'[30]

Then again, a year later, there is more advice which reveals a corner of the minds of the now 19-year-old girl and 62-year-old grandmother and godmother. '*Don't* try to check tender & loving feelings or to try & appear as if you were hard & ashamed of shedding tears. That is *not* feminine or womanly & the more you show your feelings the better it is . . .'[31]

When Victoria's young brother Ernie showed signs of laziness or of too great a fondness for sweets, Victoria was asked to make the necessary corrections. When Victoria herself wrote to deplore another English colonial war – in this case the Ashanti War of 1892 – reflecting Hessian distaste for colonialism and war in general and her own horrifying memories of tending the wounded with her mother in the Franco-Prussian War, the Queen wrote back stoutly defending England's action: 'I quite share your feelings abt. War & shedding blood – but we were driven into this – & as every thing in this world more or less – is the *sacrifice* of *few* for the *benefit &* *safety* of *many* – we can but hope & think that this War, wh. *cannot* be a long one will be of great use . . .'[32]

Nor could Victoria accept the Queen's anti-Russian feelings. The Queen was always irritated by the lavish annual hospitality offered by the Hessians to their Russian relations. 'I *hope* you will not get at all Russian from the visits to Jugenheim,'[33] she entreated Victoria one summer when the Tsar and Tsarina and their family were staying with the Battenbergs. She always referred to the country as 'that dreadful Russia'. 'You will be glad to see Papa safe back from that dreadful Russia,' she wrote on another occasion.

The range of these letters is wide, and they never descend to the dull or commonplace: a well-informed and highly intelligent and interestingly prejudiced old lady exchanging thoughts with an alert-minded, highly intelligent and responsive girl. When Victoria was still only 17, but '*quite old* enough for me to speak or write to you about', the Queen had offered her grandchild her observations on marriage in general, together with some warnings:

'Dear Papa will, I know, be teazed and pressed to make you marry, & I have told him you were far too young to think of it, & that your 1st duty was to stay with *him*, & to be as it were the Mistress of the House . . . I know full well that *you* have *no* ideas of this sort & that *you* (unlike, I am sorry to say, so many *Princesses abroad*) – don't wish *to be married* for *marrying*'s *sake* & to have a *position*.

'I know darling Child that you would *never* do this, & dear Mama had a horror of it; but it is a very *German* view of things & I wd wish you to be *prepared* & on your *guard* when such things are brought before Papa . . .'[34]

Two years later, when news of Victoria's imminent engagement reached Windsor, the Queen was right in thinking Victoria would be 'anxious to know what *I* think'. She continued:

'I think that you have done well to choose only a Husband who is *quite* of your way of thinking & who in many respects is as English as you are – whose interests must be the same as yours & who dear Mama liked. Besides,' (and we can imagine the speed at which quick-reading Victoria's eye covered that page!) 'you do *not* leave dear Papa who needs your help as much as the dear *Geschwister* do. One only drawback I see – & that is "the fortune". *I* don't think *riches* make happiness, or that they are necessary, but I *do* think a certain amount is a necessity so as to be independent. And that I *hope* you will be able to reassure me upon.'[35] (Alas! that she was not able to do.)

Over the following months serious Marriage Advice was added to the Queen's injunctions. 'You are so good and sensible that I am sure you will be a steady good wife & *not* run after amusements, but find your happiness chiefly in your own home. Beware of London & M. Hse [Marlborough House, a "dig" at her dissolute son!]'[36]

Queen Victoria told all her own children how pleased she was at the forthcoming wedding between her favourite naval officer and favourite granddaughter. 'I am very glad she has found a person, kind, good & clever & whom she knows thoroughly well,' she wrote to Vicky. 'Of course people who care only for "gt matches" &c will not like it – But they do not make happiness . . .'[37]

As to Louis, his family appears to have been slower off the mark than Victoria's. Neither Sandro nor his father perceived the significance of Louis's refusal of the invitation to Tsar Alexander III's coronation – and Louis was never a one for missing coronations. Nor did they link this refusal with his cousin's refusal of her invitation to Balmoral.

Almost every morning during that magical spring of 1883 Louis took out from Heiligenberg stables two magnificent black Hungarian light horses which his father had given him, and harnessed them in tandem to an outsize dogcart he had had specially built in England – all dark green with brass fittings and brass mounted black harness: a real lady-killer's equipage. Then he would drive fast (there was one nasty spill) over to the Hessian hunting lodge at Seeheim to pay court to Victoria.

There were picnics, rides, walks in the forest. 'At last one day,' Louis wrote for the benefit of his own children, 'on a bench in Seeheim grounds, I plucked up courage and asked your dear mother if she would marry me. All the happiness of my life begins with that memorable day . . .'

A day or two later, and in a state of ecstatic happiness, Louis wrote to his old shipmate Prince George, the future King:

My dearest Georgie,[38]
I have a great piece of news to tell you. Our mutual cousin Victoria has promised to be my wife! I can't tell you how happy I am. She is such a lovely darling girl, as you know, and I am nearly off my chump altogether with feeling so jolly. I hope you will be pleased to have me as a cousin. It makes me ten times happier to think that I shall be the nephew of your dear parents and cousin to you all. Everybody here is pleased about it and your Grandmother has been so kind about it. She has written to offer me the yacht. Isn't it grand? . . . I am in a deuce of a hurry and have such heaps of letters to write. However, this is the 2nd, your father's was the first.

Goodbye my dear old boy,
Ever your affectionate old shipmate,

Louis

5

'We are in the midst of love matters.'

SIR HENRY PONSONBY, *Darmstadt, April 1884*

THE wedding was planned for the Spring of 1884. Queen Victoria said she would come. Her granddaughter wrote to express her gratitude and thankfulness. The Queen replied: 'I see that you appreciate the gt effort I mean to try & make & I know you will kindly help me in making things as quiet as possible for me.'[1]

No doubt Victoria, in reassuring her on this point, truly believed at the time that this would be possible.

The affection between the old Queen and her young granddaughter ripened during Victoria's months of engagement. Queen Victoria with her deep and passionate feelings for all human relationships, for those of her family especially, and for those of her nearest and dearest family most of all, was determined to enjoy the pleasure of Victoria's company alone before the wedding.

So she invited all the family over to Osborne, arranged for one of the Royal Yachts to fetch them and for the programme to be worked out so as to allow her to be with Victoria for some of the time.

Much as she loved match-making, and the whole ideal of marriage as personified in what she regarded as her idyllic relationship with Albert, something in her flinched back from being with engaged people. Perhaps she feared some unseemly demonstration between them, or was just embarrassed at the ephemeral and false nature of the relationship.

'I have,' she once wrote to Victoria, 'a *particular* aversion to being mixed up with *Brautstand* . . . [State of being betrothed].'[2] This was of Ella's engagement. Of her son Leopold's engagement, she feared that he 'will be (as everyone is under those circumstances) very tiresome if he is absorbed with his Bride . . .'³

Victoria understood all this very well and did not know whether to be joyful or anxious when she heard that Louis would be staying with the Prince of Wales on board the Royal Yacht in the Solent during Cowes week.

The Queen's own feelings about the matter were made clear in the last letter she wrote to Darmstadt before the family left for England.

'Louis Battenberg is coming here tomorrow,' it ran, '& I shall be very pleased to see him. But I much regret that what I *told* Papa nearly a *month ago* has *not been listened to* & that he is coming to be at Cowes with Uncle Bertie, for I wished to have you to *myself*, & as you *are*, for the *last time* – how can I avoid asking him, & Uncle Bertie will be constantly wanting *you* to go to him. This *last* I do *protest* against . . .'⁴

However, it all passed off without too many or too great embarrassments. Louis and Victoria were very discreet and only rarely appeared in front of the Queen together. Cowes was as lovely as ever. The Queen's Cup was won by the Marquis of Ailsa's cutter *Sleuthhound* after the Prince of Wales *Aline* lost her foretopmast off Osborne. There was much sympathy for Bertie that night.

Later there was a tearful farewell between the Queen and the betrothed. The Hessian family – widowed father, four daughters and Ernie, now a sensitive, clever and spritely little fourteen-year-old – embarked late in the evening in the Royal Yacht *Osborne* for Le Havre. During the crossing Victoria wrote a letter of affectionate thanks to the Queen, who replied:

'To take leave of you at night, & never to see you *again* . . . as a dear girl, – as you are now, was very painful to me & I felt it terribly . . . Its being at night too was particularly sad. I always hate "goodbyes" at night or leaving any place at night. I saw the OSBORNE lit up gliding like a meteor over the Solent!'⁵

Now that the Court at Darmstadt had reconciled itself to the betrothal, it set about making this the wedding of the decade. Experience was on their side. The news that 'the widow of Windsor' was bestirring herself and intended to make the crossing and bringing with her a numerous suite (and, of course, her own bed and bedding), greatly accelerated the number and greatly improved the quality of the wedding acceptances.

The Prussians accepted *en bloc*, from the Crown Prince and Princess down (and that meant a *huge* influx of equerries, secretaries, gentle-men- and ladies-in-waiting and servants by the score), the Romanoffs sent Grand Dukes, Uncle Bertie would of course be there with dear, lovely Aunt Alix, the Hohenzollerns and Habsburgs and Badens, the Coburgs and Würtembergs and Hohenlohes, announced their inten-tion of coming in large numbers, and there would be Bourbons, and Scandinavians, too – the Christians and the Oscars and the Charles's.

Experienced as they were, the powers of organization and protocol management of the Hessian household were going to be stretched to the uttermost.

For Queen Victoria the auguries were not happy. The death of Brown in March 1883 had been a crushing blow and she missed his firm speech and firm supporting arm dreadfully all through the summer and autumn. The anniversary of 'that dreadful day' was an especially distressing one – twenty-two years a widow.

There were plenty of political worries, too, as if it were not awful enough having Mr Gladstone, that dangerous and incompetent radical, as Prime Minister. Surely a disaster was imminent in the Sudan? When Gordon was sent out to deal with things, the Queen percipiently feared that it was too late, and she worried and worried all through the Spring of 1884. On 18 March she learned that Gordon was besieged in Khartoum by the 'Mad' Mahdi. Four days later, just before she was to leave for Darmstadt, another almost insupportable blow struck her – the death of her beloved haemo-philic son Leopold.

The wedding had to be postponed for the funeral of Victoria's favourite uncle, and all the special arrangements, all the special carriages, all the special trains, had to be cancelled and rescheduled. Victoria, already in a state of nerves, was distraught. Her sisters had never seen her like this.

At last the new date was decided. It should really have been in May, but the Queen had a superstitious dread of May marriages, so it had to be 30 April.

Another worry – a domestic one this time – was Victoria's sister's engagement to Grand Duke Serge of Russia. Ella had her way at last, and got her Russian Grand Duke as she had always promised herself she would. They were to marry in June. The Queen deeply deplored the business. None of her family, by her thinking, should marry a Russian; but for her beautiful little grandchild to do so, whom she loved almost as much as Victoria, was like a personal affront. 'Russia,' she once wrote to Victoria, addressing the vast land mass dynastically, 'I cd not wish for any of you.'[6]

A further family anxiety, Victoria's father's loneliness in his widowhood, seemed to be on the way to a solution during this Spring of 1884. Grand Duke Ludwig had for some time been enjoying an affair with the wife of the Russian *chargé d'affaires* in Darmstadt, a Madame Alexandrine de Kolemine.

To everyone's relief the husband departed, and then arranged a divorce. His former wife thus became a perfectly acceptable mistress at the Court. The Grand Duke was delighted and quite recovered his old spirits, and Victoria and her sisters, who were fond of Madame de Kolemine, were greatly relieved. There was, of course, no question in this case of another morganatic marriage – a divorced woman who was not even a countess marrying into the Hessian family.

Queen Victoria arrived at Darmstadt two weeks before the wedding, confident that 'a change will be good for me', and with plenty of time in hand for settling down and meeting – very quietly – all the dear family.

She had in her suite Sir Henry Ponsonby, Lord Bridport, her doctor, Dr Reid, Lady Ely and other ladies-in-waiting, and o course her youngest daughter Beatrice, now a dumpy, kindly and much loved figure who all were convinced was destined for permanent spinsterhood.

Things began badly, the crossing to Flushing was a bad one – 'they kept assuring me it would get better, instead of which it got worse'[7] – and on reaching land she received the sad news of the death of her old and trusted friend the Duke of Buccleuch. Would fate's savage blows never cease?

The Hessian family were waiting at Darmstadt station and received her with the minimum of ceremony. The Grand Duke himself was seen to be in the highest of spirits – almost indecently high in view of his (by the Queen's reckoning) recent bereavement.

At the New Palace, at the Queen's command and even before breakfast, the Grand Duke took her to see Alice's suite, where everything was again as it had been before, and as it had been on the day Alice died, the clothes lying about just as she had left them nearly five years earlier.

Love and death were everywhere that month in Germany. After breakfast, Ella's beloved strode in – a splendid figure but full of fear for the disapproval of his betrothed's awesome grandmother, and showing it. Grand Duke Serge need not have worried. Whatever Queen Victoria might say or write about Russia and the Russians, face to face she was always courteous and kind. She noted that he was 'very tall, & gentlemanlike, but v thin, pale & delicate looking'.[8]

On the following day, recovered from the rigours of her journey, she received Louis's parents and found them 'both v kind'. After that, there was more preoccupation with death. It was the third anniversary of Disraeli's death – there were so *many* of these anniversaries now – and then the mausoleum at the Rosenhöhe had to be visited, and the statue in memory of Alice admired.

Between these expeditions, the Queen saw much of Victoria. She was looking pale and unwell. Perhaps pre-marital nerves? The Queen gave her a set of diamond stars for her golden-red hair, gilt fruit dishes in matched descending height for the dinner table, an Indian shawl, some Indian material, and Scottish shawls and plaid, some Irish poplin and lace, English lace and Welsh material – something from every part of her United Kingdom.

The Queen decided that she could not face the great Gala Opera on the night before the wedding. But she did take a drive to admire the decorations in the centre of the city, which seemed to be everywhere *en fête*.

The early morning of 30 April was clear and fine and promised exceptional heat for later in the day. She took breakfast in the garden of the New Palace with all the Hessian family, Bertie and Alix and all their children – an enormous gathering for so early in the day. The only person missing was the bride. The Queen asked after her and was told that she was not well. She was lying down on a sofa in her room.

The Queen flattered herself that she understood, and sent Dr Reid to prescribe something for her. Later in the morning there was still no sign of Victoria, and she failed to appear at luncheon too. The Queen was now very worried. At last, in the early afternoon, a message came to the Queen.

'Thank God!' she wrote, 'V suddenly got all right again and went to dress . . .'[9]

The Queen was correct in thinking that it was 'nerves' which had driven practical, sensible, un-nervy Victoria to her sofa. But it was not from a state of alarm at her own imminent wedding – it was the thought of her father's imminent nuptials which had proved too much for her.

Rumours had been circulating about Darmstadt for some time that the Grand Duke was not content to have only a mistress about the Court. His children, at first disbelieving, were forced to accept that these rumours were true when their father stunned them into momentary silence by telling them that he intended to marry Madame de Kolemine.

Louis was also told, as were his three brothers. To everyone else it was a Court secret. But of course the word spread with the pace of any Court scandal. The Prince of Wales was outraged, but could not find the courage to pass the news on to his mother. Nearer and nearer to the Queen spread the conflagration.

Sir Henry Ponsonby wrote to Gladstone lightheartedly, 'So you see we are in the midst of love matters.' But he soon changed his tone when he realized that either the Grand Duke was being diabolically cunning, or had been persuaded into this course of action by his mistress while in a stupor of love.

'The Grand Duke has behaved very badly,' he wrote now, 'in not telling the Queen before she came to Darmstadt because it places her in a most awkward position. If she goes away it will create a scandal, if she remains it will look as if she approved the marriage.'[10]

Louis was thrown into near panic. The other Battenberg boys were distressed and embarrassed. What now, they might well ask themselves, about Hessian snobbery and talk of Victoria marrying beneath her? But they did not pass such a vindictive observation because they were too kind and too polite – and, above all, they did not wish the happiness of this occasion to be put at risk.

The task of telling the Queen finally fell on Victoria herself. The last person who would risk her wrath was the Grand Duke, and he no doubt calculated that the bride and beloved granddaughter was the most likely person to turn away this wrath and persuade the Queen that it was the best thing for all.

Victoria made 'the painful communication' to her five days before the wedding day. The Queen was outraged and gave all her reasons to 'poor Victoria' for her determined opposition to the match. She confirmed them all in writing the next day. Granting him his 'excellent qualities' and acknowledging 'how happy he made dear Mama', she was forced to remind Victoria that she could not have the Grand Duke near her so much as before (which really meant not at all), for 'his marrying such a person – a divorced Russian lady – would lower him so much.

'He cannot say,' the Queen continued, 'that this intended union is for the sake of his Children or for his Country – it wld be the vy reverse of *both*, it can only be for what *he thinks*, (& I am afraid he is much mistaken) will be for his *own* personal happiness. It will do him immense harm in his own Country – in England he will lose the position he held & enjoyed & I cld *not* defend such a choice . . . I do *most earnestly* ask him to *pause* & put off at least for a time – & to think, that the difficulty of doing so – or even of breaking off such an engagement is *infinitely less* than the *pain* & *suffering* of hurting all those he loves best & of offending his best friends & subjects by such a marriage which would be the inevitable result.'[11]

Queen Victoria was, however, quite prepared to offer the Grand Duke some consolation.

'If dear Papa,' she told Victoria, 'should feel lonely when you 3 elder are married – I should say nothing (tho it must pain me) if he chose to make a morganatic marriage with some nice, quiet, sensible & amiable person – who would at any rate command the respect of us all as well as of his Country.'[12]

On the day of the wedding, the matter was still unresolved and a worry for everyone. 'Darling child, how I feel for you all in this gt trouble,' the Queen told Victoria.

But the Queen, anxious though she was, believed that after the very clear statements of her own position, a decision was, so to speak, only pending. She did not know – as the bride and groom and all the inner circle knew – that the Grand Duke was more hell bent than ever on his suicide course of action. The only question – and a Damoclean one it was too – was when?

The Queen, then, was in a state of comparative emotional calm when she went upstairs on that afternoon to dress for the ceremony – 'just one of my usual evening dresses, pearls, diamonds'.

Downstairs again, she awaited the other ladies: first her two daughters Vicky and Beatrice, and her daughter-in-law Alix, then her granddaughters – oh, so many of them now, and each one so precious – all of them in white, too.

Victoria was the last to appear. She was looking pale yet radiant – as close to pure beauty as she would ever look, in her mother's wedding dress: Honiton point lace patterned with roses, orange blossom and myrtle over white satin, a long veil, a sapphire and diamond diadem, and a wreath of orange flowers and myrtle which the Queen had given to her.

It was a stunningly beautiful dress, but with only a short six-foot-long train in deference to the state of court mourning.

The whole population of Darmstadt seemed to be out on the streets for there had not been a wedding on this scale for a generation or longer. The Queen listened to the cheers and waved with practised style. She sat with Victoria beside her in the open state coach. The Grand Duke, looking as if he had not a care in the world, sat opposite.

First there was the civil ceremony, a dry, quick affair conducted by the Prime Minister, at which both said '*Ja!*' Then this august gathering, half Europe's royalty and some more, moved off in carriages to the Castle chapel, which they all entered in order of rank, first the Queen and then together Uncle Bertie and Aunt Alix, Uncle Fritz and Aunt Vicky of Prussia.

Victoria entered between her father and Louis's father. She was seen to be limping slightly as a result of an accident. Even at 21, with the double solemnity of mourning her Uncle Leopold and preparing for her own wedding she could not entirely suppress her tomboy spirit. A few nights earlier she had tried, and failed, to leap over an outsize coal scuttle and twisted her ankle.

She was followed at once by Louis in Lieutenant's full dress naval uniform, superbly cut tail coat, and wearing the Grand Cross of the Order of the Bath (a wedding present) and the Star of the Hessian Order of Louis and Chain. Only a few days before, his cousin Ludwig IV has placed him *à la suite* of the Hessian Artillery Brigade, and had given him to the *Ludwigsorden*.

Louis and Victoria made an impressive couple standing side by side while the aged Court Chaplain conducted the ceremony. The chorale was sung, then there was the address and the couple exchanged rings. A gun salute was fired, and after a hymn and prayers, the Chaplain pronounced the benediction in the Lutheran style.

The old Queen stepped shakily forward. Her arthritis was bad and she still missed good Brown's strong arm.

'I went up to dear Victoria & embraced her tenderly,' she wrote, '& also kissed Ludwig [Louis], shaking hands with dear Louis [the Grand Duke] & Pce Alexander . . . I could hardly restrain my tears when I thought of the last wedding 2 years ago [Prince Leopold's] at St George's, & how soon that happy marriage ended, & of the terrible uncertainty of life.'[13]

After they left the Chapel there was a reception in the Drawing Rooms at the New Palace, and the Queen made a public appearance on the balcony for the crowds before bidding farewell to the happy couple – off into their own uncertainties of life.

Nobody ever knew just how the news got out that the Grand Duke had married his mistress secretly almost immediately after he had slipped away from the chapel where he had given away his daughter. Ponsonby said it 'oozed' out. 'Everyone went about pretending they knew nothing about it. The great marriage ceremony of Prince Louis and Princess Victoria was duly performed and then came the thunderclap. The Grand Duke married Mme Alexandrine de Kolemine *the same evening!*'[14]

A terrible royal question mark now hovered above every head – who was to tell the Queen this time? This time the wrath could *not* be turned away.

When no volunteer was forthcoming from the English, German, Russian, or any of the other royal families, the Prince of Wales decided that a lady-in-waiting should be asked to volunteer. Lady Ely was the first choice, and she really had none herself. That evening she ventured into the Queen's suite and gave her the tidings.

Faced with a real and sudden crisis the Queen could always be relied upon to keep her head; this was one of the royal responsibilities she had always maintained. Rumour had it that the Queen was thrown into a state of tantrums. But that is unproven and unlikely. All that is known for sure is that Bertie was called in for a discussion.

Meanwhile, solutions were being offered just as if it were not already too late. Miss Jackson, speaking with the steady voice and firm disciplinary sense of an impatient English governess, wanted Madame de Kolemine sent back to Russia where she belonged. Ponsonby had the temerity to ask, 'But if she won't go?'

'Ah, but she must!'

The Prince of Wales's instructions from the Queen were to interview the bride and inform her that the marriage would have to be annulled immediately. This was a minor embarrassment by contrast with the next task – that of passing the same news to the Grand Duke. Such a breach of protocol was unacceptable to any of the royal families, German, Russian, British, Scandinavian, and so on . . .

Love was never blinder than in Darmstadt that Spring. The Grand Duke was as shocked at this reaction as his guests had been by the stealth of his wedding. What could he say? His life was in ruins whether he obeyed or disobeyed these orders. In fact, of course, there was no alternative to obeying. He had broken the most inviolable of all the royal rules, and as reigning Grand Duke of a state that prospered virtually by its grand alliances, he clearly had to conform – cruel though it was.

At length he told the Prince of Wales that he would see the law officers about the legal process of annulment. 'We are,' commented the Prince of Wales, 'a very strong family when we agree.' To make doubly certain the Queen instructed Lord Ampthill, her ambassador in Berlin, to bring pressure on the German government to speed the annulment.

The Prussians considered that all these delicate negotiations were best handled by the English party, and on receipt of 'advice' from Bismarck, made a quiet and hasty departure from 'this contaminated court'. Others were doing the same thing. The German *chargé d'affaires* went off suddenly to Karlsruhe, the Prime Minister was diplomatically ill, although spotted by the sharp-eyed British consul out driving. Only the Queen and her eldest son kept their heads and took any steps to right the wrong. They stuck out their time, too.

'We don't hurry,' pronounced Ponsonby. 'But we go as settled on Monday. And we trust nothing will become public until we are well away.'[15]

These were strange and tense days in Darmstadt. The flags and bunting still waved in the spring sunshine but all joy had left the city. The Queen took short informal drives in a carriage but was recognized by few of the people. The Grand Duke and his family remained unseen in the palace. Royal life, and royal love, seemed to sleep uneasily in this city of betrothals and dynastic arrangements.

But love was not after all dead in Darmstadt. During these three weeks of alternating joy and anxiety in the Hessian capital, Princess Beatrice herself had found love. Just as Louis, the one Prince the Queen had feared, was safely and satisfactorily out of the way, her last unmarried daughter, upon whom she so depended, had fallen in love with his youngest brother.

Liko – Prince Henry of Battenberg – although a year younger at 26, returned her love with ardour; and the plump, shy Princess who could scarcely bring herself to speak to a stranger, and the last of the handsome, dashing Battenberg boys, came to a secret understanding before parting at Darmstadt station.

So when Ella left with the English Royal Party, to stay alone with her grandmother for the last time, as Victoria had done (and it was as well to be away from her broken-hearted father), hers was not the only love-sick heart in the suite. Beatrice steeled herself to ask her mother's permission after they reached Windsor. It might be easier there, away from the difficulties of Darmstadt . . .

The last words on the strange yet romantic events of that Spring in Darmstadt belong to Queen Victoria's private secretary.

'These Hessians have been so kind and civil to us that I am really sorry for them,' wrote Ponsonby. 'The glory of the Hessian Court is its alliance with other great ones – Baden, Würtemberg, Bavaria, etc. may swagger – but a family event in the Hessian family brings to Darmstadt Royal England and Imperial Germany and all this to be lost for the sake of [Madame de Kolemine].'[16]

For Louis and Victoria, the machinations of Madame de Kolemine, whom the Queen's suite had described as 'depraved' and 'scheming', provided an unsettling start to their married life, and it was not for several days of their all-too-short week at Heiligenberg that they heard that the legal process for an annulment was getting under way.

But nothing could quite spoil the joys of Heiligenberg for Louis. Victoria, who knew the castle almost as well as her husband, loved it too. She now looked on it in the light of her real home, at least when Louis was away at sea.

From Heiligenberg on the day after his marriage Louis wrote a letter to his parents which at once told movingly of his love for them and the happiness that had stemmed from that other morganatic union of thirty-three years ago.

My dearest parents,[17]

I want to take this opportunity on the first morning of my married life to say to you what my heart was too full to express yesterday. I thank you with all my heart and soul for the great and endless kindness and love you have shown me all my life. You have given me the opportunity to bring home my beloved Victoria as my wife, and few men can have found such an angel as she is. To my life's end I shall owe you my thanks for that. My happiness is so overwhelming that I cannot yet take it all in, and my heart is full of thankfulness to everyone who has helped me to find it. I can look into the future with confidence, because I am sure that our married happiness will resemble yours – I cannot wish and hope for more, for such perfect domestic happiness as yours must be the rarest that two people on this earth have ever enjoyed.

God bless you and reward you for all you have done for me.

Ever your grateful and loving son,

Louis

The couple returned to England. Louis had been appointed to the Royal Yacht *Victoria and Albert* the previous September – a comfortable sinecure which would leave him plenty of time with his bride, especially as the yacht was still undergoing a refit. He had taken a lease of a house called Sennicotts near Chichester on the south coast and conveniently close to Portsmouth. Here they enjoyed a further three weeks of honeymoon; then it was time to return to Germany before another wedding, this time in Russia.

Darmstadt still reverberated with the echoes of that double wedding a month earlier, and Louis already found himself with the family responsibilities of a married man. His first task was to persuade his father-in-law that there was still some hope in life. The Grand Duke had been invited to Windsor by the Queen as a gesture of renewed goodwill after his great unhappiness.

Queen Victoria found him 'in *such* a state of distress & grief that it is terrible to see'; and had enjoined Victoria to 'do *all* you can for him, for he feels your both marrying terribly'.[18] The Grand Duke was quite as distressed as the Queen had reported. Nor was his unhappiness in any way lessened by what the Queen later described as his 'being shamefully teazed by everybody to marry at once'.[19]

Louis and Victoria were gentle and kind with him. With the support of Ella and Irène they succeeded in reviving his spirits somewhat.

'That dreadful woman,' as the Queen now described Mme de Kolemine, had long since retreated to Moscow, but she took with her all the Grand Duke's love letters, and early in June Queen Victoria got wind of blackmail threats. These came to nothing, and it is not difficult to imagine the scale of the counter-threats if she should do any such thing.

In fact Mme de Kolemine did herself rather well in spite of her blackmailing failure. After despatching to everyone of influence at first importunate and then threatening letters, she was granted a title and given a large annual allowance. This did not cease when she married M. de Bacharacht, another Russian diplomat, nor when the Grand Duke died and she outlived him by many years.

The disturbed state of Europe's royal relationships was again exposed at this second Hessian wedding. The Grand Duke's scandal was largely forgiven and forgotten in Prussian and Russian eyes since the annulment proceedings were continuing apace and would shortly be concluded. (The marriage was finally dissolved on the 9 July 1884.)

It was Ella herself who remained as one source of discord – the beautiful Hessian daughter who had refused Willy (and for that the future Kaiser never forgave her) and 'Fritz' of Baden. Neither of these families was pleased to see her going to the Romanoffs. The Romanoffs, for their part, had not been pleased with the marriage of Louis and Victoria. Nor had the Prussians who had remained on uneasy terms with the Hessians since the war of unification and were very bigoted indeed about the distinction between Serene and Royal Highnesses.

Louis was regarded by the Russians as a turncoat, their close relative who had chosen English nationality, England as his home and the Royal Navy as his career. England was Russia's traditional enemy and competitor. It was England that opposed any Russian expansion into Asia and the Near East and insulted the Russian armies by sending her Navy up the Dardanelles – with this very officer serving in one of the battleships.

Now this same officer had married the sister of Grand Duke Serge's bride and would become his brother-in-law.

Louis's marriage to Victoria was viewed with the same disfavour by the Tsar and his family as Ella's marriage to this Russian Grand Duke was viewed by Queen Victoria and her family. There was no more romantic royal couple in the whole world than Louis and Victoria, but politically this match was not made in heaven.

This was the Hessian children's first visit to St Petersburg, the first time they had travelled so far by train and so far north, where the nights in June were so short that the light seemed never quite to leave the sky. The journey was a long one, taking three days and two nights.

There was something especially momentous about these long royal marriage journeys from Darmstadt to St Petersburg since the first one in 1773. It was not only their distance and frequency but their dynastic significance which marked them among the most important for the Hessian family.

Nearly half a century had passed since little, delicate Marie of Hesse, Grand Duke Serge's mother, had made the journey by royal carriage. Ella's reception was to be no less extravagant. Beside her in the train, and looking out as eagerly at the unfamiliar countryside, sat little Alicky, now twelve years old, who was to follow her sister on this same journey in another ten years to become Empress of All the Russias.

Victoria, too, thought the countryside lovely. 'I never saw any so rich in water before. From the frontier on, it is full of fine rivers and the most beautiful little lakes,' she told Queen Victoria in her first letter from Russia, which greatly interested the Queen, but may not have altogether pleased her when she continued: 'The vegetation is much the same as in Scotland, especially the trees. Great forests of firs and the grassland studded with birches.'[20] The grass she described as 'much richer' than Balmoral grass.

The Russian Court was at Peterhof in the Great Palace built in the rococo style by Tsar Peter I some twenty miles from St Petersburg on the Gulf of Finland. They were met by the Tsar and Grand Duke Serge and the rest of the family at the railway station, and were driven away in gilded coaches drawn by white horses. The Grand Duke of Hesse and his unmarried children were to stay in the Grand Palace, Louis and Victoria at a mansion next door.

The wedding was still a week away and during that time there were many joyous royal reunions as more and more relatives arrived from the palaces of Europe. Uncle Affie and Aunt Marie of Edinburgh were especially solicitous. She loved reliving happy childhood memories at Peterhof, knew every inch of the gardens and parks, and after dinner, and the sunset at 10.30 p.m., led a procession of carriages around them in the long colourful twilights, admiring the fountains and waterfalls and patterns of vast flowerbeds.

Not everyone knew Serge as well as Ella and Victoria and the other Hessians. But here, in the privacy of the palace and its grounds, there was every opportunity of watching the groom and judging his character. 'He was,' wrote one of Alicky's future ladies-in-waiting, 'a real *grand seigneur*, of high culture, artistic temperament and intellectual pursuits, though a certain shyness made him seem outwardly stiff and unresponsive.'[21] He did indeed look as if he was to be a rather solemn bridegroom with his long, lugubrious face made to seem even narrower by the brown beard.

Serge already had a reputation for being a political reactionary and believed in stamping out the smallest embers of liberalism for fear they might grow into revolutionary flames. There was a brooding, mystical element in his character that alarmed some people. But amongst people he knew well he was lively and fun. Alicky had adored him since she was an infant and they were always laughing together and teasing one another. Alicky went bright scarlet when she was teased, and sometimes when Serge wanted to score off her he would remind her in front of others that he could remember watching her being bathed as a baby.

Victoria, who had also known him for as long as she could remember (he was six years older), wrote to the Queen, 'I like him so much. He is graver than his brothers & much more refined in every way.' He was, she noted, full of 'little attentions' to Ella and had had the mansion, the *Ferme*, they were to live in done up 'charmingly and most comfortably'.

In addition to these rooms, Serge and Ella would have the huge Sergueivsjia Palace in St Petersburg and a country estate by the river outside Moscow called Illyinskoje. This was to be the home Ella would love most. Serge was immensely wealthy, and Ella was to have everything – jewels, clothes, carriages, horses and priceless antiques from anywhere in the world – for the asking.

'I don't think Ella's head is easily turned,' Victoria assured the Queen. 'It is true that she received magnificent jewels . . . but where everybody has such a quantity of fabulous stones it makes a small impression.'[22]

Ella had been warned by her Aunt Marie that you have to be strong and fit to marry into the Romanoffs, and she had been well briefed on what she was expected to wear. Her dressing and coiffure took several hours. The wedding dress was the Russian Court dress, white and cloth of silver, immensely heavy in itself. Grand Ducal crown, diamond tiara, ear-rings and necklace had all belonged to Catherine the Great, and once in place, strained her neck muscles to the uttermost. The ear-rings were so heavy that they had to be supported round the ears by a wire which slowly buried itself deeper into her flesh.

No one knew better than the court officials at St Petersburg how to put on a good show, and the people of the city joined in with a will. The entry by coach into the city went off perfectly, and the weather was clear and sunny. Victoria wrote to the Queen:

'The streets of St Petersburg which are so broad as generally to look emptier than they really are, were prettily decorated and filled with a very orderly crowd who cheered the whole procession lustily. The whole town turn out was a magnificent sight, the beautiful old gilt coaches being drawn by handsome horses covered with gorgeous gold trappings.'[23]

The bride's family looked as grand and magnificent as they always did on grand and magnificent occasions. The Grand Duke of Hesse, huge and vast-bearded, seemed to have lost none of his presence by his peccadillo. He had recently put his son Ernie *à la suite* of the Hessian Guard Regiment, so that he could wear uniform, too, and the girls matched up to their reputation for being the most handsome as well as the most dynastically desirable in Europe. Alicky had her hair loose, and both she and Irène wore white muslin dresses with flowers – they were so lovely that they needed nothing more.

The Grand Duke of Hesse had insisted, as a condition of consent, that Ella should keep her own religion; so the interminable Greek Orthodox wedding ceremony was followed immediately by a scarcely shorter Protestant one. 'Ella bore the fatigues remarkably well, in spite of the great weight of her dress and jewels,'[24] wrote Victoria.

The wedding breakfast followed – almost as long and formal an affair as the ceremonies – and then bride and groom, according to Russian tradition, were taken by coach to the Serguievsjia Palace where the Emperor and Empress, representing the bridegroom's dead parents, were received with an offering of bread and salt.

The social round continued for several more days. There seemed to be no limit to the number of relatives distant and less distant, young and middle-aged and old, Grand Dukes and Princes and Princesses – especially Russian ones – whom they had never met before.

The gigantic Tsar Alexander III took a special fancy to Alicky. She rarely started the laughter, but when the fun was going she joined in with vast enthusiasm and evident happiness. Perhaps it was this pretty and unselfconscious laughter that caught at the heart of the Tsar, and then of his eldest son the Tsarevitch.

Nicholas was sixteen, a kind, good-looking, enchanting but rather solemn lad. At a party for the younger relations which Alicky was allowed to attend, Nicholas gave her a brooch. She thanked him, accepted it for a while, then, uncertain of the propriety of the situation, handed it back to the future, and last, Emperor of All the Russias. Nicholas was puzzled and rather offended, and offered it instead to his nine-year-old sister Xenia, who accepted it eagerly.

Victoria said nothing in her letter to the Queen about the series of events which detracted from the glories of the Royal Wedding. These she would recount to her personally later because the security of the Russian mails was not to be trusted. These events, noticed by all but especially affecting her family, related to matters of precedence – a subject of the greatest delicacy and importance among those who lived by it. In England it was comparatively relaxed, in Germany as stiff as anywhere, in Russia scarcely less stiff.

The Russian Court had determined to put Louis in his place and demonstrate, as only the manipulation of precedence could, their disapproval of him and of his marriage.

The Royal Yacht *Osborne* had arrived at St Petersburg a few days before the wedding in order to convey the English and Danish contingents back to their homelands afterwards. The officers, who were always drawn from the better quality families, were naturally invited to take part in the festivities, though at a somewhat humble level. However, this included the wedding breakfast, which was a gargantuan feast following the Protestant ceremony.

Louis entered the banqueting hall with Victoria and her family from the Malachite room in the Palace. Along with the other guests, they were then led in turn by menservants to their seats. To his astonishment, Louis found himself being taken far down the table to the section reserved for the *Osborne*'s officers, where he was placed below the captain. Mortified but helpless, Louis took his seat, and no doubt covered up his indignation by talking to his fellow Naval officers in the most natural manner.

In fact, those who noticed did not regard his seat placing as a slight, but rather that Louis, as a naval officer, had chosen to sit among his shipmates. It was, all the same, a great insult, and the Grand Duke later took the matter up with the Tsar who agreed that it had indeed been unfortunate but after 'what he had heard from Berlin he could *not* place [him] with the family'.

From Berlin? So the Prussians were ganging up to insult him and his rank!

'Thank God,' Louis wrote to his father from England after his return, 'my fate has brought me to this wonderful free country, where I can live without being troubled by such petty chicanery.'[25]

Louis welcomed the salt air and the wind as he left the land behind. Not that there was much of 'the quiver and beat of the sea' about this gentle cruise through the Baltic in the *Osborne*, with a yacht-load of elegant and titled ladies, never out of sight of land, to Copenhagen. The *Osborne*, commissioned ten years earlier, was a three-masted paddle-wheeler yacht of 1,850 tons, as elegant and stylish in her appearance as in her accommodation.

Every day and all day the sun shone, and in the heat some of the Baltic islands stood out as a mirage in reverse high in the sky. There was sightseeing around Copenhagen, dinner with the Crown Prince and his family and a drive about their park before they continued across the North Sea, which lived up to its evil reputation and all the ladies took to their beds and were very sick indeed.

The aftermath of the Darmstadt weddings had not yet spent itself. When the Grand Duke came to Balmoral at the Queen's invitation, he was still a shattered figure. Even deer stalking in the Scottish heather, his favourite recreation, failed to cheer him up. The Queen wanted him to get away altogether to some distant place like India in order to expunge the memory of his mistress from his mind. She remained deeply concerned about him.

But soon another worry of such dimensions occupied her mind that the Grand Duke's love life was almost forgotten. For Princess Beatrice – 'Baby', 'Sweet Child' – had confessed that she had fallen in love and wanted to marry Louis's youngest brother. For most of that summer of 1884 the Queen refused to discuss the matter.

Beatrice's determination surpassed her mother's, to Ponsonby's delight and the delight of many others at Court. It was quite time she was married, they were saying, and once you had got over the surprise, it could be seen as the ideal match.

The pressure on the Queen increased relentlessly. By November the first cracks began to appear in her defences, and by the middle of the month she was writing to Louis that she might be becoming reconciled to the idea.

'Of course it remains a shock to me,' she wrote to Victoria,'& there will be things very difficult to get over with my feelings – Still as he is so amiable & prepared to do what I wish – I hope all may be for the best & may turn out well. Of course,' she added, 'I *can't* spare Auntie, & especially at first they must *not* think of travelling or paying visits.'26

The sting was, of course, in the tail. No travelling, and the couple were to live with her. Beatrice's duties as secretary-companion would remain unchanged. Liko, astonishingly, was prepared to put up with this savage condition. He had come to feel a great affection for the old Queen. The betrothed couple were very circumspect and there was no public kissing, 'wh Beatrice dislikes', the Queen noted with relief.

Louis was delighted at the outcome. To have his youngest brother, to whom he was devoted, always in England was the perfect arrangement. Society and the general public were less pleased. Too many of these royal girls had married Germans and it had been hoped that the last one might be spared for an Englishman.

Victoria had been in on Beatrice's secret from a very early stage. Another wedding was not the only pleasure to look forward to in 1885. On her return from Russia and Ella's marriage, she knew that she was expecting a child. That autumn she lived quietly at Senni-cotts following the Queen's advice that she should not ride. She went out for walks with the dog Aunt Louise had given her, drives exploring the Sussex countryside in a trap, visiting Arundel Castle and Chichester and calling on friends, while Louis worked in Ports-mouth on a torpedo course.

It was a quiet, domestic life for her, as befitted a young woman of the 1880s, *enceinte* for the first time. She did a little gardening, a gentle walk a day, and as always much reading. She met her father in London when he came over in September *en route* to Balmoral but did not accompany him to Scotland, preferring to be with Louis, who was working especially hard, and reserving herself for the journey to Darmstadt when the Grand Duke returned.

The Queen was determined that Victoria's child should be born in England and at Windsor, in the same room and the same bed in which Victoria had been born. With her highly developed sense of occasion, nothing else would satisfy her, and after the pain she had suffered over Beatrice's engagement, Victoria was anxious to appease her in every way. She was also inclined to agree with her Grandmother that Germans were clumsy and insensitive by contrast with English gynaecologists and accoucheurs – witness Willie's withered arm, caused, the Queen believed, by carelessness in delivery.

So, early in February 1885, Louis and Victoria left Sennicotts to stay with the Queen to await the baby's arrival.

Victoria slept restlessly in the Tapestry room on the night of 24 February. The Queen awoke early, and visited her and found 'she was very suffering'. All that day the Queen and Louis who 'was most helpful and attentive', remained beside her, 'till at length, at 20m to 5 in the afternoon, the child, a little girl, was born . . . Baby is very small, thin and dark,"[27] she noted, but added next day that she thought her 'very pretty'.

She was to be named Victoria Alice Elizabeth Julie Marie, known as Princess Alice, who, after giving birth to four girls herself, became the mother of the present Prince Philip, Duke of Edinburgh, thirty-six years later.

It had been almost as exhausting for the Queen as for the mother, and the accoucheur was amazed at how she had stood up to the physical and emotional ordeals of the long day. But there was no limit to the strength the Queen could give to an occasion when it was as domestically joyful as this, and her satisfaction knew no bounds at attending to the new born child, rubbing life into her little arms in just the same way that she had – such a short time ago it seemed – rubbed Victoria's little arms when her own Alice had given birth to her here.

This had been no ordeal. An ordeal was something quite different, like appearing before a crowd or attending some important assembly. To the Queen the giving of life was as glowingly satisfying as the loss of a life was intolerable and appalling. She had just heard that an old fiddler who always used to play at the gay balls at Balmoral when her children were young had just died. '*Every*, every *link* with the *past* is being swept away!' she wrote in despair. He was 90. The loss of one of her numerous dogs – an aged collie called Noble – occasioned almost equal grief and led her to write a long letter to Victoria reminiscing about the old days with him, and how he loved to recover sticks.

But on that February evening she was content and all those dread thoughts about Beatrice's marriage had been driven from her mind by the sound of the little Princess's first cries.

Alas! those morbid thoughts were soon to return. Almost every day something occurred to remind her of the dread event. In May Beatrice's annuity had to be approved by Parliament. Some anti-royalist Irish members and the Liberal republican Henry Labou-chère opposed it, though it got an overwhelming vote.

Things were not made easier for her by the very strong Prussian opposition to the match. The long gap between the birth of Vicky in 1840 and Beatrice in 1857 meant that Vicky, already a grand-mother four times over, would once again have a new brother-in-law. But by Prussian standards a mere Battenberg 'Serene' was not good enough for the future German Empress, whatever Vicky herself might feel about it. The old Empress Augusta, Vicky's Fritz, and their eldest son Willie all made their feelings clear.

The Queen now leaped to Liko's defence. Then she bore into the attack against the Prussians – and a formidable assault it was, too. Dealing with them in turn as 'insolent', 'foolish' and 'unkind' she reserved a special diatribe for Willie. She had never much liked him and regarded him with her shrewd and prophetic eye as a future menace to Europe with all his militaristic posturings and sycophantic allying himself with that dangerous man Bismarck.

'That very foolish, undutiful and, I must add, unfeeling boy, I have no patience with and I wish he could get a good "skelping" as the Scotch say . . .' Of his wife, that 'poor little insignificant pcess' she felt it suitable to quote Lord Granville: 'If the Queen of England thinks a person good enough for her daughter what have other people got to say?'[28]

A war with Berlin on this scale distracted her mind from the real fear she felt, which had nothing to do with dynasty building, for the forthcoming event on 23 July 1885. It was a temporary palliative only.

'I am *very depressed*,' she wrote to Victoria from Windsor. 'How I dread the week after next – & how I wish it was months and years off! The nearer the fatal day approaches the more my invincible dislike to Auntie's marriage (NOT to dear Liko) – increases. Sometimes I feel as if *I never* cld take her myself to the Marriage Service – & that I wld wish to run away & hide myself!'[29]

In the event, it was not as bad as she had feared. There had to be a certain degree of ceremony for the wedding of the last of her children, and a certain degree of grandeur – Buszards of Oxford Street made a wedding cake 9 feet high and weighing 450 pounds. But, while there were droves and droves of royalty present from all over Europe, including the Grand Duke and Louis's mother and father, the ceremony was performed in the little village church at Whippingham, which for the Queen had the double merit of having been designed by Albert and being so small and remote that the crowds were few. The going-away was rather much for her, and she shed some tears. But that was all.

It was another great step up in status for the Battenbergs, an even greater one than Louis's marriage, for this one was direct into the line of the English Queen's children. Commenting cheekily on the speed of Liko's 'Yes' at the wedding ceremony, a gossip columnist of the time noted that 'It is not vouchsafed to all of us to become demorganaticated, bridegrooms, Royal Highnesses, and Knights of the Garter in the twinkling of an eye.'[30]

As the years passed the Queen came to realize what a blessed event it had been. She had not lost a daughter but had gained a son, in the full literal meaning of that comforting old cliché. It brought a man into her household again, one she loved and trusted, who was charming and gay, and brought her out into the world – even brought her out onto the dance floor.

In due course there was the patter of tiny feet about her palaces, the cry of young voices, and then the presence of children who needed her wisdom and guidance. She loved it all because she loved to re-live her idyllic past and it reminded her, with ecstatic little stabs of pain and pleasure, of those dear days with Albert – and Vicky and Bertie and Alice and Affie and . . .

Louis and Victoria observed with relief this reawakening of the Queen to the pleasures and responsibilities of life. What a happy and unexpected outcome it was to those anxious, turbulent days of their own wedding at Darmstadt!

At the end of 1885, Louis and Victoria could look back on nearly two eventful years of married life. There were sadnesses and anxieties. The Grand Duke's future was still a worry. The death of his mother, Elizabeth, in March was a sadness to the whole family. Their relations with the Russians were not good, and this was a great sadness for Victoria who deeply missed her sister Ella. Their relations with the Prussians were so bad that they were best not discussed. And that was sad, too, because it cut Victoria off almost completely from Aunt Vicky. Louis's chief worry was for his brother Sandro who was having a bad time of it in Bulgaria and had already proved that his own anxieties about his dangerous and ill-defined job had been justified.

On the credit side they had much to be thankful for besides the happy marriage of Beatrice and Liko. Alice was an angelically beautiful baby and they worshipped her. On 25 April she was christened at Darmstadt on the same day that Ernie was confirmed, and Serge and Ella came for the ceremonies and that was wonderful.

Louis had been promoted Commander on 30 August and had gone onto half pay for the winter which allowed him to join Victoria at Darmstadt for Christmas. It was, as always, a joy to be at Heiligenberg with the snow on the mountains, with tobogganing and skating and so many of their families around them.

Their own marriage, like so many stemming from childhood friendship, was a real one – comradely and with much unstated understanding as well as deep passion. Queen Victoria, for once, failed to understand it completely. She saw its competitive elements and sometimes heard the sharp words. She observed Victoria's careless appearance and careless – almost slovenly – ways, and she was right when she judged that these grated on Louis, who was always so careful and trim and punctilious. She worried that Victoria took nothing at its face value, questioned and analysed relentlessly until she had found the answer.

The Queen thought, with some reason, that Victoria was neither gentle nor suppliant enough with Louis. There was truth behind all these strictures, but they failed to take into account that Louis, who had known Victoria from infancy, saw what he was in for and recognized his own need for an exacting marriage. He liked the competition between them and the occasional fighting. It was what he had chosen. He loved her restless mind, just as Prince Albert had enjoyed the Queen's intelligence and analytical skills.

The two marriages had much in common. Victoria lacked Queen Victoria's power. She was also far less emotional and nervy, and in fact demanded much less from Louis than the Queen had demanded from Albert. On one subject Victoria did not need the Queen's advice. She got it nonetheless. 'Let me again ask you to remember,' wrote the Queen, 'that your 1*st duty* is to your dear and most devoted *Husband* to whom you can *never* be *kind enough* & to whom I think a *little* more *tenderness* is due *sometimes*.'[31]

Louis received all the tenderness any man could ask for. It was just not served up to the Queen's formula, and it did not need to be specified as Queen Victoria liked it to be specified. This was something that shrewd old lady, to whom sentiment was so important, never understood.

6

'I felt as if I could have jumped for joy!'
QUEEN VICTORIA *at the age of 67 years.*

THE Queen was among the first to acknowledge what a good match her youngest daughter had made. 'I thought you would like to hear how well all is going on,' she wrote to Victoria from Balmoral only two months after the wedding, 'how happy dear Auntie is & they are together – & yet so sensibly etc. – so that I feel but little change. Liko is delighted to go out stalking but not to go out 2 days running away from Auntie.'[1]

While Liko pursued the deer on alternate days in the Highlands, two of his brothers, Louis and Franzjos, were becoming increasingly worried about Sandro's situation in Bulgaria – and becoming increasingly involved in it. Ever since he had been pressed into the job of Sovereign Prince of Bulgaria, Alexander of Battenberg's life had been a misery. Sofia, he discovered to his horror when he first arrived, was a capital city of a few thousand hovels, without paved roads, drains or services of any kind. The 'palace' for the new ruler was an old two-storey house which was falling down – various parts of the roof did fall in and had to be supported by props in his bedroom.

As to the people, they were 99% illiterate and 100% corrupt. In addition, 'All the scum of Russia has taken refuge here and has tainted the whole country,' he wrote home to his father. And the poverty, of course, was frightful. This was the land Sandro was supposed to mould into a reformed, efficient and prosperous autonomous country. Only a deep sense of duty doubtless supported by the consideration of glory if he succeeded, kept him at his post.

At least he had the support of the Tsar, his uncle Alexander II, for his first two years in the job. When the Tsar was assassinated and succeeded by his son, that brooding, mean-minded tyrant, Alexander III, things became much worse. The Russian officials and army officers in Bulgaria, who disliked Sandro's stiff formal regime as much as his reforming policies which – among other things – marginally reduced the bribery, had been busily poisoning Sandro's reputation for some time. Sandro's uncle Tsar Alexander II had not listened; Sandro's first cousin Tsar Alexander III did.

All liberal foreign policy was cast out of the Kremlin windows under Alexander III, and a nationalist, aggressive, anti-German and Russia-for-the-Russians policy gathered strength.

Poor Sandro's position became more and more untenable and Gilbertian. On the one hand the southern Bulgars, excluded under the Treaty of Berlin, wanted to be unified under his rule. On the other hand Russia opposed this nationalist movement because it would upset the status quo. The educated liberal movement in Bulgaria favoured the unification and worked up a strong anti-Russian nationalist campaign in the country, which Sandro found it difficult not to support.

Even Sandro's love life became involved in this confused situation. For many years Aunt Vicky's and Uncle Fritz's second daughter, Cousin Vicky, had been in love with the tall, noble, handsome Battenberg soldier-prince, and Sandro now wanted her as his wife because, first, it was time that he was married, second, he loved her, and, thirdly it was terribly lonely in Sofia anyway. Aunt Vicky encouraged the match, and so did Uncle Fritz later. Both of them hated the Russians with a loathing almost as deep as Queen Victoria's.

But the Tsar was furious about the proposed match when he heard. He had brooded long and bitterly about Sandro and that dreadful family at Potsdam, and had worked himself into a state of implacable hatred as a consequence. He made it clear first to Sandro, and then to the German Emperor, and to Bismarck, that he would not allow such a marriage to take place. To give offence to Russia was no part of Bismarck's policy, so he forbade it too.

While all this unpleasantness was going on behind Sandro's back, and while he was on a visit to Heiligenberg, more dramatic events were occurring in Bulgaria. With their Prince away, the southern Bulgars, still supposed to be under the control of Turkey, rebelled and thrust themselves onto the liberals in Sandro's part of Bulgaria. This suited almost no one but the Bulgarians and Queen Victoria, who suddenly perceived a reunited Bulgaria under that nice Battenberg boy as a very useful buffer against the predatory Russian bear. Sandro hurried back to his post, accompanied this time by his younger brother Franzjos who was by now a fully qualified officer. He might be needed.

But the first to react violently were not the Russians (who blamed the whole thing on Sandro, struck his name off the Army List and withdrew all Russian officers from the Bulgarian army), nor the Turks nor the Austrians, but the Serbs. They marched into Bulgaria, probably under pressure from Russia but it was difficult to prove anything in the Balkans.

Now the most unfavourable time to invade a nation is when it is in the full flush of nationalist enthusiasm, hot from victory. In this case military zeal was allied with an experienced army commander. Sandro's prowess on the field of battle was as notable as his powers of diplomacy were wanting.

The powerful Serbian army was routed in a bloody three-day battle at Slivnitza. Sandro found release on the field of battle for all his frustrations and fury. 'I was everywhere at once,' he told his father proudly, 'in front, behind, right, left.'[2] After that, he led his victorious troops deep into Serbia and he could have taken them all the way to the Adriatic such was their enthusiasm and momentum. But the Serbs sued for peace.

Nowhere was the joy greater than at Windsor Castle. 'We are,' the Queen wrote to Victoria who was in Darmstadt with Louis, 'constantly occupied with Bulgaria & dear Sandro's wonderful success & splendid conduct. *No one* CLD sympathise *more truly* with your anxiety & your joy & pride, than I do. How proud you must all be of him! Please God! all looks so much better now.'[3]

Slivnitza was the most splendid of all the Battenberg military victories, especially praiseworthy (and especially insulting to the Russians) because it was carried through without the Russian field officers who were supposed to provide the backbone to the Bulgarian army. It was also the crowning moment in the strange story of Sandro's rule of this turbulent and victimised Balkan state.

Tsar Alexander III's reaction was ferocious, and he now bent all his power and wealth to the destruction of Sandro's rule. Throughout the early months of 1886 he used millions of roubles to bribe and corrupt the liberal and pro-Sandro elements in Bulgaria, and especially the army officers. Every device was used to discredit Sandro throughout Europe – he was filthy in his ways, was a homosexual, kept a harem in Sofia, was destroying the country ... Some of it stuck, especially in Germany and Austria.

In spite of many warnings that his own and Franzjos's lives were in danger, Sandro stuck to his post. 'He has grown thin,' Franzjos wrote to Louis, 'and looks very strained. Sometimes he has melancholy moods, to which he is very prone. But he has a great deal to cope with; nothing but enemies, intrigues and deceit on all sides.'[4]

These intrigues reached their culminating point on the night of 20–21 August in Sofia. At 2.30 in the morning Sandro's servant heard noises and footsteps outside and peering from a window saw the garden filled with shadowy shapes. 'He rushed into Sandro's bedroom, awakening him with the words, "Fly, the Palace is surrounded by soldiers, you will be murdered,"'[5] Louis recounted to the Queen later. Sandro attempted to escape by a back door but was spotted and fired at by four soldiers.

He returned to his room, dressed in his general's uniform, and descended the stairs to the hallway with his servant. He was at once surrounded by drunken, rebellious, shouting soldiers wielding revolvers and bayonets. Their leader tore a page from the visitors' book and tried to write out a statement of abdication, but he was so drunk that it resulted in nothing but ink blobs. Another soldier tried with little more success. Sandro was puzzling over the scrawl which appeared to have no meaning when an officer put a cocked revolver to his face and shouted, 'Sign or I'll shoot.' Sandro signed with a steady hand.

He saw they had got Franzjos, too, and they were both being shouted at, insulted and threatened. The drunken cadets were worst, and both the brothers believed that it could only be a matter of time before they were killed. 'This wouldn't have happened if you had made me a major,' Sandro heard one officer say to him. Clearly, the Russians had promised him promotion to Colonel – that was how Balkan military coups d'état were started.

There were carriages waiting outside. Surrounded by cursing, threatening soldiers, Sandro was hustled into one, his brother into another. Then they rattled off into the night and that was the last that was seen of them for some time.

Victoria was in Darmstadt, Louis in Portsmouth, when the telegram arrived telling of the brothers' abduction. Louis was granted leave and left at once for Germany. By the time he arrived at Heiligenberg, where his father and mother were in a state of shock and agonising worry, another telegram had arrived, this time from

Sandro in Russian Besserabia, saying that they were safe, but 'I am absolutely shattered by the fearful anguish I have suffered,' he ended. Louis determined to go to their aid. He knew the depth of the Tsar's wrath and was now more fearful than ever for his brother's safety.

Again the tide of revolt changed in Bulgaria. This time the people rose up against the corrupted army Palace guards and demanded their Prince. 'Go back to Sofia!' the cry came from Darmstadt and Balmoral, as well as from the people who loved their tall, handsome, soldierly Prince. 'What dreadful anxiety we have been living in since that awful 22nd!' wrote Queen Victoria, '& those *3* days before we knew where dear noble brave Sandro was! When we heard his dear life was safe & the enthusiasm so great for him, & that wicked, villainous, atrocious Russia failed – I felt as if I cld have jumped for joy!'[6]

And what a joyful reunion of the three brothers it was! 'You may imagine what were my feelings on seeing my beloved Sandro again,' wrote Louis who had ridden much of the way and was almost as weary and dusty as Sandro and Franzjos. They fell on each others' shoulders and thanked God that they were all safe.

Sandro recounted in detail the perfidious events leading to their capture, their long journey in the carriages with curtains drawn, a twenty-four-hour halt when they were locked in a monastery with hardly any food, and then to the Danube where the Bulgarian Royal Yacht awaited them in darkness. The brothers were at the limit of their endurance. They were starving and half dead from the heat, for whenever they attempted to open a window in the carriage or a porthole in the yacht they were threatened with a bayonet or revolver.

They were taken downstream to the Russian border. It seemed unlikely that they would survive the journey with these wild, drunken Bulgars; and if they did the Russians would shoot them at the end of their journey. In fact the Russians did not know what to do with them, and in a state of acute embarrassment tried to send them back to Sofia.

Louis wrote to the Queen: 'I have not yet got over the effect produced on me by the account of all that unparalleled baseness, duplicity & brutality ... I found S. quite crushed and broken, longing to lay down his weary head far, far from the scene of all his suffering, sick to death of the mere word "Bulgaria". And it was then that his grand nature shewed itself again to the full. No sooner had he taken in the whole situation and had found that it was his *duty* to go back, as things had turned, then his resolve was taken –

telegrams announcing his intention were despatched, a special train ordered at once to bring him here with all speed. At 2 o'clock we started on our eventful journey amidst the frantic delight of the populace.'[7]

In Bulgaria he was greeted with joy and enthusiasm. But Sandro knew better now. Russian Machiavellism was still at work – of that he was sure. It was confirmed when he was nearly assassinated in the Cathedral one day. What was the use of staying on? Insulted, threatened, utterly disillusioned, Prince Alexander of Bulgaria, who had ruled as well as he could for seven years, confirmed the abdication he had signed at bayonet point and left the country with his two brothers.

Sandro never returned to Bulgaria alive, though his name, as the country's first Sovereign Prince, was revered by the liberal element and the peasants. Nor did this skilful and brave soldier ever fight again. His spirit never recovered after his abdication, his pride permanently wounded by what he regarded as his failure. He was as sickened by German as by Russian perfidy, and, like his father before him, offered his services to the Austrian Emperor. He gave up his Princely titles and was granted the Hessian title Count Hartenau and given command of a brigade.

The intense and continuing love between Sandro and the lovely Cousin Vicky developed into a tragic domestic and political issue. Even after Fritz's death in 1888, his widow, supported by the Queens conspired to bring about this marriage which Bismarck so implacably opposed. With Willie's accession to the German throne the chance, for his sister's love match were even further reduced, Bismarck and Kaiser Wilhelm seeking to discredit everything that his father had stood for.

Vicky's heart was as broken by her son's callousness as her daughter's by the opposition to their marriage. Louis and Victoria tried to make peace in the German family, but as Victoria wrote to the Queen, 'at Berlin people are only too glad to widen the breach'.[8]

Sandro at length found solace in a beautiful opera singer, Johanna Loisinger, and married her in 1889. 'Oh! dear Sandro! it is a sad thing,'[9] wrote the Queen. But for Sandro it was the happiest thing that had ever happened to him. For four years he lived at last in peace and harmony. Then he went down with appendicitis in November 1893 and died suddenly of peritonitis.

The blow was an especially hard one for Louis. Sandro was his favourite brother and they had always been very close. The Queen

THE INHARMONIOUS BISMARCK.

Empress (sings). What shall we do with our daughter?
Bismarck.   Don't know. If the wedding's to be,
                   When over you hand her
                   To Prince ALEXANDER,
                   You'll then have to do without *me!*

Ensemble.

Empress.   { What shall we do with our daughter?
Bismarck. { What will they do with their daughter?

(*Spoken.*)
Bismarck. I think your Majesty is singing a little out of tune.
    Empress. Pardon me, Prince; but it is you who are a great deal too sharp.
    Bismarck. Um—well—we'll take two bars' rest, and then sing together—
    Both (in unison). Vaterland! mein Vaterland!
                      La Li-e-ty! La Li-e-ty!
                                            [*Left jödelling.*

had dearly loved Sandro and soon forgave him his hasty and improper marriage. From Graz where Sandro had died, he wrote to her:

'I reached here, after many delays owing to snowfalls, towards two o'clock this morning. My poor sister-in-law was sitting up for me. I was aghast at the change in her appearance. She, who I last saw as a tall, fine woman, is shrunk into nothing ... a thin,

frail, whitefaced girl . . . She led me in silence to Sandro's room . . .
I believe I realized for the first time that he was in truth gone. I
completely and utterly broke down. She stood there all the time, not
a tear in her eye, not a sound escaped her . . .'[10]

The Bulgarian government, and their new monarch, Prince
Ferdinand I, asked that the body of their revered first Prince should
be buried in Sofia. The interment took place later in the year in a
solemn ceremony in the Cathedral and his two children were given a
special Bulgarian pension, which was very useful as they were hard
up.

Cousin Vicky married another prince a year after Sandro met
his opera singer – Adolphus, Prince of Schaumburg-Lippe, who died
in 1916. Eleven years later, and to the surprise of the surviving
relations she married again, this time morganatically to a young
man of twenty-seven, an ex-waiter called Alexander Subkov.

The first years of Louis's and Victoria's marriage were marked by
other family marriages and intrigues, some of which contributed to
the fatal military alignments of 1914. There were, too, other tragic
deaths which, in the tradition the Queen herself had established,
preoccupied deeply, publicly and for long the bereaved families.

In 1888 Germany lost two Emperors, and Louis lost his father.
Emperor William I died on 9 March and was succeeded by his
son Fritz, who was already dying of cancer of the throat.

So bad were international relations that even a man's prolonged
and painful death became a political issue. The Queen had persuaded
her son-in-law to take *English* medical advice. Sir Morrell Mackenzie
disputed the German doctors' diagnosis of cancer and decision
to perform a tracheotomy, and dark rumour had it that Bismarck
wanted the new Emperor Frederick out of the way and his more
pliant and reactionary son on the throne.

For a while Fritz believed that he had been cured in England
without an operation. By November 1887 Sir Morrell had to agree
with the German surgeons. All Europe knew that the new German
Emperor had only a short time to live, and Queen Victoria made a
diversion to Potsdam on her way back from Florence where she had
been staying in order to see her son-in-law for the last time and to
comfort Vicky.

The Prussians regarded this as a purely political move by the
wily old Widow of Windsor, and were certain that she had really

come to cause mischief and support Vicky in her fight for Sandro's hand for her daughter. The Queen remained aloof from all gossip, kissed the dying Emperor, who was beyond speech but gave her a bunch of forget-me-nots, and received Bismarck in audience.

Historians have been arguing ever since as to who came best out of that confrontation. But it is known for a fact that Bismarck was mopping his brow when he emerged, and was heard to remark, 'That was a woman! one could do business with her!'

The Emperor Frederick died on 15 June, and with him any hope that Bismarck's aggressive expansionism might be held in check. Willie leaped onto the throne with indecent alacrity, and Vicky's long political ordeal at the hands of Bismarck and her son began. She wanted to escape from it all and come to England for a while. But at the last minute she lost her courage. For, as *Vanity Fair* put it, 'If she left Berlin, she would never come back to it.'

Louis was deeply concerned about the German situation, and Victoria who had watched the boy from whom she had once learned cigarette smoking grow into a dangerous and powerful young man, wrote anxiously from Germany to her grandmother:

SEEHEIM[11]
June 16th 1888

Darling Grandmama,

How sad this news about poor Uncle Fritz is; though so long feared & expected, the blow is none the less hard to bear, & I feel so dreadfully sorry for poor Aunt Vicky. You will understand her grief better than any one . . .

The future is uncertain and doubtful, & people feel it to be so. In all our part of Germany Uncle Fritz was truly loved & admired; & the lower classes every where trusted & honoured him. It was he who reconciled the bitterness caused by the war of '66, everybody knew & felt that was hard & unjust in it, found no sympathy with him, & the French themselves honoured him as the best & noblest of men who fought against them. Had he been spared, I think he would have won a more true & lasting affection throughout Germany than any sovereign before him.

For Willy I feel a sincere pity. He is so young for his position [29 years], & so greatly needs a wise & honest friend to help him . . . I greatly fear, that for want of such a one, his faults rather than his good qualities will develop. When I think how warm hearted & nice he was as a boy, how greatly he changed during the last years, I cannot but think it is in a great measure the fault of his surroundings. Now that the chief cause of bitterness between him & his mother [the projected marriage of Cousin Vicky and Sandro] must come to an end, if there were some one to work

143

on his better feelings, I believe he would get on better with his mother . . . It is a sad lookout . . .

Hoping you are well, & with much love from all of us,

I remain

Ever your loving Grandchild

Victoria

The Queen, never a one for mincing her words, replied sharply on 4 July: 'It is too dreadful for us all to think of Willy & Bismarck & Dona [the new Emperor's wife, Empress Augusta Victoria] – being the supreme head of all now! Two so unfit & one so wicked.'[12]

Prince Alexander of Hesse's death later in the year was more personally tragic for Louis and much less politically ominous for Europe. A few weeks after the German Emperor's death, Louis heard that his father was in pain and was losing weight. He got leave from the Navy to see him, realized that he was dying but did not extend his leave for fear of alarming the old man.

It was a time of great suffering for Louis. 'He is so miserable & unhappy knowing how ill his father is,' Victoria wrote to the Queen shortly before his father's death, and confessed that 'it is hard to have to appear cheerful and hopeful when one's thoughts are so sad. This was such a united, happy family that it is terrible to think of the change coming, & I do not know how my poor mother-in-law will ever be able to bear it.'[13]

Louis, Victoria and little Alice were recalled urgently in December, and on the 15th Prince Alexander of Hesse – brave and much-decorated warrior, rebel, and diplomat – died at Heiligenberg. He was a full-blooded Prince in the best meaning of the rank – gay, adventurous, dashing, yet a steady, wise counsellor and father to his four boys. Now he was dead of cancer at 65.

The Queen, tortured by the agonies his sons were suffering during their father's last days, pondered over this terrible disease – '*This illness* . . . which I think *justifies* EVERY *attempt* to *arrest* the progress & *relieve* the pain.'[14]

Julie, once the Polish orphan girl, survived him for another seven years at Heiligenberg. Louis was at sea when she died on 19 September 1895. He felt her loss deeply, and the Queen wrote in commiseration, 'To be unable to see your so dearly loved Mother once more, or even to follow her to her last peaceful resting place is cruel indeed – no wonder you feel broken hearted!'[15]

Within a few weeks the Queen's own heart was to be broken,

yet again, by the sudden and unexpected death of the late Princess's youngest son, Liko. 'The sunbeam in our home is GONE!' the Queen cried out in anguish.

Liko had found life increasingly oppressive as a full-time 'ray of light' (as the Queen also described him) at Windsor, Osborne, Buckingham Palace and Balmoral. Dutiful as he was, he had his share of Battenberg energy and extrovertism, which did not find full expression on the hunting field or in the Highland heather with a gun under his arm or handling his yacht in the Solent.

The Queen did not much like him to go away and told him so. When he went out to shoot in Albania she complained that it was 'a very foolish expedition & I hope he wont be very long away & come back safe'.[16]

When Liko heard of the proposed Ashanti Expedition to the Gold Coast late in 1895 he determined to fight for his country and show that he was a Battenberg to the core. 'I told him it would never do'[17] reported the Queen. But Liko showed unexpected obstinacy, and in the end the Queen agreed, and even commented that it was 'a very gallant thing for him to do'.[18]

On 7 December 1895 Princess Beatrice watched his regiment go with tears in her eyes. A military band was playing *Auld Lang Syne* and patriotic fervour was everywhere evident.

Liko was eager for combat, and on the way out to Africa he studied the topography of the country and was proud that he was one of the few to withstand the rigours of the Bay of Biscay. But he never met the enemy. He was struck down with fever soon after landing and died at sea on the way home. Neither the Queen nor her youngest daughter fully recovered from this blow, although Beatrice amazed her mother by her stoicism and dignity in her bereavement.

Deaths came with ever increasing frequency in the last decade of the Queen's life but her capacity for grief, and the depth of expression of her grief, never failed her. Sometimes her talent for the melodramatic got the better of her. The death of the Grand Duke Ludwig of Hesse in 1892 was a sad event for her and for his children, but it was not entirely unexpected. He had been treated for heart disease the previous year and had been in poor health for some time. But the Queen, in expressing her '*quite overwhelming* grief' also referred to the distress of the youngest children, 23 and nearly 20 years old, living in comfort and style, surrounded by servants and court officials, as 'poor dear Ernie and Alicky alone – *Orphans ! !* It is *awful*.'

Each shared grief brought Louis and Victoria closer than ever to the Queen. So did shared worries, of which the accession of Willie as German Emperor was only one. Nor was Sandro's morganatic marriage the only one that gave them all concern.

Considering the weight of her influence, the time and energy she gave to it and the depth of her feelings, Queen Victoria's match-making in the last twenty years of her life was surprisingly ineffectual. She was particularly and bitterly disappointed in the marriages of the Hessian children she regarded as her own, and she never succeeded in reconciling herself to them, although, like any good family woman, she never ceased to love them and their children and was always eager to welcome them to her homes.

After Ella's marriage and the Queen's prophesies of doom for it, she became worried about Irène's future. As always she relied on Victoria's influence to help guide her young sisters and brother to the *correct* marriage at the *correct* time. This was very hard on Victoria because she did not always agree with her grandmother, nor did she always have so much influence over her sisters as the Queen supposed. They were all spirited and strong-willed girls, and no one could have prevented Ella from having her Russian Grand Duke whom she had known since she was a child.

In 1886 Irène fell in love with Henry of Prussia, the sailor Prince. Irène had known him ever since those days, before their mother's death, when they had stayed at Potsdam and Victoria had always wanted to climb his ship's mast in the palace grounds. This match did not suit the Queen at all. She had other plans for these two grandchildren – the double closeness of their relationship did not bother her, but she regarded Henry as weak in will and body (which was perhaps putting it rather strongly), and she forecast problems like those Vicky had suffered from the division of the Bismarck-dominated Prussians and the Hessians.

Early in 1887 Henry was due to go off on a long voyage and the Queen succeeded in extracting from Irène an assurance that she would not promise herself to him before he left. But naughty Irène broke her word, and it was left to Victoria (as usual) to tell the Queen. The shock made her feel 'quite ill'.

'And she *assured* me *again* & *again* that she wld *never do that*! How CAN I trust her again after such conduct?' the Queen demanded of poor Victoria. 'This *want* of *openness* has *hurt* me *deeply*.'[19] It was particularly offending that she had read of their engagement 'from the papers 1*st*'.

The couple got married at Charlottenburg Palace on her birthday, 24 May. The Prince of Wales attended but the Queen said she could not, she was otherwise engaged; and told Victoria that she could not have brought herself to go even if she had not been.

It was a sad as well as a grand affair. The Emperor Frederick had only a few weeks to live but insisted on coming in full uniform, his tracheotomy tube providing a discordant accompanying note to the proceedings. Field Marshal Moltke, the Franco-Prussian war hero, remarked that he had never seen anyone as brave as the Emperor. Bismarck, overhearing him, commented that an Emperor who could not talk should not be allowed to reign.

Recounting this ugly exchange to his mother, Bertie remarked, 'If I had not taken into consideration that good relations between Germany and England were essential, I should have thrown him out.'[20]

Once it was settled, the Queen as usual determined to make the best of it. Henry, whom she had rather despised for allowing himself to be bullied by Willie as a boy and by the Prussian court as a young man, was now to become an even closer part of *her* family. 'Henry must be brought round to a *right* view of things & not become a 2*nd* enemy as it were in the midst of the family wh is too painful,'[21] she wrote to Victoria.

So much for the third Hessian daughter. Now, what of the fourth and last, that enchanting, quiet and rather mysterious figure, Alix? Alicky would soon need a husband. With Irène's departure, she would lack all sisterly company at Darmstadt: she would be alone with Miss Jackson, who had not improved with age and with what the Queen described as 'her bad health, hard ways & crabbed, bad temper',[22] was *not* a suitable companion.

The Queen, of course, had plans for Alicky. She revealed them in a long letter to Victoria on 2 March 1887, although she prefaced them with this bitter comment and harking back again to Ella's unfortunate Russian marriage:

'I feel very deeply that my opinion & my advice are never listened to & that it is almost useless to give any. – It was not before Ella's marriage was decided on wh dear Mama wld never have allowed to come abt.' The Queen continued severely: 'As Irène has been lost to us here – I must tell you, who have so much influence with Papa & generally in the family, that my heart & mind are bent on securing dear Alicky for either Eddie or Georgie.'[23]

Now Eddie, the Duke of Clarence, was in the direct line of

succession. If the Queen lived for another decade or more, as she appeared quite capable of doing, the Prince of Wales would be well past middle age when he came to the throne, and his heir could be King-Emperor in twenty years. The Queen was, then, nominating Alicky as the future Queen of England and Empress of India, a measure of her regard for Hessian blood and this grandchild. Although, as always, claiming that she was no matchmaker, the Queen pursued this plan assiduously for more than two years, and Eddie seemed genuinely in love with her – as well he might be for with every month that passed Alicky bloomed more beautifully.

But other powerful forces in Germany and Russia were working against the Queen's designs. Bismarck discerned political advantages in securing another and even more powerful bond between the Hessians and the Romanoffs. Nicholas, the Tsarevitch himself, must have the hand of this Hessian Princess. Tsar Alexander III approved, too, and so did all his court. The Grand Duke and Grand Duchess Serge were brought into the plot, and Ella was delighted at the idea of having her baby sister with her in Russia – and as the future Tsarina.

Alicky, 15 years old, innocent in all things, unknowing that plans were afoot to make her either the future Queen of Great Britain and Empress of India or Empress of All the Russias, was confirmed and came out on her 16th birthday, 6 June 1888, amidst all the upheavals caused by the successive deaths of the German Emperors and the lightning appearance of Queen Victoria at Potsdam.

It was arranged that her father should bring her to St Petersburg in the winter for her first ball. Soon after this, but just too late, came the Queen's invitation to Alicky and her father to come to Balmoral. Both invitations were accepted: it was to be a busy winter for the young Princess.

It was nearly five years since she had last been in St Petersburg and had been given a brooch by the gentle, kindly boy who would one day rule Russia. Royal life at Peterhof in the winter was a magical experience with a constant round of tobogganing parties, balls, carnivals and dancing and skating to music in the moonlight. Everyone encouraged Nicky and Alicky to be together as often as possible, and Ella was always there with her loving kindness and advice.

After all this, Balmoral was something of a let-down. And so was Eddie, Duke of Clarence. Neither Alicky nor her father had received warning that there was any expectation of an 'understanding' being reached with Eddie.

Poor Eddie did not make strong competition for the handsome young Nicky. One of the few excitements in his life had been that terrifying storm he had endured with his younger brother in the *Bacchante*, and after that he had favoured the Army over the Navy. He did very little and had little to say for himself, and he looked the archetypal Victorian Hussars officer with little chin, less forehead, a tiny waxed moustache and protuberant eyes. Alicky rebuffed his advances as kindly and gently as she could. But poor Eddie could not be consoled. 'I don't think she knows how I love her or she could not be so cruel,' he wrote in his sadness to his mother.

The Queen was not pleased at Alicky's refusal. She wrote to her daughter Vicky, 'She shows gt strength of character, all her family and all of us wish it, and she refuses the gtst position there is.'[24] The Queen did not expect any help from this quarter. But to her granddaughter Victoria she addressed a final appeal. 'Is there *no* hope abt E? [Eddie] . . . she shld be made to reflect seriously on the folly of throwing away the chance of a very good Husband, kind, affectionate & steady & of entering a united happy family.'[25]

But, ever resilient, ever flexible, the Queen was soon singing quite another tune. After some rather fast affairs – the turn of a pretty ankle was one sight that brought life into Eddie's eyes – he became engaged to the stately, respectable Princess Mary ('May') of Teck.

'I must say that I think it is far preferable than ein kleines deutsches Prinzesschen with no knowledge of anything beyond small German Courts,'[26] the Queen wrote.

But Eddie died of pneumonia before the marriage could take place and May married his younger brother Georgie instead and in 1910 became Queen-Empress anyway.

All this, with its tragic outcome, in no way diminished the Queen's anxiety about Alicky's future. 'Those dreadful Russians' must not be allowed to have her, Alice's loveliest and last. Victoria was the one person who could save her from such a terrible fate, while Ella, on the other hand, she suspected of being a ringleader of the Russian conspiracy.

The Queen noted with disapproval that the Grand Duke was taking Alicky to Russia again in 1890, and she asked Victoria to '*tell* Ella that no marriage for *Alicky in Russia* wld be allowed'.[27] When the Hessians returned to Darmstadt, the Queen wrote again, this time anxiously interrogative: 'I *knew* there was *no question* of a *marriage* for *her* in *Russia*, and that you have brought her back safe & *free*?'[28]

By this time the Queen had convinced herself that all was well. But the Prince of Wales, who was more knowing and cynical, thought Ella would 'move Heaven & Earth' to get her Russian. A year later the Queen was still on tenterhooks and, glancing through the *Almanac de Gotha*, picked on Prince Max of Baden as a possible contender. This, too, came to nothing. But her anxieties were temporarily allayed by the death of the Grand Duke of Hesse which turned all Alicky's thoughts away from marriage.

Alicky was a deeply spiritual girl who had been the most affected by the Darmstadt tragedy of 1878 in which she had lost not only her mother but her youngest, and nearest in age, sister May. After this she had experienced moods of melancholy and became lost in deep dark pools of Lutheran introspection. She placed her trust in her Hessian divine, Dr Sell, who prepared her for her confirmation, and she came to depend on him as in later years she put her trust in Rasputin. The death of her father affected her deeply, and all thoughts of taking up another religion as the price of marrying a Russian were dispelled.

By early 1894 the Queen was confident that all was over with the Russians. 'I wonder if poor dear Alicky has talked to you abt the *end* of Niki's hopes,' she asked Victoria. 'At Alix [Aunt Alix, Princess of Wales] & Victoria say he is miserable & that our dear Ella *always* encouraged him instead of doing the reverse.'[29]

It was only a temporary reprieve, and in two months time she learned that she had lost the battle. The last impediment had been removed. Ella had herself been converted to the Greek Orthodox faith and was among those who persuaded her youngest sister that it was in no way an ordeal and that there was much in favour of the Russian religion. But the most enthusiastic and persistent 'converter' was Willie who had politically encouraged this match from the start.

Victoria's role in this long drawn out campaign had been a difficult one. She saw what was right on both sides – a characteristic which the Queen deplored – and always knew that much anguish would be experienced whichever side won.

Victoria understood the attractions of the Russian way of life which had drawn first Ella and then Alicky to that country – the fierce and beautiful winters, the vast spaces, the beech forests, the exciting intrigues of the extravagant Court, the intellectual stimulus of the arts. She did not fear for their future as the far-sighted Queen did. But she understood, too, how sad it was for Queen Victoria to see in turn two of her grandchildren whom (as she constantly reminded them) she regarded as her *very own*, go to the country she feared and distrusted more than any other.

'Oh! darling Victoria,' the Queen wrote in the last letter in which she referred to the affair, 'the more I think of sweet Alicky's marriage the more unhappy I am! *Not* as to the personality, for I like him *very much* but on acct of the Country the policy & differences with us & the awful insecurity to wh that sweet Child will be exposed. To think she is learning Russian & will have probably to talk to a Priest – my whole nature rises up agst it . . .'[30]

But once again, as realistic as ever, now that she knew the worst she was determined 'to make the best of things', as she put it herself. She made herself responsible for all Alicky's arrangements until 'she is taken by Russia'.

Like her three sisters before her, Alicky was invited to stay for the last time unmarried in England. It was to be a hectic time for her, and Victoria was again deputed the task of immediately supervising her programme. The Queen wanted plenty of time alone with her in order to 'prepare' her for married life. These talks always included plenty of sound commonsense about looking after her health and the health of her family. She also wanted to talk to her about her new religion, court protocol, and no doubt in her case, how to deal with the Russians.

Alicky was to have treatment for the sciatica which had been bothering her, lessons in Russian from a Mlle Schneider, and – oh horrors! – religious instruction in the Greek Orthodox faith from the Tsar's own personal confessor, Father Yanishev, who made the long journey to England for this purpose.

The Queen was anxious to see Nicky, too, for some long talks, so he was invited from Russia. All her relations in England wanted Alicky to come to stay: she was suddenly the most wanted guest in the country. Uncle Bertie and Aunt Alix made the strongest claims on her time and invited her for as long as she could come to Sandringham. Uncle Affie and Aunt Marie pressed her to come to Clarence House. The Queen took offence and considered that she was being deprived of her share of her granddaughter's precious time.

'It was cruel to wish to take [Alicky] away from me who knows best and am losing so much of her,' the Queen told Victoria. 'Marlborough House [i.e. the Wales's] I do *not* wish for more than *a night*, or *outside* 2 nights & I don't wish her to go to Clarence House [i.e. the Edinburghs] either.'[31] As usual Victoria had to patch things up and put the Queen's case to the Queen's sons and Alicky, as tactfully as she could.

Early in June Alicky travelled to Harrogate to take the sulphur water cure, all German cures having failed. It was not to be a rest cure, however. For company she had her relentless Russian teacher, and her luggage included Russian language and history books.

The tedium was broken with the arrival of Victoria to keep her company for a few days. The oldest and youngest Hessian sisters had a gay time together. They went about the town incognito in tricycle bath chairs pedalled by a man at the rear. 'We used to urge them to race each other,'[32] Victoria remembered.

At this time Louis and Victoria had a house by the river at Walton-on-Thames, not far from Windsor, and it was here that a Russian idyll was to be played out during three days late in June.

It was a burning hot summer in England, and for day after day no cloud appeared in the sky. On 20 June Louis travelled to London to meet Nicky, who had arrived that morning at Gravesend in the Russian Imperial Yacht *Polar Star*.

Louis took him back to Walton where 'I found myself in the arms of my betrothed, who looked lovely and more beautiful than ever,'[33] Nicky wrote to his mother.

There was no programme for the young lovers, no chaperone, the world did not know where they were, and they lazed about in the sun, went for walks by the river and for boating picnics. 'Nicky was a good oarsman,' Victoria recalled, 'but so energetic that by the time he got back he had taken off all the skin under the finger on which he wore his engagement ring to Alix.'[34]

For much of the time the couple presented a touching domestic scene under a big chestnut tree in the garden, Alicky doing embroidery while Nicky read to her. On 24 June the idyll was over and all the Walton villagers realized suddenly that they had had royal guests in their midst when a carriage emblazoned with the royal arms and with an outrider arrived and departed again with Louis and Victoria and the betrothed pair for Windsor Castle.

Nicky and Alicky were very demonstrative together and the Queen was hard pressed to restrain herself. Others found their open affection touching, and one gossip observed that 'they behave in a way that gives every confirmation that theirs is a love match'.[35] All the family had the opportunity of meeting them and everyone admired Alicky.

'We all loved her,' her cousin, Princess Alice, Uncle Leopold's daughter then eleven years old, remembers. 'She was so delighted and happy,'[36] There was a mystical radiance about this lovely young woman which struck many people at that time.

Opinions of Nicky differed. Everyone found him agreeable, kind and gentle in his ways, and he was undeniably handsome. But did he have the authority of a future Emperor of All the Russias? Among those who came to Windsor that summer there were many who understood the nature of personal authority. If they did not themselves possess it, they lived close enough to it to recognise it in others. Some who watched his manner both with those who were older and had known power and with those younger who would never know it, doubted whether he would ever have the style and confidence of a great autocrat.

Princess Alice and her mother used sometimes to chaperone the couple on drives around Windsor Park. 'I remember him once saying – and it was typical of him – "I really dread becoming Tsar because I shall never hear the truth again." Isn't that defeatist? I never forgot him saying it. What a dreadful thing to say! – and it suddenly came out in the normal course of conversation. It impressed me at the time and I have never forgotten it though I was quite a small girl. I thought it was quite frightening. You would think that he would stand up to these people who would never tell him the truth and say, "I'm not going to have them around me when I am Tsar."'[37]

Louis and Victoria took part in all the festivities laid on by the Queen for the young couple, and felt themselves – for they had three children of their own now – to be married veterans. On the third day the Duchess of York (Georgie's May) gave birth to a boy, the future King Edward VIII and Duke of Windsor. It was the first time that there had been alive at the same time a sovereign and three direct heirs to the throne of England. Nicky and Alicky were chosen as Godparents. 'What a nice healthy child!' noted Nicky warmly.

The wealth of the Romanoffs was illustrated in spectacular style at Windsor when, watched by the Queen and Louis and Victoria, Nicky presented his engagement presents, among them an immense sapphire and diamond brooch and a chain bracelet decorated with a huge emerald. He also presented her with the Tsar's engagement present, a great Fabergé *sautoir* of pearls which had cost him a quarter of a million golden roubles, Fabergé's biggest ever single order. That was not all. The party moved to Osborne in mid-July, and from there Nicky embarked in the Imperial Yacht for the passage back to St Petersburg.

He left behind another present. Alicky showed it to Uncle Leopold's Princess Alice with its engraved dedication in German. It was another diamond brooch. Crying, she spelt out the words to the little girl: 'Nicky's Goodbye Tear'. It was like 1840 at Darmstadt all over again, when Nicky's grandfather had left behind a tearful little Marie.

From this time Victoria took complete charge of her youngest sister. After closing down their house at Walton, she returned to Osborne and boarded the Royal Yacht *Victoria and Albert* which the Queen had lent to her and Alicky. In it they crossed to Flushing and took the train to Jugenheim to stay at Heiligenberg for the rest of the summer.

After the hurly-burly of Windsor and Osborne, they were both in need of peace and quiet. Victoria's three children were sent away to stay with relations. But it turned out to be a very brief hiatus in a year that was to be eventful and anxious from beginning to end. The Tsar became very ill in October. A kidney disease was diagnosed. His condition rapidly worsened. Victoria recognized the importance of Alicky seeing him in case he should die, and hurriedly made arrangements to get her to his bedside as soon as possible.

Nicky was in Livadia on the Crimean coast with his father. He was due to stay at Wolfsgarten but that visit was cancelled. Travelling as ordinary passengers, for there was no time to arrange a royal train, Victoria accompanied Alicky to Warsaw. There her sister Ella took over as companion and guide.

At Simferopol Nicky was waiting at the station, and for a moment the sight of Alicky stepping down and coming anxiously towards him drove away his fears and worries. Then there was a four-hour drive to Livadia. The Tsar was awaiting Alicky, looking huge and yet gaunt, white and with the look of death on him. He had insisted on getting up and presenting himself to the future Tsarina in his full-dress uniform.

Ten days' later, on 1 November 1894, Emperor Alexander III was dead at the age of 48 and Nicky was Tsar.

It had become an unfortunate fact that dramatic events occurred at royal weddings in Germany. It was at the wedding of Ernie, the new young – too young some said – Grand Duke of Hesse, that Queen Victoria heard the dreadful news that Alicky was, after all, to 'go to Russia'.

The Hessian sisters' only brother had seemed rather reluctant to marry at all. He was good looking, excitable, wayward and high spirited. He had inherited little of the military tradition and prowess of his father and grandfather, and he was inclined towards the arts rather than militarism. He drew and painted well, encouraged new enthusiasm for the theatre in Darmstadt, and brought about a notable revival in all the arts. He liked pranks and practical jokes and forgot to answer letters.

He was only twenty-three when his father died. He had been spoilt and pampered by his parents and his four sisters and from the moment he became Grand Duke the Queen gave long and anxious thought to finding him the right wife.

At this time Irène's little boy, Waldemar, was giving the first dread signs of haemophilia and there was now not a member of any royal family anywhere who did not fear this disease. The Queen had had plans for Ernie to marry the Prince and Princess of Wales's daughter Maud, neatly tying up two more of her grand-children simultaneously. But Maud was not a strong girl, and in the early state of understanding of haemophilia in 1891 it was thought she might be a carrier.

Later in that same year chance brought Affie's and Marie's lively little daughter, Malta-born Ducky (Victoria Melita) and Ernie close together. They laughed at the same jokes, rushed about together in a private, carefree world of their own. They both came to stay at Balmoral in October and the Queen was enchanted at the colour and liveliness they created wherever they went. Here, she thought, was a marriage made in heaven and she encouraged the couple to be together as much as possible. 'Ernie looks very well & is in high spirits,' the Queen told Victoria, and added that the two of them 'are very funny together'.[38]

Victoria was not the only one to worry about this affair. They were too much of a likeness, this pair, for her taste. Together they might be too feckless and eccentric for the responsibilities that still rested on the Grand Duke and Grand Duchess of Hesse. Other doubts were expressed in Darmstadt. Another doubly-related marriage? What about the dangers of haemophilia? Better a German marriage, many people were advising.

A year later the Queen was suffering from doubts of her own, and as usual expressed them to Victoria and at the same time gave her instructions. In January 1893 the Queen arranged for Ducky and her parents, and for Ernie, to come to Osborne. Victoria was to '*hint*' to Ernie 'to be very kind and posé [sedate] & not teaze Ducky or make silly jokes, wh might destroy our *hopes & wishes*'.

At this time the Queen had taken advice from Sir William Jenner on the haemophilia risks in such a union and was reassured by his report. Victoria was not so sure. Her fear of the disease, which was to endure for all her life, had increased with the discovery of the deafness of her own first-born. Was that due to 'the royal disease' too?

She wrote anxiously to her brother from London: 'I still worry rather at the thought that Ducky & you are so nearly (doubly) related. Could you not in a general way ask Eigenbrodt [physician to the Hessian Grand Ducal family] why he is so much opposed to relations marrying.

'If he has other reasons besides the fear of an illness like Uncle Leopold's, against our family especially intermarrying, it would be as well to know them, for I think it is one of the duties of a man in your position especially, to try & have healthy descendants, & I know besides from experience that to see one's children not quite strong, or with some little ailment, like Alice's hearing, is a cause of worry & pain . . . I hope you won't think I am fussing you, but I so fear the newspapers will soon be discussing engagements between you & Ducky, & then Grandmama etc & Uncle Affie will again try to hurry you . . .'[39]

Warnings like these added to Ernie's own doubts about marriage in general, and to the spritely, mercurial Ducky in particular. He was uneasy about being an adequate husband and of not being able to have children – and now perhaps of their being deformed in some way if he were successful. Later in the year the Queen tried harder than ever to persuade the young man to make up his mind.

'I have written *twice* to Ernie abt the *necessity* of his showing some attention & interest,' she wrote to Victoria, who was now feeling harassed about the whole affair. 'Pray tell it him & say he *must answer* me. – Aunt Marie [Ducky's mother] fears *he* no longer wishes it, wh I am sure is not the case . . .'[40]

This, or some similar prod, appears to have driven Ernie to a decision. The wedding was fixed for 19 April 1894, and it was to be a full-scale affair, this time at Coburg because Affie was now the reigning Duke there.

Nobody would refuse an invitation to the wedding of the Grand Duke of Hesse, whose family had contributed so much of its blood to Europe's royal families. Old disputes and prejudices were forgotten, and to Coburg there came Ella and Serge and Nicky from Russia, Henry and Irène and Willie from Prussia, Uncle Bertie, Aunt Beatrice and Queen Victoria herself from England, all the Battenbergs, and of course the Hessians, including the bridegroom's youngest sister, Alicky.

At some moment during the social hurly-burly in the days before the wedding – they never divulged just when – Nicky proposed formally to Alicky. Everybody knew what a shock this would be to the Queen and it was left until the morning after the wedding before anyone told her. It was not quite as bad as the *fait accompli* at Darmstadt, but very nearly as bad. But the Queen recovered quickly, her mind already busy with plans, and it was at this time that she decided to bring Alicky back to England with her.

As to Ernie and Ducky, their marriage was at first as merry and colourful and exciting as everyone had expected it would be, and they were as wayward and irresponsible as the Queen had feared. 'Already there are gt complaints' about their failure to answer letters and even telegrams, the Queen complained to Victoria, who was also supposed to correct the faults of all the members of her family, married or single, and at once. 'I *do* wish you *cld* get Ernie to be less neglectful.'[41] Eleven months had passed since the wedding and they had not yet thanked for all their presents.

But Ernie was beside himself with joy. His doubts had been settled in the happiest way possible, for within less than eleven months Ducky had given birth to a lovely little girl, who was christened Elizabeth.

'I wld have preferred its being called Alice,'[42] the Queen commented obtusely. She always gave the impression that her pleasure as a result of a successful match was as brief as her displeasure when her ambitions were thwarted. But by this time, in March 1895, Alicky was already the uncrowned Empress of All the Russias, and later in the year was to give birth to her own first child, the first of her four beautiful girls, the Grand Duchess Olga.

7

'I wld *earnestly* warn you agst trying to *find*
out the *reason* for & explanation of
everything.'

QUEEN VICTORIA's *advice to Princess Louis
of Battenberg*

THE year 1887 brought mixed fortunes to Louis and Victoria, professionally and domestically. For many months Louis had been
hoping for an appointment. He had been on half pay since the
previous August. Although every officer experienced periods of half
pay in their naval career, Louis had hoped that he would not be left
unemployed for quite so long, especially after his service in the
Royal Yacht. The blessing was, of course, that he saw much more
of his family than he could have otherwise hoped for.

Louis's love for Victoria had grown deep and full and intellectual
and he adored his chubby, happy baby Alice. To his shipmate from
the North America Station, the Hon. Freddie Spring-Rice, whom
he had not seen for a long time, he wrote, 'Now that I am married,
I positively hate going to a ball, as I could not dance with the only
woman I could care to.'[1]

In the midst of all the worries about Irène's engagement to her
cousin Henry of Prussia, and close in time to all the great Golden
Jubilee celebrations for the Queen at Windsor and London, Victoria
caught typhoid. Little Alice was taken away, and Louis gave up all
his time to attending to her through this dangerous and debilitating
disease. 'There never was so kind a nurse,' Victoria commented, '&
in my illness I have once more seen and felt how good he is to me.'[2]

By the beginning of June, to Louis's immense relief, Victoria began to show signs of improvement, and even wrote a short letter to the anxious Queen. The Queen replied:

'I cannot say with what joy I received your dear little pencil Note & what thankfulness to God fills my heart for your preservation through this horrid illness! You have been most tenderly lovingly nursed by one of the kindest & best of Husbands whose love & unbounded devotion you can never sufficiently repay.'³

Still in a very weak condition, Victoria was able to go to London with Louis on 15 June. The Queen had made special arrangements for them so that Victoria could rest as much as possible. She and Louis stayed at Buckingham Palace, little Alice with the Mistress of the Robes, the Duchess of Buccleuch, in her old house in White-hall, with its garden reaching right down to the Embankment.

Louis rode in the great Golden Jubilee procession, looking as splendid as he always did on horseback in his full dress uniform – even amongst the most grand and the most handsome of Europe's royalties – while Victoria was given a carriage.

'The heavens,' noted one lyrical *Illustrated London News* observer, 'draped themselves in their glorious mantle of blue, from whose central expanse the god of day beamed down warmly upon the warm-hearted millions.'

After that, Victoria went with the Queen to Windsor and took no further part in the London festivities; but that did not matter very much as everyone came to Windsor to pay their respects to the Queen there. It was the biggest gathering of royalty for many years, dozens and dozens of them of all ages and rank, from every corner of the empire and the world, from the King of the Belgians to the Grand Duchess of Mecklenburg-Stretlitz, from His Highness the Maharajah of Cooch Behar to the Infanta Eulalia of Spain, from the King of Saxony to the Thakir Sahib of Goudal, His Highness the Maharajah of Bharatpore, the Prince Antoine of Orleans, Her Majesty Queen Kapiolani of Hawaii and the Queen's own daughter Princess Christian of Schleswig-Holstein.

Having observed or taken part in thanksgiving services, state operas, processions and balls, and leaving behind an exhausted but gratified Queen Empress and the dying embers of celebratory fires on half the hill-tops and cliff-tops of the United Kingdom, the visitors began to disperse in early July. Amongst them Louis, Victoria and Ernie left for Darmstadt, Victoria much strengthened by the care and attention lavished on her by her grandmother, and Louis much gratified by an excellent appointment at last.

Captain Sir Harry Stephenson, a close friend of the Prince of Wales, had asked for him as his 'Commander' (executive officer and second-in-command) of the battleship *Dreadnought* in the Mediterranean.

The *Dreadnought* displaced 11,000 tons, had the thickest armour plate of any battleship, and carried a one-calibre armament (like her namesake twenty-five years later) of four immense muzzle-loading 12.5-inch guns. She looks in our eyes today something like a giant oval barge with the two gun turrets and two masts stuck on top, for she was fully rigged for sailing. At the time she was regarded as the Royal Navy's finest man-o'-war and was often referred to as the naval officer's 'beau ideal of a battleship'.

A number of these naval officers, especially the more articulate and the less successful (which of course included those who had been on half pay for an inordinately long time) resented the appointment of such a young and junior commander to such a plum post. Only favouritism could have got Louis the appointment, they were saying – a Jubilee Year bonus for the Queen's beloved German Prince. Quick to make political capital out of it, John Redmond, Home Ruler and Irish Nationalist, asked in the House of Commons (1 August 1887):

'Is it true, as reported, that Prince Louis of Battenberg has been appointed to the command of Her Majesty's Ship *Dreadnought* over the heads of 30 or 40 officers having superior qualifications?'

Amidst ironical laughter from other Irish members, the First Lord of the Admiralty corrected the member as to the appointment – commander of, not in command of – and told him he had been selected because 'he is best qualified for the post'. Another Irish member 'gave notice that if Prince Louis was appointed he would move that his salary should be disallowed'. Other members got up in protest, there was uproar, and the Speaker had to call for order.

The storm, brief but sharp, in and out of Parliament, raged at its worst while Louis was still in Darmstadt and he heard nothing until he arrived back in England.

But he had plenty of defenders. On the day he left Darmstadt a service paper summarized the situation intelligently and fairly. The outcry, in their judgement, was 'no doubt a plausible spasm of national indignation when viewed from the anti-foreign-competition standpoint'. But it arose 'as it seems to us somewhat illogically . . . No one in the House of Commons or elsewhere need feel surprise if a young commander is drawn over the heads of his seniors in rank.

The arrangement has no doubt worked well. It obviously enables patronage to have an easy and a graceful swing. Interest finds an outlet for its generous impulses. The Court favourite finds himself well placed, without, it would appear, the Court having a thing to do with the nomination.

'It would be, of course, an act of impertinence to question the spirit in which the gallant captain of the *Dreadnought* has chosen his chief executive officer, but unquestionably if a high power had expressed a wish that Prince Louis should receive employment becoming to his personal wishes, why, hey presto, the captain would be found to gratify the illustrious desire.' The writer summed things up succinctly:

'If German princelings are to be denied promotion they should not be admitted into the Service, even when the promotion takes the form which is perhaps open to objection as a system of "taking care of Dowb". This is really the crux.'[4]

The *Dreadnought* appointment affair was the most serious and most public attack Louis had so far suffered. There had been unpleasant incidents before this. His vulnerable situation made them inevitable in a closely competitive service, built on an elaborate class and patronage structure. As well, this was an arrogant and xenophobic time in England, and the Royal Navy was strong in both characteristics.

In order to conform to its manners and cults Louis had had to make an immense effort of adaptation. The spirit of the wardroom – jovial, hearty, hostile to the unfamiliar and anything smacking of culture and 'fanciness' – was as far as the moon from the manner and style of living and thinking in Hesse, where culture, non-conformity and the enquiring mind were all taken for granted. No wonder Louis nearly quit the service several times in his early years!

Brought up to sustain a long tradition of service, and with an abiding hatred for failure, Louis had stuck it out – just as Sandro stuck it out for seven-and-a-half years as Sovereign Prince of Bulgaria – and adapted himself as far as he was able. But there was no possibility that he could conform exactly to the pattern of the typical mid-Victorian naval officer. For one thing, he never quite lost his German accent and his speech phrasing bore German traces, too.

Of course his rank brought him advantages and privileges. Of course his 'illustrious desires' as the writer put it, were usually met. But the price was sometimes steep, the wound sometimes deep.

Increasingly as he rose in the service hostile fellow officers and politicians with an eye on the main chance and searching for a chink in the Battenberg armour were ready with their lances. One day they would find that chink and strike to kill.

Louis travelled from Darmstadt to Malta via London and arrived in the city at the height of the uproar over his appointment. He concealed his anguish and his anger with a demeanour of dignity and proceeded to Windsor to say goodbye to the Queen.

She did not expect to see him for three years and she was especially kind and sympathetic to her 'Ludwig', as she invariably called him, and told him to ignore the cheap jibes – good gracious, had she not had her fill of them in her time! Brown, Dearest Albert even; nothing was sacred to low newspapers and low politicians.

Georgie was at Windsor, too, now a lieutenant and more madly in love with the sea and the navy than ever. They were to travel together out to Malta where Georgie was to serve under his Uncle Affie in the flagship *Alexandra* (its name had been changed from *Superb* in honour of Uncle Bertie's wife). Prince Alfred had now risen to the rank of full admiral and to be Commander-in-Chief of Britain's premier fleet. There had never before been such a strong Royal Family flavour in the Mediterranean Fleet.

These were easy, tranquil years. The Russian war scare was long since past, Britain's relations with France were better than they had been for some time, and so vast was her fleet, there was no other maritime nation she had to fear. The fleet was in a better state of readiness and efficiency than it had been when Louis had last served here five years before. The spirit and morale was sustained, as it had been for many generations and all through the Napoleonic wars, by a relationship between the officers and lower deck which at its best was unique and yet always difficult to define.

It stemmed from a compound of sharp rank division, severe discipline and a paternalistic understanding among the officers that the men were as valuable as they were and came before their own interests in the community of the ship and the team. The Royal Navy fostered the belief that every officer was responsible for every seaman's welfare as well as for their discipline and efficiency, that sailors who might one day die together beside their guns should learn to work together as equals but within the strict framework of discipline demanded on board ship. It was the spirit which led to Napoleon's defeat at sea, and to Germany's defeat twice over in the next century. Many navies tried to emulate it but none succeeded.

In his fifteen years of service Louis had long since absorbed this naval spirit, which was so remote from his father's and brother's experiences in the Army, and now took it for granted. Only occasionally, perhaps after coaling ship – a dirty and disliked but frequent task before the days of oil-burning boilers – did it occur to him that there was no other service in which all worked together as equals so hard and sometimes under such dirty conditions. In a letter he wrote a year later, in the full heat of summer at Smyrna, he gave a glimpse of what coaling ship meant, even to senior officers.

'We have had a heavy job coaling from a collier alongside us. From Saturday, 4.30 a.m. until Monday forenoon I was in my clothes, having my meals almost always standing, and only lying down on the deck, all dirty and greasy, for an hour's sleep at a time. It was very hard on the men, who worked incessantly, two halves relieving each other every two hours night and day and, having to work all through Sunday, they required a good deal of humouring. The heat was intense, and with a burning sun.

'On the third day I was so worn out that I could hardly drag myself along. We hoisted in close on 1,000 tons; that is, 11,000 bags which had to be filled, then hoisted in, emptied, and sent back for refilling. I wonder what a Lieutenant-Colonel of the British Army would say if he was expected to do that in time of peace as a matter of ordinary routine?'[5]

Very soon after this, with the *Dreadnought* back at Malta, Louis would, by contrast, be going ashore in the Admiral's barge with Uncle Affie and with all the ceremony and style accorded to the C.-in-C. It surprised nobody, least of all the bluejackets.

Louis had determined to bring Victoria and little Alice out to the island although, as he also wrote to Spring-Rice, 'we are not blessed much with earthly goods'.

'I am sure you must miss dear Ludwig, one of the kindest & best of Husbands, very much,' the Queen wrote to Victoria at Heiligenberg, 'tho' you rejoice in his being again employed.'[6]

Soon after this, grandmother and granddaughter met again, but for the last time for many months. Cholera had appeared on the island that summer and there had been some deaths, but by October it had been cleared and Louis considered it safe for his wife and baby to join him.

They took passage in the P & O *Coromandel* on 20 October, and after a very rough passage arrived at Valetta on 29th. Louis was still away in his ship and Victoria and Alice stayed with the island's

Governor, Sir Lintorn Simmons, 'a fine looking old man with bushy side whiskers'[7] and a friend of Empress Eugenie's.

This was Victoria's first experience of service life abroad, and she realized that there were many things she would have to get used to besides the climate and the strangeness of living on a rather barren island. The food was poor. There was no refrigeration and the only fresh meat was from the small grey cattle brought from Russia, which was tough, and some equally tough sheep.

Goats were the things you remembered most about about Malta in those days. They were everywhere and they smelt abominably. Everybody drank their milk – it was all there was – and ruined the one lovely fruit, the little strawberries, with their cream. Malta Fever, which often broke out on the island and could be fatal, was at last traced to the goat's milk and their filthy teats.

The bread was sour, there were no cultivated flowers, it was very hot in the summer, often wet and cold in the winter. But there were compensations, and she had known before she married that her life would be nomadic and often spent in places less congenial than the Rhine valley and the English countryside. Everyone was very friendly and there was always plenty going on.

The whole fleet, with the exception of the *Dreadnought*, had arrived in Valetta harbour on the same day as the *Coromandel*, offering Victoria a brave and impressive sight – if not her longed-for husband. When Uncle Affie came ashore he asked her and Alice to stay at his large and impressive residence, San Antonio, in two days time, and he soon made his niece feel at home.

His own family arrived a week later – and as usual the island seemed to shudder from their impact as if a full broadside of solid shot had struck the cliffs. Every child, from three-year-old Beatrice (Bee), seven-year-old Melita (Ducky), to thirteen-year-old Alfred – five in all – seemed to have inherited all of the mother's Russian ebullience. Then Louis's ship came in and there were more noisy, loving reunions.

During her first days on the island Victoria had managed to find a home, although that was a flattering term for the little furnished house situated on a dusty, draughty corner of the battlements, Number 1, Molino Avento.

But most social life occurred out of doors that autumn and winter, which was uncommonly warm and fine and she was often at San Antonio. She took the older Edinburgh girls riding on the ponies they had brought out from England, and then they would return to

San Antonio and Victoria would have tea in the garden with Aunt Marie while Alice and little Bee played about them. She would often dine, too, with her Aunt when the fleet was away. Theirs was a very happy relationship.

When their husbands' ships were back in port everything suddenly changed and social events were crowded and freshly charged with the sight of splendid uniforms and the sound of deep voices and masculine laughter. You could never be lonely at Malta, whether the fleet were in or at sea.

From the beginning of her stay in Malta Victoria was struck by the astonishing determination of English people abroad to maintain under the most adverse circumstances their way of life at home. Just as the male sports and pastimes – the hunting and shooting and fishing – were maintained in the fleet from the moment when they could get ashore, so at Malta there had been developed a fair imitation of the seasonal round of entertainments.

There were 'drawing rooms', dinner parties and balls at San Antonio, Malta's equivalent of Buckingham Palace with the Duke and Duchess of Edinburgh as the 'reigning King and Queen'. When the Duke's younger sister, Princess Louise, and her husband Lord Lorne*, came for two weeks in January 1888 it was indeed a royal visit.

At Christmas all the family gathered about Aunt Marie at San Antonio like they would gather round the Queen at Balmoral. In spite of the inappropriate climate there was a snow-decked Christmas tree and the usual presents for all. In the morning Victoria made a tour of the decorated mess decks of the *Dreadnought* with Louis just as Queen Victoria might tour the decorated poorer areas of a big city with her Albert.

Malta was very strong on opera and there was a magnificent opera house in Valetta. The air was supposed to be good for the voice, and the Maltese were very proud of producing so many fine singers. Great opera companies would come from Italy in the winter to entertain the Maltese aristocracy and the British naval officers and their families. There was shooting – after a fashion – and parties, and picnics, and polo, and gymkhana, and for the less active, golf.

'We used to play golf in the great ditch of the Floriana lines,' one officer recalled. 'The "greens" were sanded asphalt, and when there was a strong wind, the player was allowed to place his feet

---

* Princess Louise, Queen Victoria's fourth daughter, married the Marquess of Lorne, later 9th Duke of Argyll, in 1871.

close to windward of his ball to keep it from being blown off the green. At some of the holes it was necessary to loft over the bastions, and the royal and ancient game became something like rackets, for after two or three shots you might find your ball behind the tee from which you had started; but it was a game, and as fair for one as the other.'8

The fancy dress ball at the Governor's Town Palace, like a great charity ball at the height of the London season, was one of the most notable events of the year. Many of the more ambitious ladies ordered elaborate fancy dresses from London well in advance.

One year the P & O ship due to bring them out and due to arrive only a few days before the event had difficulty in getting into Valetta harbour because of a gale. The captain's efforts were watched in great anxiety by the wives who had hoped to be belles of the ball. But it proved too dangerous an undertaking and the ship steamed off to Brindisi. 'Then there was weeping and wringing of hands, and hastily prepared substitutions.'9

An event that was part social, part service and also possessed ominous prophetic overtones, was the visit of a German naval squadron. The officer in command of one of the battleships was Captain Alfred von Tirpitz, who was soon to create the great battle fleet, the High Seas Fleet, that was to challenge the Royal Navy's dominance at sea. 'I found him extremely friendly and agreeable, and quite the hearty tar,'10 commented one British officer innocently.

One of the squadron's cruisers was commanded by Prince Henry of Prussia, now captain and recently married to Irène, and later to be C.-in-C. of von Tirpitz's great fleet. The cruiser was the *Irène*, and moreover Victoria's sister, after whom the man-of-war was named, was onboard.

So there were great celebrations at Valetta and San Antonio which lasted for long after the squadron left for home, Irène remaining on the island and being joined soon by the Grand Duke her father and Alicky from Darmstadt, who stayed on the island for three weeks.

The C.-in-C.'s flag lieutenant, Mark Kerr, was deputed to look after the Hessians. Alicky became very attached to him and called him 'my Malta aide-de-camp'. Alicky was just seventeen. Louis and Victoria got to know this little Scotsman Kerr well, and to like him for his liveliness and perky good humour.

It was a happy, relaxed time for all these royal visitors – German, English and future Russian ones – to which they would look back with nostalgic wonder and sadness when they were on opposite sides in war and their lives were all at risk.

During their first long married period at Malta, which lasted from 1888 to 1892, Victoria paid visits to Russia, many times to Germany, and once or twice to England. It was a restless way of life and she wondered sometimes whether it was harmful to her young children to grow up without roots. With the death of his father in December 1889 Louis had so much family business to attend to that he had to ask to be relieved of his appointment and went onto half pay.

It was a strange and eventful as well as a sad winter. The cold was intense. Louis and Victoria went to stay with Henry and Irène at Kiel after Prince Alexander's funeral. The railway lines in Germany were blocked with immense snowdrifts, and when at last they broke through they were met by their host and hostess in a sleigh, and were taken to watch the children skating round the battleships in Kiel harbour. It was a refreshing change from the heat of Malta.

Victoria had been reprimanded more than once by the Queen for not walking enough when expecting Alice – not like Irène, the Queen remarked, who had more sense and a quick delivery. Victoria was expecting her second child that summer of 1889 in Hesse and took a great deal of exercise, with the result that a rough drive on a rough road brought the child on prematurely.

The nurse arranged for by the Queen arrived in the middle of the night and only in the nick of time. The baby – Louise – was, Victoria commented, 'rather a miserable little object'. Her truthful frankness applied to her own children as to everyone else.

Victoria now, at 26 and the mother of two, possessed a more sharply etched personality than she revealed at the time of her wedding. Her friends discerned nothing radically new in her character – only in her enthusiasms. A rationalist since her questioning childhood, she was more than ever one now. It made the Queen cross.

'I wld *earnestly* warn you agst trying to *find* out the *reason* for & explanation of *everything*,' she would reason with her granddaughter. 'Science can explain *many things*, but there is a spiritual as well as a material World & this former *cannot* be *explained*.'[11]

Uncaring of her appearance as a little girl, she sometimes presented a comically dishevelled appearance. Hair ribbons would disappear by the yard in her best tomboy romping days.

'I was always dirtying and spoiling my dresses,' she recalled. 'One summer I remember scrambling through a hedge in my best frock, tearing great holes in it. My mother to impress greater carefulness in future, obliged me to wear the darned frock when visiting the Empress of Russia's family at Heiligenberg.'

As a young married woman she showed no greater interest in her appearance – the adolescent interest had been fleeting. Her hair was always done in the same way, brushed and tied tight back, which was not becoming nor right for the shape of her head. What a pity that was for it was such a lovely russet gold! As for her clothes, it is doubtful if she could tell you at any time what she had on if suddenly blindfolded.

When going out together in the evening, it was the same story all through her married life. On time with naval precision, Louis would appear in immaculate clothes, close the door of his dressing room and with measured tread go downstairs – later in life perhaps with a slight limp from his gout. He would then allow himself a good hard look in a full-length looking glass, dusting off a fleck, adjusting his tie, and stand patiently holding his gloves and hat.

Rather late, Victoria would then appear, still pulling her dress impatiently into shape, and with some untamed wisps of hair trailing, scurry down the stairs without a glance at a single looking glass, and join her husband with apologies.

Victoria was not an absentminded nor eccentric person in the usual meaning. It was just that, in the order of her thoughts, what she was to wear and when she should put it on, figured rather low. But her mind was busy all the way down those stairs, and before Louis was really in earshot she would be chattering away to him . . .

Victoria missed little with her eyes (which remained good into very old age) or her mind. Always there is evidence of her powers of observation. She drew and painted as well as Louis, and that is to say much. She loved painting flowers and drawing maps. She has left behind a brief account of a funeral cortège for a girl in Malta. The corpse was carried exposed, and Victoria sees not just the little face as it passes, but the crossed hands on her bosom jogging up and down as the cart bumps over the cobblestones. No doubt she could have written as well as illustrated her own short stories.

In Italy she always headed for the galleries and the salerooms. She was a good judge of a painting. In Venice she once bought an unsigned oil of the Virgin and Child for 500 francs because she liked it. It later turned out to be a Sasso Ferrato. After the galleries she would go to the museums – any museum, anywhere. All through her life she dragged people to museums when she was travelling –

her friends, her children while they were still quite young and her grandchildren later, including Prince Philip who sometimes became rather restless. In fact she was a marvellous and very well informed guide.

Best of all she liked archaeological or geological museums, or museums embracing any of the sciences. Malta is a good place to start on geology; and it was the curious rock formations on the island that first excited her interest. Before she left she had produced an accurate and beautiful geological map of the whole of Malta. It could still be used with benefit today. In the winter of 1892–3 she engaged a professor of geology in London to give her a full course on the subject.

Victoria inherited her interest in archaeology from her father. When they were both staying with Serge and Ella in Russia, Serge arranged for some burial mounds to be opened for them. They were full of pots and bracelets, horse trappings and necklaces, a number of which she and her father took back to Darmstadt. She helped in a number of 'digs' in Malta, too, when they were living there, and excavated the ruins of a convent at Heiligenberg.

In later life and in times of sadness, gardening was a great solace. Even when her hands were giving her so much trouble and when bending was difficult, the little garden she kept at Kensington Palace was a miniature wonder of rare and tenderly cared for plants, as neat and trim as she herself was uncaring of her appearance. Again Malta sowed the seeds of her enthusiasm, though the soil there was so unsympathetic.

During the previous October, at the end of his half pay period in 1889, Louis had got his first command, a momentous event in any naval officer's career. H.M.S. *Scout* was a 'torpedo cruiser' of no great distinction. But Victoria threw herself into the *Scout*'s affairs with an enthusiasm equal to Louis's, getting to know all the men by name, joining in the church services and helping anyone who needed her. There was no chaplain on board such a small ship and Louis played all the parts, acting as clergyman and then hastening to play the accompaniment on a harmonium.

They both felt veterans at Malta now. A new C.-in-C. relieved the Duke of Edinburgh who was replaced in his turn by Admiral Sir George Tryon. He flew his flag in the brand new battleship *Victoria*, so soon to sink in the collision that was to drown him.

Tryon was an able, impatient flag officer whose demeanour proclaimed to all those on board his flagship and to the world at large: 'I do not suffer fools gladly'. He was one of a very small body of late Victorian naval reformers, a strict disciplinarian, an innovator who liked to test out his captains with unorthodox evolutions and signals, which was to be his undoing.

He liked his subordinates to show initiative but so terrified them that they rarely did so, which made him even more choleric. He was not an easy taskmaster. But Louis liked him and got on well with him. After he was drowned, along with more than 350 of his officers and men, in a daring but suicidal evolution, Louis wrote his explanation of the affair to the Queen:

'He was extremely masterful, marvellously quick of perception, and proportionately impatient with others less quick and above all that he would never put up with any contradiction. On all executive matters he was an absolute autocrat, taking no man's advice, feeling himself head and shoulders above his subordinates in all matters . . . We all had blind confidence in him.' And as a possible explanation of maritime history's most famous collision, he added, 'He may have argued: "It is risky but we can just do it."'[12]

Tryon once wrote of Louis: 'I desire to express my high appreciation of your zeal and ability . . .' There were very few commanders who received praise of that order from this flag officer. Louis considered his death four years later as a great loss to the navy.

Before Tryon was drowned, Louis was able to show him the ingenious navigating instrument he invented and which he called a Course Indicator. It was a typical product of his scientifically inventive mind and gave him more satisfaction than anything he ever made. He worked on this during the winter of 1891–2 when the *Scout* rarely went to sea, and it was soon adopted in large numbers. Its basic principle was adopted in fire control instruments and bombing sights. If he had taken out patent rights he would have made a great deal of money.

Some years later Victoria heard a Russian Captain trying to persuade Tsar Nicholas II to adopt the Course Indicator for the Russian Navy, and she enjoyed telling Nicky that its full name was in fact The Battenberg Course Indicator. The Tsar turned to the Captain and proudly said, 'It may interest you to know that my brother-in-law invented this instrument.' The Captain thought that very funny and burst out laughing at what was obviously a jest for he could not imagine any relation of the Tsar having sufficient scientific knowledge to create such a complex and effectual invention.

Louis had recently succeeded, indirectly and with Victoria's help, in getting naval rank for the Prince of Wales. Louis recounted the episode that led to this success to a fellow officer who recorded it in his diary.

It seems that Louis and Victoria were breakfasting out of doors with the Queen at Windsor:

'One morning the Queen said, "They have been wanting me to make Bertie an Admiral of the Fleet, but I shall not do so." Battenberg said nothing, but pricked up his ears, and when alone with his wife they talked it over, so two mornings later Princess Louis [Victoria] said to the Queen, "What was it about Uncle Bertie you were saying the other morning?" upon which the Queen said, "When I asked the Admiralty some years ago, soon after my marriage, to make my husband an Admiral of the Fleet, they refused," etc. etc. Battenberg, evidently with much tact, told the Queen how much the Navy would appreciate it, etc., but she said nothing, but a few days afterwards made the Prince of Wales one.'[13]

Without need for encouragement, the Queen was pursuing promotion for Louis himself. She was certain that his seniority entitled him to promotion to captain. 'She hopes and expects,' she wrote to the First Lord of the Admiralty, 'that Prince Louis of Battenberg, to whose merits everyone who knows the service well can testify will get his promotion at the end of the year . . . There is a *belief* that the Admiralty are afraid of promoting Officers who are Princes on account of the radical attacks of low papers & scurrilous ones, but the Queen *cannot* credit this . . . She trusts there will be no further delay in giving him what he deserves.'[14]

Louis was a captain at the end of the year – 1891 – as the Queen hoped, and as befitted his seniority, was given command of the cruiser *Andromache* for the summer naval manoeuvres.

During his service in the Mediterranean in the 1890s Louis showed himself to be both an innovatory and a democratic commander and was popular in the wardroom, the gunroom and on the lower deck. It was very different from the sniping and backbiting he suffered ashore in England, and it is no wonder that he always longed to be away at sea.

With officers who served with him he was almost invariably popular – his enemies were elsewhere, usually drinking too much port in the clubs or in home establishments. At first in the wardroom

171

they might be cautious and suspicious, and then were sometimes surprised at how easy this 'German' was to get on with. 'I find Battenberg a very nice fellow,' one officer confided to his diary at this time, 'and have had long talks with him. He is no doubt zealous, hard-working and determined to get on in the service.'[15]

Louis's influence at court at a time when this could make or break a man was widely recognized. The system of preferment and patronage was so deeply established in the nation's mechanism that officers like Louis in a privileged situation were generally respected rather than envied. The same officer, after a long 'yarn' with Louis, gathered that 'regarding the Yacht appointments, not only of Commanders, but of Lieutenants, he had a great deal to do with them, and has much influence.'

He continued in his diary, 'The Prince of Wales and the Queen evidently are very fond of him, and refer things to his judgement.'[16] The officer writes all this as a statement of fact without any sign of the resentment that would be felt today – and was felt then by those who had been passed over for promotion and therefore resented the system and those who operated it.

It was a practice of Queen Victoria to escape the worst of the English winter by retiring to an enormous hotel overlooking the Mediterranean above Nice. As a courtesy to Her Majesty the Royal Navy customarily provided a guardship in the nearest harbour and was available to land guards of honour and escorts. Louis's cruiser the *Cambrian*, his next command, was selected for this honour in 1895, and 1896. Louis was often ashore dining with the Queen who found his company soothing and his gentle advice sound.

During the second of these guardship years his wife Victoria and the children stayed nearby with Beatrice – then a very sad widow after the recent loss of her husband. Victoria often went for long drives with the Queen in her open landau drawn by grey horses and preceded by an outrider. This made her very conspicuous, but what made these drives especially embarrassing for her companions was her practice of throwing franc pieces to everyone who begged for them.

The local children soon caught on to this and came out in hordes, grabbing any old wild flowers to offer to 'Madame la Reine', and even the most blatantly incorrigible beggars all received coins. The Queen would never have played the part of lady bountiful at home for she disapproved of begging and was careful with her money in small ways. Abroad, to Victoria's astonishment, she loved to toss coins from her carriage as a generous gesture to children who were unfortunate enough to have been born both poor *and* foreign.

A more suitable custom at Nice was the series of visits by relations. The Prince of Wales always called on his mother, too. He liked a surreptitious flutter at the tables at nearby Monte Carlo, and he liked to visit the *Cambrian* to take luncheon with Louis.

In 1895 a very rich English nobleman who had a villa at Villefranche gave Louis a crate of 'Trafalgar' brandy – a magnificent ninety-year-old vintage, although Louis rarely took liquor as it was considered to be bad for his gout. At the end of luncheon, Louis offered Uncle Bertie a glass of brandy and put before him a liqueur glass. The Prince of Wales pushed aside the glass with the somewhat ungracious remark, 'There's only one brandy worth drinking. It's wonderful stuff which I found in Monte Carlo and was made in 1805.'

'But this is it,' Louis told him with satisfaction.

'Then give me a claret glass to drink it from,' Uncle Bertie ordered.

The Prince of Wales, supported by the Queen, was again pressing Louis to take over command of the Royal Yacht *Osborne*. She wanted him to come back from the Mediterranean so that she could see more of him, of Victoria, and of her great-grandchildren who were almost never in England; and Bertie wanted him for his company.

Louis was now more practised at dealing with these royal pleas. He gently explained to the Queen that it would be the end of his real naval career if he accepted this appointment – already they were calling the *Cambrian* 'Prince Louis's Yacht' because it was so often on royal affairs.

Louis recounted to a fellow officer how 'he explained [to the Prince of Wales] that he was most anxious to live down the general idea floating about, viz., that he would be pushed on in Royal yachts; and the Prince of Wales quite understood his desire to work his way up, the same as anyone else.'[17] That might be so; but from 1868 until his death in 1910, Uncle Bertie never ceased trying to push privileges at Louis.

These royal favours and honours placed an extra heavy burden on Louis. He certainly could not afford to be anything but a first rate officer and his ship to be the smartest and most efficient in the fleet in order to prove that he was worthy of his command in departments where royal favours could not count.

He succeeded in all this. At competitive games, at gunnery, at evolutions and general smartness, the *Cambrian* was on top. But few people outside his family realized what a tremendous effort this demanded of him. It is possible that the physical and mental strain all this imposed helped to bring on the inherited gout which attacked him with increasing frequency and severity from this time.

No one wanted to take over the *Cambrian* from him – she carried too deeply the impress of his personality and his innovations. The officer who was finally persuaded to do so decided to do nothing and to speak to no one except when absolutely necessary for three months. At the end of that time he called the second-in-command to his cabin.

'I am glad I had the sense to wait and watch,' he told him, 'and now I wish to tell you that this is the smartest, most efficient, and happiest ship that I have ever seen. In fact, I did not know that such a ship was possible. I at first disagreed with many things which are innovations, but I kept quiet, and now I want you to keep everything going as it was in Prince Louis's time. I fear there is nothing I can add to the ship, as she has every record and cup on the station except the Veteran Officers' Race at the Navy Athletic Sports. I am not much of a runner, but I will train for that in hopes that I may be able to add one little thing to the Roll of Honour.'[18]

Louis did not hear of this tribute until many years later. He could scarcely have asked for a finer one.

Louis's Mediterranean naval career was temporarily ended when he was appointed flag-captain of the battleship *Majestic*, flagship of the Channel Fleet. In the summer of 1897, when he left Malta with Victoria and the children, he was a post captain of forty-three and clearly destined for high responsibility. By now he could claim as wide a knowledge of the Mediterranean Sea as anyone alive. Since he had first served under the Duke of Edinburgh he had sailed off almost every coast, entered almost every anchorage, harbour and roadstead, noted every island from the Aegean to the Balearics, and seen it in every mood.

As for Malta itself, Victoria knew every inch of the island and could talk at length about its botany, geology, archaeology, history and climate.

She also spent many hours during the winter months helping Louis with his first book. It was called *Men-of-War Names* and covered 'what may be called the sentimental aspect' of the world's warships – 'why a ship bears a particular name and how she came to receive it'. Its mundane title hides a fascinating work of scholarship covering mythology, geography, natural history, archaeology, history and anthropology. It was published in 1897 and has been a standard work ever since.

They had long ago moved from the funny little dusty house in Molino Avento, and for some time had occupied a comparatively palatial place on the Piazza Regina. They were now a little better off, and, anyway, with their growing family needed more space. After the two girls, Alice and Louise, Victoria had given birth to a son while she was at Darmstadt in November 1892. He was christened Louis after the Grand Duke, Victor after his great aunt Vicky, George after Prince George Wales, Henry after Liko, and Serge after his Russian uncle – and he was always called Georgie.

Queen Victoria, as usual and at her expense, sent over her own favourite doctor, distrusting German doctors more than ever – and a few days later, on hearing the news, wrote 'to wish you joy with all my heart of the birth of your dear little Boy wh you so much wished for . . .'[19]

The future King George V was almost as gratified as his grandmother about Louis's and Victoria's son and gladly agreed that he should be named after himself. That autumn he was working at a German university, and used to come over to Darmstadt whenever he could. His professor insisted on accompanying him, so there was no relief from the constant correcting of his German grammar. Victoria remembered vividly his increasing exasperation 'until one day George broke out, "Der, die or das Sonne is really very hot to-day – choose which, Professor!"'

His only relief was in the evenings when, living *en famille*, the Professor read, his wife and daughter worked at their embroidery in silence, and Georgie occupied himself with his stamp collection, which was already the most important hobby in his life and at that time was of manageable proportions.

When Alice was five they decided it was time she had a governess. She had to be an especially good and understanding person because of her deafness. It was a long time before this was diagnosed. At first Victoria thought she was slow, absentminded and disobedient. 'The child . . . is very lively & quick with her fingers,' Victoria wrote to the Queen before the disability was diagnosed, 'but decidedly backward of speech, using all sorts of self-invented words, and pronouncing others very indistinctly.'[20]

It was Julie, then an old lady, who first suspected deafness. Victoria took her to an ear specialist in Darmstadt who confirmed it.

When she was next in London with her, Victoria visited an aurist who told her that the deafness – and it was almost complete – was due to thickened Eustachian tubes and that it was not possible to operate on them.

Alice was taught lip-reading as early as it was possible and because she was exceptionally quick and intelligent was a fluent lip-reader by the time she was eight. She shared the aptitude of all her family for learning foreign languages. At Darmstadt or Jugenheim when the families were gathered at Christmas or in the summer as many as five different languages might be heard and unless you knew at least three you were lost. By the time she was about fifteen Alice could lip-read in three languages – German, French and English – and easily follow the conversation as it crackled round the table, switching from one tongue to another. Later she learnt to lip-read Greek as well.

Alice's deafness was a great worry to Louis and Victoria all through her childhood. From the beginning Victoria was strict with her about drawing attention to her disability. However confused she might be she was never allowed to show it nor to ask anyone to repeat what they had said, but to cover up as well as she could. It was sometimes very hard on the girl, but it was less cruel than to be regarded as someone for whom special allowances had to be made. As it was, strangers could be forgiven for failing to notice any defect, and for thinking this was not only a normal and healthy little child, but also the most beautiful Princess in all the world – which indeed she was.

The arrival of the first Battenberg governess, Miss Joey Rolleston, conveniently coincided with Louis's longest time away from Malta through this decade. In the same month that Georgie was born Louis was given his first inter-service appointment, as Naval Adviser to the War Office and Chief Secretary to the joint Naval and Military Committee of Defence – according to the Queen a 'very flattering and gratifying' appointment. And she was delighted that she would again be seeing her favourite relatives more often.

London was expensive after Malta and the Battenbergs had to economise. Victoria found a house to rent in Eccleston Square, a cheap and unfashionable part of Pimlico. Uncle Bertie, who never understood that anyone could have less money than he had, even though he did not know how much that was, asked her why she had chosen such a strange place. 'I thought only pianists lived there,' he commented.

But there was one great advantage. It was within walking distance of a small rear entrance to the gardens of Buckingham Palace, and the Queen had given her a key to the door. While Louis was away at his committee work in Whitehall, the entire family entourage of Victoria, the three children, the governess and nursemaid all disappeared daily from the noise and smell of Grosvenor Place into the royal palace paradise.

Christmas was spent at Osborne, and there were visits to Sandringham and Balmoral, to great country houses, and – as always – to Germany. Victoria delighted in her children, loved to give them their lessons and to instil in them a sense of pleasure in knowledge and inquiry. There were always a dozen enterprises going on no matter where they were living – new projects, new ideas to discuss, new controversies, new inventions to see. They were all reading at a very early age, while Victoria herself was, say, discussing archaeology with Professor Wallstone, the professor of archaeology at Cambridge, or taking her winter course in archaeology in London.

Louis was often away from London inspecting forts that might have kept Napoleon at bay but had scarcely acknowledged the invention of the high explosive shell, visiting factories and naval and military headquarters. He was on seven influential committees, one dealing with the invasion threat, France then being the likely enemy in war, another on submarine mining, a third on the use of electric light on warships, a Colonial Defence Committee, and so on.

He was regarded as the perfect committee man, which he considered a mixed blessing. Revelling always in perfection, judging himself by the highest standards, Louis still did not enjoy office work. He longed for the tang of salt air again.

The first reason why he had been chosen for this job was his exceptional exercise of tact and diplomacy, a quality he had inherited from his father but which had *not* been passed on to Sandro. At this time the Army and Navy were more than usually at loggerheads over the invasion threat, guns, policy and their respective shares of the defence cake. Louis was a marvellously soothing influence. He was at first listened to because he was a Prince, then because of the sense that he talked, which often came as a surprise to those who had not known him before and who assumed that he had reached his position only through royal favouritism. He was prepared to acknowledge faults on the Navy's side and was one of the few officers who could do so without bringing the full weight of Admiralty opprobrium down on his shoulders.

At the end of his term of office a famous soldier, the Adjutant-General Sir Redvers Buller, wrote to him, 'I suppose you like a ship better than a joint Secretaryship, but you have the knowledge that you will seldom do better or more valuable work than you have done in the past two years.' And the Army Commander-in-Chief wrote of 'the mutual feeling of goodwill and unanimity' he had implanted and praised him for his 'tact and sound judgement'.

A new dimension was being given to Louis's naval career in the last years of the century as a new appreciation of his qualities and his unique social position grew in the Admiralty hierarchy. It depended on an unquestioned acceptance of his loyalty to his adopted country. If this had not been the case, he would never have been appointed to a committee job which granted him access to the innermost secret plans and papers concerned with the nation's defence. It was now increasingly recognized that, with his family connections and privileges, he could be of great value to the Navy's Intelligence Department.

In 1894 the rising power of the German Navy was already giving anxiety. Bellicose speeches by the Kaiser and the Chief of his Ministry of Marine made much of German rights to the world's oceans and the breaking down of power monopoly. Even before the beginning of the great German colonial expansion in 1884, Admiral Albrecht Stosch was claiming that 'the most effective defence of the coasts of the Fatherland is without question a victory in a battle on the high seas'.[21] From inflammatory remarks like this there emerged the huge High Seas Fleet of 1914.

The most powerful advocate of German sea power was the most powerful man in Germany. Kaiser Wilhelm worshipped the Navy, and was inconsolably jealous of his grandmother's Royal Navy. Wilhelm dreamed of battleships and doodled designs of world-beating men-o'-war during dull meetings.

On one of Louis's visits to Kiel the Kaiser proudly showed some drawings to Louis. They were of super-battleships, designed with typical German thoroughness but not much experience. Louis patiently pointed out one small flaw, and, before he realised that he was not properly playing his part, a second and more fundamental impractical feature.

This was too much. Willie petulantly folded up his plans and walked off without a word.

Naval architecture was never again discussed, although from time to time, and almost to the outbreak of war, Willie would boastfully show off the latest items in the German Navy's arsenal to Louis and indiscreetly divulge future German plans. By this means Louis was presented with intelligence that not even the sharpest naval attaché could hope to acquire.

As early as 1894 the Kaiser invited Louis to inspect some of the ships of the German Manœuvre Squadron in the North Sea. Louis's subsequent report was full and detailed, covering 'everything from masthead semaphore to training methods, gunnery (range of guns, rate of fire) . . .' The Secretary of the Admiralty congratulated him on his 'useful information' and his 'powers of observation'. These powers of observation were to prove useful in the years that lay ahead.

Russia was another likely enemy, and in Russia, too, Louis had several relatives in high places; his brothers-in-law Tsar Nicholas and Grand Duke Serge were only two among a large number of useful informants.

Long before Britain had an oil-burning battleship, Prince Louis returned from Russia with startling news. 'Jacky' Fisher was the first person to hear it. He wrote at once to the First Lord, Lord Selborne:

'The new Russian battleship *Rotislav* burns oil fuel *alone*, and her Captain (the Grand Duke Michael) assured Prince Louis personally that it was a success.'[22]

In June 1899 Louis was appointed Assistant Director of Naval Intelligence. Three-and-a-half years later and after another command at sea he was promoted Director, then one of the most powerful and influential posts in the Admiralty.

This time there were no questions in parliament about his appointment, no public attacks on him. But his enemies were only temporarily silent.

8

'No one knows what the morrow will bring
forth, what cherished tradition will be
trampled on.'[1]

THE HON. HEDWORTH LAMBTON *to*
Lord Selborne

No twentieth century royal celebration or ceremony has ever
equalled in their glittering magnificence the coronation of the last
of the Tsars and his Tsarina in 1896, and the Diamond Jubilee of
Queen Victoria the next year. Whatever the detractors of the
monarchical system may say they cannot deny that the royal sunset
over Europe was a golden one.

As sister-in-law, sister, and granddaughter respectively of the
three leading regal participants, Victoria was among the first of the
guests of honour at both occasions and recorded her impressions in
letters and in her recollections.

Louis approached the Russian celebrations with more caution
after his previous reception, but a new and more benign regime
treated him with all the respect for which he could ask. Under
Nicky and Alicky, the Battenbergs were again welcome in Russia,
and Louis rode with as much pride and pleasure in the coronation
procession as in the English jubilee procession.

Victoria lived through those Moscow days in May 1896 with a
growing awareness of a fatal shadow lurking behind her youngest
sister and brother-in-law. It was quite unlike her to feel like this.
There were small things she noted at the time which seemed to
hint at disaster. There was the fire which mysteriously broke out in
Serge's private chapel in his Palace on the morning of the sovereigns'
state entry into Moscow. Serge, in all his fine uniform, rushed into

the Battenbergs' rooms and saved their clothes. Thirty minutes later all eyes would have been on the procession and the fire out of control before anyone could have given the alarm.

Then on the night of the Kremlin ball, Victoria – ever curious and observant – noted a small room. 'I was much struck by the strange mixture of people standing in it,' she wrote. 'There were some men in uniform, some in plain clothes, even one or two in peasant's dress. On inquiry I was told that these people were all descendants of men who had saved their Sovereign's life, from the old Tsar's times downwards. It was an old custom to invite these representatives to the Coronation.'[2]

Their numbers was both a comment on the people's alertness to assassins and on the survival powers of Nicky's ancestors – although it seemed only yesterday that his grandfather had been blown up.

But as Victoria recounted in her *Recollections*, 'Perhaps the most talked of event during the Coronation has been the terrible calamity in which 1,300 people were killed and wounded in the great crush on the popular fete day, May 30th.'

'The scene of it, the "Hodynka", was a large barren common outside the city, where bodies of troops could be exercised. It was flanked on one side by barracks and on the other a high-road leading out of the town. On this expanse the great popular feast was to be held. A part of it had been railed in where open air plays, dancing, etc., were to take place. Outside the enclosure a row of wooden booths had been erected, from which the souvenir gifts were to be distributed . . .

'It was calculated that seven hundred thousand people, mostly peasants, had assembled from all parts of the country to take part in the festivity and to see their Emperor.

'Nobody had fully realised the danger of collecting so immense a crowd in an open space where, unlike crowds in a street, they formed a solid mass.

'When at daybreak the Moscow workers and all the riff-raff of that great city began to stream across the space along a rough country track they knew, which led straight from the town towards the booths and would place them in the front ranks of the crowds, a rumour sprang up that the distribution of gifts had begun and the towns folk would get the most of them.

'Once this mass of well over half a million people got on the move no power on earth could regulate their advance. Mounted police and troops were only then called out but though they tried to cut through the masses they were themselves soon lost in the midst of the crush.

'The common was anything but level, there were even some old covered wells and shallow depressions on it. Those who stumbled and fell in those spots were trampled down, others falling on top of them. The barriers between the booths unfortunately did not give way and were the cause of further casualties. All that morning we saw the dead and wounded carted past the Governor General's house . . .'[3]

Victoria remembered those rolling carts with the same artist's eye that had recorded that funeral cart so many years earlier in Malta. She would have made a graphic reporter of great occasions. Few other people present would have noticed the little details in this gaudy extravaganza – like the religious spitting match.

Among the notable and distinguished people present were the Papal Nuncio and Prince Ferdinand, who had taken over Sandro's task in Bulgaria. Though himself a Catholic, Ferdinand had had his son and heir, Boris, baptised into the Orthodox Church in order to ingratiate himself with the Russians. Rome, of course, was outraged. As Ferdinand passed the Cardinal on his way into the Coronation banquet he was very quickly spat at by the representative of the Vatican. Ferdinand, as sharply and neatly, spat back at the Cardinal.

These little incidents were omitted from Victoria's letter to the Queen, which nevertheless gave her grandmother a vivid picture of the coronation ceremony.

MOSCOW[4]
May 26th 1896

Darling Grandmama,

The Coronation is just over, everything went off admirably & it was a most beautiful sight . . . At a quarter to nine Aunt Minnie [Nicholas's mother and the previous Tsarina] in her crown & robes headed our procession into church. She looked marvellously young but I have never seen sadder eyes than hers & it was visible that only by a great effort of will she kept back the tears that kept starting in her eyes. It was indeed a sad & moving sight to see her standing all alone before her throne, waiting for the new emperor & empress to come . . . Nicky . . . looked very grave & serious & she remarkably handsome with hair unadorned & only a small string of pearls round her neck. She was flushed & a little trembling at first, but as the ceremony proceeded grew quite calm. Nicky's great diamond crown weighs nine pounds & as it had to fit across the scar of the wound he received in Japan which from the small nerves having been severed is very sensitive, he suffered a good deal of pain from the pressure ... When he had crowned himself Alix knelt down before him & he taking his crown off just touched her forehead with it replacing it immediately & placing Alicky's own small crown on her head with so much of gentle care that it was pretty to see ...

With tenderest love I remain
Your dutiful, loving Grandchild

Victoria

After the seemingly interminable ceremonies in Moscow were over, the royal relations and their suites all moved to Serge's and Ella's country retreat at Illinskoje. Relations between Russia and England were very bad again, but Nicky's political talks with Louis were on a friendly basis which would have outraged Nicky's ferocious father. But mostly, like the rest, they boated and fished, lazed and swam and danced in the evenings.

Of the Hessian daughters Irène could not come as she was expecting a child. But Victoria had a lovely time with Ella and Alicky. A new quality, no less loving and intimate than before, had entered into their relationship since they had married. Now they were all grown women with heavy responsibilities, the two who had married Russians rich beyond the dreams of avarice and very grand royalty indeed. This made no difference either. Victoria still remained the eldest sister, the cleverest and with the best judgement. Louis might be only a 'serene', a mere captain in a foreign naval service. Victoria might live more austerely with just one temporary lady-in-waiting (Gretchen von Fabrice). But the couple's international influence was as strong as that of anyone in this elevated gathering.

Already Louis had played minor parts as an informal go-between. This time his rôle was more important. On behalf of Queen Victoria and the British Prime Minister, Lord Salisbury, he had agreed to see the Russian Prime Minister, Prince Lobanoff-Rostofsky, to try to sort out some of the differences between the two countries which he had already discussed informally with the Tsar.

Louis left the relaxing relations at Illinskoje on 15 June for St Petersburg. Prince Lobanoff-Rostofsky talked to Louis 'with remarkable candour' – but then it was always so much easier talking to fellow princes than with commoners. Russia was worried about the Suez Canal, fearful that it might be closed to her. Even if she faced certain defeat (as indeed she would), Prince Lobanoff-Rostofsky said that Russia would fight if that were to happen. For his part, Louis expressed Britain's anxieties about the Russian alliance with France. But Russia, the Prince explained, must have friends somewhere – and in the face of the Triple Alliance (Germany, Austria-Hungary and Italy) there was no alternative.

The talks were long and covered a wide range of subjects, but no one outside knew about them. The idea was to smooth off some of the sharp edges in relations between these two great powers in the hope of reaching a more formal agreement on outstanding issues. In this they were wholly successful. Lord Salisbury was delighted with the results, and this was the beginning of a close personal friendship with Louis.

The Queen, too, was pleased about the talks, those with Prince Lobanoff-Rostofsky and the family chats with the Tsar. The evening after Louis had luncheon with her at Windsor, she wrote in her Journal that he 'gave me very interesting accounts of everything . . . He said nothing could be kinder and nicer than Nicky was, that he was much devoted to me & anxious to do anything to keep on good terms with England.'[5]

Unofficial conversations like those in St Petersburg in 1896 were of great value to the nation, the Navy and, incidentally, the advancement of Louis's own career. Many momentous and critical international events took place between 1899 and 1905 when Louis was Director of Naval Intelligence – the Boer War, the Russo-Japanese War and the signing of the *Entente Cordiale* and the Treaty of Friendship with Japan among them. The growth of the German Fleet reached provocative proportions, requiring a reappraisal of British naval dispositions and strategy. Japan, Germany and America became significant naval powers; Russia ceased to be one, temporarily. Louis was a busy and highly influential figure in all these events and at three levels, diplomatic, monarchical and naval.

All three of these roles were combined when he made several visits to Germany and Russia in these especially critical years. Germany had been thoroughly put out by the signature of the *Entente Cordiale* in April 1904, which King Edward VII had helped to engineer and had so warmly welcomed. Besides royal visits to France, the King had visited Portugal, Italy and Austria. Odious as he found his nephew, Edward VII decided that he ought to go to see him if only for the sake of reasonable relations with Germany. He would not go to Berlin but would take the Royal Yacht to Kiel and meet the Kaiser for the regatta there in June. And Louis must come with him.

Louis was always very willing to conduct private discussions with his relatives on the most delicate and inflammatory subjects. On a public level he was much less willing because it exposed to his fellow officers and the world at large his special privileged links with the seats of power in Europe, diminished the future usefulness of informal discussions, and made it more difficult for them to be private. 'Apart from the extreme inconvenience to my Chief,' Louis wrote protestingly to Lord Knollys, Edward VII's Private Secretary, 'for me to be absent when we are in the middle of preparing for our big manoeuvres, it is very unpleasant for me to go to Kiel at any time in an official or semi-official position. My relationship to Prince Henry, my German name and origin, my position at the Admiralty – all combine to make it awkward for me. I very much doubt if the Emperor would appreciate meeting me there.'[6] He did not add that he was on his back, crippled with gout, and that Victoria was strongly opposed to the trip, too.

Edward VII brushed aside these excuses and Louis joined the *Victoria and Albert*, packed with naval figures from the First Lord to up-and-coming young captains. At Kiel, where the yacht lay alongside her German counterpart the *Hohenzöllern*, there were exchanges of decorations – over-bountiful on the German side and frugal on the British side as usual – exchanges of dinners and speeches and so-called informal meetings between the two sovereigns.

The Kaiser good-humouredly chided Louis for joining the British Navy instead of the German Navy, and Louis lightheartedly protested that there had been no German Navy when he was fourteen.

Prince Henry was, of course, present in the *Hohenzöllern* and Louis and he exchanged family news, both embarrassed by this over-public conversation. When it was all over, to everyone's relief, the Press in Britain was uncertain whether it had been a worthwhile visit, but accepted that at least no harm had been done by the public exchange of amiable felicitations.

Probably the most realistic view of Germany's position at that time (when Britain and France had so recently become friends and Japan was trouncing Russia in the Far East) was obtained by Louis on the last night in a private conversation with the Kaiser. Louis gathered that Willie was more intractible than ever.

'Now that the clay feet of the Colossus over the Eastern border have been disclosed (the Emperor's actual statement to me) there will be no more coquetting with France,'[7] Louis reported afterwards. So perhaps Edward VII's insistence that his nephew should be present was after all justified.

Later that summer Louis was again asked by Edward VII to try to take some of the heat out of England's relations with Russia. England's alliance of friendship with Japan had led to any number of difficulties, especially since Russia was getting the worst of the war. Russia's Far East fleet had been so badly mauled that it could not hope to regain control of the sea without heavy reinforcements from the Baltic. This demanded the enormously complicated and dangerous business of sending a large coal-burning fleet 17,000 miles and half round the world from the Baltic to Vladivostok. Britain and France, standing on their neutral rights, refused in advance to allow it to coal in any ports they controlled – and there were few others between Cronstadt and the Straits of Tsu-Shima.

In August Louis joined Edward VII at Marienbad where he was taking the cure. They discussed the Russian situation in detail before Louis left for Peterhof where, as the King's personal A.D.C., he was to represent him at the christening of the Tsar and Tsarina's son and heir, the Tsarevitch Alexis, known in the family as Alexei. After four girls, Alicky had at last succeeded in giving birth to a boy and all Russia rejoiced.

At the end of the ceremonies Louis was to make a private assignation with the Emperor in order: '1. To present a letter to the Emperor which combined a request to give me an opportunity of speaking with His Majesty on the relations between the two countries. 2. To arrange for a meeting with Count Lamsdorff [Minister for Foreign Affairs] to whom I was to give a personal message from the King to the effect that His Majesty felt every confidence in the Count's sincere desire to help restoring the friendly relations between England and Russia.'

In his report, Louis told of his private talk with Nicky, describing his brother-in-law as 'very calm, moderate, conciliatory and fully appreciating the position in which our government found themselves'. Louis complained that certain men 'who had the Emperor's ear, like His Majesty's brother-in-law the Grand Duke Alexander, were inclined to suggest means for enforcing Russia's rights of a belligerent towards neutrals, beyond those really necessary, and intended deliberately to "*embêter les Anglais*".'

The Tsar countered by complaining of England's refusal to allow the Russian reinforcing fleet coaling facilities – 'an unfriendly act'. But when Louis contested this, saying that it would be unjust to give one belligerent an advantage over the other, the Tsar conceded: 'Of course your alliance with Japan necessitates extra precautions on your side not to assist us.'[8]

Louis then asked why Russia did not come to terms with Japan now. 'We must go on,' the Tsar replied. And what of China's unfriendliness to Russia? 'If that country gives us any more trouble I will declare war on it,' the Tsar told Louis heroically; and went on to claim that 'it was inconceivable that the Russian Giant, who was only now beginning to put forth anything approaching his full strength, could not in the end completely crush the impudent Japanese pygmy who had dared to attack Russia in so treacherous a manner'.[9]

The Tsar's summary of the war situation ended on a characteristically superstitious Russian note, with prophetic overtones. 'At the same time,' he told Louis, 'a feeling was gaining ground that the Japanese possessed some kind of supernatural power, and they are credited with being able to perform incredible feats of cunning and daring.'

He concluded with the extraordinary suspicion that the Russian fleet at Cronstadt was in danger of being attacked by a flotilla of Japanese torpedo boats, built, and the crews trained, in England. But they parted on the best of terms, and Louis returned to Marienbad five days after he had departed, rejoined Edward VII and gave him a personal account of his adventures and talks. Later a letter arrived from the Royal Yacht addressed to Victoria at Jugenheim. 'Louis will have told you much of interest relative to his Prussian visit,' the King wrote. 'There is *no* one I could have chosen who would have fulfilled the Mission I entrusted *him* with – better than himself.'[10]

There were still difficult times ahead for Anglo-Russian relations, but eventually the breach was to be healed, thanks in no small measure to Louis's private efforts.

The opportunities for pacifying the Kaiser were fewer in number and more barren in their results. However, Louis continued to do his best, encouraged by Edward VII. At the end of March 1905 the Kaiser made a belligerent and provocative speech in Morocco, supporting the independence of that country from France in the hope of weakening the Anglo-French *entente*. The Admiralty was certain that the Kaiser was also after coaling stations for his fleets in North Africa, which suggested a further enlargement of German naval influence in the Mediterranean.

'The Tangier Incident', as the Kaiser's speech came to be known, was vehemently condemned by Edward VII in a letter to Louis as 'a gratuitous insult to 2 Countries – & the clumsy theatrical part of it would make one laugh were the matter not a serious one . . . I suppose G.E. [German Emperor] will never find out as he will never be told how ridiculous he makes himself . . . I have tried to get on with him & shall nominally do my best till the end – but trust him – never. He is *utterly* false & the bitterest foe that E. possesses!'[11] Nevertheless, he once again charged his English nephew, Louis, to mediate with his German nephew at the earliest opportunity. This occurred a few days later when the *Hohenzöllern* in which the Kaiser was cruising met Louis's flagship at Gibraltar in April 1905.

Willie attempted to persuade Louis that his designs in the Mediterranean were entirely peaceful and that he had no ambition to undermine British power in that sea, or anywhere else. The Kaiser's attitude suddenly changed and his tone became bellicose when German relations with France were mentioned. 'We know the road to Paris,' he told Louis threateningly, 'and we will get there again if needs be. They should remember no fleet can defend Paris.'[12] Louis did not attempt to deny this, but he wondered again at the curious and dangerous mind of this German relative.

On his return to England, Louis reported everything confidentially to Edward VII, who passed on the information to the Foreign Secretary and the Prime Minister. 'In all he said to you there is throughout a want of sincerity,'[13] the King commented to Louis.

Six months before this meeting, on 22 October 1904, Louis was at his desk at the Admiralty when news came in that there had been a catastrophe in the North Sea. The reinforcing Russian Baltic Fleet, commanded by Admiral Rozhestvensky, had at last managed to depart from its base on its long voyage to the Far East. The Tsar and Tsarina, with the infant Tsarevitch, came all the way to Reval to see them off and wish them Godspeed and victory over the Japanese 'who have troubled the peace of Holy Russia'.

The fleet had steamed nervously through the Baltic and Skagerrack in two divisions. Still beset by nightmare visions of darting Japanese torpedo boats operating from secret bases, the Russian lookouts were unusually alert and nervous. In the middle of the night they had sighted a number of small vessels, illuminated them by searchlights, and at once opened fire – ferociously but inaccurately. Their target turned out to be a British fishing fleet. One of the boats was sunk, others damaged and there were several dead and injured among the fishermen.

The reaction in Britain was so violent that for many days war seemed imminent. The Russian Fleet had steamed off into the night after 'the bloodbath', ignoring the dead and wounded. There was no apology either from Russia or from Admiral Rozhestvensky. The British fleets were put on a war footing and began shadowing 'the bully scurrying down the Channel'. 'Situation Critical' and 'Good Luck!' were among the cryptic signals that crackled across the ether by the Royal Navy's new wonder wireless.

Fisher had taken up his appointment as First Sea Lord only two days earlier. His official residence was not ready, and he had 'flu. Louis went to his bedside at the Charing Cross Hotel, and was told that he was to act for him as First Sea Lord throughout the crisis, and 'attend the Cabinet meetings and conferences at the War Office'.[14]

As D.N.I. the Mobilization Division was included among the other Staff divisions under Louis's direction. Now it was his duty to call in the reserves at home and all who were surplus on foreign stations. 'By the time these parties arrived home we had enough officers and men for the scheme which was put into execution,' wrote Louis many years later.

This emergency mobilization was a pricelessly valuable exercise and one which would be exploited to the full by Louis on a second and more critical occasion ten years later.

Louis returned to the Admiralty from Fisher's bedside and busied himself with other contingency planning. On the assumption 'that it was decided to use force to prevent the Russian Baltic Fleet from reaching the Far East,' he presented to the Cabinet proposed dispositions. As far as Russia's ally Germany was concerned, 'If her Fleet had to be considered,' Louis informed the Ministers, 'a General Mobilisation would be necessary, as we should then require every available Battleship in the North Sea.'

The German Fleet, with his brother-in-law, Prince Henry, in high command, would have to be watched, and Louis recommended the use of a fast yacht or trawler which would unobtrusively steam off the Elbe, and in an emergency would race to the Dutch or Danish coast and transmit its message to London by wire, avoiding the German cable system altogether. This, Louis calculated, would give the British fleets at least twelve hours' notice of an impending surprise attack.[15]

For many days after this the Russian Fleet was closely and provocatively shadowed by the British. Lord Charles Beresford, C.-in-C. of the Channel Fleet (which alone could have blown the Russian battleships out of the water in an hour) thirsted for action.

While Louis prepared for the worst, the two monarchs tried to limit the crisis. Edward VII told the First Lord that he deprecated this shadowing and hoped that it would cease.[16] In St Petersburg the British Ambassador, Sir Charles Hardinge, spent an hour with the Tsar, who expressed his 'deep regret and sorrow' and promised reparations on the most liberal scale to the victims and their relatives. Privately Nicky telegraphed to the King his 'profound regrets'.

In due course the 'Dogger Bank Affair' blew over. But Britain continued to remain suspicious, and out in the Far East, ships of the China Station were ready for trouble when the Russian Admiral, after a long, anxious and fateful voyage, passed within sight of Singapore on the way to the annihilation of his fleet at Tsu-Shima.

The Dogger Bank Affair represented the more active and vivid side of Louis's purely naval work at the Admiralty. He regarded this work and his secret extracurricular pacifying activities as subsidiary to the administrative reforming work he carried out during these years. There was, for instance, his deep concern about the lack of a proper naval staff and proper plans for the preparation for war.

Louis's enthusiasm for an efficient staff behind the fighting forces – on land or on sea – originated in his boyhood. He remembered his father telling him how an unprepared Grand Duchy of Hesse, lacking any staff planning in its army, had been overrun with such ease by the Prussians in 1866. Prince Alexander had also told him what a difference it had made when in the Franco-Prussian War four years later the Hessian regiments had gone to war supported, like the rest of the German Army, by a Prussian-created War Staff.

It is not surprising, then, that more than a decade before Winston Churchill became the civil head of the Royal Navy and made one of his first crusades the creation of a proper Naval War Staff, Louis was delivering heavy broadsides against the dangerously outmoded oligarchic control of the Navy. This had been all very well in the simpler and more leisurely days when fleets sailed at four knots and could not be reached with instructions perhaps for months. Now orders could be telegraphed all over the world within hours, and fleets could be despatched from one end of the world to the other at high speed and regardless of the wind.

With the coming of the explosive shell and armour plate, coal-fired then oil-fired boilers, and multitudes of new machines and a new breed of technician to operate them, the management of a navy had become more complicated many times over within a few decades.

In wartime the nation and the Empire would be almost entirely dependent on the Navy for its survival, and the tasks of management would be alarmingly complicated and critical. And yet there was still no proper naval staff to support the civil and naval chiefs. Louis's logical and sensible German mind became increasingly concerned at this extraordinary situation. On 25 February 1902 he issued a long memorandum proposing revolutionary changes, among them the creation of a naval assistant for the First Sea Lord and the other Sea Lords, and Chief of the Admiralty Naval War Staff, a 'War Lord'.

A 'War Lord' properly supported by a powerful Naval War Staff! Reactionary elements in the Admiralty who saw their power diminishing and unwanted faces about them were appalled. The more radical elements seized joyfully on the long document. A royal reformer was amongst them, and only a few of them had realized it!

Fisher, Commander-in-Chief of the Mediterranean Fleet, who as First Sea Lord was soon to light the fuse to a keg of dynamite beneath the Admiralty building, grasped the nub of Louis's theme and within a few days wrote off excitedly to his second-in-command as if the whole idea were his own: 'What we want is an *additional naval member of the Board of Admiralty absolutely disassociated from all administrative and executive work and solely concerned in the* 'PREPARATION OF THE FLEET *FOR WAR*".' However, he did give Louis credit for the name – 'THE WAR LORD,' – 'a magnificent name'.[17]

Other causes which Louis initiated during his years as D.N.I. were commerce protection and insurance in war, the more efficient use of personnel, the creation of an Imperial Defence College and the reorganization of his own department. This he referred to as 'the (miscalled) Intelligence Department' because in reality it dealt with all purely naval staff matters. He wanted it greatly expanded, with the First Sea Lord as its head and provided with a Naval Assistant, in order to give it strength and teeth.

None of these reforms made headline news, although a number of them did so later when Fisher, the greatest publicist the Navy ever possessed, adopted some of them. But all of them were to prove greatly influential to the fighting efficiency of the navy when war came.

Louis's industry, his influence in the seats of greatest power and readiness to accept responsibility – a strong Battenberg characteristic – meant that his work extended farther and farther beyond the previously accepted terms of reference of a D.N.I. The more effective he proved himself, the more people used him, not only because he got things done but because it seemed advantageous to associate with someone who was clearly going to the top.

After a week in 1903 when Louis had been deluged by pleas and memoranda and recommendations on cruiser manoeuvres, submarine mining, gunnery, wireless telegraphy communications in time of war and goodness knows what else, he wrote to his old friend and shipmate, Cyprian Bridge, C.-in-C. China, 'My work seems to grow steadily – the D.N.I. is requisitioned by every department, even outside the Admiralty & not much of my waking life is devoted to other matters.'[18]

The strain was immense, sometimes intolerable, and then he would succumb to an attack of gout which might leave him chairbound or in bed for days on end. The gout was inherited from his father and was not caused by drink – in fact by this time in his life he was very abstemious.

It was not only the Admiralty that was a worry. In Louis's judgement, the Royal Navy was a paragon of efficiency and readiness by contrast with the Army – look at the Boer War for evidence of *that*! Inter-service committee work was an important part of his job, and he found his dealings with the Army deeply depressing.

The Army appeared to have learned nothing from the debacles in South Africa. His opposite number, the Director-General of Mobilization and Military Intelligence, General Sir William Nicholson, was described by Fisher as 'so hateful to the Admiralty, and such a thorough cad, that any two less amiable persons than Lord Walter Kerr, First Sea Lord, and Prince Louis of Battenberg would have declined to work further with him'.[19]

Louis, ever discreet, wrote in confidence that Nicholson 'suffers from a military swollen head and his views of the Navy and its functions are years behind those of his predecessor'.[20]

During the fifteen years between 1899, when Louis took office as Assistant D.N.I., and the outbreak of war in 1914, when he was First Sea Lord, the Royal Navy was not a happy service in its high command. A century of peace had created a service that was reactionary in its thinking, conservative in its *matériel*, cautious in its planning, and unprepared for war. Gunnery practice was kept to a minimum because it tarnished the paintwork and generally untidied things. Spit-and-polish and competitive games and regattas were the first preoccupations of a fleet. Intellectualism, as Louis had discovered decades earlier, was despised. It was bad form to show cleverness.

There was widespread ignorance of maritime strategy and history. Officer recruitment was from the younger brothers of rich and old families. The services tended to attract the 'duffers'. The seamen came from the same class as they had in Nelson's day, even though the press gang had long since been outlawed, and were fed the same as, and were paid relatively no better than, a century earlier. Engineer officers, like the engines they cared for, were barely tolerated on board. They were said to eat with their oily fingers and were made to mess apart from the other officers.

The rise of German sea power and politically motivated naval 'scares' about the unpreparedness of the Royal Navy offered a handful of clever, ambitious and far-sighted reformers the opportunity to seize power in the Admiralty. Fisher was their leader, a brilliant, explosive and dedicated revolutionary who loved to proclaim the creed by which he liked people to think he lived – 'Ruthless! Relentless! Remorseless!'

On the one hand he gathered about him a devoted body of disciples, all of them brilliant in their own fields. On the other hand he created a very large and powerful body of influential enemies, some who disagreed with his methods, but more who were reactionary by instinct and distrusted Fisher for his cleverness and feared him for his upsetting of sacred traditions. 'No one knows what the morrow will bring forth,'[21] wrote one traditionalist in dismay.

There was no place for neutrals in this war within the Navy: you were either in the 'Fishpond' and a dedicated Fisherite, or you were out of it and his enemy for life. Even the Court was split, though not so widely nor so hostilely. Edward VII loved Fisher and believed in all he did and thought. Without the King's support Fisher could not have prevailed. Georgie, now Prince of Wales, became increasingly suspicious of Fisher's methods and policies and increasingly sympathetic to what Fisher described as 'the syndicate of discontent' headed by Lord Charles Beresford.

Lord Charles Beresford – 'Charlie B' – the hero of the Alexandria bombardment, was becoming increasingly dotty with old age.

During the crisis with the passage of the Russian Fleet, it was later revealed that he planned to attack it with only part of his force as it would by un-British to fight with such heavy odds in his favour. He was sternly rebuked but remained in command. His flagship was like the palace of some mediaeval tyrant and he liked to have with him on board his wife, his motor car and his fat pet bulldog, behind whom there followed at all times a sailor with a dustpan and brush. His subordinates were terrified of him. But they admired him; so did the lower deck who could always be relied upon to love a grand eccentric.

Sometimes Beresford went on half pay and into Parliament in order to fight politically his numberless enemies. In the House he was regarded as something of a buffoon. Louis once told him 'he was much more use afloat than as a Member of Parliament, which he did not seem to appreciate. It is one of his hallucinations.'[22] Winston Churchill described 'Charlie B' performing in Parliament: 'Before he gets up he does not know what he is going to say, when he speaks he does not know what he is saying, and when he sits down he does not know what he has said.' Yet Beresford remained rich and powerful and, like Fisher, was worshipped by his disciples like Sir Hedworth Lambton, Sir Gerard Noel and Sir Archibald 'Arky-Barky' Milne, all of them friends of the Prince of Wales.

In the course of the Royal Navy's long and unhappy blood-letting, Louis acted in a steadying rôle, encouraging the surgeon in his necessary work but sometimes staying his knife, and always doing his best to comfort the patient. He was the only man who could have done this because his Princely rank placed him above the belligerents and he could not be accused of having an axe to grind, nor of striving ambitiously for favours. With this went his reputation for being a peerless negotiator and a cooling influence when temperatures ran high.

Fisher's appointment as First Sea Lord had for long been foreseen, and in many quarters dreaded. It finally came about as a result of firm and unremitting political and royal pressure. The King had a strong hand in it. But no support was more steadfast and effective than Louis's. For ten years, from 1900 when Louis was Assistant D.N.I., to 1910 when Fisher was at last forced to resign, Louis was Jacky Fisher's patron and guide, protector and corrector.

Years before Fisher's appointment, which took effect on Trafalgar Day (21 October) in 1904, these two far-sighted reforming officers had reached agreement on a wide range of plans, on the assumption that Fisher would inherit the most senior naval post, the professional head of the Navy, before long. Both knew that time was running out, that the German threat might at any moment become a reality.

By agreement with Fisher Louis was working on the subject of the redistribution of naval strength during the summer before Fisher took over, with the assent of the First Lord (Selborne) but behind the back of the outgoing First Sea Lord, the elderly, kindly but rusty Lord Walter Kerr.

All through 1903 and 1904 Louis brought his very strong influence to bear to make certain of Fisher's appointment. Fisher knew it, was thankful and eagerly expectant, but in his quixotic way half-pretended that he did not want the post and half disapproved of the means by which he was certain to get it. As a democrat and egalitarian he affected to disapprove of patronage and lived by it only reluctantly. He wrote to Louis several times to protest at the lobbying Louis was doing on his behalf. Louis wrote to him at Marienbad, where he took the cure with Edward VII most summers, 'As to your not coming . . . that is absurd. Your position in the Service and in this Country is now such that no First Lord, Liberal or Conservative, would dream of taking anyone but you. You must be made an Admiral of the Fleet, and a Peer a little later.'[23]

'I don't think the King ought to be brought in as my partisan . . .' Fisher once wrote. 'I don't QUITE like it!'[24] But Edward VII was indeed his partisan, and so – at that time – was the Prince of Wales, both of them heavily supporting Louis in his efforts. Two weeks later the Prince of Wales writes to the First Lord, 'I am convinced that no one in the Service is better qualified . . . nor will you find one who will devote more time & energy to working for the efficiency of the Navy.'

But when Fisher finally succumbed, and with poorly concealed enthusiasm hastened in to the Admiralty as its chief, Louis kept a keen, critical eye on him. When he showed excessive zeal and began to act like a self-caricature, Louis was the first to restrain him and advise circumspection. As early as 16 March 1905 we find him writing to an officer who had suffered, 'I do cordially agree with all you say, especially the fever which has seized hold of J.F. . . . also the senseless way in which he insults and alienates our senior men . . . However, he shall have my views in season and out of season, from high and low altitudes . . .[25] And that was a promise Louis kept through all Fisher's years of power.

The concentrating of naval strength at home and its dilution about the Empire upset a great many people, including the Prince of Wales. Only Louis could explain the necessity of doing this to his old shipmate because he was not only his cousin but Prince George admired Louis so completely – writing of him as being the best man at the Admiralty 'by miles'.[26]

Edward VII agreed with this judgement, and so did Fisher, who was no sycophant – 'He is out and away the best man inside the Admiralty building'[27] he informed the Prime Minister, underlining his comment for good measure.

Inevitably Louis made enemies, sometimes temporary, sometimes permanent, on both sides in this internecine warfare. When Fisher felt Louis's restraining hand on his shoulder he snarled at him. In Beresford and Lambton and the rest there developed a bitter hostility stemming from fear, jealousy and a corrupt and xenophobically tainted patriotism. It was more than they could bear that Louis was so naturally and so evidently proficient as well as being a member of the royal family and privileged in his intimate relationship with the King and Queen and the Prince of Wales. Everything seemed to be unjustly loaded on his side and they were reduced to attacking him for his birth.

On his return from Kiel in 1904 Louis had been promoted Rear-Admiral. Two years later it became known that he was to be made an acting Vice-Admiral – Beresford's 'spies' were everywhere, and knew that this was the work of their enemy, Fisher. This allowed Beresford time to spread his poison through the service. Edward VII learnt of it, probably through the Prince of Wales, and wrote complainingly to Fisher. Was not Prince Louis being damaged by these attacks?

Fisher replied through Knollys: 'I am not surprised at the King's question of Prince Louis feeling hurt. I have never known more malignant rancour & jealousy as manifested by Lord Charles Beresford and Hedworth Lambton as against Prince Louis & I regret to say Lord Tweedmouth [First Lord] is frightened of what these two can do in exciting the Service against the avowed intention of making Prince Louis an acting Vice-Admiral. But I earnestly beg His Majesty will not say a word as I yet am confident of carrying it through although Prince Louis (like the Gentleman he is) has sent me a private telegram begging me drop the matter.'[28] Fisher won, Louis got his promotion, and went to the Mediterranean as second-in-command of the fleet, the clean sea air once again proving an antidote to the poisonous vapours of London.

Tweedmouth had good reason to fear Beresford's power. Although many people regarded him simply as a pompous and arrogant ass, there was no limit to his vindictiveness. At one stage in his vendetta he wrote an article which belittled Louis's accomplishments as a naval officer and demanded that he should be removed from the Navy List because of his German birth. He sent this to the editor of every London newspaper asking for it to be published anonymously. One editor, without Beresford's knowledge, sent the article to Louis telling him who wrote it and reassuring him that none of his fellow editors would be a party to such an underhand attack. Louis said nothing.

But Edward VII got wind of what Beresford was up to and made it known that he was now *persona non grata* at court. This was a deadly blow to Beresford, whose wife was a fanatical snob and climber. Ignorant of the fact that Louis knew the cause of Edward VII's displeasure, Beresford approached him as the only person who could restore him to favour. Without a word of complaint, Louis succeeded in at least partially reinstating Beresford at court although the King never really forgave him for attempting to destroy his nephew's naval career.

Louis's appointment as D.N.I. was due to terminate in January 1905. Fisher was now firmly in power. 'I should have about two months with you here [at the Admiralty] before hoisting my flag [his next appointment, see below],' Louis had written to him earlier, 'and much can be done in that time.'[29]

He never spoke truer words for much indeed was done before Louis departed. Fisher's pace was breathtaking. Besides sitting on his Special Committee, Louis was among 'the best brains' co-opted onto a Committee on Designs which in a trice turned upside down every established principle on heavy warship construction and produced the plans for the revolutionary all-big-gun battleship *Dreadnought* and its armoured cruiser counterpart, the *Invincible*, later called a battle cruiser, a new class of fighting ship altogether.

These were heady days at the Admiralty in Whitehall, and Louis left with the certain conviction that the Fisher administration, as new, dynamic, fast and hard-hitting as the *Dreadnought* which was to be its symbol, would not falter in its purpose.

Edward VII was delighted with it all – with the long overdue reforms now firmly in hand, with Fisher as the revolution's Robespierre, and with Louis – protégé, nephew and friend – for his success in helping to bring it about.

Edward VII was equally delighted when the government recommended Louis for the K.C.M.G., an award more closely associated with the Foreign Office than the Royal Navy, 'for the valuable services you rendered to the Navy and the State'. Edward VII continued 'Nobody deserves recognition for all the hard work & great objects you accomplished as Head of the Intelligence Department more than yourself.'[30]

In the highest government and defence circles there was great regret at Louis's departure from the Admiralty, even if it was temporary and for a command at sea.

'I often miss Prince Louis's cool view of things,'[31] reflected Sir George Clarke, Secretary of the Committee of Imperial Defence. It was one of Louis's greatest assets.

Two years later, Fisher, in a rare and memorable speech at the Lord Mayor of London's banquet, spoke of the Admiralty's achievements which Louis had done so much to set in train. 'Our object has been the fighting efficiency of the Fleet and its instant readiness for war; and we have got it . . . So I turn to all of you and I turn to my countrymen and I say – Sleep quiet in your beds . . .'

'Sleep quiet in your beds' was an aphorism Fisher and his supporters in the service never tired of quoting. In 1907 it may have been somewhat premature. But in the face of the most determined and provocative German competition, the Royal Navy was in a very much stronger position to face the future foe than it had been at the end of the old century.

9

'Your brother has been so funny. He has put
his hat on the Grand Duchess Vera's head and
knocked her spectacles off.'

QUEEN ALEXANDRA *to Miss Nona Kerr*

IN the last weeks of the old century, Victoria found that she was
expecting another child, seven years after the birth of Georgie.
She had just returned from a visit to Wolfsgarten with the children.
Nicky and Alicky had been there with their three girls, Olga,
Tatiana and Marie, and they had played games happily together
with her own Louise and Georgie, Alice remained rather aloof.
At 14½, she regarded herself as above such childish things.

The grown-ups had had their own games. The ever-lively Grand
Duchess – Ducky – played a sort of hunt-the-treasure with the
supper, having it secretly laid out in a different part of the woodlands
every evening. It had been a lovely holiday, the only worry being
their host. After its wondrous, idyllic start, Victoria saw that her
brother's marriage to Ducky was not going well in spite of their
adored little Elizabeth.

Louis had to be in London in the autumn. It was earlier in that
year that he had been appointed Assistant D.N.I. and he had rented
40 Grosvenor Gardens, a few yards from Buckingham Palace
grounds, for his family. Victoria and the children joined him there
in October.

The Boer War had just begun and a great patriotic fever had
seized the capital. Regiments destined for South Africa passed their
door on their way to Victoria Station, their bands playing 'Soldiers
of the Queen'. The New Year, the first day of the first month

199

of 1900, was spent at Sandringham with Uncle Bertie and Aunt Alix.

Uncle Bertie, who had suffered such an unhappy childhood himself, adored young children and, while he could stand on his royal station and be choleric with adults, was endlessly patient with children. That year when they returned to London he took all the children to the pantomime and even concealed from them the awful toothache he was suffering.

Victoria's last baby was born on 25 June 1900. There were no problems, and he was a boy weighing over eight pounds. The Queen offered to stand as one of the Godmothers – her last Godchild as it turned out – and the baby was christened at Frogmore, in her mother's old drawing room.

It was a terribly hot afternoon and the Queen always suffered from the heat. Victoria thought that this was because she never seemed to perspire like other people. Her hands would be 'like hot bricks' but never damp. Servants had put buckets of ice everywhere to try to bring down the temperature, even under the loose covers of some of the chairs. This led to tragedy. The Dean of Windsor, Dr Elliott, who was to perform the christening, arrived early and sat down. He did not realize what was under the chair until he felt his legs chilled. This later led to a sciatic inflammation, and for ever afterwards he could only hobble about with the aid of a stick.

The Queen now looked very old and was very crippled and half blind. But she insisted on holding the big baby all through the ceremony while he was given the names Albert* Victor Nicholas Louis Francis. None of these would do for everyday use and a nickname had to be found. Victoria suggested Nicky, but the children pointed out that this would certainly lead to confusion with the Tsar, and they did not like it anyway, and wasn't Dickie a nicer name. So Dickie it was, a name she sometimes called Louis in private.

Dickie Battenberg showed early signs of liveliness, knocking off Queen Victoria's spectacles with one hand and entangling his other arm in her cap-veil while still at the font. The Queen, to everyone's surprise, showed no sign of annoyance. 'He is a beautiful large child and behaved very well,'[1] she noted. It was the present Lord Mountbatten's initiation into the pleasures of being indulged, which

* At the Queen's insistence. When she died 'Louis' took first place and 'Albert' relegated!

he enjoyed for the greater part of his childhood, most especially from his adoring older sisters and brother.

The old Queen had only nine months to live. Among the events which accelerated her end were her worry over Vicky who had cancer and knew she did not have long to live, the Boer War, the death of several of her oldest friends, and finally the death of Affie.

Like her daughter Alice, her whole being shrank from the idea of man killing man, yet her sense of duty forced her to become involved in the Boer War. Just as the nursing which Alice had done through most of the Franco-Prussian war agonized and exhausted her, so the loss of friends and the discipline she forced upon herself of seeing off the troops, visiting barracks and military hospitals, drained the Queen's last precious reserves. The attacks against England's South Africa policy by Germany, France and Austria added greatly to her suffering.

Early in 1901 Louis was working at the Admiralty and living with his family at yet another London rented house, 4 Hans Crescent. The girls had lessons and went regularly to MacPherson's gymnasium in Sloane Street. Alice read English literature with Miss Jackson and prepared for her confirmation, and Georgie went to Mr Moreton's school at 35 Cliveden Place, Eaton Square.

Early in January Louis and Victoria knew that the Queen was weakening, and on 11th they were summoned to Osborne. Many of the Queen's children and grandchildren were already there, including the Kaiser, who held his one good arm under her pillow for the last two-and-a-half hours of her life. It was the only worthy thing Willie ever did for England.

It was a solemn and epochal moment in British history. But amidst the national solemnity and the sorrow there was a strong thread of anticipatory excitement. Now that the impossible had happened and a record reign of sixty-three years was over there was an almost indecent interest in what the future might now bring. The Queen, God bless her, was dead: long live the King, and tell us what novelties and distractions your reign will now bring to our humdrum lives! The stout ex-Prince of Wales, the new King-Emperor, raising his tear-soaked face from his mother's shoulder, would soon show them.

On an intimate family level, the grief was overwhelming. They had hoped she would be spared a few more years of the new century. She was, after all, only 81. Victoria was especially heartbroken. For more than twenty years, the Queen had been mother, guide, confidante, comforter. 'You have indeed been like a Mother to us all, ever since dear Mama's death,' Victoria once wrote to her, '& to me especially so, & I have ever felt since I lost her that I have a second Mother & a true friend in you.'[2]

In her early life, when the Queen was a middle-aged woman, Victoria had found her an alarming figure. Their relationship quite changed after Alice's death, and the Queen assumed the guise of an affectionate, broken-hearted mother. Their shared grief was a great bond.

Later, Victoria always remembered the little details – her faint perfume of orange blossom from the scent she had made for her at Grasse, which Victoria unsuccessfully tried to buy after the Queen's death. She remembered the large collection of capes of different thickness she insisted on taking always in her carriage, and helping her on and off with them according to her ever-changing needs. She remembered the way she always took tea with two cups, pouring one into the other until it was the right temperature; the whisky and water with her meals when she was forbidden wine after her gout attacks in middle age.

When her eyesight was failing, and she was dreading complete blindness like her grandfather George III, Victoria used to put her finger on the last word she had written in her letters so that she knew from which point on the page she should continue.

The Queen loved Louis quite as much as she loved Victoria. Women could be loved, but not relied upon for advice. The Dowager Marchioness of Ely once told Victoria that 'the stupidest man's opinion carried more weight with the Queen than the cleverest woman's'. As a clever man, Louis found the Queen leaning more and more upon him, especially after Liko's death. She frequently asked him to come to Osborne (or Balmoral, or Windsor) 'to put things right'.

A typical case was that of Abdul Karim, the Munshi.[3] He was one of the Indian servants she employed in a curious period of egalitarian anti-racialism at the time of her Golden Jubilee. The Munshi positively towered above all of those who got 'above themselves'.

The gullible Queen thought he was marvellous, and believed him when he claimed his father was Surgeon-General. The Munshi was, in fact, a just-literate Mohammedan clerk on the make to whom the Queen entrusted higher and higher responsibilities, including, finally, showing him confidential papers from India. At first ignoring the protests of her most stoutly loyal and wise advisers, she agreed in the end to call in Louis 'to put things right'.

Princess Victoria's parents,
Prince Ludwig of Hesse, later
Grand Duke Ludwig IV; and his
wife, Princess Alice, Queen
Victoria's second daughter, with
the infant Princess Victoria.

Left: Prince Louis's parents, Prince Alexander of Hesse; and his wife, Julie, created Princess of Battenberg.

Opposite left: Princess Alice's first three daughters, (*left to right*) Princess Elizabeth ('Ella'), Princess Victoria and Princess Irène.

Opposite right: Princess Victoria at the time of her mother's death.

Opposite below: The four Hessian daughters in 1885, 'Ella', Victoria, Irène and Alix ('Alicky') the future Empress of Russia.

Above left: Prince Louis as an eight-year-old boy.

Above right: Prince Louis with his younger brother Prince Alexander ('Sandro').

Left: Prince Louis as a midshipman in the Royal Navy.

Opposite above: H.M.S. *Sultan* at Naples in 1877. (*Left to right arrowed*) the Prince of Wales, Prince Louis and the Duke of Edinburgh.

Opposite below: Prince Louis's drawing of H.M.S. *Inconstant* at sea in 1882.

Sunday Afternoon at Sea
"INCONSTANT"
1882.

Wedding portraits of Louis
and Victoria, 1884.

Right: Prince Alexander of Battenberg ('Sandro') as Sovereign Prince of Bulgaria.

Below: Grand Admiral Prince Henry of Prussia on the bridge of his flagship, S.M.S. *Deutschland*.

Opposite above: Prince Louis's first command, H.M.S. *Scout.*

Opposite centre: His last command, H.M.S. *Implacable.*

Opposite below: His first flagship, H.M.S. *Drake*, of the 2nd Cruiser Squadron.

Above: Wolfsgarten photographed by Princess Louise of Battenberg from a Zeppelin. Champagne and caviare were served in the gondola.

Below: Heiligenberg Prince Louis's castle.

Opposite: Four generations. Queen Victoria with her last child, Princess Beatrice, her granddaughter Princess Victoria and the infant Alice, later Princess Andrew of Greece and mother to Prince Philip.

Above: Queen Victoria in 1893 with two of her Hessian granddaughters, Victoria *(nearer)* and 'Ella', Grand Duchess Serge of Russia. The Scots gillie is Francis Clark not Brown, who died ten years earlier.

Above: Louis and Victoria in early married life, 1891. Prince Louis is a Commander, R.N., his wife, now 28, shows resolution and responsibility in her expression. Princess Alice is standing and Princess Louise is in her mother's arms.

Opposite: Engagement photograph of the Tsarevitch Nicholas and Princess Alix ('Alicky') of Hesse.

Above: H.M.S. *Implacable*, Malta, 1902. The family party in the centre is (*left to right*) Princess Alice, Prince Louis, Princess Louis, baby Prince Louis ('Dickie'), Princess Louise and Miss Nona Kerr, Lady-in-Waiting. Prince George sits at his father's feet.

Opposite: Louis and Victoria in maturity. The drawing was made in 1898, the photograph eight years later.

Above: Queen Victoria's funeral procession in Windsor. The Navy has taken over from the Royal Horse Artillery after the mishap with the rearing horses. The Kaiser and King Edward VII walk behind. Prince Louis walks beside the right rear wheel of the gun carriage.

Opposite: Victoria with her infant son 'Dickie', the future Earl Mountbatten of Burma, in 1900.

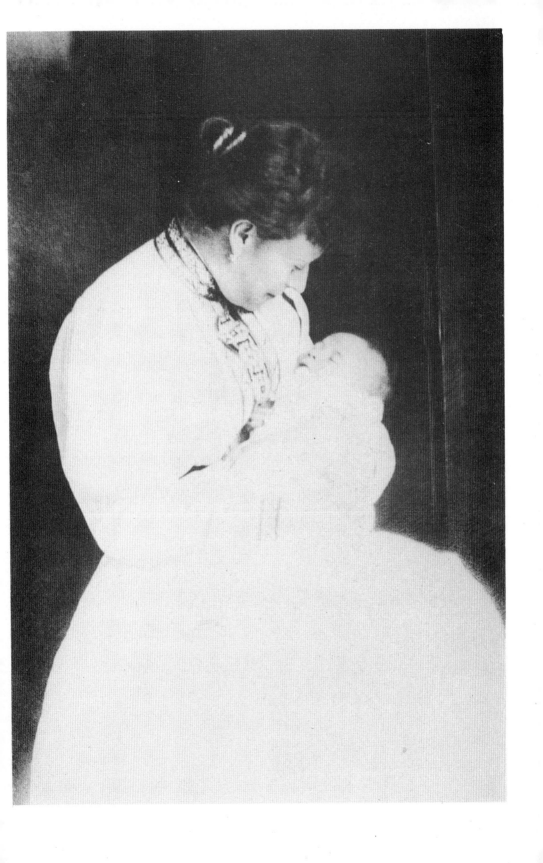

Opposite: 'Dickie' with his fancy animals which he christened 'Katuffs'; and, at the age of 3, with his elder brother 'Georgie'.

Above: Family group at Kiel, 1903.

Left to right, back row: Grand Duke Ernst Ludwig, his daughter Princess Elizabeth, Grand Duchess Serge ('Ella'), Prince Henry of Prussia.

Second row: Prince George of Battenberg, Prince Louis, Grand Duke Serge (Prince Waldemar of Prussia on his knee), Princess Henry of Prussia (Irène), Prince Sigismud on her knee.

Front row: Princess Victoria (young Prince Louis 'Dickie' on her knee), Princess Louise of Battenberg, Princess Alice of Battenberg.

Above : Prince Louis with his sons in 1906.

Below : 'Dickie' Battenberg with his nieces, Princesses Margarita on his right, and Theodora ('Dolla') of Greece.

North American visit, 1905.

Above : Prince Louis at
Toronto City Hall.

Right : Landing at Annapolis
U.S. Naval Academy.

Above: De Laszlo completes his portrait of Princess Alice. Her
husband waits wistfully on the left.

Opposite above: The Russian Grand Duchesses Marie, Olga,
Anastasia and Tatiana with 'Dickie' Battenberg. In the carriage the
Tsarevitch with Princesses 'Dolla' and Margarita.

Opposite below: A year earlier, in 1909. A day ashore on the Baltic
coast from the Imperial Yacht *Standart.* On the groyne (*left to right*)
the Grand Duchesses Olga and Tatiana, 'Dickie' Battenberg, Grand
Duchess Anastasia. On the sand the Grand Duchess Marie, whom
'Dickie' later determined to marry, and the Grand Duke 'Ernie' of
Hesse.

Left: The Emperor and Empress of Russia ('Nicky' and 'Alicky') on board the Imperial Yacht.

Opposite: Wolfsgarten, 1910. Princess Victoria with her younger widowed sister 'Ella' wearing, as always, her 'Martha and Mary' habit.

Opposite above: The Russian Imperial Yacht steams through the Kiel Canal in 1909. (*Left to right*): 'Dickie' Battenberg, Grand Duke of Hesse, Tsar Nicholas, Grand Duchesses Olga and Anastasia and Prince Sigismund ('Bobby') of Prussia. The Tsarina is below on the left, Princess Irène on the right.

Opposite left: The Russian children, all assassinated in 1918.

Opposite right: The haemophilic Tsarevitch Alexei with his sailor, Dirivinko.

Above: The present Lord Mountbatten as a Naval Cadet outside the First Sea Lord's residence in 1913.

Opposite : Soldier and nurse :

Prince and Princess Andrew of Greece, Prince Philip's parents, during the Balkan war of 1912.

Right : Prince Louis as First Sea Lord, with Winston Churchill, First Lord of the Admiralty, 1913.

Below right : Louis and Victoria in 1919 at Kent House.

The Greek family in 1922. Princesses Alice, Theodora, and
Cecile (in front of her) Prince Philip, Prince Andrew, Princesses
Sophie and Margarita.

Above: Lord Louis
Mountbatten marries the
Hon. Edwina Ashley, 18
July 1922.

Right: Victoria, Dowager
Marchioness of Milford
Haven, shortly before the
Second World War.

Left: Prince Philip at Gordonstoun School learns the ropes.

Below: With his fiancée, Princess Elizabeth, in July 1947.

He was the only man in England who could – and did – explain gently to her the folly and danger of her ways. She agreed to cancel the arrangement on the understanding that the Munshi should be known formally as her Indian Secretary, even if he saw nothing from India. The official who had been the first to protest was ignored by the Queen for twelve months; Louis remained as loved as ever.

Louis became an executor of the Queen's will, her personal Naval A.D.C., and the most intimate details of her affairs were confided in him. In spite of her son Affie being a Captain R.N. while Louis was still a boy, it was Louis who finally persuaded her to take a more sympathetic attitude towards her Royal Navy. (The Duke of Edinburgh was not good with the Queen and usually tried to persuade her of the fine qualities of the Navy after he had drunk too much wine at dinner.)

'Grandmama was essentially what was called a womanly nature,' Victoria once wrote, 'and her likes and dislikes were influenced by personal contacts. This was the secret of Lord Beaconsfield's charm for her . . .'[4] And Brown, and Liko and her own husband, she could have added.

The funeral of Queen Victoria was the most solemn occasion of national mourning until the early Armistice Day ceremonies after the First World War. As a spectacle, it was as magnificent as her Jubilee. It was the last public expression of grief in the grand Victorian manner. All her surviving children came to it, except Vicky who was too ill to travel, and great numbers of foreign monarchs, princes and grand dukes arrived in England for the mournful event.

After the procession through London, the bitter February cold in no way reducing the massed crowds, everything went off perfectly until the coffin was taken off the train at Windsor. From here six Royal Horse Artillery horses were supposed to draw the gun carriage on which the coffin rested to St George's Chapel. But the horses had become restless standing for an hour and a half in the cold. They reared and eventually broke their traces.

For a few minutes there was utter pandemonium and according to Lieutenant (later Admiral Sir) Percy Noble: 'the coffin looked like toppling off the gun carriage'. The same officer continued, 'At this moment I distinctly saw Prince Louis go up to King Edward and whisper something in his ear, at which the King nodded an assent. Prince Louis them came over to me and said: "Ground arms and stand by to drag the gun carriage."'[5]

There were outraged protests from senior Army officers that sailors should be permitted to take over where the Army had failed with horses. The King himself had to intercede. 'Right or wrong, let him manage everything,' the Sovereign ordered. 'We shall never get on if there are two people giving contradictory orders.'[6] The Navy rose to the occasion, using the snapped off remains of the traces and a length of railway communication cord to draw the gun carriage by stately, orderly slow march up the steep hill to the castle, and down again to the Chapel. Very few people present knew that there had been a drama at all.

The new reign made little difference to Louis's and Victoria's relations with the English Court. Certainly the Battenbergs were no less favourably placed with King Edward VII than with Queen Victoria. Louis and Victoria could now live rather more in the style that their station expected. Louis had been left a large sum at the death of his father, and Victoria had benefited from a number of inheritances. There was more on the death of the Queen. Victoria was sensible and careful, generous but not over-generous, with money all her life, a characteristic she passed on to her children. She had seen the dangers of too much money, and was later to be worried when one of her sons proposed to marry an heiress.

In 1897 Louis and Victoria decided that she should have a permanent lady-in-waiting. By this time they knew the Kerr family very well, Mark having been an early shipmate of Louis's. He had three unmarried sisters who helped to look after their old father. When he died, leaving them very little money, Louis thought that one of them might like to come and join them. The youngest, Nona, agreed enthusiastically and returned to Germany with Victoria and the children after the 1897 Jubilee celebrations.

Nona Kerr was engaged 'to assist us in the education of our children',[7] which was being mainly conducted by Miss Jackson and Victoria herself. But the job became much more than that. Besides assisting at formal occasions, she would do small errands, visit people for Victoria, help to look for houses when the family had to move, and carried out a multitude of minor chores. The arrangement was an informal one, and Nona often returned to her family for months on end, especially after the children had grown up.

After the Queen's death, Victoria wrote to Nona that she wanted to increase her salary. 'I know you don't absolutely need [the extra], though you have to get all sorts of different kind of clothes than you would have to get if you lived at home in England. But neither do I need the [increase] that I shall now be getting, yet it is quite pleasant to have it, & I shall enjoy having it all the more if I can feel that not only four but the five fingers on my hand share something of it with me . . .'[8]

Victoria and Nona sometimes got on each other's nerves after being together for a long time. Then Victoria would speak her mind and regret it afterwards. At the same time, Victoria always found it difficult to find the graceful word of gratitude when it was needed. 'It is against all my principles,' she once wrote to Nona when she left for a much needed holiday, 'to tell you that it seems to me that I miss you a good deal. It is quite your own fault that this should be the case. How you can stand being snubbed & plagued & ill-treated generally I don't know. You ought by rights to be very angry, & then we should both have rejoiced at your holiday & I should have felt rather less mean than I do now.'[9] That was in 1901. Later on, it appears that Nona could give as good as she got!

It was impossible to have a neutral and non-passionate relationship with Victoria. She was far too volatile for that. As the fifth anniversary of Nona's appointment comes round in 1902, Victoria tries once again – and again unsuccessfully – to demonstrate her gratitude gracefully.

'I have lots & lots to thank you for,' she writes, 'but I don't know how to express it . . . Besides my detestable incapacity to put any really true feelings in to words, as between you & me, I have also a dread of tieing you down or binding you in any way, in case you might think of me more than of yourself, which is a conceited dread I know, but is the result of your mistake. I enjoy being a tyrant, but shirk the responsibility of it, & want you to feel free & independent inspite of everything, & I am a bad hand at working conflicting feelings. If I were sure you had the necessary sensible dose of selfishness, perhaps I would not blunder so much & employ so much rebuffing.'[10]

We can only guess at what those 'conflicting feelings' are. But it seems reasonable to suggest that they are the strong-willed and impatient authoritarian at odds with the sensitive, conscience-prone egalitarian. Victoria is a true Hessian, through and through!

Louis's relations with Nona Kerr were almost as close and intimate as Victoria's and – in the purest sense – they formed for many years an almost ideal *ménage a trois*. He became for her a father-figure to whom she often turned for advice, and like Victoria, he would confide to her his most confidential problems.

In the early years of the century the children grow strong and healthy, passing through without trouble the childhood chickenpox, measles and the like. Louise has a little trouble with curvature of the spine. Victoria adores medical problems and tackles this one successfully.

She is not warm or sentimental with her first child, a fact which the old Queen noted with disapproval, but brisk and sensible, and luckily they are all clever enough to perceive the love beneath. And their well-being is close to her heart. 'Baby [Dickie] is flourishing,' she writes to Nona from Filey in the summer of 1900, 'the food and air agree with him.'[11]

While Dickie was lying on the seaside sands at Filey, his eldest sister's mind was already consumed with love and thoughts of marriage. In 1901 when she was still only sixteen, Alice had fallen in love with Prince Andrew of Greece, the fourth son of George of Denmark, who had been given the crown the Duke of Edinburgh had coveted.

Andrew was only nineteen years old himself, a lively and carefree soldier with a waggish sense of humour and winning ways. His charms had dissolved Alice in that well-known royal trysting place, the summer gardens at Heiligenberg.

To Victoria's concern the couple became unofficially engaged in 1902. Edward VII and Queen Alexandra strongly favoured the match. Had not, the Queen argued, Victoria herself become engaged at only nineteen and at a very unpropitious time? Louis and Victoria yielded. On 9 May 1903 Andrew was invited to London, alone, and without even an A.D.C.

'His engagement to Alice was announced by Uncle Bertie,' wrote Victoria, 'at a family dinner given by George and May [Prince and Princess of Wales] at Marlborough House at a sort of housewarming party . . . Very shy he was on the day that he, Alice and I assisted at a Te Deum in honour of the engagement at the Greek Church, which was followed by a reception at the [Greek] legation.'[12]

Edward VII and Queen Alexandra also invited the young couple to dinner at Buckingham Palace and a play afterwards. This was marked by a curious incident which perplexed them at the time and has puzzled the family as an unsolved mystery ever since.

The King came down to dinner resplendent in a vast expanse of stiff white shirt, but unfortunately dropped a small speck of spinach on to the white shirt front. He looked down at it and appeared to be lost in thought. Presently he took his napkin, dipped it in the spinach and rubbed it all over the shirt front.

When Alice and Andrew discussed the matter after the play they came to the conclusion that it was because he wanted to make quite certain that the spot was big enough to make it worth while changing his shirt before going on to the theatre. It certainly was!

Of all the royal weddings at Darmstadt, none was more gay and light-hearted than that of Alice and Andrew of Greece on 7 October 1903. Everything was in its favour. The weather was perfect, everybody was pleased about the match, the groom looked splendid, the bride was the most beautiful of all princesses, and Darmstadt was the most satisfactory venue for a wedding.

Everyone felt relaxed at Darmstadt where royal goings-on were so commonplace that the local population regarded them as a matter of course, pleasurably but without remark. For the guests who lived in perpetual fear (like the Russians), in a state of absurd exclusivity (like the Spaniards), or half-suffocated in protocol and ceremony (like the Prussians), a stay at Darmstadt was as relaxing a tonic as a seaside holiday for common folk.

But the colour and ceremonial were not lacking at Darmstadt that October, either, and the glories of Hesse were as bright as ever.

The new century of emancipation, revolution and egalitarianism might never have arrived for all the notice that was taken of it. Once again fine grade Hessian blood was enriching one of the European monarchies, and almost all the relations came to celebrate and wish them well.

The Greeks alone numbered nine in all, and together with their suites required half a palace on their own. There were as many Russians, from the Tsar and Tsarina down to lesser grand dukes. The King of England could not come, but the Queen was there. And there were other Queens-to-be like Ena Battenberg (Spain) and Alice's younger sister (Sweden). And of course there were Henry and Irène, Ella and Serge, and Beatrice and Liko, and so many more – two hundred and sixty at the big reception Ernie gave in the Alte Palais ballroom.

Again, there had to be three ceremonies, a civil wedding to conform with local law, then one in the old Protestant Chapel in the Castle and another in the new Russian Orthodox Chapel which had been built as a result of ever more frequent demands. To signify that all the Hessian wedding traditions were being maintained, Alice arrived in one of the old state carriages. But as confirmation that the Hessians did, after all, acknowledge the new century, the couple drove off on their honeymoon in a new Wolseley horseless carriage Nicky had given them.

Their departure was a glorious and riotous finale to the centuries of great Darmstadt weddings. There would never be anything like it again. It involved half of Europe's royal families, light-headed with champagne, 'rushing into the crowd,' as Victoria herself described the events, 'followed by excited policemen and Russian detectives in plain clothes.'[13]

Mark Kerr made a note of the spectacle he and his equally astonished sister witnessed that evening. It was, he observed, 'more like a Bank Holiday on Hampstead Heath than a Royal ceremonial. I was given the bridegroom's overcoat and hat to hold, and was standing next to the Grand Duchess Vera when Prince George of Greece seized the hat and put it on to his aunt's head, knocking her spectacles off and damaging her coiffure . . . she could not see who was the aggressor. However, she pulled the hat off and started to hit me over the head with it. Queen Alexandra . . . found the opportunity for having a little joke, so she went back until she found my sister, and told her, "Your brother has been so funny. He has put his hat on the Grand Duchess Vera's head and knocked her spectacles off." My sister evidently thought the champagne had been too much for me, and hurried forward to reprove and, if necessary, to remove me. I don't think she quite believed my statement of innocence until she heard a chuckle, and looking round saw Queen Alexandra laughing heartily . . .'[14]

The jokes continued, on all sides, amidst outbursts of cries and laughter. Everyone was issued with bags of rice and satin slippers to see off the couple, which was orthodox enough. But Nicky was not content with one bombardment.

'Come along, we can catch them again outside,' he cried, and began running. 'Everyone in their tiaras, ribbons, and stars followed him,' Mark Kerr wrote, 'the children of the party hanging on to his coat-tails. As they came out under the [new electric] light, it appeared to the detectives that something unusual was happening, for the paper bags must have looked like bombs, and the satin shoes gleaming under the searchlight appeared very like daggers. Thereupon they shouldered their umbrellas and joined the rush.' The

Emperor went straight for the backs of the crowd lined six deep along the road. 'Putting his head down he rammed them and gradually pushed his way through ... shedding the children from his coat-tails on the way, and reached the street at the moment when the [horseless] carriage was going by with Princess Alice bowing her acknowledgements to the cheering crowd.

'At this moment she received the contents of the full bag of rice, which the Emperor had carried, in her face, followed by the satin shoe, and leaning over the back of the carriage hit the Emperor on the head with it, at the same time telling him exactly what she thought of him, which so overcame him that he remained in the middle of the road shrieking with laughter, while the bride resumed her seat, with a charming smile, looking more beautiful than ever.'[15]

Never again would the laughter at Darmstadt be so carefree. Inexorably the political tensions were to tighten over the next decade as competition for arms, for commerce and political and strategic advantage all increased. None of the guests present at Darmstadt that October was to escape from the consequences of these changes, and of the revolutionary fervour in Russia and war in the Far East. There were to be personal tragedies, too, which would again confirm the savagery of the blows which from time to time struck down the Hessian families.

One tragedy was already imminent. There had been no Grand Duchess to help Ernie through the long-drawn-out festivities. One of Queen Victoria's last matches had broken up in divorce nearly two years earlier. Ducky had proved as volatile as the horses she broke in and rode at wild speed around Wolfsgarten and through the Hessian forests. She made un undutiful, careless and hostile Grand Duchess to the people of Darmstadt. There could have been no greater contrast with Hesse's last Grand Duchess, Alice.

Victoria was the first to recognize the impossible nature of her younger brother's marriage, and the inevitability of its collapse. In November 1901 Ernie wrote to her in Malta: 'Now that I am calmer I see the absolute impossibility of going on leading a life which was killing her & driving me nearly mad. For to keep up your spirits & a laughing face while ruin is staring you in the eyes & misery is tearing your heart to pieces is a struggle which is fruitless. I only tried for her sake. If I had not loved her so, I would have given it up long ago ... My last years have been a living hell to

209

me ... You have been a sister to me like there are few – God bless you for all your love.'[16]

The next month, divorce ended what had once been such a passionate marriage, and the unfortunate little Elizabeth split her life between her two adoring parents. It is said that the child died of excessive love. Medically, it was from a rare form of ambulatory typhoid. Soon after Alice's and Andrew's wedding, Ernie took Elizabeth to stay with Nicky and Alicky at Skierniewice, Nicky's shooting lodge in Poland. She died there suddenly on 15 November 1903. Ernie, almost dead with grief, came back with her body, which was placed alongside those of Grand Duchess Alice and Frittie and May in the Rosenhöhe.

Victoria left for Darmstadt to comfort her brother. The palace was as hushed as she remembered it after the death of her mother and baby sister fifteen years earlier. She was kind and sympathetic to Ernie. But her attitude to the tragedy showed a strong contrast with the late Queen's, who would *not* have approved of her grand-daughter's briskness. 'My poor brother is very quiet and resigned in his grief. Sorrow is so much easier to bear when your recollections of a person are only happy ones & no bitterness is mixed with them. He will continue missing his dear little child terribly, but there is no reason to fear he will brood and mope over his loss.'[17]

The next tragedy was quick to follow. While Louis, in charge of naval intelligence in London, was watching the movements of the German Fleet, and the Russian Baltic Fleet as it made its painful way East, Victoria went to stay in Germany, where Prince Henry was observing the critical naval situation with equal keenness from the other side. A few weeks later, and after she had returned to London, an urgent message called her to Russia. The nihilists had at last got Ella's Serge. He had in fact recently given up his duties as Governor General of Moscow, which had made him so detested for his firm rule, because he felt so out of sympathy with Nicky's new 'soft' policy.

Serge had been busy for some days clearing out his private possessions from his office, and was on his way to continue this work after lunch. Moscow was in the throes of a February thaw, and the sound of falling snow and ice from the rooftops was very like explod- ing bombs. But Ella recognized one sound as more lethal than that of falling snow. She ran for her carriage and in a minute was at the spot where the assassination had taken place. There was already a crowd, and people tried to keep her back. But she pushed her way forward.

'They were gathering up his remains,' she told Victoria when her sister arrived to comfort her, 'but my feeling at the gruesome sight was only "Hurry, hurry, Serge hates blood and mess."'[18]

When Victoria travelled to Moscow in the summer of 1906, she found Ella still in a state of deep distress – a pathetic contrast with the bright and effervescent younger sister of her childhood. She was living at Illinskoje surrounded by armed guards. She had converted one of the guests' houses in the park into a nursing home and was caring for incurably wounded soldiers from the Russo-Japanese war. The younger members of the Imperial family thought she over-indulged them and resented the way she requisitioned so many of the carriages for taking the soldiers out for drives. Ella did not care.

Everywhere Victoria saw evidence of unhappiness and unrest, as if the Russia she had known as a child was as lost for ever as Ella's old laughter and gaiety. There was the smell of burning in the air when she left Illinskoje with Nona and the light of distant flames lit up the horizon. The mounted guard remained close and alert until the train drew into the station and carried them away towards St Petersburg.

The atmosphere was just as tense in the capital. Assassinations of army officers and high officials were commonplace. At the station where Victoria and Nona arrived a General had just been shot dead while sitting on a bench with his wife and mother.

Nicky and Alicky, too, were in a state of deep depression. 'My heart bleeds to think of the disgusting things which have happened,' Nicky had just written to his mother. 'I feel very tired in mind . . .'[19]

The losses and humiliations of the defeat by Japan, followed by the uprisings all over the Empire, the mutiny of the battleship *Potemkin* in the Black Sea following the near-annihilation of Admiral Rozhestvensky's fleet at Tsu-Shima, Serge's assassination, the loss of friends and relatives – there seemed to be no end to the horrors for the Russian Imperial family.

As Nicky had feared, what he had told that little girl in Windsor Park had come true; and no one would ever tell him the truth again. Perhaps worst of all, and still a secret within the family, the court doctors and one or two of the nursemaids, was one dreadful truth.

Like Victoria's baby brother Frittie, Irène's son Waldemar, like her dear Uncle Leopold and other of her relatives, when the beloved, the precious-beyond-calculation little Tsarevitch Alexei fell down bumps and bruises appeared on his arms and legs and became dark blue swellings that sometimes made the two-year-old boy scream out in pain. Alexei was a haemophilic, and, in that July of 1906, the family's long ordeal had just begun.

Only in the faces of the four winsome little girls, Olga – now ten – Tatiana, Marie and Anastasia, did Victoria see any happiness at Peterhof.

Victoria's one public function was in keeping with the mournful times. Late in August she accompanied Nicky and Alicky to Cronstadt, the naval base from which Admiral Rozhestvensky's fleet had sailed with such imperial high hopes only two years earlier. Here, with her sister and brother-in-law, Victoria inspected the battle-scarred warships *Cesarewitch*, *Slawa* and *Bogatyr*, back from the Far East and almost the only survivors of the war. They made a sad but somehow fitting symbol of the condition of this once confident and happy country.

It was, as always, a relief to return to Darmstadt, which more than ever in the years leading to 1914 became a neutral haven from the crises that threatened to demolish the complex web of family links, from Balmoral to Athens, from Madrid to St Petersburg.

At Wolfsgarten Victoria found Dickie, now six years old. He had been by himself at this beautiful *schloss*, riding, playing in the exquisite half-life-size house Uncle Ernie had built for his little Elizabeth, and being thoroughly indulged by all the loving servants. To this day, Lord Mountbatten returns as often as he can to the last family home in Hesse to relax in the beauty of Wolfsgarten and recall childhood memories.

Georgie had become a naval cadet the previous year, and now he arrived on leave, as proud to show off his Royal Navy uniform about Darmstadt as his father had been nearly forty years earlier. Louise had travelled with him from England, and they all moved to Heiligenberg where Alice and Andrew joined them. And now Victoria was a grandmother, and Alice brought with her little Margarita, her daughter of eighteen months. Later Louis turned up, and for a short time the family was complete in their only permanent home.

Victoria was relieved to see that her brother's second marriage was a great success. They all loved his new wife, Eleonore, Princess of Solms-Hohensolms-Lich ('Onor'), and all Darmstadt went *en fête* when she gave birth to her first boy, George, on 8 November 1906. He was given the second name Donatus ('Don') 'in a sense of gratitude for the long-wished-for heir being given them'.[20]

Amidst the joys of Christmas at Heiligenberg that year, with families united and happy, tobogganing, snowballing, skating, playing with their healthy new babies, Victoria remembered the worries and fears of her two sisters in Russia; and remembered, too, these words of anguished warning uttered by her grandmother: – 'Don't let them go to Russia, Victoria . . .'

Early in the New Year 1907, Louis returned to his duties. For three more years, Victoria continued the restless, peripatetic life of a naval officer's wife which she had endured for most of the time since she had married. This meant complicated and far-sighted packing, arranging for houses, preparation for any number of contingencies, plans for family meetings and always a heavy correspondence. She often spoke at this time of 'the constant state of uncertainty of naval families'. Somehow, through all the to-ing and fro-ing, the children got educated, were taken on visits, their portraits painted by Laszlo.

On the one hand, Dickie's enthusiasm for pets had to be indulged – there was his first dog, Scamp, which his Great Aunt Louise, Duchess of Argyll, gave him, a little lamb, Milly, which he took everywhere, white mice by the score. On the other hand, Victoria somehow managed to feed her own voracious appetite for culture and self-improvement. Always, wherever she went, on P & O ships bound for Malta, on the train to Athens to visit Alice and Andrew, in rented houses in London, or hotels in Dover, Paris or Naples, there were several books close at hand, which she consumed and argued over with herself and anyone else who would listen.

She kept a meticulous record of her reading in little leather volumes inscribed 'Books I Have Read'. In a typical three-month period, there are twenty-one in May, June and July, 1903, those with a * against them being read for the first time. They included:

* Opinions Sociales par Anatole France
* A Life of Shakespeare by Sidney Lee
  Historic Oddities & Strange Events by the Rev Baring-Gould (in part aloud to L)

L'Art de la Lecture par Legouvé aloud to L & N.K. (Louis & Nona Kerr)
* A Handbook of the History of Philosophy by Ernest Belfort Bax
* A Diary of the Siege of the Legations in Peking 1900 by Nigel Oliphant
* The Prots, a weird Romance by Dudbroke (lent me by Andrea)
* The Riddle of the Sands by Erskine Childers (aloud to L)
* Gilbert White's Selborne

And 'on journey to H.B.' [Heiligenberg] Journal d'une qui sen fiche, par Gyp and Die Macht der Stunde von Paul Heyse.

Victoria relished new ideas like a gourmet sampling new tastes. Some people laughed, especially at her more radical ideas, but rarely behind her back; and certainly no one was bored by them. Not surprisingly, she adored George Bernard Shaw and all he stood for. In London in January 1907 she inevitably went to see his new play *A Doctor's Dilemma*. 'It is much the wittiest thing I have seen for a long time & was very well acted. The man is a remarkably able satirist & it is somewhat refreshing once in a way,' she wrote about it, 'to see the veil of humbug ... torn off people & things – no wonder the public winces . . .'21

Left-wing humbug angered her as much as reactionary humbug. On her way out to Malta in 1907, for almost the last time, she found that the future Lord Strabolgi and member of the Admiralty War Staff, Lieutenant J. M. Kenworthy, had been detailed to look after her on board the warship in which she embarked at Genoa. 'Though a socialist,' she noted, 'he treated our maids and servants with a haughtiness they had never met before.'

Although a restless life for her youngest child, it was a marvellously stimulating upbringing for young Dickie. During those sensitive and susceptible years from six to ten, he was much with his mother and became infected with her wide and exciting enthusiasms. These could be for subjects as distant in time as the Paleolithic Age – for her interest in archaeology was as strong as ever and she was now a noted authority – or as recent as contemporary technological revolutions.

Brother Ernie, noted patron of the arts, also supported the sciences. At Wolfsgarten the Grand Duke arranged a flight in the Zeppelin *Victoria Louise* with an extravagant caviare-and-champagne lunch on board for the whole family, which included Dickie. A visit to the first exhibition of airships and aeroplanes at Frankfurt in the summer of 1909 made lifelong aviation enthusiasts of Victoria and Dickie. 'All the flying machines had much trouble in leaving the ground and did not fly very far nor high,' Victoria noted, 'but they were very manageable and dived under ropes stretched between high poles.'[22] She was particularly impressed by the flying of de Caters and Blèriot.

Dickie, now aged nine, would have done anything to get airborne again. He had done so for the first time three years earlier when he was only six. In 1906 Uncle Ernie had arranged for a Parsifal (Blimp) airship to come to Wolfsgarten to take the family for a flip. Dickie was considered far too young for flying and had reconciled himself to watching others of the family going up. At the last second new ballast was suddenly needed to compensate for the expansion of the gas because of the sun. Uncle Ernie's hand reached down, grasped Dickie's collar, and hauled him on board.

By this time Louis was enthusiastically supporting the development of naval flying, and Victoria, Louise and Dickie on one never-to-be-forgotten occasion all in turn bumped off the ground in a Short biplane.

'The planes were not made to carry passengers,' Victoria recalled, 'and we perched securely attached on a little stool holding on to the flyer's back.'[23]

Georgie was another aviation enthusiast, and like his father saw a great future for the new machines in the Royal Navy. Describing the activities of the pioneer naval pilot, Lieutenant Charles Samson, he wrote to his mother: 'He runs down into the water & then rises off the water flying about over the ships, & right out to sea. He lands in the water between & amongst all the ships with the greatest ease, though the harbour is cram full of ships, & rises again equally easily.'[24] It all seemed wonderful and magical.

For most people of intelligence and sensitivity, the years leading to 1914 were full of apprehension. Victoria was deeply concerned about the growing threat of war while she was also proud of the leading part Louis was now playing in the preparations if the worst should happen. She could remember so clearly, when she was younger than her own youngest child, those poignant and gruesome sights at Darmstadt during the Franco-Prussian war. And even in the years the world regarded as peaceful, so many of her friends and relations, like Liko, had died in minor campaigns, or in that long and bloody war in South Africa.

In 1912 her own family became closely involved again. Greece joined with Bulgaria, Serbia and Montenegro to drive the Turks out of Thrace and Macedonia where they were persecuting the

Christian population. Andrew was given the rank of major and was appointed to the staff of his brother, Crown Prince Constantine. He went off to the front, leaving behind Alice with her three girls, one only an infant. Nona Kerr offered to go out to help her and perhaps do some nursing. 'You are a trump,' Victoria commented. 'It would be a great comfort to me if Alice had so true a friend and practical head with her . . .'[25]

News of massacres, of the butchering of prisoners on both sides, filled the newspapers. Louis was now at the very centre of power in London, and besides her anxiety about the war in the Balkans and the welfare of her precious daughter and grandchildren, she knew as well as the Prime Minister himself how acute was the danger of a much greater conflagration in Europe: Sarajevo was only two years away.

Some weeks after Nona had arrived in Greece and when she had already seen many of the sufferings of the people, Victoria wrote to her: 'I can understand how sick you must be of war & all it means, when one sees it close by. Were it not that it teaches us what a feeble thing is human life, & what a great thing the human spirit is compared to the frail body it inhabits, I do not think one could look war in the face, without breaking one's heart over it . . . The European outlook is gloomy again, Austria & Russia cannot agree over the Albanian boundary . . .'[26]

Georgie provided one brief light note to the Balkan war. He was now serving on board the battleship *Colossus* in the Home Fleet. Britain was at that time building two giant Dreadnoughts for the Turkish navy, and British men-of-war often carried a Turkish naval officer or two as observers. With the outbreak of war with Greece this was no longer appropriate. 'We dispatched our Turk to the front today,' Georgie wrote to his mother. 'I warned him not to get too close to Andrew, as he is rather fat and a good mark.'[27]

Sadly, it was Andrew's father who became a mark. A few weeks later, with the successful completion of the campaign against Turkey, King George of Greece was assassinated. His eldest son had recently marched triumphantly into Salonika, and the King – who had never believed in formality or armed escorts – arrived soon after. On 18 March 1913 he went for a walk with only an A.D.C. and was shot through the heart at point-blank range.

In 1913 Louise was a fine-boned aristocratic-looking young woman of twenty-four, with beautiful eyes, 'the Mountbatten nose', and a strong chin. She did not have any of her older sister's classical beauty, but after an awkward adolescence she was now graceful in her movements and was undeniably attractive. She had had a number of proposals but had not yet found anyone to match up to her *beau ideal* – her own father. A few years earlier King Edward VII had made it clear that he would like her to marry King Manoel of Portugal in order to strengthen the ties with 'England's oldest ally'. King Manoel had proposed, but Louise had turned him down, which displeased the Kings of both Portugal and England. Uncle Bertie wanted Louis and Victoria to press Louise on the point, but with typical Hessian enlightenment, they refused to apply pressure.

Dickie was not without his problems at this time as he was already experiencing his first trials of strength with the difficulties of being a prince. Like Georgie, there was never any doubt about his career. As night follows day, he would go into the Royal Navy. No alternative ever crossed his mind. His was a naval birth, a naval infancy, a naval childhood. At five he was the idol and unofficial mascot of his father's flagship at Malta and Gibraltar.

'He was a sore trial to me,' one officer remembered, 'for if he was not up aloft, he was down in the stokehold getting as black as a sweep; and he would have fallen overboard and been drowned several times over except that I detailed a specially chosen able-seaman to act as his dry nurse.'[28]

At nine he was dashing around Kiel harbour, in and out of German men-o'-war, in the despatch vessel S.M.S. *Carmen* with 'Uncle Harry'.[29] On holiday from preparatory school, he would be found on board his older brother's ship, admiring and learning.

Like Kaiser Wilhelm Dickie doodled warship designs at every opportunity. Not that his enthusiasms were narrowly naval. He was already fascinated by photography, and moving photography at that. He loved horses, besides his smaller pets, and was riding at three years. His lifelong love affair with cars began with the family's Wolseley Stellite.

Dickie was learning syntax in English and German at six years, and Victoria saw to his education until he went away to Locker's Park School, in Hertfordshire, as a boarder at the age of ten. The school was accustomed to having boys of elevated birth, which diminished the problems associated with being a prince. But it still made a difference if you went, say, to Windsor Castle and luncheon with the King for your Sunday outing instead of to The

King's Arms Hotel at Berkhamsted. You also had to be careful what you said to the other boys, and how you said it. It was a test for which Victoria diligently prepared him.

For example, when the King died in May 1910, Dickie had to take his part with the rest of the family at the funeral. As always, Victoria's instructions were clear and precise. 'All is arranged about your clothes, so that you need not trouble yourself about anything, as I have thought about & arranged all . . . You will try hard not to think about it,' she continued sternly, 'when your thoughts are needed for your work, also that you will not talk to the other boys too much about it . . .'[30]

Throughout Dickie's three years at Locker's Park, Victoria's letters to him are full of wise advice, affectionately expressed, filled out with domestic and family news. Early on, after receiving a good report on him, she writes: 'I am proud to know you have made such a good beginning by your conduct and diligence, for I know it was not always easy for you. Nothing makes Papa & me so happy as to see that our children are doing their best at work & are honest & brave. Cleverness is not the chief thing, it is the willingness to do right & the effort made for it that really counts.'[31]

Victoria badly missed her younger boy and she could not always keep her feelings of deprivation out of her letters. She knew, too, that he missed her. But she never allowed herself to resort to what she called 'mawkish sentiment'. 'All one's life,' she wrote to Dickie just after his tenth birthday, 'is made up of pain & pleasure, meeting & parting & I have always tried not to let my mind dwell on the sad things, but to be grateful for the pleasant things I have had & to look forward to those that are coming; otherwise ones heart aches too much. You must try to do the same & to be busy with the work & play which each day brings so as to draw your thoughts away from sadness & to make each day useful & agreeable . . .

'You know I love you very much my dear boy,' she continues, '& it makes no difference if I am nearer or farther from you in my feelings & thoughts – & if you needed me much, I would come to you from anywhere . . . In three weeks & a half we shall be together again . . .'[32]

From all accounts Locker's Park was a well run school. The headmaster, Percy Christopherson, and his wife were an efficient and understanding couple whom the boys liked. Dickie seems to have got on well with the rest of the staff, too, except – like Louis in his early days in the Navy – with the French master.

Perhaps it was because an accomplished German brings out the worst in a Frenchman – or did the Franco-Prussian war still rankle? Dickie was frequently badly treated by him. He wrote home to his mother about the injustices he suffered at his hands. 'I agree in thinking the master was unfair to you,' she replied, '& that his excuse afterwards was not quite truthful probably, but you must not forget that masters are only ordinary human beings & that this one has evidently a hasty temper; when his anger had passed . . . he probably felt he had been unfair himself & repented of it. It would have been better if he had said so, instead of giving you a fancy explanation, but the mistaken pride of a grown person towards a boy prevented him. Do not judge him too hardly for his fault & bear him malice for it.'[33]

There was so much for the young boy to learn at this time besides his school work, and Victoria's sense of responsibility for his character building and instruction was in no way reduced by reason of his being in the able hands of Mr Christopherson for most of the year. In any case, there were certain subjects that no school could be expected to teach. When he remembered family birthdays on his own he was praised; when he forgot them he was rebuked. When he received 'Cousin Georgie's' Coronation Medal, Victoria instructed him:

'You must address your letter: *His Majesty The King*[34]
        Buckingham Palace
        London
        (to be forwarded)

then it will reach him all right. You might write like this:

'*Dear Cousin George,*
 I thank Your Majesty very much for the Coronation Medal, which Papa has just sent me & which I am very proud & pleased to have.
 I hope to wear it often when I am an officer in your Naval Service.
      I remain
       Your dutiful & obedient cousin
        Louis Francis* Battenberg

More you need not write. Begin rather low down on the first page so that there are some words left over for the first inner page where the letter will end.

* the "of" is not necessary.'

There were rags and fights at Locker's Park but little deliberate ragging or cruelty. The system and the staff protected Dickie against that. It was different at Osborne. He progressed to this naval training college in the Isle of Wight in May 1913. Conditions for the cadets were not much improved over what they had been for his father in the *Ariadne*'s gun-room. Like his father, Dickie was handsome and deceptively tender-looking – a real mama's boy, his fellow cadets might have thought. On top of that he was a cousin of the King, his father was First Sea Lord, *and* German-born. Here was an irresistible target for any young bully, and there were plenty of them about.

At first, whatever he said, however he behaved, would be wrong. If he was silent or if he talked he would be accused of putting on airs. As a fat man attracts conversation about weight, so a prince attracts snob talk. At thirteen it was not easy to talk with friendly discretion about life in palaces and what the King of England is like.

Within a few days of his arrival, he wrote a letter to his parents which tells in a few words much about the boy as he was then, and the man he was to become. 'All my term greatly pity me,' he writes, 'because I have without the least exaggeration been asked over 100 times my name, whether I was a prince, our Cook's name (the only thing I refuse) etc. I get pointed at, have my cap knocked off . . . However I am now so used to this I don't mind it much.' And he concludes on a perky note: 'Have you seen my photo in the Daily Graphic, everybody shows it to me.'[35]

Two weeks later he was having his first real trouble, and showing that he was prepared to stand up for himself. Now there is a note of Mountbatten pride in achievement in his tone. '. . . I have had a fight with Scott [Admiral Sir Percy Scott's son] because, when he knocked my cap off a lot of chaps, in second term, egged me on to fight him in the end, which I did. I was expecting a 2 day's 3 [punishment] for it, but instead of that I have become a hero. My own term nearly went crazy about it . . . all came & said something like this: "Did you fight Scott?" (Yes) "Did you lick him?" (I think so) "You're a brick." And then I was patted very hard on the back . . .'[36]

But Dickie was not always the hero. There was a good deal of aggression on both sides, and he fought hard against the attempts to 'cut him down to size', though in fact the boy did his utmost to make his fellow cadets forget that he was a prince and the son of the First Sea Lord, and certainly did not act in a superior way. A year later we find him writing to Victoria: 'I have only got one real chum left now, Graham. Stopford got so ragged at being chums with me that he has chucked it . . .'

The first rigorous year at Osborne passed. Like the rest, Dickie became hardened to the spartan regime. He experienced the same sharp contrasts between the conditions of his service life and his private life on leave at Heiligenberg and Peterhof. He fell in love with Nicky's and Alicky's lovely Marie and determined to marry her. In the summer he sailed through the Kiel Canal in the Russian Imperial yacht *Standart* and stayed also with Aunt Irène and her family and talked naval affairs with Uncle Harry. He saw much of his elder sister and took a keen interest in all his nieces, though he was exasperated when Alice produced yet another girl in July 1914. 'Please congratulate Alice from me,' he asked his mother, 'but it was silly not to have a boy for once in a way. Why is she called Sophy?' (Sophie, now Princess George of Hanover, Prince Philip's sister 'Tiny', named after her aunt, Queen Sophie of the Hellenes.)

IO

'One is almost tempted to discern in some of the things he said to Prince Louis the workings of a disordered brain.'

WINSTON CHURCHILL *of Kaiser Wilhelm II*

JUST twelve years before that War declaration night of 4 August 1914, Louis and Victoria had by fateful chance been occupied, each in their own way, in major British and German manoeuvres, both of which were to have a powerful influence on the strategy of the Great War.

After the coronation of King Edward VII and Queen Alexandra in 1902, Victoria had chosen to return to Germany rather than to Malta with Louis, who was then serving as captain of H.M.S. *Implacable* in the Mediterranean Fleet and expected to be away on a cruise. From Heiligenberg, she travelled with her brother Ernie, recently divorced, his little daughter Elizabeth who was only seven and had barely a year to live, and her own Alice, Louise and Georgie, to Friedberg for the great German Army manoeuvres.

On horseback with Alice and Nona, and with a senior staff officer present to answer her questions, Victoria watched the wheeling columns of troops, the racing gun limbers, the columns of cavalry in their nineteenth-century finery and with their nineteenth-century weapons.

In one exercise Victoria saw the Kaiser on a magnificent charger place himself at the head of his Cuirassiers, Uhlans, Hussars and Dragoons, and amidst a perfect thunder of hoofbeats and cries, put to flight 'the invading infantry'. But the next day, Victoria noted, it was a different story. By arranging themselves in close formation and supported by machine-gun fire the infantry demonstrated how

222

they could resist any number of cavalry assaults. As Umpire-in-Chief, Wilhelm had to concede victory to the foot soldiers and, with his senior generals, reluctantly admit that the golden days of the cavalry in modern warfare were numbered.

Lessons in mutual fire support and the use of cover learnt by the British in the Boer War were also shown in these important 1902 manoeuvres. They were, as always, an awesome demonstration of power and mobility by the greatest army in the world, and Victoria could not restrain her fascination in all that she saw, in spite of her strong feelings of repugnance towards war.

While Victoria watched through the dust the changing patterns of colour and listened to the cries of command and the beat of hooves, Louis was planning how best to escape with his fleet from a Greek harbour in the British naval manoeuvres of September–October 1902. He was one of a small group of the Royal Navy's radical intelligentsia which believed that one of the service's basic strategical tenets, the principle of close blockade, had been destroyed by the new technology. In the Napoleonic wars British strategy had been founded upon the close blockade of the enemy's ports. For months on end and sometimes under the most appalling conditions, Collingwood, Nelson and other British admirals, had cut off the enemies' trade and close-blockaded the French and Spanish fleets, saving the country from invasion – those 'storm-beaten ships, upon which the Grand Army never looked, stood between it and the dominion of the world', as the American historian Mahan so memorably put it.

The more advanced thinkers in the Royal Navy believed that the torpedo and the mine, and the *reliable* high speed of the modern steam fleet had put an end to the close blockade. In future wars enemy ports would be watched only by swift light craft while the battle fleet remained as a distant threat behind its booms and minefields, protected by its torpedo-boat flotillas.

The fleet manoeuvres of 1902 were planned to test this theory. Three fleets were to take part. Fleets 'A' and 'B', consisting of twelve battleships, sixteen cruisers and fourteen destroyers, were ordered to blockade the Greek port of Argostoli, containing Fleet 'X', consisting of eight mainly slower and older battleships, six cruisers, seven destroyers and some small torpedo boats. The defined purpose of the exercise was 'to endeavour to ascertain what risks are involved in keeping such a close watch on a fleet in a defended port as to ensure bringing it to action if it issues therefrom'.[1]

The C.-in-C. of the Mediterranean Fleet, Admiral Sir Compton Domvile, commanded 'A' Fleet, and he had under him Vice-Admiral Sir Arthur ('Tug') Wilson who commanded 'B' Fleet. 'X' Fleet was to be under the command of Rear-Admiral Burges Watson. But he was taken seriously ill at the last moment, and Louis, as senior captain, automatically took his place. He was given the temporary rank of Commodore; but of vastly greater importance, he was given the opportunity to prove his belief that, in the new steel navy of fast battleships and faster torpedo boats, he could escape from a much more powerful close-blockading fleet. The opportunity had been given to him by a stroke of great good fortune. Now all that he had to do was to exploit it. He did so, with great panache.

The rules stated that 'A' and 'B' Fleets could steam within 8,000 yards of Argostoli and its imaginary shore batteries, that 'X' Fleet had to steam at night with navigation lights showing for the first fifty miles, but that within this distance it would be immune from torpedo attack. Louis viewed the problems of escape with a fresh eye. First he tucked his heavy ships in a corner of the harbour which it was theoretically impossible for them to penetrate but which also made them invisible from the sea. Here they were moored a mere two hundred and fifty yards apart while his destroyers carried out carefully planned attacks on the enemy's light forces watching the harbour. Their 'victims' numbered two small cruisers and eight destroyers for the 'loss' of one destroyer and three little torpedo boats.

As a *ruse de guerre* Louis had one of his colliers disguised as a German steamer, and with a torpedo boat lashed along her starboard side, sent her out too. To improve his intelligence service, he landed nearly 400 officers and men, with the most up-to-date wireless and telephonic equipment, and ordered them to spread out along the highest points on both sides of his base to give warning of his adversary's movements.

A few days later, as the light faded, he sent out his cruisers with navigation lights at full brilliancy (visible at some 20 miles) and duplicated abreast the mainmast to confuse the enemy into thinking that the battleships were emerging too. They kept extra close order to avoid wide gaps. The ether was filled with bogus wireless messages which also served to jam any of the enemy's signals, rockets were fired into the night sky and signal guns sounded out as if the whole Royal Navy was putting on some anarchistic fleet review.

Shortly after this, Louis ordered the battleships to unmoor. Their white upperworks were covered in canvas, the yellow funnels painted grey. The eight men-o'-war, averaging around 15,000 tons, crept out of the narrow, shallow anchorage in the dark, with navigation lights dimmed to the minimum legal brilliancy which meant they would be invisible beyond two miles. One of them damaged its rudder post on a rock, but the other seven continued out to sea, taking the opposite course to the cruisers and rapidly working up to their maximum speed of fifteen knots and holding it for four hours until the stokers were nearly dead from exhaustion.

The line of battleships, their wash scoring white the dark sea and their black smoke marking their passage against the stars, was eventually spotted by two of the enemy's patrolling warships. Both had been 'put out of action' in earlier engagements, but they did not know this at the time. In any case they failed to get their message through, and Louis's 'X' Fleet had a ten-hour start before 'A' and 'B' Fleets learned of his escape. He was pursued at seventeen knots but reached his destination in Sardinia safely and with hours to spare.

The reaction to this success was gratifying and spectacular. The King and Jacky Fisher were among those who telegraphed their congratulations. Less formally, an unnamed sailor was reported to have commented: 'Six b——y British Admirals outside, one d——d foreigner inside was too clever for them all.'[2]

The effect on the Mediterranean Fleet was remarkable. Very few officers, least of all Admiral Watson, had believed it possible to escape through a close blockade of faster and more powerful and more numerous ships. The blockaders had revealed a number of shortcomings, that was true, but the cheeky ease with which Louis – a mere captain – had escaped with his forces virtually intact after committing substantial damage on the enemy made a lasting impression.

Argostoli did not lead to the immediate abandonment of the strategy of close blockade any more than the manoeuvres in Germany resulted in the Army scrapping its cavalry. But Louis's demonstration proved the radicals' case that the strategy of distant blockade in a war with Germany would have to be introduced. The southern North Sea, thick with mines and submarines, would be no place for the British battle fleet of the future, except as a battleground with the German fleet. The blockade would be exercised from distant bases in the Channel, in Scotland and the Orkney Islands; it need be no less effective for that.

When Louis went back to sea again two-and-a-half years after the Argostoli manoeuvres, he had behind him the high reputations he had gained both as a naval staff administrator and as a handler of a fleet. His new appointment in January 1905 was as Rear-Admiral Commanding the Second Cruiser Squadron of six fast and modern armoured cruisers, with his flag in H.M.S. *Drake*.

In the new alignments of power in Europe during the early years of the new century, the position of the United States was attracting increasing attention. President Theodore ('Teddy') Roosevelt was demonstrating that imperialism was not an exclusive European monopoly and that America could flex its muscles as well as Germany or France or Britain. The American Navy was growing apace along with the nation's economic power, and Roosevelt and the nation were proud of their fleet. 'I wish you could have been here the other day when we had the naval review,' the President wrote to Louis after they had met. 'We had twelve battleships and four armoured cruisers in line – not much of a fleet from the standpoint of the English Navy, but good from the standpoint of any other, and every ship modern, and, I believe, of first class fighting efficiency.'[3]

In 1904 the decision was made by the British government to secure closer and even more amiable relations with the United States. Among the plans was a visit by a crack naval squadron as a gesture of friendship and a demonstration of maritime strength. What better choice for Commander of the Squadron than an Admiral who was a Prince with a reputation for charm and elegant diplomacy?

Louis formally hoisted his flag on board H.M.S. *Drake* at the end of February 1905. Four days later, on the 27th, the Royal Standard was broken at the main as King Edward stepped on board to inspect the ship and her company, to take dinner and spend the night (in Louis's cabin).

The arrival was a moving moment for Louis. He was genuinely fond of the portly monarch who had been so kind and thoughtful when he had been a raw recruit of a boy with imperfect English, and had supported him so often since. 'The officers, in full dress, were drawn up on the quarter-deck in the order of their rank while His Majesty took up a position on the top of the admiral's companion-way, and Flag-Captain Mark Kerr called out each officer's name as he passed before His Majesty and saluted. The quarter-deck was gaily decorated with flags and electric lamps . . .'[4]

It was a pleasant, intimate evening in Louis's day cabin. Edward

VII made an informal speech to Louis and his staff, wished them godspeed on their important mission to the New World, and after dinner agreed to play bridge. He lost, to Mark Kerr, but this 'did not in the least upset his temper'[5] according to Louis's Flag-Captain. The next morning he breakfasted at a quarter to nine and then went up onto the quarter-deck where he was photographed with all the ship's officers before he went off in his barge for a cruise round the harbour.

The widowed Princess Beatrice and her daughter Ena, Jacky Fisher and other notables were received on board the cruiser before she sailed. (Victoria was not among those who saw off Louis. She was in Russia comforting Ella after Serge's assassination. It would be a long time before she again saw him but they were both reconciled to these separations. She once calculated that in the first ten years of their marriage they had been together for only three.)

Louis took his squadron to the Mediterranean to work up its efficiency to the highest possible peak. But, as always, there were social occasions too. The Kaiser came on board, and so did Queen Alexandra, and later on the King and Queen of Greece and the King and Queen of Portugal. In Greece he met Alice and Andrew, saw his first infant grandchild and attended Margarita's christening.

It was not until early August that Louis headed his six big cruisers west into the Atlantic. In order to avoid giving offence to Canada, and to console its government for the loss of the North American Station which Fisher had recently closed down, there was to be a visit to the Dominion on the way.

The reception at Ottawa was typical of Louis's experiences in Canada and the U.S.A. – flags and bunting, cheering crowds held back by the police, inspections and dinners and ceremonies. An encampment of seventy tents had been set up in Cartier Square and the face of the city was given a maritime colouring with the arrival of the 3,500 British bluejackets. At a luncheon on 23 August, the youthful Mackenzie-King, then President of the Canadian Club, spoke of 'how proud we are to do honor to a prince and an admiral' but 'prouder still to honor in your distinguished person, one who has not made

> "His high place the lawless perch of winged ambitions,
> Nor a vantage ground for pleasure",

but has given to the world another illustrious example ... of one who, endowed by birth and fortune with opportunities beyond the reach and power of other men, has, under the guidance of lofty ideals and a sense of the finest honor, seen well to recognize in opportunity, a responsibility and in capacity, a duty; and has consecrated both to the service of his country and the welfare of his fellowmen. Gentlemen, I ask you to fill your glasses . . .'

This sort of thing was repeated time and again throughout the tour. Always, Louis found it discomfiting. He was, in some ways, a vain man but his vanity was a private affair – his looks, his clothes, his decorations – and these public pronouncements on his qualities embarrassed him, partly because they demanded a reply and he did not at all care for public speaking – and especially in this case because he had picked up a heavy cold and could hardly speak anyway.

The United States was more fun, in spite of the continuing formalities and speech-making. He enjoyed himself with Teddy Roosevelt at the White House and showing off the seamanship of his squadron. At Annapolis the squadron was received by Rear-Admiral ('Fighting Bob') Robley Evans, the American C.-in-C., and from the first exchange of courtesies the Annapolis and Washington part of the programme was a great success. At a White House dinner Louis talked and listened so hard to the President that he had to wave aside dish after dish. Mark Kerr was astonished to hear him say afterwards, 'I must get something to eat'.

The squadron left for New York on 8 November. Louis determined to make a spectacular run up the Hudson River, where he was to moor his ships two cables apart and two cables downstream from Admiral Robley's fleet, in order to show New Yorkers, and the U.S. Navy, what British seamanship was all about, and also to celebrate the King's birthday.

The six armoured cruisers passed Sandy Hook in line ahead at eighteen knots, black smoke streaming from their funnels. Speed was eased off momentarily in shallow water, and then increased again. The pilot schooners awaiting them were ignored and they tore past the Statue of Liberty and the Battery.

'Abreast of Government Island,' wrote a bo'sun in the *Drake*, 'we broke the stars and stripes at our main and saluted the nation with twenty-one guns, which was promptly returned by the battery. A strong ebb tide was running, but we forged up the very congested Hudson in perfect alignment, which was much commented on by the sea captains in the port . . . Great crowds on the shore cheered enthusiastically, and whistles all over the river tooted forth greetings

. . . It was truly a magnificent sight – bands playing patriotic airs, guns booming, flags flying, whistles hooting, and multitudes cheering.'6

The river was thick with traffic and sightseers' boats. One ferry-boat skipper, determined not to allow the appearance of a few foreign ships (and showing off ones at that) to break his timetable, took his boat through the line with seven hundred passengers on board. Disaster on a fearful scale appeared inevitable. But at the last second the *Cornwall*'s captain took violent evasive action and missed the ferryboat by a few yards. The big cruiser regained her station at once. The ferryboat skipper got a rocket in the newspapers the next morning.

Half the U.S. Navy, and many thousands of New Yorkers, watched the anchoring. No one had seen anything like it before. The ships' engines were ordered full astern, the anchors were let go. Affecting a calmness they did not feel, the six captains watched the water to see if their ships would bring up before the cable of the first anchor was run out to a clinch and parted.

On the bridge of the *Drake* Mark Kerr took in the reports in turn and then told Louis that all his ships were in station and every cable intact. 'That's good,' Louis replied laconically.

At the same instant the dressing flags went up with the Royal Standard, and the Royal Salute was fired, and echoed by the American ships. Within two minutes great warships which had seemed hell-bent on a suicide course were at anchor in perfect position, dressed overall with flags flying and the smoke of saluting guns rising above the river.

At New York the work of 'creating good relations' began in earnest. For eleven days Prince Louis was given the full American treatment of hospitality, and shook hands and chatted with the people from all walks of life in the great city. On every day there was a luncheon and a dinner. One dinner for Louis and his staff was in China Town, and they were served by (non-Chinese) singing waiters. Louis was allotted one to himself, and this waiter was accorded a paragraph in the newspapers the next day. His name was Irving Berlin. Some forty years later, when he was in Europe entertaining the troops, Berlin recounted the events of that evening in detail to Victoria when he came for dinner at Broadlands. 'I was very proud,' he told her. 'It was the first time my name ever appeared in print.'

For Louis there were receptions and inspections, tours and balls, all requiring speeches. Towards the end he had almost no voice left and was close to becoming immobilized first with weariness and then with a sharp attack of gout. It all culminated in a farewell ball in the *Drake*, for which the ship had brought with her a special portable dancing floor. There was room for only 1,200, and ferocious was the competition among New York society for the prized invitations.

'It was,' commented the *Times*, 'one of the most notable affairs ever held in New York . . . Cheery and genial, with a cordial handshake and a pleasant word of greeting for everyone, Prince Louis of Battenberg last night welcomed representative America on board his flagship *Drake*, moored at the Cunard Line pier at the foot of Gansevoort Street . . . the Admiral-Prince stood erect, athletic, and looking an ideal sailor.'[7]

In an editorial after the squadron had sailed, the same paper commented: 'When he dropped anchor in these waters most Americans had a confused notion that he was a British Admiral only because he was a German Princeling, and may perhaps have been pardoned for inferring that he was much disposed to stand on punctilio and possibly to exact the very letter of the etiquette of his naval rank. Had this been the case, he might have spent his time here in an atmosphere of frigid correctness instead of the genial hospitality which has in fact enveloped him. But it took nobody who had dealings with him long to find out that though hereditarily a German Princeling, he was essentially a British sailor.' The *Times* noted the 'unbroken pleasantness' of the visit, the departure closing 'an incident of the very best international experience and augury'.[8]

Louis cherished for the rest of his life the warmest memories of this American 'experience' and became an ardent lover of America, a love he passed on to his two boys. In 1973 his younger son spoke again to the Canadian Club, reminding members of his father's visit and reading extracts from the chairman, Mackenzie-King's speech of welcome, which the same chairman had re-read to him in 1947. They were as apt today as they were then.

But Louis was also glad to get away at last. 'This is such an endless separation,' he wrote to Nona Kerr. 'Oh how thankful I shall be to find myself back once more at Gibraltar under normal conditions and to have you all with me once more – for I miss you quite as much as my children & *HER*.'[9]

With the completion of the last ceremonial, Louis wasted no time in getting back. When the six cruisers had passed Sandy Hook, they were ordered into line abreast and told to race home – yes, *race*, a flat-out race of 3,327 miles to Gibraltar!

Nothing like it had happened in the history of the Royal Navy, unless you include Nelson's pursuit of Villeneuve across the Atlantic exactly one hundred years earlier. Louis's squadron accomplished the passage in seven days and seven hours. He knew that if he sought permission from the Admiralty for such a daring and extravagant exercise, he would be turned down, probably with some salty comments. So he conducted it on his own initiative and told the Admiralty afterwards.

It can reasonably be claimed that another senior officer would have been reprimanded while Louis was congratulated. Here, for a change, was one of the advantages of privilege. The exercise was a most valuable one as it demonstrated the ability of those tough old reciprocating engines to withstand the rigours of war emergency and instilled confidence in the engine-room staff.

Jacky Fisher was the only other Admiral who conducted sustained high speed trials with his fleet at this time. 'It was war we were preparing for, when high speeds would be essential,' wrote one of Fisher's subordinates, 'if high speed meant wear and tear and breakdowns, let us, said he, find it out in peace. Let our designers design engines, boilers and machinery that would stand the strain.'[10]

Victoria had reserved rooms at Gibraltar for herself and Nona, Dickie and Louise, and they all arrived there by sea from Marseilles on 27 November expecting to have at least two days before the Squadron completed the Atlantic crossing. Instead, late that evening, Victoria was told that the *Drake* was only a few hours' steaming away and would arrive in the early hours of the morning.

At the unusually long range of 96 miles, Louis's flagship had got a wireless message to the battleship *New Zealand* en route to Cadiz, which had re-transmitted the message to Gibraltar. Soon, two armoured cruisers were seen approaching 'the Rock' at high speed, flames flickering from their tall funnels and dense clouds of black smoke trailing astern. They were the *Drake* and the *Berwick*. They had been racing neck-and-neck for over three thousand miles, and the race was not yet over.

On that last night the *Berwick* crept within a few cables-length of her flagship. In order to hold her off, every officer in the *Drake* except Louis, Mark Kerr, the navigating officer and the officer of the watch, were working in the bunkers helping to carry sacks of coal to the stokeholds. The *Drake* was not getting full power from her port engine and the *Berwick* continued to gain on her.

The flagship was just ahead when, at 1.15 a.m., Kerr ordered the signal, 'Ease speed and anchor as convenient'. Ten minutes later the *Drake* let go three cables off the New Mole at Gibraltar. She had averaged over 18.5 knots across the ocean. The *Berwick*'s speed was virtually identical, and the other four big ships were only a few hours behind.

Louis came ashore at once and made for the Grand Hotel where he was at last reunited with Victoria, and with Dickie and Louise the next morning. Georgie arrived on leave from Osborne a little later, and the family relaxed together and went on expeditions into Spain and attended shipboard parties.

Only once or twice during Louis's service career did Victoria find herself with her own family and with her husband's ship at Christmas. Although she had not yet been able to throw off the sadnesses and the horrors of her last visit to Russia, and she still grieved for Ella in her loss, it was wonderful to be with Louis again and to be able to throw herself into his life and the life of his flagship.

On Christmas Day the family visited the *Drake*, which was decorated all over with traditional evergreens brought out from England, and displayed the signal: 'A very happy Christmas to you and all your friends.' The whole ship's company attended Divine Service on deck in the mild, sunny weather. 'At noon a procession was formed,' one of the *Drake*'s company recorded, 'headed by the Princess, and a tour round the mess-deck was made, while the band kept playing the tunes, "The Roast Beef of Old England" etc. The mess decks were decorated with flags, evergreens, and coloured art papers, while the mess tables were bending with the weight of turkeys, hams, puddings . . .' Later, 'cheers, loud and long, were given for our Admiral and his charming wife, the Princess . . .'[11]

From the warmth of the Mediterranean Victoria and the children travelled by sea to Genoa and then overland to the crisp cold of a German winter. Heiligenberg always called them at this time of the year – the snow was so pure, the tobogganing in the hills and the parties in Darmstadt such fun. Louis took his squadron back to England, reported to the King and to Fisher on his American goodwill trip, and received the thanks of both for its success. Then he rejoined his family for a long period of leave.

An account of Louis's seagoing commands, from the little *Scout* of 1889 to his last twenty-two years later, risks becoming a monotonous eulogy. As a fleet commander he won at manoeuvres; his ships won every sporting cup and award, were top at gunnery and at smartness, and were always the happiest ships in the fleet. 'What the lower deck thought of Prince Louis can be summed up in three words,' one of his ex-signalmen wrote recently, 'We adored him.'[12]

There is no doubt that Prince Louis had a special place in the hearts of the lower deck. 'Jack Tar' tended to love a Prince anyway. A sense of romance was not yet quite dead among the less educated people, and Louis cut a romantic and dashing figure. Add to that the affection he reciprocated, his style and manner of approach to them, and it is easy to understand why he was truly loved by them.

Louis cared most solicitously for their welfare and health and was at all times absolutely just. He remembered their names and details of their families and home life. If they had a problem he would pursue it to its solution.

Some eight years after Louis had been Commander-in-Chief, Atlantic Fleet, his younger son Dickie was second-in-command of a very small man-of-war, one of the Portsmouth Escort Flotilla. He had, as a mess-mate in the wardroom, a well-educated, socialistically inclined Warrant Officer who had a poor opinion of senior officers and shared the general dislike of having to salute them when on leave ashore.

When this Warrant Officer heard that Prince Louis had received approval to do a cross-Channel escort trip onboard, in September 1918, he was dumbfounded and embarrassed. But Louis quickly put him at his ease and after the trip was over said that the lower deck tried to avoid saluting officers on leave, but that in the Atlantic Fleet their opinion of their Commander-in-Chief was so high in 1910 that when liberty men were ashore at Dover and saw Louis walking to his hotel they not only were proud to salute him but would double round the back streets to have a chance of saluting him again.

Midshipmen felt the same respect for Louis. Two of them have told of the breakfasts to which they would be invited in turn. 'We enjoyed this,' one of them recalls, 'and tucked into a good meal, after which the table was cleared, except for a large cup of coffee in front of everyone, and there would be much talk about something interesting that was going on in the world, or locally, and even we Mids felt we could and did join in, being so encouraged.'

Louis 'always seemed to have a fresh view and was not bound by what used to be done,' this officer added. 'I had a special contact with him as his A.D.C. and found him a most attractive personality.'[13]

'We sat one on his right and one on his left,' another midshipman at this time remembers. 'He talked to us as though we were grown up and completely without any condescension. He would often discuss with us European politics on which subject he was so expert ... He was a figure of immense dignity and great kindliness and modest with it ... To us and indeed to everyone in the ship he was the greatest Naval Officer of the day and *Prince of Wales* [flagship Atlantic Fleet 1908–10] the smartest of all ships.'[14]

Chatfield, one of the greatest sailors of the century and not easily given to offering praise, was then a captain. 'To serve in his Fleet,' he wrote of Louis, 'was an inspiration and education ... Prince Louis was perhaps the outstanding officer on the Flag list. He had had a most brilliant career at sea and at the Admiralty, and was a great tactician and fleet handler ... He was severe but just, a leader who had a marked influence on the minds of officers who served under him, as he also had a definite influence on the advance in tactics and progress in efficiency of the Navy as a whole.'[15]

The archives at Lord Mountbatten's home of Broadlands in Hampshire contain a substantial file of tributes to Louis which were sent to Victoria after he died. His Flag-Lieutenant, James Pipon, who reached flag rank and died recently at a ripe old age, described him as he saw Louis then; 'Prince Louis was a masterly and born handler of a fleet; I never met his superior. He always seemed to have a complete picture in his mind of the position of every unit of the fleet. His decisions were always prompt and never at fault. I remember on one occasion when some new signals for deploying the fleet were under trial, and when we were steaming at high speed, two ships began to turn the wrong way and a dangerous situation was at once counteracted by his instant order to the whole fleet to alter course together. Any hesitation would probably have resulted in a collision.'

Louis's Flag-Commander when he was C.-in-C. Atlantic Fleet in 1908, T. F. H. Beamish, saw Louis as an unusual combination, an intellectual and a great potential fighting seaman. 'Prince Louis undoubtedly deserved success,' he wrote. 'He achieved the affection and trust of the Service, and his brilliant career shows him as a great practical sea officer and administrator. He read much and widely, and history and languages gave him great pleasure.' But, Beamish continues, 'In every phase of strategy and tactics, and in the use of ships and weapons, his absorbing intention was to put the enemy in the worst possible position, to do him the maximum of injury, and while taking precautions, to be prepared to accept and take a risk with dash and intelligence.'

Louis and Mark Kerr made gunnery history in the *Drake*. The reform in British naval gunnery was as important, violent and swift as the reform in naval design and recruitment and training. Percy Scott, strongly backed by Fisher and Louis, was the Garibaldi of gunnery. Like Mark Kerr, with whom he had served with Prince Louis in the *Inconstant*, he was a peppery little man who made enemies easily. But, in the nick of time, he got gunnery officers shooting straight and fast. 'The gunnery Lieutenant who failed to make good – and success or failure was entirely in his hands – was swept away without mercy,' wrote an officer of this turbulent and uncomfortable period. 'Those who succeeded reaped the rewards of early promotion.'[16]

Louis and Kerr and the *Drake*'s Gunnery Lieutenant worked relentlessly on the flagship's gunlayers until no other ship in the Squadron, or the Fleet, or the Royal Navy for that matter, could equal their record. On 6 December 1906, *The Times* told the world: 'The *Drake* occupies the position of top ship in the whole of the fleets for this test . . . [She] has now just completed her battle practice and shows the most marvellous shooting, shooting which is unequalled in the Navies of the world. At a range of four miles, 133 rounds were fired and 105 hits were made, or a percentage of 79 . . .' Again the congratulatory telegrams poured in, from the King, from Fisher . . . When he read of these results, Teddy Roosevelt sent his own Inspector of Target Practice to England to see how it was done.

Results like these, at target practice and in manoeuvres, were bought at a price paid both by Louis and his officers and men. Chatfield tells of the difficulties encountered in extricating the great battleships of the Atlantic Fleet out of Dover harbour with its breakwaters and narrow exit.

'The *Prince of Wales*, casting off from her berth at the Admiralty jetty, would steam out of the eastern entrance flying the signal, "Single line ahead, ten knots". Woebetide the captain who was late turning his ship and failed to follow in the wake of his "next ahead" at two cables' distance. "Take up your appointed station" would be run up at the flagship masthead. "Manoeuvre badly executed" would pillory some captain publicly; but a contrary signal would be made just as readily when justified.'[17]

Any officer arriving on Louis's bridge for the first time while at sea, and knowing nothing of his reputation, might imagine briefly that here was a bland, soft and pampered serene highness – his command a favoured sinecure. He appeared deceptively malleable and gentle, he spoke quietly and always with extreme courtesy, and was always immaculately turned out. 'We midshipmen were fascinated by the sight of Prince Louis,' Commander David Joel recalls, 'as he invariably appeared in white flannel trousers with creases at the side, in the manner made fashionable by King Edward VII, and surprisingly *brown* boots!'

But there is a different picture of him down in his cabin after his fleet has arrived at Berehaven in Ireland. One of his captains has committed the serious offence of letting go his anchor late, ruining the symmetry of the anchored fleet in the harbour. Untidiness was something Louis could not bear. It was inefficient in peace, dangerous in war. 'Up went the signal,' another of his captains remembered, '"Captains repair on board the flagship". How well do I see again the tall, handsome, black-bearded Commander-in-Chief standing on one side of his cabin table and the eight captains arranged like a lot of schoolboys on the other. Some of them were at least twelve years older than I was, elderly gentlemen, unable to march with the times, never to be employed as admirals, but doing their last service, happy in command of their ships.

'Prince Louis addressed them on their work during the cruise to Bantry Bay, lightly censuring and praising. Then, in a more severe voice, "Captain Z, you did not let go your anchor when my signal came down; if you do that again I shall send you to sea; I insist on discipline in my captains."'[18]

There was still plenty of fire in Louis in his mid-fifties. He rode hard, and this was the time when he embraced flying with such emthusiasm. Physically, he was as strong as ever. There is a story, recently come to light, of his being caught in a violent thunderstorm when travelling along the Prince of Wales pier at Dover from his flagship to his office in Naval Headquarters. He was in a hackney carriage drawn by a pair of horses, which were suddenly struck by lightning. The left horse died instantly, and the other was burnt all down one side and in a great state of panic. The driver was blinded. Louis leaped out, picked him up and carried him some two hundred yards back to Waterloo Mews where the driver kept his stables. This was the action of a man of vigour and decision.[19]

Louis had to ride out many another storm during his last period at sea – a period that was longer than he expected it would be. The six years from the time he relinquished his appointment as D.N.I. until he returned to the Admiralty in 1911 marked the increasingly discordant Fisher regime and its uncomfortable aftermath. The voice of 'the syndicate of discontent' sounded increasingly shrill and ugly as it raged and fought against the truculently introduced naval reforms. The clash of personalities and the struggle for power within and outside the Admiralty was like a precursor to the Armageddon in the North Sea which both sides knew was inevitable and imminent.

Fisher saw the fight in simple black-and-white terms. So did his enemies. For that reason Beresford, Lambton, Milne, Custance, Noel, Wemyss and other of the leading counter-revolutionaries believed Louis was a steady and blind disciple to Fisher, as well as royally privileged and German-born – a most poisonous combination in their eyes.

At this time Edward VII, according to Ponsonby, 'didn't pay much attention to Beresford';[20] and the Navy, if it was still fit to fight, would soon be locked in battle with Louis's land of birth. They did not understand how fiercely Louis was fighting against Fisher's arbitrary and provocative methods and some of his policies, too. They did not understand how uneven was the relationship between the two admirals, how Fisher would at one time describe Louis as the greatest flag officer in the Navy and fight to secure his future at the Admiralty, and at another time would be writing freely that he was not to be trusted. Fisher knew he had to have Louis with him, but he never forgave him for refusing to act as one of his 'spies', as all his followers were ordered, to report secretly to him on the activities of their C.-in-C.

For his part, Louis was outraged at the way he considered Fisher put at hazard the nation's whole naval defence structure by creating a new 'Home Fleet' in order to reduce the relative strength of the fleet commanded by Beresford, who refused to resign. Of this dangerous spitefulness, Louis commented, 'Why, it is criminal. I can use no other word.'[21]

As Winston Churchill was to write later, 'There is no doubt whatever that Fisher was right in nine-tenths of what he fought for. His great reforms sustained the power of the Royal Navy at the most critical period in its history . . . After a long period of serene and unchallenged complacency, the mutter of distant thunder could be heard. It was Fisher who hoisted the storm-signal and beat all hands to quarters. He forced every department of the Naval Service to review its position and question its own existence. He shook them and beat them and cajoled them out of slumber into intense activity. But the Navy was not a pleasant place while this was going on.'[22]

It was an unpleasant place for everyone in high command, but no one suffered more than Louis. Fisher was attacked more viciously and more publicly, and though he became tired and embittered before he was at last forced to resign, he always relished the fight. For Louis it was suffering all the way. While Fisher shot off his libellous blasts, quoting Biblical texts with double underlinings and triple exclamation marks, to all and sundry, knowing that his appeals to '*BURN THIS!!*' would be ignored, Louis was forced to remain silent.

Hedworth Lambton was as tireless and unremitting an opponent to Louis as was Beresford. Lambton was a spoilt, handsome, lazy patrician who had the ear of the Prince of Wales but like Beresford had lost the confidence of the King. From 1906 to 1911 he fought tooth and nail to hold Louis back and reduce his influence. He succeeded in delaying Louis's promotion, complained when he got it (to Vice-Admiral) and complained louder when he was appointed second-in-command of the Mediterranean Fleet in February 1907. With Beresford as his ally he succeeded in keeping Louis out of the Admiralty for some three years, lobbying ministers, spreading suspicion about his competency and loyalty.

Lambton loathed Louis's vigour, the importance he attached to success, and his manifest delight in his success when he achieved it. 'How very German!' we can hear him saying in his slurred, fruity voice. On manoeuvres Louis once succeeded in boxing in Lambton's flagship with a ship to port and starboard, a third ahead, a fourth astern. It was a ludicrous and humiliating position. 'Are you rehearsing the Battle of Trafalgar?' Lambton signalled.[23]

In September 1906 Louis was at last moved to write to Edward VII about Lambton. Lambton was protesting at Louis's imminent promotion and doing his utmost to prevent his joining the Board. Louis said that he could not understand the officer's motives. It was not as if Lambton was being deprived of 'important and pleasant commands',[24] including that of the Royal Yacht.

But it is almost the only protest we hear from him, and this was a purely private one. A year later Beresford was attacking even Louis's shooting record in the *Drake*. He had a chance forty-minutes-long opportunity to pronounce his complaints to Ponsonby, 'presumably hoping I should pass on to the King what he said'. His first item was Fisher and Louis. The *Drake*'s firing 'which had attracted so much attention was really a farce' as the 'wonderful results' had been gained 'under unfair conditions'.[25] So claimed Beresford.

The attacks continued, at every level and on every subject, during the following years. Fisher defended him hotly just as Louis had defended Fisher in the early months of his regime. He also pushed him up towards the highest office as energetically, though not as consistently as Louis had pushed him in the early years of the century.

Louis's enemies were Fisher's enemies, and Fisher watched them keenly. Louis could also be his own worst enemy. He wanted watching, too. He might be 'more English than the English' but Fisher worried every time Louis and Victoria visited Germany or had anything to do with their German relatives. It was not in Louis's nature to attempt to conceal the visits, nor did he – even at this stage in his career – apprehend their dangers and the advantage they gave to Beresford and his friends.

Early in 1908 Louis felt it necessary to apply for permission to leave his command in Malta temporarily in order to attend the funeral in Germany of his brother-in-law, Gustaf Prince of Erbach-Schönberg. Of course the whole fleet knew where he was going. He was quite entitled to go, but was it necessary, was it wise?

A month later he was proposing to take his flagship to Corfu to see a number of his German relations as well as Alice and her family at 'Mon Repos'. Fisher appealed to Edward VII to intervene. 'I do not think it would be at all wise of Prince Louis to go to Corfu,' he wrote, 'as his enemies unjustly accuse him of being more German than English . . .'[26] Other arrangements were made, but Louis did not learn his lesson.

At one stage Fisher despaired of his protégé who had once been his own patron. When Louis refused the plum appointment of C.-in-C. of the Mediterranean Fleet in case it compromised his chances of getting to the centre of power and an Admiralty appointment, Fisher exploded, 'No one would . . . have him as Second Sea Lord. There would be such an anti-German crusade – ill-deserved but none the less effective! So he's wiped out!'[27]

This was just a wild Fisherism. He was really working as hard as ever on Louis's behalf, because, first, he really believed he was the man for the top, and, second, because his appointment would be a body blow to his late enemies.

II

'You know you can't mount your
Dreadnoughts on wheels and come to your
dear friends' assistance.'

THE GERMAN EMPEROR *to Prince Louis*

THE year 1911 had started badly for young Dickie just as it was to
end triumphantly for his father. At Locker's Park he was struck
down by an inflammation of the lungs and he was in bed and
isolated for some time. Victoria visited him whenever she could, and
brought him the new Nesbit book and a large model destroyer to
cheer him up. Georgie managed to get leave and came to see him,
too. He was serving in the light cruiser *Blanche* but later in the year
he was appointed senior midshipman in the cruiser *Cochrane*. He
talked to his young brother of his life at sea with great enthusiasm.
No wonder Dickie never thought for one minute of any other career
than the Navy!

Victoria, Louise and Nona Kerr all did a lot of charity work
during the early cold months of 1911. Then in the evenings they
travelled down to Bermondsey in the slums of the East End where
they organized entertainment and games for the small boys of the
area in a school. They were called 'Happy evenings' and were a
great success until the 'Progressive' council, resentful of grand
people patronising the poor, refused them the use of the school.

Louis was briefly on half pay awaiting a new appointment and
they were living in London at 87 Queen's Gate in Kensington.
In March he was given command of the 3rd and 4th Divisions of the
Home Fleet based on Sheerness in the Thames estuary. It was
close enough to the Admiralty for canny eyes to see this job as a
temporary one. In fact it was so conveniently placed that the whole

family and their belongings moved from Queen's Gate to Admiralty House, Sheerness, by barge down the Thames.

'The surroundings of Sheerness,' wrote Victoria, 'are not beautiful and the immediate vicinity of some gunnery defences obliged us to keep our windows open even in the winter, whenever there was gun practice. Not far off lies Queensborough which had a glue factory, the smell of which was most repulsive.'

It was the least pleasant of all Victoria's billets, but they were both so busy that summer that neither had much time to notice their surroundings. Louis was often away at sea, and the rôle of an Admiral's wife included giving dinners and even a garden party. Victoria's work as President of the Friendly Union of Sailors' Wives also took up a lot of her time.

For Louis the summer and autumn months of 1911 were as critical in his professional life as they were for the nation and for Europe. Relations with Germany became worse and worse, the Royal Navy expected war to break out and many Germans steeled themselves for a surprise attack by the British Fleet.

The poison stemmed from the small Moroccan port of Agadir. Germany suspected France of planning to establish a protectorate in Morocco in contravention of the Algeciras Agreement reached five years earlier after the first Morocco Crisis. The German Navy sent a gunboat, allegedly to protect the country's interests in Morocco. The British saw their naval base at Gibraltar threatened, and again suspected that the Germans themselves were going to build a naval base close to England's most important trade route through the Mediterranean.

The summer of 1911 was also a hot summer. Edward VII had died the previous year and 1911 was the summer of the coronation of George V and Queen Mary. It was followed by a magnificent naval review. So it was a colourful and jubilant as well as an uneasy time

During the course of this dangerous year, while Victoria visited Germany and entertained her Prussian relations at Sheerness, Louis was employed as an Admiral in command of front-line British battleships, by the British court and the British government as an unofficial go-between and gatherer of intelligence, and finally at the very end of the year in a very high seat of power.

Fisher was shrewd enough to regard it as a strong mark in Louis's favour that he was 'an intimate personal friend of the German Emperor's brother',[2] and was on familiar terms with the Kaiser –

241

especially as the two German brothers remained as forthcoming as ever about matters connected with manoeuvres, *matériel* and strategical and tactical policy. But Louis did not limit his conversations with his brother-in-law and cousin to naval matters. As in the past, whenever opportunity occurred, he talked informally to the Kaiser on wider matters concerning European policies and tensions.

One such opportunity occurred when the Kaiser visited England in 1911 and his yacht was anchored off Spithead. Louis saw him several times but only once alone – on the afternoon of 20 May. Afterwards he provided the new King George V with a report on what was discussed:

[The Kaiser] spoke of his earnest wish to cultivate the friendliest relations with England politically. '. . . but you must not *differentiate* in the way you have been doing of late. You must not preface every conversation with the condition that you cannot come to an agreement with us on this or that subject if it were to affect the interests of France or Russia.' – At this point P.L. said that our good understanding with these two countries was the natural and necessary counterpoise to the Triple Alliance – At this the Emperor fired up & proceeded with more and more warmth, not to say heat, to ridicule this conception of the balance of power in Europe:—

. . . You must be brought to understand in England that Germany is the sole arbiter of peace or war on the Continent. If we wish to fight we will do so without your leave. And why? Because we Continental powers dispose of armies counting millions. Of what possible use would it be for you to land your 50,000 men anywhere? I am convinced you would never attempt anything so foolish, as those beautiful life guards and Grenadier Guards would be blown sky high by my submarines before they could set foot on shore. As to those French, we have beaten them once & we will beat them again. We know the road from Berlin to Paris. You know you can't mount your Dreadnoughts on wheels & come to your dear friends' assistance.[3]

The Kaiser became more and more bellicose, warning Britain not to attempt to interfere with the friendly relations his empire enjoyed with Russia. They were old allies. Had they not fought side by side together against 'Napoleon's yoke'? He followed this with a promise that Louis remembered six years later when he and Victoria were being driven nearly mad with worry about Ella and Alicky and Nicky and their five children: 'To us the most cardinal principle is a sacred thing. If a revolution were to endanger the throne in Russia, the Emperor of Austria & I would instantly march in shoulder to shoulder, and re-instate the Emperor Nicholas . . .'[4]

Louis was not given an opportunity to reply to this diatribe. By chance or intention – probably the latter – a woman's voice broke up what Willie described as 'our conversation'. It was the Empress calling 'Tea's ready.'

George V sent this confidential report to Churchill, who replied: 'I am much obliged to the King for letting me see the enclosed. I will not speak of it to anyone but Grey [Sir Edward Grey, Foreign Secretary 1905–16]. The Emperor has long since ceased to have any settled policy, and is (I believe) every year taken less and less seriously by his own subjects. One is almost tempted to discern in some of the things he said to Prince Louis the workings of a dis-ordered brain; but (even if that were so) they are none the less dangerous . . .'[5]

Louis continued right up to the war to be used as a source of inside knowledge and wisdom on both German and Russian affairs, and his opinions were highly regarded at the Foreign Office and the War Office as well as at the Admiralty.

For example, in June 1912 Louis writes to the Prime Minister, Asquith, on the naval situation in the Baltic, which is of close relevance to British naval policy. He outlines Sweden's likely role, and gives it as his opinion that 'the rise of Russia's sea power in the Baltic is viewed with considerable apprehension in the Berlin Admiralty . . . The threat of a Russian fleet, even in small numbers, should in time ease the situation in the North Sea. I know that Emperor William is much more disturbed at our friendship with Russia than with France . . .'[6]

In the same way that the fitness for war of the Royal Navy was carefully investigated after 'The Dogger Bank Affair' in 1904, so plans and dispositions were retrospectively examined when the Agadir Crisis of 1911 began to recede in the late summer. What would have happened if the worst *had* come to the worst?

The answer was – the worst or the serious risk of it. Since early in 1910 the team of McKenna and Fisher had been replaced at the Admiralty by McKenna and Wilson. As Lord Selborne, that highly respected figure and old veteran of the Admiralty, wrote, 'The Cabinet was shocked and amazed to find . . . that the Admiralty could produce no war plan for the Navy. It was so secret that only the First Sea Lord knew what it was! It was locked up in his brain!'[7]

Both McKenna and Fisher were blamed for this state of affairs.

Fisher had gone. Now Asquith decided that McKenna must follow him. A strong hand was needed at the Admiralty, one that could swiftly and efficiently create a Naval War Staff that would prepare this vast and expensive war machine for war. 'I bequeathed that task,' wrote Selborne sadly, 'as an urgent legacy to Fisher nearly seven years ago and gave him all the material for its fulfilment . . . I thought it would have been a job after his own heart, but obviously I was wrong.'[8]

Selborne always regretted that virtually nothing had been done to create a Staff at the Admiralty since Louis's long and detailed memorandum on the subject he had prepared ten years before. Fisher paid lip service to the idea of a Naval War Staff and collective decision-making but did nothing to create one during his long regime. In this respect he was even worse than all the reactionaries he had been so busy fighting.

He claimed that for security reasons it was safer for only one man to have the war plans locked in his head. That might be true. It is also true that he did not want to see his power diluted. At sea he had been an autocrat. He never divulged his plans to anyone. At the Admiralty he was equally dictatorial and secretive. The first reason why Fisher had put forward Wilson as his successor when he was forced to resign was because he was even more hotly opposed to any Staff structure at the centre of power.

Wilson's reasons for his opposition were fundamentally different from Fisher's, however, and had nothing to do with megalomania. Wilson was the archetype of the naval officer who is frightened of brains, and especially desk-bound brains. These officers believed in seamanship and the inspiration and experience of the man on the spot – as St Vincent, Collingwood and Nelson had done. They preferred to disregard all the new-fangled rubbish like torpedoes, submarines, wireless and mines, and still resented secretly even the steam engine. Only recently Wilson had described the submarine as 'underhand, unfair and damned un-English', and had disallowed the claims of submarine commanders to have 'sunk' battleships on manoeuvres. The powerful body which Wilson represented had been brought up in the Royal Navy to be suspicious of centralised control, of land-bound smart-alicks, and was passionately opposed to war at sea being directed by a brainy élite. It was said, perhaps apocryphally, that Wilson's war plans were on a single sheet of paper somewhere – in a cupboard, some thought, but no one could find the key during Agadir.

McKenna had quite failed to bring about a change of heart in Wilson and his loyal party. It would require a man of ruthless drive to do so. Asquith's choice was Winston Churchill. Churchill's ambitious eye had been trained on the Admiralty for some time. He was restless, and not altogether successful, at the Home Office. War there was confined to shooting up anarchists in Sidney Street: he needed to stretch himself and concern himself with 15-inch guns rather than police revolvers.

Asquith approached Churchill informally. Would he like the Admiralty? 'I accepted with alacrity,' Churchill recalled. 'I said, "Indeed I would."'⁹

McKenna was told, and was very upset and pleaded for time. This was not granted to him. On 25 October Churchill and McKenna swapped jobs, to McKenna's dismay.

Even before Churchill took up office he realized that he would not be able to work with his most senior Admiral. If all the reforms he desired were to be rapidly implemented, and if a Naval War Staff was to be set up rapidly, he must work in harness with a sailor who thought as he did.

Fisher, as always, and in spite of being retired and of his claims of being out of the fray, had advice to offer – dogmatic advice on every aspect of naval affairs. The rising young politician and the 70-year-old Admiral had a close understanding and a mutual admiration. What little Churchill knew of naval affairs he owed to Fisher's instruction, and Fisher's influence on him was profound and long lasting.

On the day Churchill took office, Fisher wrote a long letter packed with strongly worded advice. The most important appointment Fisher told Churchill to make was Louis as First Sea Lord in place of Wilson. '. . . *Private, Wilson is no good ashore!* . . . He [Battenberg] is the most capable administrator in the Admiral's list *by a long way* . . . I think also this should please the Liberal Party – they will say what better proof could we give of our confidence to Germany than selecting a man as First Sea Lord with German proclivities. In reality he is more English than the English . . .'¹⁰

It was curious that Fisher, who had himself refused to consider creating a Naval War Staff in his own time was now recommending for his old job an Admiral who was fiercely pro-Naval War Staff. But then Fisher was always a contradictory man and it was not *his* power that would be diminished by its introduction.

Louis, then, was Churchill's man to lead the Admiralty forward into its new age of reform and modernisation and preparation for war. He was, as Fisher and so many others had told Churchill, a brilliant administrator. He was easy to work with. As a Prince he would not forever be seeking kudos and power like some – these had been granted to him, without struggle, from birth. So he would not be trying to take credit for everything and would be content for the First Lord, who was still on the way up, to take as much credit as he wished. And, finally, it was no disadvantage at all that he was one of the innermost court circle and knew more about the German Navy than anyone outside Germany. Moreover, he understood the German mind.

Churchill consulted his Prime Minister. Herbert Asquith agreed that Louis was by a wide margin the right man for the job. But when he consulted some of his colleagues, he was surprised at their cool reaction. Fisher's prediction had been quite wrong. This Liberal Cabinet was more cautious about German-born Louis's suitability than the most fiercely reactionary Conservative Cabinet could ever be. It was not, they protested, his loyalty they doubted. Oh no! It was what other people might think, and especially what those who had put them into power might think. Thus spoke the radicals.

On 4 October 1911 that *eminence grise* of Britain's defence counsels, Lord Esher, reported to the Secretary of State for War: 'Prince Louis is the ablest by far, but the P.M. "tried it on" with Lloyd George, who was horrified at the idea of a German holding the supreme place. Asquith says L.G. is an excellent foolometer and that the public would take the same view. Still, he is the most competent man . . .'[11]

It was only a short time ago that Lloyd George, who regarded himself as forward looking, tried to get rid of Fisher and replace him with Beresford![12] What was Lloyd George up to now? Was he truckling to the low press, as Queen Victoria might have said, thinking of his own skin at the next election, or showing political responsibility and prescience? Who can say, but when he read a violent piece on the subject of Prince Louis's unsuitability in *John Bull*, written by that scandalmonger Horatio Bottomley, he must have derived dark satisfaction:

'Should a German "boss" our Navy,' ran the headline. 'Bulldog breed or Dachshund?' It would, Bottomley claimed, be 'a crime against our Empire to trust our secrets of National Defence to any alien-born official. It is a heavy strain to put upon any German to make him a ruler of our **Navy** and give him the key to our defences . . .'¹³

Asquith told Churchill and, after toying with the idea of making Louis Controller, in charge of *matériel*, appointed him Second Sea Lord. This gave him responsibility for training, personnel and appointments. As First Sea Lord he selected Francis Bridgeman.

Admiral Sir Francis Bridgeman was the undramatic and rather unwell C.-in-C. of the Home Fleet. He was on record as favouring a Naval War Staff and would, it was expected, do as he was told. Churchill did not think he would last for long. Then he would automatically be replaced by the man he really wanted.

Fisher saw through the ruse at once. 'Nos 1 & 2 you have arranged splendidly,' he wrote slyly to Churchill, '– as on reflection I am sure No 2 will run No 1!'¹⁴ And to Louis himself, Fisher wrote jubilantly: 'I almost think my greatest satisfaction at the present moment is the delightful "*smash up*" for Beresford, Hedworth Lambton, Noel (and others needless to mention!) in your being Second Sea Lord and in due course succeeding Bridgeman!'¹⁵ He then reminded Louis of the long and arduous nature of the battle of attrition he had been forced to wage in order to bring about this result against all the prejudices of the powerful Beresford lobby. 'I hardly think you know to what malignant lengths they went! However, they are all now safely "*on the beach*".'

For a man who was renowned for the uncanny accuracy of his prophesies this was a singularly unprescient comment.

Old 'Tug' Wilson, a man who had given his whole life to the Navy – he had never married – was sacked with scarcely a word of thanks. Louis moved into the Admiralty with Bridgeman on 5 December 1911. Bridgeman, who was astonished at his unexpected elevation, got a lukewarm reception from the Press. Louis's arrival was privately and publicly welcomed, except by Beresford and his supporters who were, as Fisher had predicted, not at all pleased.

Selborne wrote to Churchill to congratulate him on his choice of Louis as Second Sea Lord. 'He is the ablest officer the Navy possesses,' he wrote, 'and, if his name had been Smith, he would ere now have filled various high offices to the great advantage of the country, from which he has been excluded owing to what I must characterise as a stupid timidity. He has in fact nearly had his naval career maimed because he is a Prince & because of his foreign relationships . . . a better Englishman does not exist or one whom I would more freely trust in any post in any emergency.'¹⁶

Victoria was delighted. Her husband, she knew, had been held back long enough by his enemies. And now he had won – and no thanks to Fisher, whom she cordially despised and mistrusted (though she rather liked his homely wife). Excitedly she sent telegrams to her children with the news.

Dickie's headmaster at Locker's Park was asked to break the news to him. Then she wrote to Dickie: 'The papers have all said very nice things about Papa being the right man to go to the Admiralty & praising his work as an Admiral and former work as D of NI. I should like to have been there when Mr Christopherson told you the news . . .'[17]

The relationship between Churchill and Prince Louis was a curious and complicated one. The young Churchill recognized, as clearly as those who were close to him, his own genius and the almost limitless potential of his political career. After an uncertain start, the Admiralty offered him the opportunity to demonstrate to the public, who were suspicious of him, and his political enemies, who were vigorous and numerous, that his belief in himself was justified.

Today Churchill's magnificent record is generally regarded as inviolable. For his prophetic warnings before the Second World War and his unsurpassed leadership during it, he stands for all time as one of the really great Englishmen. In 1911 he was about to plunge into the turbulent waters of the nation's defence at a most dangerous moment in history. He knew the hazards and relished the risks he faced. The waves and the currents proved too much for him this time, and he was eventually sucked down and all but drowned.

But that was four years hence. For the present he was burning with zeal, boundlessly energetic and ambitious, personable, charming and almost wholly ignorant of the Navy he loved. As well, although he shared his love for the Royal Navy with his Admirals, he was far removed from all of them – even from Jacky Fisher – in style, temperament and motive. His Admirals were all veterans in a career to which they had dedicated their lives. They were close to, or had reached, the summit. They were not much interested in what went into the record for future examination and judgement. By the standards of politicians they were selfless men.

Churchill was a highly bred political animal, already experienced in the cut and thrust of parliamentary life, ruthless, opportunistic and arrogant. (He was many other things as well – too many to discuss here although one must bear in mind always his emotional-ism.) He wanted brains and energy and experience about him. In Louis he had all three, with two massive pluses: direct access to George V, and the greatest knowledge of War Staff requirements in the Navy.

It was mischievous old Fisher, muttering jealously and resentfully in the wings, who later first spread the belief that Louis was 'Winston's servile dupe'. Historians have picked this up and per-petuated it, sometimes with seeming satisfaction. It is, after all, more satisfying to denigrate a prince than a commoner. Churchill wanted Louis as a partner in what he regarded as the greatest opportunity of his lifetime, eventually got him in face of many difficulties and obstructions, and held on to him more tenaciously than was good for his own political reputation when the wolves closed in on Louis. The fact is that for all but the last weeks of three vital years from October 1911 to October 1914, these two excep-tional men operated with mutual respect and the closest under-standing. There were disagreements, but they were few and mild considering the fundamental contrasts between their characters and working styles.

The belief that Louis was no more than Churchill's servant has gained ground because Churchill's exaggeration of the part he played in guiding the Royal Navy to its 1914 war stations was as successful as he intended it to be, in spite of his later fall from grace. Like all politicians he needed to take as much credit as possible for all that he accomplished. His methods were as old as politics itself (as any civil servant knows) and, to him, almost instinctive. He sought advice, received it, redrafted it, saw to it that the documents got into the right hands and were preserved for the record, and expunged from his memory the facts of their origin. Any acknow-ledgement or thanks were likely to be verbal – the telephone was already proving invaluable in this respect, and Churchill was an enthusiastic early user. Original documents prepared by his advisers went the way of the first drafts – or most of them did. Some have survived.

It is October 1911. The creation of a Naval War Staff is, for Churchill, to be the first priority. It is the first reason why he has been selected for the job of running the Navy. Louis is still at sea in his flagship. Even before Churchill has taken up office, or before the present First Lord or First Sea Lord know they are to be relieved,

Churchill is addressing himself to Louis. On 22 October Louis replies with a long letter containing his observations on the duties of a Chief of Staff, providing 'a classical picture' of the functions of naval staffs.[18] Churchill paraphrases this in his own style and in his own handwriting but occasionally using Louis's phrases, word for word.[19] Then he presents it to the Cabinet as a draft scheme.

'The War Staff,' runs his definition, 'is to be the means of preparing and training those officers who arrive ... at stations of high responsibility, for dealing with the more extended problems which await them there. It is to be the means of sifting, developing, and applying the results of history and experience, and of preserving them as a general stock of reasoned opinion as an aid and as a guide for all who are called upon to determine, in peace or war, the naval policy of the country ...'[20]

The scheme varies in only one fundamental respect from the one Louis has prepared. Haldane provides the clue in his memoirs. 'Churchill wanted it [the Staff] to be put directly under him as First Lord. To this I objected stoutly, saying that it would be inert unless it were under the First Sea Lord. Prince Louis of Battenberg ... agreed with me and the staff was placed directly under the First Sea Lord.'[21]

As Admiral Gretton has pointed out, Churchill made no mention of the real origin of 'his' scheme in his account of these times in the first volume of *The World Crisis*, nor of the controversy about its control.[22]

On more mundane matters like manning the Fleet, recruitment and mobilization it is possible to see time and again Louis's beliefs expressed in Louis's own language in official memoranda emanating from the office of the First Lord and above Churchill's initials. 'This is my first draft,' scribbles Louis on his *Memorandum by the First Lord on a Naval War Staff*. 'You will be able to improve it very much I am sure.'

After reading it Churchill notes beneath Louis's signature, 'No, it is exactly what is wanted. It shd be printed for confidential use.' And again: 'It would be impossible to express my views more clearly,' Churchill comments on one of Louis's drafts. 'I approve entirely the course proposed.'

In one brief letter, marked 'Secret' and covering a wide range of topics, we can read: 'All your arrangements ... appear to be most suitable', 'If you approve, I see no objection to ...', 'The [classifications] you propose are excellent', 'I cordially agree with your proposals', and 'I am much impressed with your admirable plan . . .'23

This is not the language of a man who regards his partner as a cypher. It is the language of a man who intelligently recognizes the reality of his situation. Louis is twenty years older than he is. Louis has been in the Royal Navy for forty-three years, Churchill (in the case of the *War Staff Memorandum*) a few hours.

We can hear other voices at this time. It is not difficult to discern Fisher's, especially on warship design.

Like the Kaiser, Churchill loved to sketch designs for super-Dreadnoughts; and like the Kaiser he had to be brought down to earth. ('The original idea which I put before the Chief Constructor for a 30 knot 8.15″ gunned vessel,' he told Louis sadly, 'is much too costly.')24

Here he is on his idea of new battle cruisers: 'Broadly speaking, the money and the weight are taken from the armour & put into the guns. The increase in muzzle-energy is of course prodigious, & the governing principle, that yr own fire is the best protection against the enemy's, appears orthodox & sound.' It proved to be neither. It proved to be disastrous. He should have listened to others besides Fisher on this subject.

A glance through some surviving but unpublished memoranda and letters of this period reveals the truth of the relationship between Louis and Churchill. Louis is the target for broadsides of letters and memoranda demanding his opinion on manning improvements, dispositions, the quality of individual officers, the scrapping of obsolescent ships, the status of the Mediterranean Fleet, and countless other subjects.

Time and again we read, 'Please write privately by special messenger what you think of . . .' Louis provides his opinion, and the information, and suggests certain action. 'WSC I agree', is found in Churchill's familiar handwriting at the bottom of Louis's memoranda. It is Churchill who, more often than not, concurs with Louis rather than the reverse, which has been the popularly held view.

This was a normal and proper relationship between the political and professional heads of the Royal Navy. But because Churchill went much further than usual in claiming credit for himself for the work of others, and because he became such an esteemed and famous man thirty years later, the largely unrecorded part played by the professional sailors who kept him steady and helped him to survive is too easily forgotten today. Louis, the most notable and responsible of them, did nothing whatever to claim any credit for himself in any surviving letter or memorandum, and certainly not in the memory of anyone who knew him then.

If one considers the stature and performance of Churchill when he was a young man, or later for that matter, it does not add to his dignity nor to the veracity of his reputation to judge him blameless and perfect. He was not so in 1911–14, and those who knew him and loved him recognized this fact.

A great airman, Sir John Slessor, who worked closely with Churchill in the Second World War, has written that 'it is a mistake to believe that because Winston is such a great figure nothing must ever be said against him. It would be incredible if he was always right, or if he always behaved well. I don't think it diminishes his ultimate stature or his position to point out that he was human and that he sometimes did improper things.'[25]

Churchill was boundlessly arrogant at 38, before he had suffered the humiliation of dismissal and public excoriation. His overbearing manner and peremptory language greatly irritated Bridgeman, and Louis had to agree that it was not customary for the civilian Lord to address senior professionals as Churchill addressed Bridgeman: 'I will want to see you on so and so . . .' or 'I want you to make a series of proposals . . .' The slightest delay in response to a request would result in a note couched in the language a commander might use to address an erring sub-lieutenant. Bridgeman complained bitterly, but privately, about this.

The news was received with interest by the great Conservative and future First Lord, A. J. Balfour:

'Winston,' he was told by J. S. Sandars, Balfour's secretary, '. . . has outraged official decorum by the language of his official minutes . . . Bridgeman and Prince Louis met & agreed that respect & authority could not be maintained if Winston were allowed to issue papers couched in these terms. Bridgeman, therefore, met Winston . . . and plainly told him that he must mend his manners or his Board would have to take action. Bridgeman pointed out that as Winston could not give a single order outside the Admiralty building without the consent of the Board & that he was only *primus inter pares* the terms in which he had been addressing his colleagues was most improper.'[26] Churchill, it seemed, argued the case hotly before capitulating 'abjectly'. 'He broke into tears and talked in such a melancholy manner about himself that Bridgeman thinks he must be ill. I assured Bridgeman that I had never known the time when sympathy was not asked for Winston on grounds of health.'[27] Sandars concluded tartly.

With George V, however, Churchill could be fulsome and in-gratiating, and he was transparently anxious not to displease him. His letters were over-elaborate, over-long, and over-frequent. Once, when the King was *en route* to India, he received a very long telegram by cypher about the date of announcement of his new Board, asking for his assent. This time, tactfully through third parties, Churchill was requested to economise in future and cut the guff.[28]

Churchill's appointment of several of George V's favourites and Fisher's foes, against any considered judgement, led to widespread protests, especially from Fisher. On 28 March 1912 Churchill wrote to his King, that he had 'the honour to submit for Your Majesty's approval the appointment of Sir Hedworth Meux [he had recently changed his name by Royal Licence from Lambton in order to secure the inheritance of a brewing fortune] . . . as Commander-in-Chief at Portsmouth, and that of Sir Berkeley Milne . . . in the Mediterranean.' Churchill claimed to be 'confident that both these appointments are the best that could be made and will greatly conduce to the advantage of the Service.'[29] They did not.

In spite of all this currying of favour the King remained suspicious of Churchill, whom he regarded as brash, over-ambitious and conceited. George V remained a naval conservative to the end. He had disapproved of almost every reform put in hand by Fisher, and was equally suspicious of everything Churchill was up to. This was where Louis again proved so valuable. He was the only naval officer who could talk on equal terms with his sovereign.

After sending Milne to the Mediterranean, Churchill had agreed with Louis that the strength of that station must be much reduced in favour of the fleets in home waters. Milne, and George V, were greatly upset. McKenna, at the Home Office and really out of the picture now, naughtily sent a critical memorandum to the King. Louis invited himself to lunch at Buckingham Palace and tried to explain things to George V. Louis told Churchill later: 'I found HM in complete ignorance of the naval aspect. I think he found my statements fairly unanswerable . . . It is sad to think that our Sailor King stands on McK's level as a naval strategist!'[30]

Nonetheless, Louis retained a real affection for his cousin, and their relationship remained to the end as it had been when Georgie was an eager young midshipman in the *Inconstant* in admiring awe of

the older officer who had seen so much of the world, of life, and of women.

Louis also remained firm friends with Churchill, and Victoria liked and admired Churchill's wife, Clementine. They often dined at each other's houses in the years before the war, exchanged copies of their published works (*Lord Randolph Churchill* for *Warship Names*) and they were often in the Admiralty yacht *Enchantress* together. Although Churchill very quickly deprived his Admirals of their yachts as a measure of economy (it made no difference but sounded good at the Treasury), he loved his own perquisite and spent an unprecedented proportion of his time on board. Louis was sometimes asked to accompany him. He did so reluctantly because every voyage resulted in a new accumulation of paperwork in his office.

In May 1912 he agreed to accompany Churchill, Prime Minister Asquith and his daughter Violet, David Beatty the naval Secretary and future dashing Commander of the Battle Cruiser Fleet, on a Mediterranean cruise, taking in Malta. They travelled together overland, halting for a lavish dinner in Paris.

Violet Asquith was vastly amused by the whole business, and kept her eyes open, as usual. Louis she recorded as 'tall and blue-bearded, with a simple, natural beauty.'[31] Churchill and he scarcely drew breath during the long journey, and as the train emerged at last from the Mont Cenis tunnel, she heard these two men of war deep in discussion about Napoleonic strategy.

Then, to Louis's dismay, he discovered that the itinerary included a secret call on Fisher at Naples. Louis knew what plotters these two cronies were and feared an upset of carefully laid plans. 'They can't resist each other for long at close range,'[32] Violet Asquith observed. There would, he knew, be much stirring up of muddy waters and inflaming of old passions. Churchill wanted to persuade Fisher to chair a royal commission on oil supplies to meet the new needs of the Royal Navy. Louis was determined not to become involved as this was a purely political subject and he disliked intrigue. 'Prince Louis hates it and keeps out of the way as much as possible,'[33] Beatty wrote home to his wife.

If Louis's relationship with Churchill was less intense and explosive than Fisher's, it was a good deal more soberly productive. Nor did it contain the ingredients of spontaneous combustion which was later to blow asunder the careers of both Fisher and Churchill and create the great political and military crisis of 1915.

Louis had the advantage over Fisher of possessing in common with Churchill an aristocratic and ancient lineage. As well, the two men were liberal democrats with a strong sympathy for the under-privileged. This may at first seem to be an irrelevant advantage for men concerned with the running of a great naval service. But in 1911–14 compassion and practicality together made a democratizing influence at the Admiralty an invaluable asset. The Navy was feeling the rumbles of working class industrial unrest outside, and this at a time when expansion of the fleet to meet the accelerated German programme after Agadir made new recruitment an urgent necessity.

Fisher had done much to improve the lot of the lower deck during the early period of his regime. But a new restlessness against the low pay, poor food, brutal punishments and primitive living condi-tions made itself felt in 1911 and 1912. 'You will have a Mutiny at the Nore if you don't handle the Lower Deck grievances,'[34] Fisher had warned Churchill. And an observer close to the lower deck wrote at this time: 'If we think things can go on as they are going, we make a mistake. They can't. Human discontent is the highest of all explosives.'[35]

Lionel Yexley, the editor of the lower deck paper *The Fleet,* was the moderate but clever and determined leader of a campaign for improvements, 'an ex-bluejacket with a positive genius for advo-cacy'.[36]

'When I joined the Navy in 1907,' a one-time ordinary seaman remembers today, 'I had the same pay as my father had had and the same pay as my grandfather, who had fought in the Crimean War.'[37] Pensions, fixed in the time of William IV, worked out at eleven-pence a day after twenty-two years service – a halfpenny for every year's service!

Yexley worked hard on Churchill and Louis. They made a sympa-thetic audience, especially Louis who had been championing the cause of the lower deck before Churchill entered politics. Sub-stantial improvements in pay, conditions and opportunities for promotion from the lower deck were pushed through by Louis during his period as Second Sea Lord – unglamorous and mainly unacknowledged work, but as important as the increase in gun calibre of the new battleships. Relations between officers and men improved. So did recruiting. So, above all, did general morale at all levels in the Royal Navy.

Louis was also responsible for the introduction of 'The Mate Scheme', a real naval revolution which attracted a lot of attention outside the service, especially amongst high Tories who regarded it as one more Liberal nail in the coffin of the nation.

This Mate Scheme allowed certain selected young warrant and petty officers to reach a commissioned grade of Mate, with possible promotion to Lieutenant in two years and eligibility for rank up to Commander. An early sailor to benefit by promotion from the lower deck, Henry D. Capper, tells a moral tale against himself. It seems that he was asked to come to see Louis ('a thoughtful and shrewd observer', Capper described him) and give a report on his experiences because he and his fellow proletarians had had some trouble with their fellow officers. The conversation went like this:

P.L.: What games do you play?

CAPPER: None at all.

P.L.: Don't you play cards, billiards, tennis, hockey, cricket, golf or football?

CAPPER: No, all my recreation time is spent in reading and writing.

P.L.: Well, Capper, this is probably the main cause of the aloofness of the officers which you tell me of.

Louis went on to urge them all 'to find their proper level in the ward-room, use the facilities you have to advise them to cultivate playing the same games as their messmates play, and thus create a companionship with those who belong to the new sphere they are entering.'[38] Capper went away a wiser man, and was so struck by this advice that he published it in the *Naval Warrant Officers Journal*. But you could not root out overnight a tribal caste system as deeply entrenched as the Navy's. It had been difficult enough, ten years earlier, to rationalise officers' training so that the lowest form of commissioned life, the engineer officer, shared his early training with the élite executive officer, who came from a very different class of home.

However, a start had to be made, and Louis began with the Mate Scheme – amidst mutters of 'German socialist' from some of the more aged service fossils. Amongst the politicians and general public it was Churchill who took all the kicks, and the credit – and it was 90 per cent credit. 'Don't let [these personnel reforms] be forced on you!' Fisher had advised him early on. '*Get the credit my dear Winston!*'

Churchill needed no encouragement to do so. With his unerring eye for publicity, he had a telegram sent to the very first sailor to emerge from the lower deck to reach the rank of Commander for a hundred years. It bade him to travel by special transport to Holyhead where the *Enchantress* was anchored in order to receive the personal, and much publicized, congratulations of the First Lord himself. The breathless officer was then dragged off to Scotland to have luncheon with his own wife in company with Churchill and Clementine.[39]

Louis succeeded in getting away to sea in the summer of 1912 as commander of one of the opposing fleets in the manoeuvres. It was a marvellous relief from the burdens of administration which had reached a new level of pace and weight under Churchill. The First Lord travelled to Spithead and with the Prime Minister saw off the Fleet – something he loved to do, 'Prince Louis looked vy imposing on his splendid *Thunderer*,' he wrote to his wife later in the day. But this time it was the briefest respite, and Louis was soon back at his desk at the Admiralty, and to face a new crisis, this time an internal one.

'Sir Francis Bridgeman has again been ill,' Victoria wrote to Nona Kerr. 'It is more than likely, that he will resign his post before long & then the Prince, who is doing B's work as well as his own now, will succeed him – in which case you will probably find us already in Archway House [the new extension to the Admiralty] on your return . . .'[40]

Victoria was correct in her prediction. But between the writing of this letter in mid-November, and the Battenbergs' move into Mall House, the First Sea Lord's residence, a political storm burst over Louis which made the controversy about his appointment to the *Dreadnought* twenty-five years earlier seem a very minor affair.

Fisher was correct in his prediction. During the eleven months Louis had held office, Bridgeman had been consulted by Churchill not only brusquely but also infrequently. Neither man made much effort to get on with the other. Although Bridgeman had backed the creation of a Naval War Staff, it was Louis who did all the planning and who helped Churchill to push it through. The situation for Louis was embarrassing, and it says much for his tactful handling of it that the two senior officers remained on amiable terms.

The condition of Bridgeman's health is revealed by one of his

257

letters to Louis written as early as April 1912. 'I propose if all goes well returning this day week,' he writes. 'The Dr says I ought to be fit again by then. I have had a rotten time of it . . .'[41] For most of the summer Bridgeman continued to nurse his ill health up in Yorkshire, making only brief descents on London.

On 14 September he wrote to Louis saying that he would have to defer again his projected return to London. 'I hope you will not be seriously inconvenienced,'[42] and offering to come up for a day or two at a time if he was badly needed. It was no more inconvenient for Louis than the absence of his chief had been for most of the time since Bridgeman had taken over office.

Two and a half more months passed, and still there was no sign of Bridgeman at the helm. On 28 November Churchill wrote him a nice letter saying how concerned he was at the continued ill health of his 'colleague and friend', and suggesting that it might be a relief for him to retire. The next day Churchill told George V, as if it was already a *fait accompli*, that Bridgeman would be giving up his post, and hoped that His Majesty would approve of 'Prince Louis of Battenberg to fill the office of First Sea Lord, and that of Sir John Jellicoe to succeed him as Second Sea Lord'.[43]

Louis, too, thought that the matter was as good as settled when on the morning of 4 December he received a rather defiant letter from Bridgeman saying that he would return to the Admiralty in a few days and stay for a week or ten days before returning to the country for Christmas; that after the New Year he would return to the Admiralty 'for good', and that there was nothing 'organically wrong' with him.[44]

On the same morning Bridgeman received a letter from Churchill making it rather clearer that Bridgeman was expected to resign, which crossed with a letter Bridgeman had written saying he was fine and 'I don't think there is a necessity to resign'.[45] But on receiving Churchill's second letter, he took up his pen and wrote sadly, but somewhat resentfully, 'I now understand that you expect me to resign and I am happy to be able to meet your wishes.'[46]

The news was made public, there were regretful comments about Bridgeman in the Press, and complimentary ones about Louis on his accession to the senior post. Ten days passed. Then the Conservative *Morning Post* came out with the 'revelation' that Bridgeman's resignation had been forced on him for reasons of policy disagreement and had nothing to do with his health. Churchill, it was suggested, was up to some dirty tricks.

Beresford and his friends had caught the scent of blood again. Here, they saw, was a chance to deliver a body blow at the Liberal Party, at Winston Churchill and his naval reformers, and above all it was a golden opportunity to discredit Louis. They had persuaded Bridgeman, himself a Conservative, now weak from long illness and sad at losing office, that he had been badly used; that it was a Liberal plot to get him out, to which Louis (with his Liberal views and Socialist wife) was a party.

Churchill demanded from Bridgeman that he should make clear that there had been no policy disagreement between them. Bridgeman, confused and frightened, concurred and telegraphed that he had 'no idea where the *Morning Post* article came from'.

But that was not the end of the affair. The Opposition demanded a debate, and there were extraordinary scenes in the chamber on 20 December when Churchill was accused of ill-using the Admiral and of (by implication) lying. Churchill fought back angrily, but was finally forced to reveal the contents of a private letter Louis had received from his colleague saying how depressed he was about his health, how weak he felt and how he sometimes felt inclined to give up his post. 'The fact is, I really ought to go somewhere warmer than England to spend the winter – an impossibility so long as one stays at the Admiralty.'[47]

This clinched the matter in favour of Churchill and Louis. But it left behind an unpleasant odour which clung about the corridors of the Admiralty for some time. In fact relations between the civilian and professional Navy chiefs had not been happy and it was untrue that there had been no disagreements. Bridgeman accused Churchill of 'meddling' and of exceeding his duties. The brash young politician obviously rubbed him up the wrong way. Bridgeman also opposed Churchill's and Louis's intention to raise the pay of the men.

Victoria was resentful about the fuss. 'The papers have spoken a lot of nonsense about Bridgeman's retirement,' she wrote, '& party politics have caused it to be made use of against W.C. in parliament – the simple truth is that he was always complaining of his health when heavy and quick work fell upon him ... he really was not physically fit for his post & the strain it entails; could often not sleep, had to leave board-meetings before their end & forgot & muddled things from mental strain. Though he did not himself realize that he was not up to his work, the people at the Admiralty did, not only W.C. & L.'[48]

In Bridgeman, idleness led to bitter brooding. He never forgave Churchill, whom he considered a bounder, to the end of his life. Nor did he forgive Louis, whom he ever after regarded as a leading player in the conspiracy to depose him. The antipathy embraced all the Battenberg family, and years later, after the First World War, he had Lord Mountbatten blackballed from the Royal Yacht Squadron, even though David Beatty, by then First Sea Lord, had put him up.

Once again Louis had been placed in a false and horribly vulnerable situation, and one which was none of his making. Everything about his record and his character favours innocence. He was an ambitious man but not a devious man, nor a man who would plot with a politician again a fellow officer and friend. None the less the fact was noted by his thwarted enemies that Louis had overcome all opposition to his ambitions, and had not only survived twelve months at the Admiralty but had now reached the very summit.

During this difficult time Louis was sustained by the support of his relatives and some of his fellow officers – and especially of his fellow officer and cousin, King George V. In reply to the King's letter of delight and confidence at his appointment, Louis thanked him 'with all my heart'. He continued, 'I deeply regret the cause of my advancement & wish it cd have come about otherwise. The only advantage in the matter, leaving personal sympathy with my good friend Bridgeman out of count lies in the fact that I have now for some considerable time, with short intervals, acted as "understudy" to my new office.'[49]

The community of small boys at Locker's Park reflected in miniature the response of the country. '. . . how awfully nice it is about Papa's promotion,' wrote Dickie to his mother. 'Mr Christopherson is frightfully pleased & if our work is good enough he wishes to give an extra half-holiday on Tuesday, to commemorate the fact. Of course, needless to say Walkinshaw [an old enemy] . . . had to grumble & insult Papa, he called him a sea-donkey & doesn't seem to honour the R.N. in the slightest. I hope he does not get into the Navy [he didn't] if that is the way he thinks about it . . .'[50]

12

IN the last years before the war Victoria still contrived to find time in a busy life to visit her three sisters and brother. She saw Irène most often because she was the nearest, and she and her children usually came once a year to stay with the Battenbergs either in England or at Heiligenberg or Wolfsgarten. Russia was more difficult in a number of ways. It was a wearisome journey. Security arrangements were tiresome. And there were special problems connected with Alicky.

Ella remained as loving and sane and as good company as ever. This once-upon-a-time fairy-tale Princess who had become one of the grandest and richest of all Grand Duchesses had now given up the material benefits of her position and devoted her life entirely to a religious nursing Order she had founded, the only one in Russia. She lived humbly close by her own Convent of Martha and Mary where she and her nuns nursed the poor sick of Moscow, and now always wore the grey robe and white veil of her Order, her 'Martha and Mary garb' as Victoria referred to it.

When Victoria visited Ella in July 1912, she and Nona were given the use of a few rooms in a humble little house next door to Ella's convent. It was so full of bugs that after one restless night they moved in with Ella. There was only one living room, simply furnished with basket-ware chairs. 'There we took our meals and visitors were received, mostly old friends and abbesses from other convents,' Victoria wrote of this time. 'In spite of taking Russian lessons . . .

my powers of conversation were extremely limited, and as a number of the abbesses could only speak Russian, I was at a complete loss when Ella left the room.'[1] It was unusual for Victoria to find herself nonplussed!

The summer of 1912 was an especially hot one in Russia. It was also a difficult summer for Victoria. Quite apart from the anxiety she felt over the troubles between Greece and Turkey – in which Alice and Andrew were deeply involved and at risk – her youngest sister was becoming an increasing burden on the family.

The strains and stresses of her life had proved too much for Alicky. Her deeply introspective and mystically religious nature was incapable of dealing with her family worries, Russia's worries, and the worries about her own spiritual and physical wellbeing. She had become a neurotic and difficult woman, a bad wife and a disastrous Empress. Her dependence on Rasputin was now widely known and firmly established.

'Alexandra Feodorovna spoke of herself as a "great worrier", and this was true,' wrote one of her ladies-in-waiting, 'but when anxieties gained the upper hand, Rasputin's pious outpourings and her faith in his prayers and prophesies gave her confidence. The Emperor found a certain peace of mind in the hopeful assurances that in the end all would go well, and was glad to see the comfort the Empress derived from her trust in Rasputin's healing powers.'[2]

The state of her own health and that of her precious Alexei were her constant preoccupation and the first reason for her increasing dependence on that priest. 'What can I say about my health,' she asks, somewhat unnecessarily, in a letter to another and devoted one-time lady-in-waiting, Princess Bariatinsky. 'For the time the Drs are contented with my heart . . . But have again strong pains in the legs and back . . . – tho' gentle massage, mere stroking, it has made the pains worse. You see I have many complaints. What is necessary for one thing is harmful for another, it's all complicated. Am very tired & weary . . .'[3] And later, with a note of defiance: 'If people speak to you about my "nerves", please strongly contradict it. They are as strong as ever, its the "overtired heart" & nerves of the body & nerves of the heart besides, but the other nerves are very sound. Very bad heartaches [sometimes], have not what one calls walked, for three years, the heart goes wild, fearfully out of breath & such pain . . .'[4]

Like most hypochondriacs, Alicky had some reason to be concerned about her health. The sciatica, for which she had been taking the cure at Harrogate before her marriage, had grown more acute with the passing years, and her numerous pregnancies had been difficult. One of her doctors stated that she had 'inherited a family weakness of the blood vessels'. This is hardly a specific diagnosis, but it is worth noting that Victoria's one weakness was in her circulation. Alicky found movement of her legs increasingly difficult and painful and spent the greater part of her life after the age of forty-five lying down.

'There was a curious atmosphere of fatality about [the Empress],' wrote Queen Victoria's grand-daughter Princess Marie Louise. 'I once said – in the way that cousins can be very rude and outspoken to each other – "Alix, you always play at being sorrowful: one day the Almighty will send you some real crushing sorrows and then what are you going to do?"'5

The worst of these 'crushing sorrows' was of course Alexei's haemophilia. A glance at any of her letters at this time reveals how thoughts of her son dominated her whole life. Alexei was very poorly when Victoria stayed with Nicky and her sister at Peterhof in August 1912 after leaving Ella in Moscow. By December he was better again. 'Thank God [he] progresses favorably,' the Empress writes to Princess Bariatinsky, 'sledges daily & one hopes he may be able to stand by Xmas.' She then describes his treatment – electrical, mud compresses, physiotherapy – in detail. 'He is patient & good poor wee Sunbeam – looks well, sometimes less of course as nights are often restless . . . By the eyes one sees he has suffered much.'6

There was much suffering to be seen in many eyes at Peterhof that August. And there was much fear, too – fear of death by violence as well as from this dread 'royal disease'. Russian social and political problems appeared insoluble, and violence and lawlessness threatened anarchy.

Less than a year had passed since the Prime Minister, Peter Arkadyevich Stolypin, one of the few great figures of this era, had been assassinated. Nicky was there when it happened. Stolypin was in the first row at the opera and had turned, with his back to the stage, in the interval, when he was shot twice in the chest. 'Women were shrieking,' wrote the Tsar, 'and directly in front of me in the stalls Stolypin was standing. He slowly turned his face towards me and with his left hand made the sign of the Cross in the air. Only then did I notice that he was very pale and that his right hand and uniform were bloodstained . . .'7 Olga and Tatiana were beside their father, early witnesses to political assassination.

As in 1906, when Victoria had been at the palace and her sister had just become aware that her baby boy was a haemophilic, and in all the visits she had made since, it was only the irrepressible gaiety of her four darling nieces – and of her lively eight-year-old nephew when he was well – that made life at Peterhof endurable.

As well, these visits to her youngest sister now had about them an air of duty. For, while Louis was going about his duties with his fleet at sea – and for the last time – Victoria was doing her best to create better relations at the Russian court, to make peace between her two sisters, and to ensure that Rasputin would be banished forever from the royal palaces.

As Ernie had begged Victoria earlier, '. . . try to make her understand that through ruining the position of her friends she is ruining her own future, that I am sure she would not like'.[8]

All Hessian pressure had been brought to bear on Alicky to get rid of her evil priest since news of Rasputin's position had filtered out of Russia some three years earlier. The political pressure to banish Rasputin had been intense, too, ever since the first threats to expose the situation in the Russian parliament, the Duma.

Rasputin was at last winkled out of the Russian court in 1911, but no official announcement was made, and when Ernie was making his plans to go to Russia in April 1912 to see his sisters, and like Victoria, to attempt to create better relations between them, he was still uncertain of the situation. 'I will have to be very careful in what I say,' he wrote to Victoria, 'as it means they have sent him away & their hearts will be very sore, as they have had to accede to public opinion & if I harp on the same subject after he is gone, it might embitter them still more.'[9]

It was a great sadness for Victoria and her brother that they never succeeded in bringing about a complete reconciliation between Ella, the dedicated nursing sister and abbess, on the one hand, and the ailing, confused, pathetic and highly-strung Empress on the other. Rasputin was soon back in favour and the fateful last years of the Romanoffs ticked by like the timing device of a giant bomb.

As she made her way back to Hemmelmark, where she had left Dickie and Louise with Irène and Henry and their children, Victoria surely must have thought back again to those earnest pleas made by her grandmother to save the Hessian girls from Russia.

But Victoria was always grateful that there was one last happiness which they all enjoyed. The following summer, the Battenbergs with their three unmarried children and Andrew and Alice and the three grandchildren, and Nicky and Alicky and their five children, all met at Wolfsgarten for what was to be the last of 'the Russian invasions'.

Much has been written of those 'golden summers' just before Armageddon. Perhaps not all of the summers enjoyed those halcyon qualities which sentiment and nostalgia ascribe to them today. But if ever the setting and the occasion and the company perfectly combined to create the last joyous gathering of Europe's royal families, surely it was at that *schloss* set in the magical German woodlands of Hesse, and in the ballroom and gilded reception rooms of Heiligenberg.

Lord Mountbatten remembers his lovely Marie. 'I was mad about her, and determined to marry her. You could not imagine anyone more beautiful than she was, and we were both the same age, just thirteen.' He remembers, too, how proudly he wore his cadet's 'round jacket' at dinner – 'just as my father had been proud of his uniform when he first came home from England. We played tennis and rode through the woods and up into the hills, there was diabolo – oh, every sort of game. And there were parties and picnics and dancing. There we were together – just one great family like any other family.'[10]

They all spoke English among themselves, all fluently of course as if it was their only language. Then they spoke German to the German locals, French to the aristocracy, and the Russians spoke in Russian to their own servants. A happy, tightly knit community, relaxed in their own private insulated world.

Louis had stolen a few days from the Admiralty to relax with his relatives at Wolfsgarten and Heiligenberg. It was the last time he saw two of his sisters-in-law and all his entrancing young Russian nieces and nephews. In less than twelve months everyone here, relations, courtiers and servants alike, would be enemies or allies, while he would be in command of Britain's first line of defence and attack.

Louis's greatest achievement during his two years as First Sea Lord was, without doubt, to work harmoniously with his uneven, dynamic and brilliant partner. The record speaks for itself: in what was accomplished by the partnership in these twenty-three critical months (add twelve more for the period when he was really Second and First Sea Lords), and in the fact that his two predecessors with

Churchill lasted respectively one and twelve months, and the first of his successors with Churchill (Fisher) for less than seven months.

After that, under other First Lords, Admirals Jackson, Jellicoe and Wemyss failed to come within sight of Louis Battenberg in quality, style and accomplishment as he performed up to the first days of October 1914.

Churchill was a handful and it is doubtful whether any other senior naval officer at this time could have worked successfully with him. He did not hesitate to step far beyond the limits of his responsibilities and duties as political head of the Navy. In the 1912 manoeuvres, when he had been First Lord for only a few months, 'he not only gave wireless instructions to the Commanders-in-Chief from Whitehall, but on the return of the ships to harbour he lectured to the flag officers on how the manoeuvres should have been conducted, and this even before the Umpire had completed the report!'[11]

Perhaps his worst sin, in the eyes of senior officers, was the way he tended to encourage insubordination by ingratiating himself with the lower deck and junior officers alike. The naval historian Arthur Marder cites the case of Able Seaman Jones, word of which spread rapidly through the fleet. Jones was one of a ship's company being inspected by Churchill with the ship's commander

'So you know your men by name?' demanded Churchill.

'I think I do, Sir; we have had many changes recently, but I think I know them all.'

'What is the name of this man?'

'Jones, Sir.'

Churchill persisted: 'Are you quite sure that the man's name is Jones?'

The commander confirmed his belief, whereupon Churchill turned to the seaman and asked him his name. The seaman told the First Lord that his name was indeed Jones.

'Is your name really Jones or do you say so only to back your officer?' Churchill asked.

'My name is Jones, Sir,' rejoined the seaman.

It was later reported that the commander and his officers were in a state of 'choking wrath' on Churchill's departure.[12]

Louis sometimes had the delicate task of smoothing ruffled feelings and reviving the *amour propre* of offended senior officers, while at the same time endeavouring to restrain his partner's worst excesses. Admiral Sir Richard Poore, a very highly esteemed officer, was C.-in-C. Nore. On 5 November 1913 Poore wrote to Louis complaining, with good reason, of Churchill's behaviour during a four-day visit to the dockyard. 'On Sunday, 26th October,' wrote the Admiral, 'an inspection was held [by Churchill] of the "Vengeance". He was accompanied by General Sir Ian Hamilton, Mr John Churchill, Colonel Greely, 19th Hussars, & I think there were others . . .

'The ship was inspected, also the Ship's Company at Divisions, & the after turret cleared for action & worked.

'At Divisions the officers of Divisions were asked their names & general history of individual men as they were inspected. The men were openly questioned as to the correctness of their officers' replies.

'This procedure before the men without doubt tends to lower the position of the officers.

'This inspection was also carried out without the slightest reference to myself as C in C . . .'[13]

The worst Churchill crisis arose during this same visit. The captain of the Naval Air Service parent ship, H.M.S. *Hermes*, had had a minor disagreement with one of his lieutenants. Encouraged by Churchill, the lieutenant gave him his views on the matter, and sufficiently impressed Churchill for him to command the captain to his presence to tell him that the lieutenant's decision was the right one and must be complied with. Later, the brash young lieutenant told his commanding officer that Churchill had told him to write to him at the Admiralty if he did not get his way.

Admiral Poore took up the case and complained vehemently to Louis, who consulted his Second Sea Lord, Jellicoe, as matters of discipline came within his province. Churchill, suspecting that there might be trouble, and perhaps tipped off by the lieutenant, ordered Jellicoe to let him see any correspondence relating to the affair – and affair it was rapidly becoming!

But Jellicoe, deeming Poore's language too intemperate for Churchill's eyes, returned the letter to Poore with a private letter making suggestions for toning it down *without* telling Churchill – who, alas, got wind of what was going on, and telegraphed the General Post Office ordering the letter to be intercepted and returned to him. He got it back, read it, but claimed later in his defence that he did not read Jellicoe's private letter attached to it. But he also told Louis that he was going to order Poore to haul down his flag.

The indignation of the Board was ferocious, and the Second, Third and Fourth Sea Lords told Louis they were prepared to resign in a body. The crisis lasted six days, with Louis meeting in turn

Churchill, attempting to persuade him to modify his stand, and then with his fellow Sea Lords to report on his negotiations. On 10 November Louis had three meetings, first with Churchill, then with his colleagues, and in the evening with Churchill again. Peace rested on the manner in which Poore should tender an apology in exchange for a stay of execution. After each meeting Churchill put everything stiffly in writing, like minutes for the record, and sent the document to Louis.

Louis replied the next day after again talking to the rest of the Board, and then sent Churchill a memorandum which told him that he did not possess the power to force Poore to resign, and that if he insisted on doing so, the entire Board would resign. This thoroughly frightened Churchill who was behaving more and more like a thwarted spoilt schoolboy, and knew that this could lead to his own sacking. So he called back the weary and exasperated Louis and told him that he would after all withdraw the order to Poore if the Admiral said sorry properly.

That left Louis and his colleagues with the task of persuading a furious and affronted senior Admiral to do this, and not to resign, or demand a court martial. Poore agreed, 'under vast pressure' as Sir Francis Hopwood, the Additional Civil Lord, put it to George V's private secretary, Lord Stamfordham. 'Winston would not be flattered if he knew the arguments used by the Naval [Sea] Lords to keep the Commander-in-Chief from going. They were in short that he (Churchill) was so much off his head over the whole business that Poore need take no notice of it!'[14]

The next day Louis ordered the young lieutenant who had started the whole uproar to his office and gave him a dressing down; and that was the end of that.

Louis had dealt with the whole ludicrous episode with great tact and skill. But he deplored the amount of time and energy he had to expend on this and numerous smaller excesses of Churchill's which threatened discipline or gave offence to valuable officers.

But this in no way diminished his very high regard for Churchill's brain-power, exuberant vigour and ability to learn fast. Louis, Fisher and Jellicoe were thrusting naval knowledge into the young politician like new oil from new tankers into the new oil-driven super-Dreadnoughts Churchill was responsible for laying down.

Merely to work alongside Churchill was a daily stimulation. To create what they created together, with other fine 'brains' like Pakenham, Moore and Madden, with Fisher keeping rather more than a watching brief (in fact there was some very noisy intervention from time to time!) on all that was going on, was an invigorating and never-to-be-forgotten experience. Louis revelled in it all, while regretting that with every passing month war with the land of his birth grew increasingly probable.

As overall operational commander, Louis was associated with every decision and action taken by the Board during these two vital years from the massive expansion of the fleet in all its categories and the introduction of the 15-inch gun and of oil-fired boilers, to the plans for the blockade of Germany and the strangulation of its trade in the event of war; from the provision of protection of British commerce in time of war to the problems created by the rapid naval expansion of Turkey, Italy and Austria. The detail work was immense and unceasing. So were the meetings – Board meetings daily, committee meetings, sub-committee meetings, Committee of Imperial Defence meetings, Cabinet meetings at which his special knowledge was called for.

But through this locust cloud of paper and decision-making there stand out several naval achievements for which Louis was more particularly responsible either because of a life-long enthusiasm or because the subject fell within his special knowledge and province.

Besides handling many of Bridgeman's responsibilities, Louis was given the task when Second Sea Lord of forming a Naval Air Service. It was a job after his own heart, and he always regretted he did not have more time for it, and that later as First Sea Lord his work could only be supervisory.

The Navy's first efforts to get into the air came about as a result of private enthusiasm, and Louis was involved from the earliest stages. A rich aviation pioneer, patriot and benefactor, Frank McClean, promised to provide the Admiralty with the machines if authority could be granted for a number of naval officers to learn to fly. Other pioneers like J. T. C. Moore-Brabazon, Percy Grace and C. G. Grey supported McClean, and early in 1911 the Admiralty agreed that four officers should begin their training. This took place at Eastchurch on the Isle of Sheppey in the Thames Estuary, and it came under Louis's control from Admiralty House, Sheerness.

The Hessian enthusiasm for flying dating back to 1906 with the visit of an early German lighter-than-air machine to Wolfsgarten had already deeply infected Louis, and he could claim to be one of the first naval officers to become airborne. He therefore warmly welcomed these first trainee pilots and followed their activities with paternal interest. He flew several times himself with the pilots' commanding officer, Lieutenant C. R. Samson RN, during that summer, and did all he could to support them in their fight for recognition.

In August Samson remained in the air for just short of five hours – 'my warmest congratulations'[15] signalled Louis. Before he left for the Admiralty he was able to give Samson good news. 'I hope to get out to Eastchurch next week,' he told him, 'to have a yarn with you and your messmates & see the new machines. The new First Lord [Churchill] has told me that he means to develop the aeroplane in connection with fleets for all he is worth.'[16]

Churchill placed the whole and now rapidly developing Naval Air Service in Louis's hands when he came to the Admiralty in Secember 1911, and for the next twelve months Louis presided over the vital debates on whether the Navy should concentrate its first efforts on heavier- or lighter-than-air machines. The claims of both were powerful. The airship party could cite the airship's long range, superior lifting power and ability to hover for long periods scouting for the fleet in the murk of the North Sea. But by a series of mischances, Britain's first effort to build a sizeable airship – inspired by Fisher when he was still at the Admiralty – had ended in disaster. The unfortunately-named *Mayfly* never did.

These were heady days for aviators. Louis was a stout aeroplane supporter from the first. And so was Churchill. Under the stress of competition, and spurred on by the youthful enthusiasm of the early flyers and Churchill's energy and far-sightedness, long-term plans were made based on the confident assumption that the aeroplane had an almost unlimited future. A chain of air stations was planned for Britain's southern and eastern coasts, there was talk of torpedo aircraft at a time when the latest machines could scarcely get off the ground with a single passenger, a workable floatplane was contrived and rapidly developed during Louis's regime, and even before the end of 1911 Samson had taken off from the forecastle of a battleship.

At first it was decided to press ahead with heavier-than-air craft alone, but as more information was gathered from Germany of her zeppelin programme and of the size of the dirigibles – up to one million cubic feet capacity – 'it became apparent that the use of airships as an adjunct of naval warfare was passing beyond the region of experiment into one of fact';[17] and, as the Committee of Imperial Defence decided in December 1912, 'we cannot afford any longer to neglect airships'.[18]

With the advantage of hindsight, it is interesting to line up and identify the protagonists with their cause. Louis's strongest supporter in the heavier-than-air lobby was, of all arch-reactionaries, 'Tug' Wilson. 'Sir Arthur Wilson seemed to think that experiments should be first made to land on a ship,'[19] Samson told Louis. Jellicoe became an airship man, and so was Fisher, that arch-innovator. Churchill vacillated from violently supporting Louis to pressing for a full-scale airship programme after all – Fisher saw to that.

It was a blessing for the nation that no one succeeded in 'shooting down' the aeroplane, so that at the outbreak of war the Navy was far ahead of the Army in air development and could muster nearly a hundred sea- and land-planes and a substantial reserve of pilots as well as the seaplane carrier *Hermes*.

Early in 1914 eight large rigid airships were under construction, too. But they were not ready at the outbreak of the war, and Britain never built anything to match the enemy's zeppelins. On the other hand, the Royal Navy remained well ahead of the German Navy in its development of naval aircraft and was far ahead of the rest of the world with its carriers and torpedo and bombing planes at the end of the war. Much of the credit for laying the foundations must go to Louis.

At the end of 1913 Louis recommended to Churchill that the burden of responsibility for the Air Service should be transferred from the Second Sea Lord to the office of the Fourth Sea Lord who 'cannot in any sense of the word be described as a very hard worked or a very fully occupied Official'. He told how hard-pressed he had been as Second Sea Lord although 'I am not a slow worker, I think'.

'I had been intending,' scribbled Churchill characteristically in the corner of Louis's *Personal* note, 'to propose something of this kind myself'.[20] He did so in a formal memorandum to the Cabinet, without, of course, any reference to Louis or Jellicoe, who as Louis's successor as Second Sea Lord was to be relieved of the burden. Perhaps it is not surprising as this occurred when the battle over Admiral Poore was at its height and relations between the Board and its political chief were atrocious.

In 1913, with the Naval War Staff taking its first hesitant steps and a Naval Staff College already open, there remained one yawning gap in the nation's defences, the question of the insurance of merchant shipping in time of war. History showed its importance, especially in the Napoleonic Wars, and it is difficult to see why it had been so neglected ever since, unless it was that any fuss about it in peace hinted at lack of confidence in the Navy in time of war. Neither was it a very glamorous subject nor one which suggested kudos or honours for anyone who raised it. But, as history showed, a panic rise in marine insurance rates could clear the seas more effectively, and starve the nation more quickly, than any number of commerce raiders.

Louis had first become interested in the subject when serving in the Mediterranean in the early 1890s. Tryon had been campaigning for some sort of state control of marine insurance, and he infected Louis with his enthusiasm. Louis had been pressing for it ever since but did not get sufficient backing either from the Treasury or from Fisher during the Edwardian period.

It was not until he became First Sea Lord that Louis could insist on action, and at a meeting of the Committee of Imperial Defence on 6 February 1913, he initiated a debate. He showed how 'a few early captures' of merchantmen would send insurance rates rocketing, and cited his experience as D.N.I. during the Russo-Japanese War. Then a few Russian cruisers, ineffectually stopping ships and searching for contraband, had sent insurance rates shooting up. What could be expected, then, asked Louis, when this country was actually conducting a maritime war? As a result of this meeting there was set up – in the nick of time as it turned out – a Standing Sub-Committee on Insurance of British Shipping in time of War.

This led to the implementation of a state insurance scheme against war risks, which kept British commerce alive in spite of four years of ferocious U-boat warfare – and actually made a profit for the state! 'To this one measure, above all else, was due the uninterrupted flow of seaborne trade through all the vicissitudes of war,'[21] wrote the official historian on trade in the First World War.

When the progress of Louis's proposal was being debated in the Committee of Imperial Defence two months before the outbreak of war,[22] Churchill pointed out that the seas would become safer as war progressed because the Royal Navy would soon eliminate any German surface raiders, as indeed proved to be the case. But no one present – not even Louis who was 'in favour of substituting submarines for a battleship'[23] in the building programme, nor Churchill – whose mind was without an horizon – could bring himself to believe that any nation would ever conduct unrestricted submarine warfare against merchantmen.

Only Fisher believed that a future war would be so merciless and so cruel that barbarism at sea would become a commonplace. 'This submarine menace is a terrible one for British commerce and Great Britain alike . . .' he wrote in a memorandum on the subject on 1 January 1914. 'All that would be known would be that a certain ship and her crew had disappeared, or some of her boats would be picked up with a few survivors to tell the tale . . . The essence of war is violence, and moderation in war is imbecility.'[24]

Louis considered the memorandum was 'marred by this sugestion', and Churchill thought that 'this would never be done by a civilized power . . . These are frankly unthinkable propositions'.[25]

It is ironical that the one man in a position of power who predicted the dangers of U-boat warfare took no steps to implement a national insurance scheme to protect the nation's commerce; and that this was left to the milder and more balanced Louis Battenberg. He, in turn was backed by Churchill, who was to see Britain all-but-throttled to death by the dread U-boat in two World Wars.

There is little light relief, and there are few domestic intrusions, in Louis's professional life during these two years at the top. Only occasionally do we catch a glimpse of the family man, the man who loved to be with his wife and children and away from the desks and committee rooms of Whitehall.

Just one month before war broke out, in the course of one of his tours of inspection, Louis visited the training ship *Empress*. Once this ship's name had been *Revenge*, and Louis told the boys of his stormy Atlantic crossing to Halifax in her forty-five years ago, a voyage which had taken thirty days. He had been aloft when a gale was at its height, he recounted, and a spar had fallen and crashed to the deck below – there, there was the patch (and he pointed to the deck) the carpenter's crew had inserted in the timbers. Cadet to Admiral and First Sea Lord! And with all the honours and all the power his adopted nation had granted him . . .

At the end of 1913 the Royal Navy had three Princes of Battenberg on its List* – Georgie was a lieutenant in the battle cruiser *New Zealand*, and Dickie was still a cadet at Osborne – doing well enough but not exceptionally well. He had had a bad year with his health and had been laid up with scarlet fever and mumps for some weeks. Christmas brought all the family together at Kent House on the

---

* So had the Army. All Beatrice's sons were in the Army, including the haemophilic Prince Leopold. Prince Alexander ('Drino') had transferred from the Navy into the Grenadier Guards.

Isle of Wight, the guests of Aunt Louise and Uncle Lorne. On Boxing Day Georgie invited his younger brother on board his battle cruiser. The *New Zealand* was decorated for Christmas, just like the *Drake* in 1905, and Georgie took his younger brother round his great ship. Dickie wore his cadet's uniform with pride. On his breast was the Coronation ribbon – the first of so many medals that would one day grow to eight rows.

When Princess Louise had no further use for Kent House she gave it to Victoria in anticipation of a clause in her will. And so, just before the outbreak of war, the Battenbergs at last had a home of their own in England in addition to Louis's official residence at the Admiralty in London.

Princess Louise's brother, the Duke of Connaught, had recently called on Victoria at Mall House when Alice was staying there with her three daughters. Victoria introduced her grand-daughters to their 'Great Great Uncle' – to which, she said, he replied in a horrified voice, 'My dear Victoria, you are making an ancestor of me!'

In fact, Great Great Uncle Arthur, Duke of Connaught, became godfather to Cecile's first boy, yet another Prince Louis of Hesse, his great great great nephew. The Duke of Connaught's daughter, Lady Patricia Ramsay died as this book was being completed, leaving only Princess Alice, Countess of Athlone, as the last of the old Queen's grandchildren.

Louis's Christmas break in 1913 was a brief one. His work at the Admiralty, an especially difficult political situation at home, and the ever worsening international scene, were all combining to exert an almost intolerable burden on his shoulders. Several times that winter he was laid low with attacks of gout, the pain of which added to his exhaustion. They lasted a week or ten days; and on his return to his office he inevitably faced an accumulation of work. But there is no doubt that he was on top of his job at this time. He fought the good fight alongside Churchill as bravely, and as successfully, as ever.

Their greatest struggle was over the 1913–14 Estimates, which continued for five bitter months of that winter. It was mainly an internal and political struggle in which Churchill was always in the van, and exposed, and Louis and his three Sea Lords took up the rearguard and provided him with the ammunition and support.

The fight must be seen against the disease of rearmament which had infected the whole world, from Chile to Russia, from the U.S.A. to Australia, and of course to every European nation. In the naval field the statistical competition centred upon Dreadnought-type battleships. Everybody was building or buying them – Chile and Turkey, Brazil and Greece, Japan and Austria, as well as the great powers in vast numbers. It was as if every country in the 1970s was building up their batteries of I.C.B.M.s, and not just the super-powers. The race had become a sort of insane statistical game, with a wide variation of the interpretation of the figures according to the weight of armour, the speed and the number and calibre of guns of each Dreadnought.

Britain, with its small professional army, its great Empire, and its dependence on freedom of trade for its very life, had by 1913 been watching the increasing size of the German Navy with proportion-ately growing alarm.

As late as January 1914 Churchill defined the situation to the Cabi-net: 'Defeat to Germany at sea means nothing but the loss of the ships sunk or damaged in battle. Behind the German Dreadnought line stand $4\frac{1}{2}$ million soldiers & a narrow sea bristling with fortresses & batteries. Nothing that we cd do after a naval victory cd affect the safety or freedom of a single German hamlet . . .'[26]

Such a statement shows how incomplete was Churchill's under-standing of sea power at that time. For a man with such monumental powers of prophecy and strategic thought it is amazing that he did not predict the decisive throttling power of the British blockade in war.

When Churchill was called to the Admiralty after the Agadir Crisis, the Cabinet had agreed that a 6 : 4 superiority over Germany in Dreadnoughts was minimal for the security of the Empire. That meant that Britain had to build at least four Dreadnoughts *every year*, which with the appropriate proportion of cruisers, destroyers, sub-marines and auxiliary craft (to say nothing of ammunition, dock-yards, anchorages, shore and coaling facilities) placed a fearsome burden on the nation's resources.

The political struggle, in the simplest terms,* was between the left wing of the ruling Liberal Party, and the right, or navalist, wing, which was supported by the opposition Conservative Party. In the centre of the field of battle, like some cynical but keen-eyed umpire on military manoeuvres, stood the Prime Minister Asquith.

The left-wing Liberals, fighting for political as well as for genuinely

---

* For the best account of this political contest see Marder, *Dreadnought to Scapa Flow* i pp. 311–27.

compassionate motives for a reduction in money for arms and an increase in social security for the poor, the old and the under-privileged, had as C.-in-C. David Lloyd George, that devious, shrewd Chancellor of the Exchequer. The navalists, of course, were led by Churchill – who, only a few years earlier, had fought *beside* Lloyd George against Fisher and McKenna for a *reduction* in naval expenditure.

The newspapers, then commanding much greater influence than they do today, took up pro- and anti-armament sides on all matters, and especially violently over the Estimates battle. For example, predictably the *Daily Telegraph* powerfully supported Churchill and his Board throughout; while C. P. Scott's Liberal *Manchester Guardian* wanted to be rid of Louis, and Churchill, too, if need be. 'An imme-diate change is needed at the Admiralty,' Scott wrote to Lloyd George. 'Fisher must come back. If the present First Lord can't work with him, then surely he shd make way for some one else . . .'[27] It was a curious experience for a Hessian to be accused of being a reactionary warmonger, and Victoria especially felt it deeply.

Hopwood tried to keep the Sea Lords away from the front line and hinted, through Lord Stamfordham, that the King might use his influence on his cousin to show restraint and not allow Churchill to drag him forward.[28] In the end the four Sea Lords, like many who work behind the lines in war, took all the knocks and got none of the credit, which partly accounts for Scott's hostility. At one stage, and with Churchill's encouragement, they threatened to resign in a body in his support. When a compromise was reached, with no reduction in Dreadnought building, but with some substantial concessions from Churchill, he swung round on his Board and told them that he wanted no rebellion, or else.

'If you or your naval colleagues,' he wrote to Louis, 'are not con-tented with the Estimates for which the Government propose to ask Parliament, I shd be willing – though I shd regret the change – to relieve the Board of the duty of signing them, & to present them to the House of Commons as the Army Estimates are presented upon the sole responsibility of the Minister. This is a step wh has been vy strongly pressed upon me during the last two years & I have on several occasions resisted it with difficulty. I cd not help being dis-appointed by the reception wh was given to the great & successful exertions I have made on behalf of the Navy.'[29]

Churchill concluded with the thinly disguised threat that he could well survive should they persist in resigning in a body. Only days before Louis and his Board were being complimented on their loyalty. It was hard for simple naval officers to keep pace with political manoeuvrings, and Louis could be forgiven if he had likened working with Winston to sharing an office with Humpty Dumpty. The threat was pure bluff. Churchill, in fact, knew very well that if he toppled his Board off the Humpty Dumpty wall beside him he would go too; and that there was no one to whom he could turn to replace Louis at this stage of events.

Louis was spared any more of the informal and unofficial missions to his influential and ruling relatives during his period of office as First Sea Lord, but both he and Victoria discussed politics and international relations with the Russian Emperor and Prince Henry, and less often with the Kaiser when they were together.

The burden of these talks was always reported to the King, verbally or by letter. For example, we find Louis writing to George V: ' . . . may I take this opportunity of pointing out that Henry of Prussia (who presumably reflects his brother's view) does not appear to realize that if war were to break out between Germany & Austria v Russia and France, we here cannot permit either of the two latter countries, esp France, to be crippled – consequently we *cannot* stand out in certain circumstances. I was glad to hear from him that William has really tried to moderate Franz Ferdinand's military ardour.'[30]

Louis had originally arranged to take Dickie to join Victoria, Louise and Nona in Russia in August 1914. In that event it was planned that he would have conducted one more semi-official diplomatic mission. There was a good deal of pressure in both England and Russia to bring about a naval agreement, Russia having now recovered from the losses of the war with Japan and being on the way towards creating a modern navy. This would threaten Germany in the Baltic and Turkey in the Black Sea. Conversations during the summer were to be concluded, and any outstanding points tidied up, by Louis when he visited Nicky and Alicky with Victoria. But Wilhelm had marched against Nicky before he could get there, and Louis never again saw Russia.

One of a number of minor economies to which the Board of Admiralty agreed at this time was a cancellation of the customary full summer manoeuvres, which cost little short of a quarter of a million pounds in fuel. Instead, there was to be a full test mobilization of the Navy's Royal Fleet Reserve and of the Reserve officers, and the reactivation of the whole of the powerful reserve Third Fleet.

Louis had been pressing for a full mobilization of Fleet Reserves for ten years, and most strongly as Second Sea Lord when the Mobilization Division at the Admiralty came under his control. The machinery was there, massive and elaborate on paper, but would it work? It could be fatal to the nation if it did not.

The subject of a test mobilization had come up in conversation with Churchill on a number of occasions since they had both come to the Admiralty at the end of 1911. When Jellicoe took his place as Second Sea Lord, Louis discussed with him, and then again with Churchill, the possibility of a full scale test. Churchill quickly recognized the political and financial advantages of such a test in the face of looming difficulties over finance with the Treasury and Parliament.

In June 1913 Louis received one of Churchill's numerous 'as you know' memoranda. 'As you know,' this one began, 'this has been in my mind for some long time. I should hope next year to obtain a mobilisation of the whole of the Royal Fleet Reserve . . .'[31] Louis, of course, assented, and Churchill put the proposal to the Cabinet on 13 December 1913.

Some 20,000 reserve officers and ratings answered the call in the summer of 1914. The world was at peace, and although there had been some recent unpleasantness, and a nasty assassination down in the Balkans, very few of these men realized that it would be a long time before they saw their homes again, and for a number of them there would be no return. To Louis, Churchill and the Board the international situation appeared more ominous, and there was a sense of urgency in the corridors and offices and committee rooms of the Admiralty which had been experienced recently only during the two Moroccan crises, and the threat of war with Russia a decade earlier. Let Churchill himself take up the story briefly:

'Officers specially detached from the Admiralty watched the process of mobilization at every port in order that every defect, shortage or hitch in the system might be reported and remedied. Prince Louis and I personally inspected the process at Chatham. All the reservists drew their kits and proceeded to their assigned ships. All the Third Fleet ships coaled and raised steam and sailed for the general concentration at Spithead. Here on the 17th and 18th of July was held the grand review of the Navy. It constituted incomparably the greatest assemblage of naval power ever witnessed in the history of the world. The King himself was present and inspected ships of every class. On the morning of the 19th the whole Fleet put to sea for exercises of various kinds. It took more than six hours for this armada, every ship decked with flags and crowded with blue-jackets and marines, to pass, with bands playing and at 15 knots, before the Royal Yacht, while overhead the naval seaplanes and aeroplanes circled continuously . . .

'One after another the ships melted out of sight beyond the Nab. They were going on a longer voyage than any of us could know.'[32]

Among those who had been temporarily appointed to the great Dreadnoughts were the cadets from Osborne. Dickie found himself in his brother's battle cruiser *New Zealand*. He arrived on board, full of anticipatory excitement, with a small valise and was issued with a hammock and told off to his quarters. This was the real thing, but mercifully softened by the presence of Georgie. 'I was in great awe of him,' Dickie recounted, 'as he showed me all round his huge ship.' Together they watched the searchlight and flying displays, and later their father came on board with the First Lord.

'Papa arrived & we had church, after which we had lunch with the Skipper,' Dickie wrote to Victoria in Russia. 'After lunch we went on board the 'Enchantress' & saw Winston Churchill. Mrs and Miss Hogier [Hozier] or something, also Admiral Jellicoe, & the 4th Sea Lord, and Admiral Hood etc. Georgie took the female Winston Churchills back to the *New Zealand* for tea . . .'[33]

The ships of the Reserve Third Fleet were due to return to their home ports on 23 July. The officers and ratings who had supplemented the regular complements were already beginning to disperse to their homes, though most were still on board, when news arrived at the Foreign Office on the afternoon of 24 July of Austria's threatening ultimatum to Serbia. The First Fleet, and the Second Fleet with its high proportion of Reservists, were intact, replenished, ready for war, in Portland Harbour. These Reservists were due to pay off on Monday morning, 27 July. Very large numbers of regular officers and ratings were at the same time due to go on summer leave.

On Friday evening 24 July, at 6 p.m., Louis was still at his office. Churchill returned from the House of Commons, where the Foreign Secretary had given the news of the Austrian note. There was now, Churchill stated, a real risk of war. 'Europe is trembling on the verge of a general war,' he had, a few minutes earlier, written to his wife.

The question of 'standing the fleet fast' – that is to say, cancelling the dispersal of ships and the release of the Reservists, and the summer leave – would have to be considered urgently. It was not only a strategical and tactical question. It was also a political question. To cancel a demobilization could aggravate a crisis and provoke a possible enemy as seriously as ordering a mobilization.

On the next morning, Saturday 25 July, Churchill and Louis met again at the Admiralty and discussed this question, which was so delicate yet so critical that the security of the Empire could depend on the decision reached. Churchill chose this moment to tell Louis that he was going to the country for the weekend by the 1 o'clock train. His wife, who had been poorly, was at the seaside at Cromer, 138 miles away.

> 'The cosiest corner for holiday whiffs
> Is found in a hollow of Cromer cliffs'

ran the Punch couplet.

The fastest train took three-and-a-half hours. But there was the telephone. He told Louis that he had arranged to have a special operator placed in the Cromer telegraph office day and night, and that he would telephone every few hours for news. Asquith, Grey, Haldane and Lloyd George would also all be away for the weekend.

'Ministers with their week-end holidays are incorrigible,' Louis told his younger son when Dickie arrived at Mall House from Osborne a few days later. He could have added that naval officers, too, are incorrigible for the Admiralty was empty of almost everyone except the resident clerk.

All through that Saturday and the following day the despatches and memoranda arrived in a steady flow. In the afternoon a note from the Foreign Office indicated that Serbia had accepted all Austrian demands. When Churchill telephoned from Cromer at 6 p.m. Saturday, Louis was able to give him this better news. 'I went to bed with a feeling that things might blow over,'[34] Churchill later recalled.

Louis was telephoned at breakfast time Sunday morning. What was the news? Churchill asked at once. Louis told him that things were not so good. There was a rumour from the Foreign Office that even Serbia's craven acceptance had not satisfied Austria. Telephone me at 12 o'clock, Churchill requested. And then went down to the beach to make sandcastles with his children. 'We dammed the little rivulets which trickled down to the sea as the tide went out. It was a very beautiful day.'

Churchill returned to his hotel, and Louis's telephone call came through promptly at noon. The line was bad and both men had trouble hearing what the other was saying. But it was clear to

Churchill that 'the items of news' were 'all tending to a rise of temperature'.[35] Louis asked him what advice he had about the demobilization of the reservists. If orders were not issued very soon, all the reserve officers and men would be dispersed and thousands of regulars would be scattering to the four corners of Britain. Many were joining their families at the seaside and recall notices would therefore not reach them, at least for a week or two.

Churchill warned Louis of the political implications of cancelling the demobilization and standing the fleet fast, but made it clear (and of this there could be no doubt in spite of the poor line) that, as the man on the spot, it must be Louis's decision alone. Churchill added, as a crumb of comfort, that he had decided to cut short his weekend and would return that night.

It may well have occurred to Louis that Churchill might have absented himself from London for another reason than concern for his wife and for the opportunity of playing with his children on the beach.[36] At some time that week-end the decision would have to be made whether or not to stand the fleet fast. The wrong decision now could seriously damage and even destroy the career of the man who made it. During the early part of that Sunday afternoon, almost alone in the huge Admiralty building, Louis wrestled with the problem. He had no one to discuss it with.

The Austrian ultimatum to Serbia was due to expire at 6 p.m., and Austria had refused to accept Serbia's reply. Louis decided that if Austria remained implacable and unyielding by this time, then he would issue the orders himself, while Churchill was – presumably – in the train on the way back to London.

All the messages that came in during that long summer afternoon of 26 July suggested a further sharpening of the crisis all over Europe. Diplomatic relations between Serbia and Austria were broken off. At 6 o'clock Louis began writing out the orders himself in his own hand, assisted by the resident clerk, and within five minutes the top priority message was singing along the wires to Portland – cancel leave and demobilization of Reservists, First and Second Fleets to remain concentrated.

Then Louis sent an urgent despatch to George V and another to the Foreign Office telling of what he had done.

A combination of good luck, prescience, exact planning, and finally the decision to take a brave risk, had resulted in the Royal Navy being ready, concentrated and on a war footing in the nation's most anxious hour since Trafalgar. Marder has called it 'a master stroke', and Churchill later referred gratefully and publicly to Louis's securing of 'the timely concentration of the Fleet'.[37] It was the first time any acknowledgement had been made to Louis's part at the outbreak of war. But by then the sounds of catastrophe drowned all claims of credit to him.

Louis cared little for the credit (which was as well for he got none publicly and little privately at the time, or in published works since for that matter) and never referred to that Sunday afternoon and the decision he had made except to his family. It was enough that he had done his duty, and a blessed bonus that George V and the Cabinet approved and that when Churchill raced into the Admiralty at half past nine he supported him in what he had done.

There had to be an announcement the next day. When it appeared in the newspapers it became only one of a large number of items telling of the worsening situation, and the wording was cool and reserved – 'No Manoeuvre Leave', 'Orders to First and Second Fleets'. The tone was more urgent in the signal that was despatched from the Admiralty on that same day:

July 27, 1914

This is not the Warning Telegram, but European political situation makes war between Triple Entente and Triple Alliance Powers by no means impossible. Be prepared to shadow possible hostile men-of-war and consider dispositions of H.M. ships under your command from this point of view. Measure is purely precautionary. No unnecessary person is to be informed. The utmost secrecy is to be observed.

During that week, as the clouds darkened, step by step the well-prepared contingency naval plans were put into effect. Coastguards were alerted, guards were set up on bridges, magazines, oil tanks, and harbour entrances, shore batteries fully manned, the ports watched for unwelcome foreigners, foreign warships building in British yards – including the two great Dreadnoughts for Turkey – were taken over for the Royal Navy.

On the morning of 28 July Churchill, Louis and his Chief of the Admiralty War Staff, Rear-Admiral Doveton Sturdee, discussed the timing of the despatch of the First and Second Fleets to their war stations. Louis and Churchill agreed that there could be no further delay. The First Fleet, later renamed Grand Fleet, included all the most modern ships, six Battle Squadrons numbering thirty-three battleships and four battle cruisers supported by cruisers and dozens of destroyers. Under the distant blockade strategy only recently implemented by the Naval War Staff, this Fleet was destined for bases in Scotland, while the Second Fleet, which would cover the passage of the Army to France and seal off the second entrance to the North Sea, was to be based at Portland. With these fleets at their stations, Germany was cut off by sea from the rest of the world until her Navy emerged from its bases, confronted, and destroyed in battle the Royal Navy.

The British First Fleet could reach its Scottish bases by two alternative routes – to the west or to the east of Britain. The west route was safer, but it was longer and while the fleet was *en route* it left open to attack every port in Britain from the north of Scotland to the south of England. The east route was quicker.

'[The Fleet] could go through the Straits of Dover and through the North Sea,' wrote Churchill, 'and therefore the island would not be uncovered even for a single day.'[38] It was the dangerous route, the brave route – and, inevitably, it was the route chosen by Louis and Churchill.

Cabinet approval was called for. Louis, who had always believed in acting first and obtaining authority afterwards, supported Churchill wholeheartedly when he decided to issue secret orders, and *now*, without formal approval, though the Prime Minister was told.

On Tuesday 28 July 1914, Louis transmitted this signal to the C.-in-C. at 5 p.m.:

To-morrow, Wednesday, the First Fleet is to leave Portland for Scapa Flow. Destination is to be kept secret except to flag and commanding officers. As you are required at the Admiralty, Vice-Admiral 2nd Battle Squadron is to take command. Course from Portland is to be shaped to southward, then a middle Channel course to the Straits of Dover. The Squadrons are to pass through the Straits without lights during the night and to pass outside the shoals on their way north . . .

The Fleet had been stood fast; now Louis sent it on its way to its battle stations. But it is best left to Churchill's graphic and romantic pen to follow this massive fleet on its northward passage: 'We may now picture this great Fleet, with its flotillas and cruisers, steaming slowly out of Portland Harbour, squadron by squadron, scores of gigantic castles of steel wending their way across the misty, shining sea, like giants bowed in anxious thought. We may picture them again as darkness fell, eighteen miles of warships running at high speed and in absolute blackness through the narrow Straits, bearing with them into the broad waters of the North the safeguard of our considerable affairs.'[39]

On top of all his vast and complex duties, Louis had the additional burden of worry about Victoria, Louise and Nona Kerr in Russia. He had already telegraphed to say that he and Dickie could not after all join them. Now he despatched an urgent telegram to St Petersburg asking that they should be given safe conduct home through Scandinavia as soon as possible. The idea of war with Germany was terrible enough. But war with Germany with his beloved family trapped, or in German hands, was more than he could bear to think about.

Louis's anguish at this time was indeed deep and painful. He was no lover of war. His whole soul flinched back from the prospect of material and human destruction on an unprecedented scale that opened before the nation. For him it would be 'brother against brother, friend against friend', the prospect he had faced as a young man in 1866, and a prospect his own father had had to face on a number of occasions. His nephew Prince Maurice of Battenberg was in the 60th Rifles, his son Georgie was serving with Admiral Beatty in the Battle Squadron, and he had relatives in the German Army and Navy.

On Sunday 2 August, Louis ordered this signal to be despatched to his naval commanders:

At 2.20 today, 2 August, the following note was handed to the French and German Ambassadors. The British Government would not allow the passage of German ships through the English Channel or the North Sea in order to attack the coasts or shipping of France.

Be prepared to meet surprise attacks.

On Monday 3 August, eight days after Louis had 'stood the Fleet fast', the King of the Belgians made his direct appeal to Britain for assistance as the German armies poured across his frontier. Now at last the Liberal, and mainly pacifist, British Cabinet recognized the inevitability of war, and those who wanted no part of it resigned. The British ultimatum to Germany demanding the maintenance of Belgian neutrality was despatched from the Foreign Office. It was disregarded. At 11 p.m. 4 August 1914 the British Empire was at war with the German Empire and its allies. When the Prime Minister made the announcement in the House of Commons the next morning, it was observed that tears were coursing down Churchill's cheeks.

At the precise hour of 11 p.m. – midnight German time – Louis had ordered the war signal to be telegraphed to all fleets and naval establishments:

COMMENCE HOSTILITIES AGAINST GERMANY

Louis's grief was necessarily more private than Churchill's. It was no less profound. 'I well remember,' wrote one senior officer, 'that on the historical 4th of August I had had occasion to visit Prince Louis at his office in Whitehall. I went into his room and found him bowed over his writing-table with his face buried in his arms. He remained for some minutes without moving or speaking in that attitude and I was beginning to feel some little alarm, when he looked up and said, "Fremantle, it's war at midnight, and no one seems to realize what it will mean to us and to the world".'[40]

Louis was thankful that he was not alone that evening. Dickie and the other Osborne cadets had been put ashore before the fleet's Channel exercises, and the boys – too young and still too inexperienced to fight – were granted their usual summer leave. He came up to London by train from Portsmouth to join his father at Mall House. He knew now that he would not be going to Russia after all, and to console himself, and to amuse himself during the long days that inevitably lay ahead until his mother and sister returned, he went to his favourite pet department at Selfridges and bought some white mice in a cage.

Those last, desperate summer days of peace in London are remembered today by Lord Mountbatten for the rare satisfaction of being alone with his father at meals, and hearing from him the inner truth, stage by stage, of the nation's march towards war. Louis always talked to his sons, as he did to his midshipmen, as if they were his equals in age and understanding, and this made even more memorable those evenings of early August when Louis, after one more day of urgent meetings, urgent plans and urgent orders, came down for dinner with his son in the First Sea Lord's dining-room at Mall House – two naval officers together, separated by all the ranks in the service between cadet and full admiral, and by forty-six years.

Louis, as smart in his admiral's uniform as if onboard his flagship, and Dickie – already emulating his father's concern for his appearance – sat at the long polished table with its silver and glass shining in the candlelight, waited on by stewards in white jackets.

On the evening of 4 August they both knew that the last hope of peace had died with the sunset. There would be no answer to the British ultimatum which was due to expire in three hours' time.

The moment was solemn enough, but it was not a sombre meal. Now that the die was cast, the talk was of action and likely outcomes, of the German assault on France and Belgium, of the respective strengths of the great fleets, of what the submarines might do, of how, already, the great processes of organization were transporting the British Army to the Channel ports for passage, under the shelter of the Navy's battle fleets, to the Continent.

Outside the crowds were gathering in Trafalgar Square on one side of the Admiralty Arch, and all the way along the Mall towards Buckingham Palace, calling out fervently for the King and singing patriotic songs.

After dinner the admiral and cadet went their separate ways. Louis went by the special direct stairs and corridor to the Admiralty War Room where a great map on the wall showed the position of every fleet, squadron, flotilla and individual Royal Navy ship in the world.

They were all correctly at their war stations. There was only a thin scattering of enemy warships outside the German home bases – a battle cruiser and cruiser in the Mediterranean, a squadron of cruisers in the Far East, one or two more scattered cruisers which would soon be rounded up. Within days every German merchant-man would have sought the shelter of a friendly or neutral harbour. Even before the expiration of the ultimatum, the distant blockade of Germany was taking effect. When would the High Seas Fleet come out to fight?

Dickie had his evening duty, too. He played with his white mice for a while, watched them spin their wheel, gave them their food and water, and went to bed for his first night of war.

13

'It is a promise. It will be fulfilled. I take
entire responsibility.'
PRINCE LOUIS *on the despatch of the Ostend
troopships*

THE Battenbergs were a widely scattered family on the first night
of war. Georgie was away with the Fleet; and while Louis and Dickie
were dining in the Admiralty Victoria and Louise, with Nona Kerr
and Ella, were in a train drawing into St Petersburg railway station.
They were tired and fussed, and Louise and Nona were severely
ill with tonsilitis. They were met by the British ambassador, Sir
George Buchanan, and Baroness Buxhoeveden, one of Alicky's
ladies-in-waiting, and hurried off to the Winter Palace, which had
been specially opened up for them as it was midsummer.

Now there was the real fear that the family might be split for the
duration of the war that was already raging in Russia, Belgium,
France and Serbia.

The expedition, which also included the necessary ladies-in-
waiting, maids and other servants, had started from Nijni Novgorod
(now Gorky) in the Imperial river yacht down the Volga. It was
hot and dusty, and even when they were able to see the banks of the
wide, muddy river, 'the shores were not very picturesque'. The
Volga's tributary, the Kama, was more interesting, and they stopped
at many towns and villages. At each the routine was the same – the
people turned out in their best clothes to greet and do honour to the
two sisters of the Russian Empress. Ella and Victoria would then
pursue their own enthusiasms, as they had always done since they
were children, Ella going at once to the local convent, Victoria for

brisk walks to see any historical, architectural or archaeological sights, studying the people, noting their appearance, their clothes and characteristics.

At the town of Perm the party broke up, and their journeys took on a portentous character. Ella visited a convent at Alapaevsk, where she was later to be incarcerated in the schoolhouse and so cruelly murdered in four years time; and Victoria, Louise and Nona concluded their journeyings through the Urals to Ekaterinburg, where their arrival was treated as a formal one – a royal visit.

In this ugly mining town there was an ominous feeling of hostility in their reception, quite unlike anything they had previously experienced. 'I did not think the town attractive,' wrote Victoria, 'and there the population did not seem particularly pleased at the official visit. I noticed it, especially, at an evening entertainment of fireworks, where the crowd was quite unenthusiastic.'[1] Driving through the town, Victoria's attention was caught by a large house on a square in the centre, and she asked who it belonged to. 'It is owned by a rich merchant,' she was told.

When she was mourning her youngest sister and her brother-in-law and nieces and nephew, she remembered the picture she carried in her mind of that square, plain yet theatening house where the family were murdered, and of the tour they had made outside the town and past the shafts of iron and gold mines afterwards.

It was at Ekaterinburg that the message from Louis about the imminence of war arrived; and here, too, Louise and Nona picked up their virulent tonsilitis, which was accompanied by a high fever and much pain. The journey back from this unhappy town by trains and steamer to St Petersburg was a nightmare. Doctors, summoned to the train by telegraph, awaited them at several of the towns through which they passed. But little could be done for the unfortunate pair, except to treat them with caustic.

Ella rejoined them for the last part of their journey, and in the Winter Palace Victoria enjoyed the pleasure of seeing her two younger sisters together, seemingly reconciled, at least for the time being and with Rasputin banished – perhaps for ever? – from the court. Olga and Tatiana, now tall, lovely girls of eighteen and seventeen, came with their mother. The parting was sad for they knew that the separation might be a long one.

Fighting was now raging along Russia's western borders, and all Europe must soon be drawn into the war. Getting home was going to be a difficult and possibly a dangerous business. Alicky had, 'with loving foresight, equipped us with thick coats and other serviceable clothing for the sea journey' as they had only light summer clothing with them. They were also given little bags of golden sovereigns which they wore round their waists under their dresses, although Victoria had to leave behind all her family jewels.

The first part of the journey was simple and comfortable, a special train having been laid on for them to the Russian frontier at Torneo at the head of the Gulf of Bothnia. Here their carriage was shunted into a siding alongside another carriage. But it was no ordinary carriage. It was, they saw, a special royal one, luxuriously fitted out. Scattered royal relations from all over Europe were hurrying to their home courts.

Victoria at once recognized its occupants – they were Aunt Minnie, Tsar Alexander III's widow, and her daughter Olga Alexandrovna, old friends and relatives from so many happy summers at Heiligenberg. They, too, were heading anxiously for home – Aunt Minnie from England – but there was just time for Victoria to climb down to the line and run to wish them farewell through the window.

Here Victoria and an official from the British Embassy had to help her convalescent companions over a high wooden footbridge, which was the only connection between Russia and the first Swedish town. There was a train due to leave shortly for Stockholm. But they found that it had been entirely taken over by officials of the Austrian Embassy in St Petersburg, and there was not a seat left for them. At the cost of £75 in gold they managed to persuade the Swedish authorities to hitch on to it the carriage which the Dowager Empress and her daughter had just vacated.

From Stockholm, where they were looked after by the Crown Prince of Sweden, conditions improved, but the last stage of their journey was difficult and rugged. They managed to get on board the last ship from Bergen in Norway. It was packed with tourists and anglers who had been holidaying among the fjords and were now desperate to get back to England before a blockade shut them out. The ship took a circuitous journey, going far north to avoid the risk of attack, and arrived in Newcastle at last on 16 August. At Mall House, where they were greeted with thankfulness and joy, 'we found,' wrote Victoria, 'Louis absorbed in his work which went on at night as well as by day,' and Dickie, who was 'finding occupation in the care of some white mice'.

'War,' Thomas Hardy wrote, 'makes rattling good history.' But the history can vary according to which side you are on, and through whose eyes you view the battle. Prince Louis of Battenberg's experience of war was brief, tumultuous and agonising. But for 'good history' it is necessary to stand back to survey and judge what was accomplished, what went right, and what went wrong, during and immediately after Louis's period of office as First Sea Lord.

The German Navy which Kaiser Wilhelm and Grand Admiral Alfred von Tirpitz had created over the past twenty years was highly professional and well led. The quality of the ships, and their equipment, was very high. So was the gunnery and seamanship. Their staff work was highly developed. Neither their spirit nor their *matériel* was conditioned by the undue regard for tradition which still gripped the British Navy. The British Naval War Staff was still raw to its task and lacking experience. The German Naval Staff had many faults, too, but at least it was well run in – a process which Louis calculated could take 25 years.

Louis, from long familiarity, recognized all this, and had the highest respect for the young and ardent German Navy which had germinated and matured so rapidly in its un-maritime Teutonic soil where militarism had for so long been the only crop. He also knew the German weak spots, an advantage which Churchill had long ago appreciated in his German-born partner. Louis understood the tendency to inflexibility in the German mind, the over-confidence they felt in equipment and their skill with it, and the sense of inferiority they suffered in experience and tradition by contrast with the Royal Navy. He knew his old homeland would make a tough antagonist, even though Britain had been fighting, mainly successfully, at sea for some four centuries, while the German Navy had scarcely existed a quarter century ago.

The balance of strength between the two battle fleets was very fine; finer than either appreciated in view of the as yet unrecognized superiority of German gunnery, shells, torpedoes, mines, and the strength of her ships. Germany, hemmed into her corner of the North Sea, also had the advantage of surprise enjoyed by any blockaded fleet – remember Louis at Argostoli. Nor did Germany depend, in the short term, on keeping her sea communications open. The German Navy could afford to sit back in its base, and watch with satisfaction its antagonist exercising the arduous demands made on blockading fleets in high winter seas, wearing down engines and consuming fuel while always at risk from mine and torpedo.

By means of these new underwater weapons and carefully timed forays, the Kaiser hoped slowly to whittle down the strength of the British battle fleet until the High Seas Fleet had gained parity, or even numerical superiority. A credit and debit account of the opening phase of the war at sea reads something like this, with the Royal Navy achievements first:

1. The safe transport of the entire British Expeditionary Force across the Channel without the loss of a single life.

2. The total blockade of Germany, excluding only the Baltic Sea. Within a few weeks of the outbreak of war, not a German merchantman was on the high seas and German maritime trade was dead.

3. In the first naval battle of the war on 28 August 1914, the intervention by Admiral Beatty's battle cruisers into an engagement between British and German light cruisers and destroyers led to the sinking of three modern German cruisers and one destroyer, and to the damaging of three more German cruisers. It was a confused, ill-coordinated action in which luck played its full part on both sides. But at the end of the day, the British could justly celebrate an invigorating success. The material losses to the Germans were nothing compared with the moral damage inflicted on them by the heavy guns of the battle cruisers. The British had penetrated German waters, had struck hard and retired with negligible damage. The German offensive spirit, already muted, was reduced still further, and the unspoken suspicion of British invincibility at sea seemed to be confirmed.

4. The almost total destruction of the only German Naval Squadron outside the North Sea on 8 December added a further fillip to the Royal Navy, and a wonderful Christmas present for the British public, depressed by the stalemate and slaughter in France.

5. Britain had been prepared for heavy losses during an early *guerre de course*. They were on a much smaller scale than might reasonably be expected considering the number of German men-of-war and armed merchantmen loose on the oceans at the outbreak of war, and the great difficulties in tracking them down and destroying them. Within a few months every German commerce raider had been eliminated.

6. The successful interception at the Dogger Bank in January 1915 of the German battle cruiser squadron by Beatty – the first ever Dreadnought engagement – in which the Germans lost the

largest and most powerful armoured cruiser ever built, and suffered severe damage to another of their big ships.

All but the last of these achievements occurred during or immediately after Louis's term of office as First Sea Lord. The successes during this early period were ignored or forgotten by his detractors. The Royal Navy was a victim of its own successful propaganda, its own tradition of victory in the dramatic manner.

For decades, and at an increasing intensity, naval propagandists from the Navy League and the proprietors of patriotic magazines and newspapers, down to the picture postcard publishers and manufacturers of children's sailor suits, had been projecting the image of the Navy as the nation's sure shield. The launch of every battleship, the promotion of every admiral, the annual manoeuvres, the cruises round the coasts, the part the Navy played in every international crisis, every imperial activity, added to its grand and heroic reputation in peace.

The faces of Jacky Fisher (pugnacious), David Beatty (cap aslant) and of Louis himself ('our handsome sailor Prince') were as familiar to the public as the silhouettes of the Dreadnoughts they commanded. The Royal Navy was not just 'the nation's sure shield'; it was to Britain the apotheosis of greatness and gallantry, summed up in the names of such monsters of steel as His Majesty's Ships *Invincible*, *Inflexible*, *Implacable* and *Indefatigable*.

With the coming of war the British people expected a sudden, swift and annihilating victory at sea, in the style of Nelson at Trafalgar. Had not the young Japanese Navy – British trained in mainly British-built ships – annihilated the great Russian 'bear' at Tsu-Shima?

The historical but dull fact that war is 99 per cent alert inactivity was scarcely considered. When setbacks occurred, it was natural and proper that questions should be asked and the quality of the men at the top examined.

And setbacks there were. The first was immediate and negative. There were only two German naval units in the Mediterranean, the modern and fast Dreadnought battle cruiser *Goeben* and the light cruiser *Breslau*. It was essential that they should be tracked down and destroyed without delay by the superior British forces. These were three battle cruisers of a slightly earlier vintage than the *Goeben*, four good armoured cruisers, four light cruisers and sixteen destroyers – an overwhelmingly superior force.

At one stage of the long and eventful chase, in the early hours of 7 August, the armoured cruisers under the command of Rear-Admiral Ernest Troubridge, could have engaged the German ships with every expectation of at least damaging them so that they could have been finished off by the battle cruisers. But, using as an excuse the greater range of the German guns, the Admiral withdrew. The *Goeben* and *Breslau* got away to neutral but sympathetic Turkey, which, influenced by this failure of British, and success of German, arms soon entered the war on the German side.

Six weeks later, on 22 September, three old British armoured cruisers, patrolling in an area where they should never have been, were intercepted by a German U-boat, and were sunk in turn, the second and third while hove to and misguidedly attempting to rescue the victims of the first disaster. 1,200 men drowned and the importance of the submarine, in German eyes especially, was greatly increased.

The submarine's torpedo had other victims during these early weeks, but it was a mine that gained for Germany her first Dreadnought success.

Soon after this came the news of Admiral von Spee's victory on 1 November off the coast of Chile over the British squadron sent to destroy him – Coronel, the first major British defeat since the days of sail. Invasion 'scares' and the bombardment of East Coast towns by tip-and-run raiding German battle cruisers were additional heavy blows to the reputation of the Board of Admiralty, of Churchill and of Louis.

The Admiralty gets no praise for successes at sea – that goes to the gallant commanders who secure the victories, and the sailors who serve under them. Conversely it gets the first knocks when things begin to go wrong, especially if the expectations of the public are as high as they were in August 1914. Judged historically today the record of the Royal Navy during those first six critical months was good, if not excellent, considering the vast burden of responsibility it carried and that it had had no experience of war at sea for a century. Except for the scandalous behaviour of Admiral Troubridge (Louis referred mildly to 'Troubridge's amazing misconduct'[2]) the commanders at sea performed bravely and ably. Any failures were in staff work and in communications.

In view of his later and unsurpassed record, it is easy to forgive Churchill his excessive zeal in the conduct of naval affairs during his term as First Lord in war, which was not much longer than

Louis's as First Sea Lord. He was aching for combat. One politician who knew him well, summed him up at this time: 'From his youth Mr Churchill has loved with all his heart, with all his mind, with all his soul, and with all his strength, three things – war, politics, and himself. He loves war for its dangers, he loves politics for the same reason, and himself he has always loved for the knowledge that his mind is dangerous – dangerous to his enemies, dangerous to his friends, dangerous to himself. I can think of no man I have ever met who would so quickly and so bitterly eat his heart out in Paradise . . .'3

Churchill's pious pronouncements on his responsibilities as First Lord read curiously in the light of history. 'I exercised a close general supervision over everything that was done or proposed,' he wrote. 'Further, I claimed and exercised an unlimited power of suggestion and initiative over the whole field, subject only to the approval and agreement of the First Sea Lord ... Besides our regular meetings the First Sea Lord and I consulted together constantly at all hours. Within the limits of our agreed policy either he or I gave in writing authority for telegrams and decisions which the Chief of the Staff might from hour to hour require. Moreover, it happened in a large number of cases that seeing what ought to be done and confident of the agreement of the First Sea Lord, I myself drafted the telegrams and decisions in accordance with our policy, and the Chief of the Staff took them personally to the First Sea Lord for his concurrence before despatch.' 'Only the First Sea Lord,' Churchill wrote in the same book, 'can order the ships to steam and the guns to fire.'4

We now know, of course, that Churchill did, on his own initiative, 'order the ships to steam', and not always in the clearest naval language. We now know that the loose wording of his telegram to the C.-in-C. Mediterranean led directly to Troubridge's withdrawal and the escape of the *Goeben* and *Breslau*. We now know that he not only despatched signals without the concurrence of the First Sea Lord and the Chief of Naval War Staff, but marked them 'First Sea Lord to see after action W.S.C.' This was his style of administration in peace. In war, then, who could be expected to hold 'the raging warrior'? The answer is no one – not even, later, a rejuvenated, reinstated Jacky Fisher.

Asquith's daughter Violet had an engaging story of Churchill, which reveals the nature of the man better than any number of official memoranda and Board minutes. A few years before the war

she and some friends had been teaching themselves climbing, and
considered themselves 'salted climbers' when along came Winston
to join them briefly. It was his first experience. Although 'he was
a raw novice, he always took command of every operation,' she
recalled, 'decreeing strategy and tactics and even dictating the
correct position of our arms and legs'.[5] Of course such a man would
'oredr the ships to steam and the guns to fire' when war came.
Moreover he was usually right in his judgements. But he was
sometimes wrong.

From time to time Louis and his Chief of Naval War Staff,
Sturdee, did what they could to stay his hand. But it must be understood that the pace and volume of work at the Admiralty at this
time were excessively demanding – demanding enough to keep the
men at their work all day and every day with time off only to eat
and sleep. Louis's decision-making alone was enough to fill a sixteen
or eighteen hour day, and that left little time to remonstrate with
Churchill.

To add to the difficulties of his task, Churchill was not only trying
to do everything at once at the Admiralty; he also tried to fight
the war himself, in person. In the midst of everything, it will be
remembered, he precipitately left England and was away for four
days supervising the arrival and then the dispositions of the Royal
Marines whom he had rushed in to help defend Antwerp. 'Our
friend must be quite off his head!'[6] the King's secretary wrote to
Hopwood.

Churchill became, in effect, C.-in-C. of the military forces there;
and, to Asquith's mixed horror and amusement, even offered to
quit his post as First Lord in order to take over formally in the field.
(He had resigned as a junior officer 15 years earlier.) This suggestion
was smartly rejected by the Prime Minister, and Churchill returned
reluctantly to London.

There had been, before this, a number of day trips to France and
always, as on that fateful August Sunday, Louis was left in complete command of all naval affairs and doing both jobs. This also
entailed special meetings with the Prime Minister and special reports
to the Cabinet, who were disconcerted by the absences of their
colleague at this critical juncture.

Without his political chief and partner, Louis's responsibilities
went far beyond those normally carried by an Admiral, and included
political and military matters of the very highest importance. The
Seventh Division of the Army was due to sail for Ostend. It was

desperately needed to stem the German advance. Lord Kitchener (Secretary of State for War) had appealed to Louis in Churchill's absence. Could he rely on the Navy to transport the troops immediately? Louis assured him that he could. Sturdee was appalled when he heard and argued vehemently with Louis. 'The transports will be vulnerable to enemy mines and torpedoes,' he claimed. 'It is against all principles of strategy to send transports unless you hold complete control of the sea.'

An officer who was present recalled that Louis 'courteously and gently and firmly' reminded Sturdee that he had promised the Army and that he could not let them down.

'But any losses involving transports will have a disastrous effect on public opinion,' Sturdee argued.

Louis repeated: 'It is a promise. It will be fulfilled. I take entire personal responsibility.'[7]

The transports sailed on the night of 5–6 October. All arrived safely. Decision-making in war can be an agonizing business. As Asquith wrote of Louis the next day, 'Getting the transports to Belgium thro' the new minefields is an anxious job, which I can see keeps him awake at night.'[8]

A master and now a veteran in leadership, Louis took the rigours and the demands in his stride during those early weeks of war. One of the most painful tasks, because it was so personal, came to him at the very outset. The C.-in-C. of the First (later Grand) Fleet was Sir George Callaghan. He was a contemporary and a friend of Louis's. Louis carried on his nose a scar caused by Callaghan from an occasion of youthful high-spirits. Many years earlier, Louis was being ragged by his fellow officers for going to his cabin so early to study. Callaghan made as if to throw a jug of water over him. But the handle broke and the jug as well as the water struck him in the face, causing a deep cut.

Callaghan became an able but not a dynamic admiral, and he was due to retire in October anyway. Churchill and Louis reluctantly decided that he should be replaced on the outbreak of war by Jellicoe, who was ten years younger and had long been groomed for the job. It was a painful business to deprive an old friend of supreme command at sea just when the event occurred to which his whole life had been directed.

Jellicoe was deeply embarrassed and appalled at this arrangement. 'Am firmly convinced,' he signalled to Churchill, 'after consideration, that the step . . . is fraught with gravest danger at this juncture and might easily be disastrous . . . I beg most earnestly that you will give matter further consideration with First Sea Lord.'9

Churchill and Louis overrode Jellicoe's protests and it was left to Louis to tell his old friend, 'kindly and gently', that he was being retired two months early. Whether the Admiralty's decision was a correct one will never be known. Jellicoe possessed a masterly brain and was a great handler of fleets. But there was insufficient fire in his belly and he was prone to whining. He loathed taking risks, frequently complained about the numbers and quality of his ships, was terrified (with good reason but he could have been more stoic about) of mines and torpedoes. He turned away from torpedo attacks three times at the only confrontation between the two fleets at Jutland and let slip a never-to-be-repeated opportunity of annihilating the High Seas Fleet.

'I thought he looked like a frightened tapir,' Lord Mountbatten recalls today. 'Beatty was my hero. I thought he was marvellous. My father said, "You are quite wrong. Beatty has élan, dash, he is a great polo player, and he possesses everything I admire in a commander of the battle cruisers. But he has not got the brains and the experience and the judgement of Jellicoe."

'But later he did agree that Jellicoe made mistakes at Jutland and should have turned his ships towards the torpedoes to comb their tracks.'10

Lord Mountbatten in later life, on mature reflection, and when the German records became available, agreed with his father about the turn that lost Jellicoe contact with the enemy battle fleet. He also recognized that Jellicoe made the wrong calculation about the choice of channel through which the High Seas Fleet might escape, partly as a result of the Admiralty's failure to pass on information. But he believed that Jellicoe handled his fleet well and that the deployment on sighting the enemy was masterly.

Louis and Jellicoe had worked closely together for many years, and long before they became two of Fisher's 'brains' back in 1904. Louis thought he knew the Admiral's mind like his own. But over the weeks that followed Jellicoe's appointment to the command of the Grand Fleet, Louis became increasingly concerned at the Admiral's flow of appeals for more ships and his cries of anguish when he was threatened with the loss of any of his strength, however small and temporary. This was eventually to lead to tragedy, the tragedy of Coronel.

By late August the whereabouts of the German China Squadron was giving Louis and the Naval War Staff increasing concern. The two biggest ships, the *Scharnhorst* and *Gneisenau*, were powerful armoured cruisers with a high reputation for gunnery and all round efficiency. With their attached light cruisers, they were lost somewhere in the Pacific. From time to time they were reported at some remote island, and then they again disappeared into the limitless wastes.

It was an unnerving situation for the Admiralty because it was impossible to provide superior forces to meet the Germans at every point at which they might turn up. One of the cruisers, the elusive *Emden* which the squadron had detached, was already busily mopping up British merchantmen in the Indian Ocean and had brought British trade in that area to a temporary standstill.

The most likely destination of the squadron was the west coast of South America. Here they could refuel and proceed either through the newly opened Panama Canal to the Caribbean, or round Cape Horn to destroy British coaling stations at the Falkland Islands and elsewhere, and prey on British trade off the Plate estuary. In the end they might make a dash for home. They were unlikely to pierce the British blockade, but before surrender in a neutral harbour, or destruction, they could do untold material and moral damage.

The force ordered to meet this threat, commanded by the gallant and impetuous Sir Christopher 'Kit' Cradock, consisted of a mixed bag of men-of-war – two old and inferior armoured cruisers partly manned by reservists, a fast modern light cruiser, a slow and ancient battleship and an armed liner of no military significance. If it were concentrated this force might repel an attack by the German squadron. Because of its lack of speed, it could certainly never pursue and destroy it. The most that Cradock could hope to accomplish was to use his faster ships to go out to damage the German ships sufficiently to make them easy game for a reinforced British Squadron at a later date. But even that would be a hazardous undertaking as the German guns outranged the British guns.

Only Churchill calculated that the British Squadron was powerful enough for the task of seeking out and defeating Admiral von Spee, the skilful and ingenious German commander – so long as he kept his mixed force concentrated. Spasmodically, and when time allowed between trips abroad and preoccupation with other naval crises, Churchill gave his attention to the problem of the lost Germans in the Pacific. From time to time he composed telegrams to

Cradock, and like his earlier orders to the C.-in-C. in the Mediterranean these telegrams were not always precise and clear in their intention.

Meanwhile the Naval War Staff recommended that Cradock should be heavily reinforced with three armoured cruisers and a light cruiser from the Red Sea and the Mediterranean. Louis considered this proposal and decided against it because these ships, and others too, were needed to hunt down the *Emden* and another German cruiser operating off the east African coast. But Louis did recommend a more dramatic proposal for Churchill's consideration, and that was to detach two battle cruisers from the Grand Fleet and rush them out to the South Atlantic without delay.[11] These 'ocean greyhounds', as Fisher called them, had a much higher speed and a much heavier and longer-ranging broadside than the *Scharnhorst* and *Gneisenau* which, once located, must be mopped up in no time.

When this proposal reached Jellicoe's ears he was appalled and claimed that the temporary removal of the ships could lead to disaster. Churchill was so impressed by Jellicoe's plea that he overruled his First Sea Lord and Chief of Naval War Staff, and instead ordered from the Mediterranean a single armoured cruiser to join Cradock. Then this vital ship was diverted by Churchill, without Cradock's knowledge. So he got nothing before he met the foe.

Leaving behind his battleship, against Churchill's intention, because it was so slow, Cradock doubled Cape Horn and made his way up the Chilean coastline in search of von Spee. When he located the German Squadron, which had now been further reinforced, he bravely yet foolishly attacked it with his two armoured cruisers, *Monmouth* and *Good Hope*. They were blown to pieces without doing damage to the hard-hitting Germans who outranged them. Neither he, nor a single one of his officers and men survived in the cold, choppy dusk water off Coronel.

14

Done to death by slanderous tongues
Was the hero that here lies . . .
Much Ado About Nothing, V iii 3

NOT long after Dickie Battenberg had watched his father leave the dinner table at the Admiralty and go off to the War Room to see the Royal Navy through its first hours of world war, he was writing an anxious letter from Osborne, to which he had just returned for his fifth term.

'What d'you think the latest rumour that got in here from outside is?' he asked his mother. 'That Papa has turned out to be a German spy & has been discreetly marched off to the tower, where he is guarded by beefeaters. Apparently the rumour started (outside the college of course) by the fact that an admiral or somebody has been recalled from the Mediterranean to find out about the Goeben & Breslau escaping. People apparently think he let the German cruiser escape as he was a spy or an agent . . . I got rather a rotten time of it for about three days as little fools . . . insisted on calling me German Spy & kept on heckling me & trying to make things unpleasant for me . . .'[1]

The tenure of one of the highest defence offices in the land by a German-born Prince at the outset of a war with Germany was bound to arouse all sorts of passions and doubts among the people, some of them in positions of responsibility. Most of all, it brought out from the darkest recesses of St James's clubs Louis's old enemies, who had recently limited themselves to spasmodic attacks, and had expected he would resign his office when war was declared. In spite of the fact that Louis had been a naturalized Briton since boyhood, and the fact

300

that he had given great and loyal service to his adopted country for forty-six years, it was still seen by many people to be an invidious position for him to hold.

It is almost impossible today to understand the depths of jingoistic nationalism and xenophobia aroused in the early weeks of the First World War when dachshund dogs were reviled and stoned, shops with German names had their windows smashed, and people with even faintly foreign names publicly insulted. It was a very unpleasant hysteria, inflamed by the popular newspapers and magazines. The Prime Minister's daughter Violet, recalling this time shortly before her death, commented, 'The witch-hunt of the First World War is one of the blackest pages in our history . . . & our family were not immune. Because he refused to abandon friends with German names I was once asked whether it was true that my father drank the Kaiser's health after dinner.'[2]

Louis's Naval Assistant, Rear-Admiral Tufton Beamish, later claimed that for years before 1914 Prince Louis realized and stated that if war came his position would be made very hard, if not untenable, and that two peaks were for him unattainable, first and the most desired C.-in-C. of the Fleet in war, and second, First Sea Lord.[3]

But everything in Louis's character, and in the tradition and training of his family, points to the fact that if war came before his appointment terminated he would have continued at his post until it was clear that he was no longer wanted. Battenbergs were not easily made to resign before their work was done – look at the way Sandro had stuck to the dreadful tasks in Bulgaria; Liko to the deadly dull duties at Queen Victoria's court until military endeavour which cost him his life offered relief; his own father to the Emperor of Austria.

A Prince's upbringing, a Prince's mind, does not encompass the act of resignation, which in an ambitious politician is always a consideration and can be a means to an end. Resignation suggests a withdrawal from responsibility, and the acceptance of responsibility is the very lifeblood, the *raison d'être*, of royalty.

Churchill and Asquith needed Louis as First Sea Lord in war even more than they needed him in peace. Aside from his very real merits and experience there was, in any case *no one else*. George V knew it, Asquith knew it, the whole War Cabinet knew it. 'There is no one else suitable for the post,' Churchill is on record as having told Asquith – and no doubt he said it more than once. There was no one in the service with Louis's experience of staff work and administration as well as command at sea, no one who knew the enemy so well, no one who knew both how to tame Churchill without fighting with him, encouraging him without being outraged by his excesses. The nation and the Royal Navy needed Churchill in war, and with him they needed Prince Louis as the *only* possible working partner.

The Court knew that in war there could be trouble for Louis. Five years earlier, Edward VII's secretary had predicted that if Louis became First Sea Lord, Asquith would have trouble with his naval team in time of war, Churchill because he was suspect in the country, Louis because of his German blood. But Asquith reckoned that they could ride out a few early storms, and then if the Royal Navy showed itself efficient and destructive of the enemy, the country would at least be reconciled to the pair.

But the great clash of arms in the North Sea did not take place, the German fleet stayed in its harbours, and aside from the early Heligoland Bight battle, the Navy's record of getting the Expeditionary Force to France safely, the blockading of Germany tightly, was a negative one. The public clamoured for sunk German battleships – not half a dozen and more British cruisers on the seabed in the first three months of war, and an intact High Seas Fleet. There was little enough good news to report from any of the fighting fronts on land, and it was reasonable enough for the public to expect victories from the mighty Royal Navy.

The murmurs against Churchill and Louis began early in the war. Louis, as 'the Germhun' (the unhappy term coined by Horatio Bottomley in *John Bull*) was the meatier target. Gossip spread rapidly in those anxious August days when it seemed as if nothing could ever stop the German armies, in Russia, France or Belgium. If the canard about Louis being despatched to the Tower of London was amusing the boys at Osborne, it was having more serious repercussions in the wardrooms of the fleet and the drawing-rooms of Belgravia. In Fleet Street it was soon being printed – only as a rumour of course, but . . .

On the evening of 28 August a group of members were standing in the hall of the Carlton Club.* Among them was Lord Charles Beresford and Arthur Lee, one-time Civil Lord of the Admiralty, a

---

* The account which follows is drawn from an unpublished draft written by Randolph Churchill and deposited by him in the Broadlands Archives. On his death Martin Gilbert wrote more briefly of this incident in Volume iii of the official life of Churchill.

keen and influential follower of naval affairs, and a future First Lord. According to Lee, 'The conversation having turned upon German spies, Lord Charles Beresford expressed the opinion that *all* Germans, including highly placed ones, ought to leave the country as they were in close touch with Germans abroad.' Louis's name was not mentioned at this time, but soon after – according to Lee – Beresford said that 'his good taste' should lead Louis voluntarily to resign his position. However good an officer he might be, 'nothing could alter the fact,' continued Beresford, 'that he is a *German*, and as such should not be occupying his present position. He keeps German servants and has his property in Germany.'

Lee protested, singing Louis's praises. 'I admit all that,' said Beresford, 'but none the less he is a *German* and he entered the Navy for his own advantage not for ours. Feeling is very strong in the Service about his being First Sea Lord – it is strongly resented.' When Lee expressed surprise at this judgement, Beresford added: 'I am entitled to speak for the Service – I know the opinion of my brother officers on the subject. It is very strong.'

Lee, fearing another Battenberg crisis at this difficult time for the Navy, referred the matter to Churchill, who took it up with Beresford in these strong terms: 'In time of war spreading of reports likely to cause mistrust or despondency is certainly a military offence.' Beresford immediately got onto Lee by telephone and 'assailed me with a torrent of abuse . . . He also threatens to raise the matter in the House of Commons . . . & might attempt to make some kind of scene on Monday.'

Beresford at first denied Lee's 'atrocious and untrue statement', then said that it was 'not my intention to cast aspersions upon the First Sea Lord's character'. Churchill, frantically dealing with the aftermath of the Heligoland Bight victory (though the battle could not have been fought at a more appropriate time for the demolition of Beresford), deputed the responsibility for carrying out the last rites to his Naval Secretary, who told Beresford that Churchill had no doubt 'from the evidence submitted to him, not from one quarter only, that you are in the habit of talking in a rash and loose way about Prince Louis of Battenberg and his German origin, and that persons who hear you are liable to put the worst construction on your language, with the result that alarm and mistrust is created'.

Although Churchill considered the incident closed, Beresford rose from the death bed of his reputation and told the First Lord that what went on in London clubs was private and that Lee had no business, therefore, to draw attention to his statements. With remarkable restraint and attention to language, Churchill replied:

ADMIRALTY
2 September 1914

Dear Lord Charles Beresford,

  I am clearly of the opinion that the safety of the state over-rides all questions of club etiquette and that personal ties must give way to public requirements at a time like this. Free expressions of opinion which are legitimate in time of peace, cannot be permitted now. Everyone has to uphold confidence or be silent.

  From week to week the Admiralty have to take steps which may turn out well or ill but which are full of risk. It would be disastrous if we did not feel sure enough of ourselves and of the trust of the nation to do so and to face losses as well as victories.

  We have an absolute right to your aid and influence in this and I hope it is on this footing that I may continue to address you.

Yours sincerely,

This did succeed in closing the incident. It did not end the gossip. September was a bad month at sea. The sinking of the three big cruisers with such terrible loss of life did not raise questions only of the Board's competency; it stirred up ugly rumours of collusion, of the very highest in the land being in secret touch with the enemy. It was impossible to deny officially such loose and ludicrous talk. But as the month advanced the first recognition of the gossip together with general criticism of the conduct of the Board, began to appear in the cheaper newspapers. Horatio Bottomley, as always with nostrils flared to catch the stink of malevolent gossip, renewed his campaign against 'Germhuns' in high places. Scurrilous letters addressed to Louis began to appear in the Admiralty post, and more serious and reasoned ones, too, arrived at the newspaper offices.

Churchill and Asquith rode out the rough weather for several weeks. When Churchill got back from his private intervention on the Antwerp front, he knew that the climate of opinion towards the Admiralty was steadily deteriorating, and he had to think carefully and anxiously about his own future. How much longer dared he carry Louis? One good victory could save them both – if, say, Kit Cradock could corner and destroy von Spee. But over the next two weeks (7–21 October) he recognized the first fatal signs of loss of self-confidence in his partner.

The strain on Louis of those four days when Churchill was absent had been immense. With the full support of Asquith and the Cabinet he could have carried the burden without flinching – the burden of worry about Admiral von Spee, the new submarine menace and the security of the Grand Fleet in its bases against the torpedo, the intermittent threat of invasion and of bombardment of the East Coast ports, and a hundred others. This is what he had been training to do since 1868. But with the knowledge that he was day by day losing the confidence of the people and of his fellow officers and the Cabinet, both his health and his capacity for work began to falter.

It had not been possible to keep from Louis the calumnies uttered that evening at the Carlton Club. Nor could all the vicious and wounding letters that arrived privately for him at his office and at Mall House be hidden from his eyes. Inevitably when near the end of his tether, the gout struck him down, with all its pain and disablement. Decision-making became more difficult and he faced it with ever increasing reluctance. It is no exaggeration to say that his heart was being broken, and in public. But no one who knew him at this time remembers hearing from him one word of complaint.

Asquith and Churchill knew Louis would never resign. Yet they knew he had to go. 'Winston has been pouring out his woes into my ear,' Asquith wrote to Venetia Stanley (Churchill's cousin) on 20 October. 'I think Battenberg will have soon to make as graceful a bow as he can to the British public.'[4]

Churchill knew that this was now becoming inevitable, but he was at his wit's end to know who could take Louis's place. The puzzle which appeared insoluble at the outbreak of war was in no way simplified with the passage of time. Haldane had an idea, though. (Haldane, who had done as much for the Army as Louis had done for the Navy, was to go to the stake soon, too – and he had only been to a *German university*!)

On 19 October Haldane wrote to Churchill telling him that he must not consider leaving the Admiralty because of the attacks against himself and Louis. 'Do not pay the least attention to the fools who write & talk in the press. It is this real thing that counts, & the nation thoroughly believes in you. I should like to see Fisher & Wilson brought in, & Prince Louis kept with them as Second Sea Lord. The advent of the first two would make our country feel that our old spirit of the navy was alive and come back.'

Churchill, in his half drowned condition, recognized buoyancy when he saw it, and grabbed the pair of 'septuagenarian sea-dogs', as Asquith dubbed them. Wilson was seventy-two, Fisher a year older, but they personified in the popular view the Navy's greatness of old. Fisher would replace Louis, eight years his junior, and Wilson was offered the job of Chief of Naval War Staff – a Gilbertian suggestion in view of his sacking three years earlier for his antagonism to Staff work. But ever loyal, ever steady and patriotic, 'Tug' Wilson yielded to Churchill's appeal to come back to the Admiralty from retirement as general unpaid adviser with no formal position. Churchill took the plan to Asquith who exclaimed that it was a grandiose scheme, but agreed that it might work.

On 24 October Bottomley returned more violently to the attack. Now he blasted: 'We shall further repeat our demand that Prince Louis of Battenberg be relieved of his present position . . .' Two days later the more responsible *Globe* came out with a considered editorial which could not be ignored by anyone in public life. 'We receive day by day a constantly growing stream of correspondence, in which the wisdom of having an officer who is of German birth as the professional head of the Navy is assailed in varying terms. We would gladly dismiss all these letters from our mind, but we cannot. They are too numerous, too insistent, and too obviously the expression of a widespread feeling.'

Louis read the papers but knew nothing of what Churchill was up to. His personal crisis, the greatest and most deadly in his life, which would leave his enemies dancing with satisfaction, still lay a week ahead. There were many problems to be considered at the Admiralty, and from his bed of pain he dealt with them as well as he was able. Enemy mines was one. They had very effective explosive power – far greater than their British counterparts, of which there were too few. The results of the first naval air raid on Zeppelin sheds in Germany had to be examined, and arrangements made for the further bombardment of German positions from the sea. News was still awaited from Cradock. That was one tragedy still to come, but there were already enough problems to break the heart of a tired and nearly broken man.

A number of those in the *Aboukir*, *Hogue* and *Cressy* who had died were senior cadets from Osborne who had taken up their appointments on mobilization. From Osborne, Dickie wrote home sadly about these drowned boys whom he had known and were less than a year older than him. Another cruiser, the *Hawke*, had taken down one of the doctors from Osborne, Surgeon-Lieutenant Custance. Dickie was deeply affected by his death. 'I really loved him,' he wrote home. 'When I heard the news that he was not saved my head sort of swam, but cleared after I had run round Collingwood in the cold air several times. That night I cried myself to sleep. I suppose he is happier where he is, but still . . .'5

On 27 October the Royal Navy suffered its greatest loss since the beginning of the war. A mine – a single mine – was struck by the powerful new Dreadnought *Audacious*, and she went to the bottom with ominous speed – though, thank goodness, with only one lost life. But the explosion of that mine sounded Louis's death knell.

Louis was the first in the Admiralty to hear of the disaster and, according to Churchill, 'he hurried into my room with the grave news' that morning. 'I do not remember any period,' Churchill wrote of this time in *World Crisis*, 'when the weight of the War seemed to press more heavily on me . . . The sense of grappling with and being overpowered by a monster of appalling and apparently inexhaustible strength on land, and a whole array of constant, gnawing anxieties about the safety of the Fleet from submarine attack at sea and in its harbours, oppressed my mind. Not an hour passed without the possibility of some disaster or other in some part of the world. Not a day without the necessity of running risks. My own position was already to some extent impaired . . .'6

Before lunch on that same critical morning, Churchill made his way to 10 Downing Street. Later in the day Asquith, in one of his wildly indiscreet letters to Venetia Stanley, wrote: '. . . Winston came here before lunch in a rather sombre mood. Strictly between you & me he has suffered today a terrible calamity on the sea . . . He has quite made up his mind that the time has come for a drastic change in his Board; our poor blue-eyed German will have to go, and (as W. says) he will be reinforced by 2 "well-plucked chickens' [Fisher and Wilson].'7

Flippant about it all as Asquith sounds in this note to his lady, in his heart he was deeply grieved over the tragedy that was about to be played out. 'I shall never forget the personal grief & *shame* my father felt in being obliged to acquiesce in accepting [Prince Louis's] resignation,' wrote his daughter. 'He felt it to be a stain on his own honour to part with one to whom the Navy & the nation owed such an incalculable debt.'8

Next, Churchill went to the Palace. King George V received the news sadly and calmly that Churchill wanted to ask his cousin to resign, and reluctantly assented. '. . . poor Louis B's resignation',9 the King wrote to his Uncle Arthur Connaught.

The last of Churchill's calls was the worst. Louis had just heard that his nephew, poor Liko's and Beatrice's son Maurice of Battenberg, had died from his wounds received in the retreat from Mons. Churchill expressed his deep sympathy, and then told Louis that he and the Prime Minister were, with the utmost regret, going to call on him to consider resigning his appointment. 'Louis behaved with great dignity & public spirit,' Asquith noted, '& will resign at once.'[10] And Churchill himself recorded: 'The uncomplaining dignity with which he made this sacrifice and accepted self-effacement as a requital for the great and faithful service he had rendered to the British nation and to the Royal Navy was worthy of a sailor and a Prince.'[11]

The last rites had to be observed. On the following morning, a letter from Churchill arrived at Mall House suggesting a possible wording for his public letter of resignation, and outlining how Churchill would reply. 'I cannot tell you how much I regret the termination of our work together,' Churchill continued, '& how I deplore the harsh and melancholy march of events wh lead to yr temporary withdrawal from active employment . . . Will you consider vy carefully whether there is any way in wh I can be of service . . . No incident in my public life has caused me so much sorrow.'[12]

Louis was utterly shattered by this turn of events, and if he had suspected that he might be asked to go, he gave no sign of it. The Prince of Wales, then aged twenty, called in at the Admiralty to offer his sympathy. 'The hurt showed in his tired, lined face,' he commented. '"This is indeed an ignominious end to a lifetime of loyal service to the British Navy," he said, "but I shall not allow this to embitter me against my country of adoption".'[13]

The formal letter of resignation and Churchill's longer reply appeared in all the newspapers on 30 October. 'Honest men,' commented *The Times*, 'will prefer the brevity of the retiring Admiral to the rhetorical document which accepts his decision' – a testy comment but indicative of responsible judgement of the two men.

October 28, 1914[14]

Dear Mr. Churchill, –

I have lately been driven to the painful conclusion that at this juncture my birth and parentage have the effect of impairing in some respects my usefulness on the Board of Admiralty. In these circumstances I feel it to be my duty, as a loyal subject of His Majesty, to resign the office of First Sea Lord, hoping thereby to facilitate the task of the administration of the great Service, to which I have devoted my life, and to ease the burden laid on H.M. Ministers.

> I am,
> Yours very truly,
> LOUIS BATTENBERG,
> Admiral

October 29, 1914

My dear Prince Louis, –

This is no ordinary war, but a struggle between nations for life or death. It raises passions between races of the most terrible kind. It effaces the old landmarks and frontiers of our civilization. I cannot further oppose the wish, you have during the last few weeks expressed to me, to be released from the burden of responsibility which you have borne thus far with so much honour and success.

The anxieties and toils which rest upon the naval administration of our country are in themselves enough to try a man's spirit; and when to them are added the ineradicable difficulties of which you speak, I could not at this juncture in fairness ask you to support them.

The Navy of to-day, and still more the Navy of to-morrow, bears the imprint of your work. The enormous impending influx of capital ships, the score of thirty-knot cruisers, the destroyers and submarines unequalled in modern construction which are coming now to hand, are the results of labours which we have had in common, and in which the Board of Admiralty owes so much to your aid.

The first step which secured the timely concentration of the Fleet was taken by you.

I must express publicly my deep indebtedness to you, and the pain I feel at the severance of our three years' official association. In all the circumstances you are right in your decision. The spirit in which you have acted is the same in which Prince Maurice of Battenberg has given his life to our cause and in which your gallant son is now serving in the Fleet.

I beg you to accept my profound respect and that of our colleagues on the Board.

> I remain,
> Yours very sincerely,
> WINSTON S. CHURCHILL

Louis responded to Churchill's offer to be 'of service' by suggesting: 'If on quitting office I could receive some sign indicating that I still commanded the confidence & trust of HM the King & his Govt it would have a great effect on my position in the country . . . What I should value above all else would be to be admitted to the Privy Council.'[15]

The King at once agreed to this and wrote a letter thanking him for all he had done, and on the same day, 29 October, Louis replied:

My dear Cousin George,[16]

I cannot sufficiently thank you for your generous letter. I will treasure it as something to bequeath to my son. The admission into your Privy Council fulfills the ambition of my life & coming at this moment is of inestimable value.

The Board Meeting was a dramatic scene, which I will never forget. The sympathy & warm friendship shown by my colleagues including the Chairman was such that I could not utter a word for fear of breaking down.

It is a comfort to me to think that my brother officers will feel for me.

Mr Churchill again assured me that when peace was reestablished he hoped to see me employed once more & this thought will buoy one up in my temporary retirement.

Thanking you once more with all my heart for your kind words.

> *I remain as ever,*
> *Your devoted and loyal subject,*
> *Louis*

Over the next few days the letters of sympathy, some of them very angry ones, arrived in shoals, from high and low, from old Admirals like Lord Walter Kerr and Lord John Hay, who had grown up with sail when France and Russia were the likely enemies instead of allies, and younger Admirals like Jellicoe and Beatty. There were predictable ones from old friends, and unexpected ones like the long and enthusiastic ones from members of the Labour Party, including one of its leaders, J. H. Thomas. In the newspapers there appeared letters of protest and dismay, including one in *The Times* from Lord Selborne which ended: 'I would as soon mistrust Lord Roberts as Prince Louis, and that anyone should have been found to insinuate suspicions against him is nothing less than a national humiliation.'

When Louis's final crisis began Victoria had just returned from Cromarty, the naval base in Scotland where Georgie's battle cruiser had anchored earlier in the week. She had gone to stay near him for a few days. Nona Kerr had just arrived in France to nurse the wounded, and to her Victoria addressed a happy letter telling of the meeting with her son. 'Georgie is flourishing & looks just like Franzjos with his beard, which is not an adornment,'[17] she told her. She enclosed a sprig of heather in her letter 'for luck'. It did neither of them much good. Nona's brother was killed by an enemy shell in France a day or two later.

Victoria took the night train and arrived at Mall House just as Louis received the news that the *Audacious* was sinking.

It was a blessed comfort that she had got back in time to help her broken husband through the next forty-eight hours. On the day the news of his resignation was made public, she wrote again to Nona:

MALL HOUSE
SPRING GARDENS
Oct. 30, 1914

My dear Nona,

What we hoped might not happen, has had to be & when you get this letter Louis will be a simple Admiral on half-pay.

It is the penalty of serving a democracy, the 'man in the street' is mighty ... This government is made up of men whom, with the exception of Lord Kitchener, few greatly respect or trust – therefore when the clamour against a German born 1st Sea Lord grew stronger, Louis spoke again with Churchill (the only one in the Cabinet who would have fully been willing to face the clamour), & they agreed that it is best he should resign ... What a pain & wrench it is you can imagine ...

We are not going to mope or hang our heads; all those whom we like & respect know that the 'man-in-the-street & Clubs' is quite in the wrong ...

Your loving
Victoria

Louise had taken her mother's place in Scotland, so that – to Victoria's relief – she was able to pass the grievous news to her brother in person. Victoria worried most of all about Dickie. How would her sensitive younger son respond to the catastrophe, surrounded by robust and mainly insensitive boys of thirteen and fourteen? Dickie, in fact, cared not one jot for what his fellow cadets thought about the resignation of his father. But it caused a deep and terrible wound in his pride and his soul, and he has never forgotten the agony.

It has been said that, when the news of the resignation of Prince Louis reached Osborne in the Isle of Wight, Dickie Battenberg was seen to march out alone on to the flagstaff and stand to attention with tears streaming down his cheeks. The story, says Lord Mountbatten, without evident emotion, is absolutely true. What he has always regarded as the unjust public humiliation of his father acted as a cordite charge to his professional life, which from that late October day rose with the trajectory of a 12-inch explosive shell from his brother's battle cruiser.

For Louis the crumbs of comfort were in the letters of praise and condolence, and in the assurances he was given that his active service was not yet over. Churchill, as good as his word, wrote to Arthur Balfour, his successor as First Lord from May 1915: 'I told Prince Louis that if I was in office at the close of the war I should offer him Portsmouth. Later, he wrote to me stating that the Mediterranean was his great desire as the finale of his naval service; and I replied that I would do my best. I consider most strongly that he should be employed again at the end of the war; or earlier if you think fit.'[19]

Poor Louis, he was not to know that peace still lay more than four years ahead, and that the golden days of the Mediterranean Fleet – a dozen or more great battleships with a hundred attendant vessels in shimmering Valetta harbour – were gone for ever.

For his younger son there was a sudden short-lived renewal of hope seven months later. Fisher had resigned and the furore over Churchill's Dardanelles adventure was at its height. 'What are things coming to,' Dickie wrote to Mama. 'Do you think they'll want Papa back. Every body here seems to think he is sure to go back . . .'[20]

There is no doubt that among those who worked with him, were closest to him, and loyal to him, there was a feeling that Louis had done the right thing in resigning. Like Churchill, Louis had been waiting for a shaft of sunshine through the storm clouds that October – a brief one would have been enough. In those volatile times, it could have transformed popular regard for the Board, for Churchill and Louis, and the calumnies and innuendoes would have been drowned. It came just too late. Two days after his resignation, Coronel was fought, and the urgency to seek out and destroy von Spee's roving China Squadron – which Louis and Sturdee had recognized seven weeks earlier – was dramatically accelerated.

Churchill recalled Louis's suggestion that battle cruisers were the only answer to the threat, and passed on to Fisher this suggestion as if it were his own panacea. Churchill put it modestly – one battle cruiser. 'But I found Lord Fisher in bolder mood. He would take two of these powerful ships,' Churchill recalled – the number Louis had originally suggested in early September.

This time Jellicoe could hardly complain, so serious was the situation. Nor was it the time to point out to him that if he had complied with Churchill's earlier request, Kit Cradock and 1,600 men and boys might still be alive and two armoured cruisers might not be lying on the ocean bed.

On 8 December, off the Falkland Islands, Louis's late Chief of Naval War Staff had the satisfaction of avenging Coronel, sinking the *Gneisenau* and *Scharnhorst*, their colliers and two of their three supporting cruisers. The circumstances of the victory, with the two great grey vessels pummelling to pieces the hated German raiders in a gun duel – the last ever to be fought unhindered by mines, torpedoes or aircraft – was romantic in the extreme, and provided a great fillip for the Navy and the nation. For Louis it came five weeks too late.

The question has often been asked: did Louis and Victoria indirectly contribute their own share to the weight of public opinion that brought about Louis's downfall? It is certainly not a question from which a biographer can escape; no more is it easily answered. The situation was exacerbated by the deep passions that were flowing through Britain at the time, the mass hysteria which had seized the country in August, referred to by Violet Asquith. If the Prime Minister could be widely rumoured to toast the Kaiser nightly at Number 10, Downing Street, anything might happen to anybody!

But other people close to the seats of power before the First World War remember events and situations which could not have strengthened the position of the Battenbergs with 'the tumbrils toiling up the terrible way'.* They were sometimes accused of flaunting their German connections. If this is manifestly absurd, it was the impression that a number of people received, at a period of growing hostility towards Germany, from their frequent visits to their relatives and friends, their widely reported sojourns at Hemmelmark, Wolfsgarten, Darmstadt, and of course at their own home at Heiligenberg.

The advantages recognized by Churchill in having a First Sea Lord who understood the German mind and knew the German Navy and many of its senior officers, and who was closely related to the Kaiser and Grand Admiral Prince Henry of Prussia, must also arouse suspicions amongst the common people, and most especially among those members of British society whose views were narrow, crabbed, prejudiced and hostile to foreigners – and there were a sizeable number of them. In October 1914, in the midst of all this tragedy and unhappiness, it is worth once again listening to the voice of the old Queen begging these Battenbergs to live more in England and have a home here.

One person who knew Victoria well at this time has commented: 'She did talk a very great deal, and not always tactfully. She could

* Prince, I can hear the trumpet of Germinal, The tumbrils toiling up the terrible way ...

G. K. CHESTERTON, *A Ballade of Suicide*

not have been more absolutely English and patriotic, but she talked too much. She had a very strong influence over Prince Louis's professional life, and it was partly because of her that he lost his position. She knew so much because she was sister-in-law to Prince Henry. She was very valuable to Prince Louis because she would get so much information about the German Navy, about their ships and so on, from him. And because she also told everybody else who cared to listen to her, people wondered what she would be saying about the British Navy when she went to Germany. All the family knew this and they all regretted it.'21

Of course it would have strengthened the position of the Battenbergs if they had, long before, changed their names and set up a permanent home in England as soon as Louis's duties ceased to be those of a junior seagoing officer. It would have strengthened their position if they had made fewer trips to Germany, sold Heiligenberg and taken a more prominent part in English life. They would have made more friends in England, and Louis would have made more in the Navy.

Fisher, with his usual love of exaggeration, claimed that Louis 'has no friends at all – probably only you [Churchill], me and Mark Kerr'.22 In fact he had fewer than most senior officers, but these were very close friends.

In 1910 Louis and Victoria did nearly buy a house in England, and Louis did once broach the subject of selling Heiligenberg. But the house deal fell through and the Grand Duke of Hesse begged him not to sell his German estate as it would suggest that he was cutting his last German roots because he thought it was inevitable.

The Battenbergs' failure to understand the need to embrace English life was their one blind spot. You can call it arrogance and pride. But it was really deeper than that. It was a failure of imagination. A lack of imagination has been the undoing of many dynasties since the earliest days of the Hessians – and as we saw at the beginning of this book that was a long time ago.

Compared with commoners, a Prince's life is little occupied with considering how others view him; and the loftier the rank the less exercised are the mind's imaginative processes. (Nowadays this failing tends to be limited to politicians.)

With all their charm, their brains and their good looks, this lack of imagination often damaged the Hessians and sometimes broke them. Alicky suffered from it, too, and with more disastrous results for the world. So did Irène, and all the Battenberg boys.

As well, the German mind is not noted for its ability to see itself through others' eyes. This has let them down in war and in peace. Add to this shortcoming the tight closed circle in which the Hessian royal families have always lived and it is easier to understand why in his own career and in his father's career, this blindness led Louis astray. In a man of real greatness, it is a tragedy that it was incurable, and that, with all her exceptional cleverness, Victoria suffered from it equally.

After Louis and Victoria left Mall House, 'the shaking down process,' as Louis wrote at the time, 'was long & painful'.[23] They stayed in the country for a week or two while their possessions were moved out of the Admiralty, and then took up residence in Kent House in the Isle of Wight where 'there is a holy calm over everything'.

While Dickie completed his training at Osborne a couple of miles away and then graduated to Dartmouth Naval College, Georgie led an eventful and sometimes dangerous life with the battle cruisers – he was in the *New Zealand* at the Heligoland Bight engagement in August 1914, and in the chase and destruction at Dogger Bank in January 1915. Louise was nursing in France. Louis and Victoria buried themselves in their house and their work. Mercifully, there was an immense amount to do for several months. They built on a wing, Victoria got the garden in hand for the spring, and Louis arranged his own rooms to suit his needs.

'All my cabin pictures are now hung in my dressing room,' he told Nona Kerr, '& I am sitting here in the small study with my dear old things – writing table, armchair, &co a bit crowded but cosy . . .'[24] Here he began work on his mammoth three-volume history and catalogue of naval medals of all nations, a definitive work if ever there was one, based on his fine collection. He also wrote his *Recollections* of his life up to the time of his marriage.

To 'a well-wisher' he wrote, 'I endeavour to live here in strict seclusion, making myself useful in any way I can, but I am obliged to confine myself to this small island. I have resolutely declined all manner of invitations which involve public appearances since I resigned . . .'[25]

It was a very muted, very narrow and very quiet existence after the hurly-burly and worries of the Admiralty. Now, suddenly, Louis and Victoria lived their lives mainly through their children and close relatives. Victoria visited Louise several times in the hospital where she worked in Nevers near Rouen. They saw a lot of Dickie, especially while he was at Osborne, and they hastened to London, or anywhere else, if there was a chance of seeing Georgie, even for only a few hours.

Like everyone else, they mourned lost friends and those who were so cruelly bereaved. Forty-four years had now passed since, as a girl of seven, Victoria had first helped her mother tend the wounded from the Franco-Prussian war in Darmstadt. She would walk through the wards at Nevers, or at the naval hospital at Haslar with Louis, talking to the maimed and the dying.

One afternoon, at the end of a long visit, Louis's eye was caught by the sight of a face that was young and fresh but had evidently known much suffering. He asked the boy his name and what had happened to him. The nurses called him 'the Baby' but his real name was Christopher Jenkins, and he told Louis that he had had his leg smashed in the Dardanelles. A Turkish shell had exploded against the barbette armour while he had been writing a letter home on the main deck of the battleship *Albion*. His leg had eventually been taken off, and he had lain close to death in an Egyptian hospital for some weeks before being shipped home.

Louis called over Victoria and they asked the boy about his life in the Navy and at home. When they returned to Kent House they talked again about the boy, and Louis wrote to the commanding officer at Haslar suggesting that 'the Baby' should convalesce with them, and they would later try to find him a job. It was little enough that they could do, but Louis and Victoria changed that boy's life; and ever since – until his death in 1974 – the family helped Jenkins through the difficult life of a cripple and sustained his morale and his outstanding character.

To Victoria it sometimes seemed that all her life had been spent in the preparation for war and in war itself with its bloodshed and cruelty. As always, she derived comfort from writing her thoughts to her confidant in all things, Nona Kerr. Louis and Victoria are in London, snatching a few hours with Georgie, who is on leave:

'We have spent a pleasant day together,' Victoria writes with passion and frankness, '& now he and L. have gone to a play. I can't face the theatre somehow just now ... [They] have talked lots of shop, it is nice to see how the boy loves his profession. And while I have been rejoicing to-day, others have lost their dear sons – an hour ago we got a telegram from Lady Leicester to say that Arthur Coke has been killed in action in the Dardanelles. I grieve so for her &

them all ... I trust & pray that there is enough of a fighting stock in me, that if I have to face what Lady Leicester is now facing, I may yet be able to take pride in the thought that death in battle & war is a fair & fine end for those men I love.

'However don't think I am dismal by writing like this. I have never shrunk from the thought of death, either for myself or mine – it has always seemed to me that ours has been a cowardly age in its blind worship of life & dread of death, & surely the sign of a very poor faith, not worthy of calling itself Christian. And now that we all are forced to think of it & realize it daily I hope it will make us braver & wiser & better.'[26]

There were times when she and Louis came close to facing the challenge which had confronted her friend Lady Leicester, and so many thousands of others. At the Battle of Jutland (31 May–1 June 1916) the *New Zealand*, first to sight the enemy, participated in the furious gunnery duel with Admiral Hipper's battle cruisers with five of her consorts. Three of the battle cruisers blew up with almost no survivors, and at one time Georgie's ship steamed, guns blazing, through the falling debris from the exploding 26,000-ton battle cruiser *Queen Mary*.

After the battle, Louis broke his own rule and took a train north to Scotland to welcome back to Rosyth the battered battle cruisers and talk to his son. This is what Louis himself had trained for during all those years in North America, the Mediterranean, the Channel and the North Sea – and now it was a comfort that a Battenberg, his own son, had *fought* with the Royal Navy at last.

At Rosyth, he saw the toll of Jutland, too. Commodore 'Barge' Goodenough's light cruiser *Southampton*, the most effective and gallantly-fought man-of-war at Jutland, was there, battered almost to pieces. Louis wrote in anguish of the 'twelve shell holes on one side' of the light cruiser, and of the 'many dead and burnt wounded'.

Louis could not wait for Dickie to leave Dartmouth and join his brother with Beatty's battle cruisers. Dickie broke his leg just before the passing out examinations in 1916, and had to take them strung up in hospital. 'I'm very hopeful of seeing him appointed Midshipman of the "Lion" on 1st June of Glorious Memory,'[27] Louis told his old Second Sea Lord, Admiral Sir Frederic Hamilton, referring to Admiral Howe's victory over the French and Spanish fleet in 1793.

To Dickie's fury, he just missed the big naval battle. 'We most unfortunate of "terms" had the bad luck to be crawling about the dusty parade ground of Devonport Gunnery school on our bellies with fixed bayonets at the time that Jutland was going on,' he wrote to his old tutor. The *Lion* was badly knocked about. 'We joined her the day she came out of dock . . . We were then kept at short notice for a month or more, & with the exception of trips up here & to [censored] we only went to sea once.'

Hopes ran high a few weeks later, though. On 19 August the German fleet càme out again 'to bombard Sunderland, to force the English fleet to come out and show the world the unbroken strength of the German fleet', according to the German Official History. In fact, the High Seas Fleet scuttled for home when faced with the threat of again meeting Jellicoe. But the exciting brush, as Dickie's account confirms, was marked by the highly effective use of the air, for reconnaissance, and the submarine, for attacking with torpedoes ('mouldies' in naval parlance).

'That day,' he wrote, 'everybody was certain there was going to be an action. The C-in-C & Beatty were quite sure. I was on the bridge at the time attending on the captain [Chatfield] & he told me to report to the engine room, "Will probably be opening fire in 15 or 20 minutes time". We sighted 5 or 6 Zeppelins, who gave us away & prevented an action. Our seaplane carrier sent up a sea plane & one of our light cruisers opened fire. Five minutes after going off watch one of our screen, the Nottingham, was "mouldied" & on our return, the Lowestoft went up (another of our screen), about 10 minutes before I went on watch. We had 3 "mouldies" miss us on the way back & every B.C. [battle cruiser] had 2 or 3 fired at them.'

Later, the *Lion* heeled hard over while the midshipmen were having tea in the gunroom, and they all rushed up on deck 'to find we were in the middle of a minefield laid for our benefit & while we were still altering course to avoid mines a torpedo was fired that missed us by a matter of feet . . .'[28]

From time to time Louis received invitations to carry out public tasks or sit on committees. He refused them all. Never again was he going to lay himself open to attack, nor risk further the disfigurement of the Battenberg name. 'I am truly grateful to you for your kind proposal,' he answers one invitation, 'but I feel very strongly that it would be inconsistent of me if I undertook any job – even a manifestly Half Pay job on a committee like this – in the Navy, in view of the cause why I thought it right to resign my original job. There are not wanting people even now (such as Lord Beresford of the Nile) who would make it a reason for further attacks on me . . .'[29]

There is a wretchedly sad picture of him in 1917, when the U-boat war was at its height, the country was so close to starvation, and the Royal Navy was again being savagely criticized. 'He looks very white, but even better looking than ever,' Dorothy Seymour, lady-in-waiting to Princess Christian noted in her diary on her return from Russia, 'so tall & upright, but so sad. Trying to do work in odd jobs in hospital or writing, but obviously eating his heart out to be doing his own work. A waste of a great brain & a very loyal personality. Not one word of grumble or longing & with the same ease in conversation as before only the gayness gone . . .'[30]

Louis and Victoria suffered another blow a month later, but this time, although it was shared by all surviving members of royal families in Britain, it struck at the deep, sensitive roots of their lives. The agitation against those in power with German names was reaching a new height in the summer of 1917, and it included now the King himself – although, ludicrously enough, not even the Editor of *Burke's Peerage* could say what the Royal Family's name was! However, the pressure was on, and it was Lord Stamfordham's unhappy task to inform all those affected that a decision and choice of new name must urgently be made. This situation would have such a fundamental effect on his children, that Louis at once took the train to Scotland to see his two sons, Georgie, still in the *New Zealand*, and Dickie in the *Lion*. To Louise in France he wrote:

> *6 June 1917*[31]
> KENT HOUSE
> EAST COWES
> ISLE-OF-WIGHT

My beloved Louise,
I have very serious news of far-reaching effects on us all to tell you. George Rex telegraphed to me last week he wished to see me as soon as possible. I took the next steamer & was closeted with him for a long time. The upshot of a long statement about his being attacked as being Half-German & surrounding himself by relatives with German names, &c. was that he must ask us Holsteins, Tecks & Battenbergs to give up using in England our German titles & to assume English surnames . . . It has been suggested that we shd turn our name into English, viz: Battenhill or Mountbatten. We incline to the latter as a better sound . . . Of course we are at his mercy. We only are allowed to use our German title as the Sovereign has always recognized it, but he can refuse this recognition any moment. If so we are plain

Mister, which would be impossible . . . For you, my dear children we feel deeply . . .
It is a terrible upheaval & break with one's past – another consequence of this
awful war. Mama is splendid & is determined to give up her own title & rank,
which is quite her own & not due to marriage with me, & to call herself by my
name and title only . . .

Newspaper comment will be unpleasant, but unavoidable. Whether the republicans
will be satisfied remains to be seen. I fear the throne here is beginning to shake also . . .

Goodbye my dear dear child. All this is very terrible. I
shall miss my old & laboriously write a new fancy name

Ever yr old loving
father

The 'new fancy name' was indeed going to take longer to write
than the mark which had appeared at the tail of countless hundreds
of documents during his working life. After the consideration of
numerous alternatives, it ended up thus: Marquess of Milford Haven,
Earl of Medina, and Viscount Alderney.

'I shall quite understand,' straight-talking Victoria wrote to Nona
Kerr, 'if the Peerage takes it as no compliment, our being foisted
into it – personally I say the honest truth in telling you I would
prefer to be a "citoyenne" & beholden to nobody, but we are the
passing generation & must look ahead for the position of our descendants.' However carefully she attempted to cover it up, there
was a bitterness in Victoria which she could not quite conceal.
'Forgive me,' she concluded to Nona, 'if I have said anything
offensive to you as a British born woman & one descended from a
very old Peers family [Lothians], but I am unduly influenced by the
recollection of brewers, lawyers, bankers Peers.'[32]

In fact, the children, though interested, were not in the least
upset by the news. Louise, now Lady Louise Mountbatten, who
would eventually become a Queen anyway, was too busy dealing
with the wounded to bother much. 'Dickie treated our change of
names etc. . . . as a huge joke & laughed uproariously,' Victoria
reported. 'They both agree it will be a wise & good thing for them
. . . Of course Dickie had to ask me hundreds of questions about
Peers & their positions & families, & whether he & Louise could
marry whoever they like without the King interfering, & whether
his sons would be plain Mr or Honble . . .'[33]

Instead of there being two H.S.H. Prince Louis of Battenbergs in the Royal Navy – one Admiral and one Midshipman – and one Lieutenant H.S.H. Prince George of Battenberg, there was now a Marquess of Milford Haven, a Lord Louis Mountbatten and an Earl of Medina, Georgie having assumed his father's second title. Louis himself, who had begun life as a Count, been promoted to Prince and Serene Highness, was now back as an English Marquess.

Victoria thought at this time that Ernie would probably deprive the family of their titles in Germany, too, but he had the courage not to do so.

It was a come-down, no one could deny it; and the Battenberg title resurrected some sixty years earlier to help straighten a rather bent branch in the Hessian tree, fell back into its old obscurity.

It was a struggle to keep up with the news of their relatives in Russia and Germany, but by devious means through neutral parties in neutral countries like Sweden, Spain and Holland, some sort of communication was kept alive, at least with Germany, all through the war. Louis and Victoria learned, early on, that it was not only in England that hysteria against the enemy was seizing the people. From Louis's sister Marie they learned that 'there was "grosse Wut" on the outbreak of war & many threats of setting the H.B. [Heiligenburg] on fire, so that gendarmes had to guard it'.[34]

Early on, too, Irène and Victoria agreed that it would be wise to do a straight swap of their personal maids, Irène's being English and Victoria's Eugenie a German. The returning English girl brought welcome news with her. 'She says Irène has lots to do & is well, though grown thin. Henry evidently lives on board his flagship, but is fairly often home'.[35] Their two sons were also serving with the German Navy at Wilhelmshaven, other relatives were on the Russian and Western fronts in the Army.

It was not until May 1915 that Victoria received news of her brother Ernie. She commented on it: 'Poor boy, he hates the war; he is always with his troops & full of admiration for their bravery & for the spirit of unity and self-sacrifice the whole country is showing & he feels as if they are undefeatable. For his sake I am glad he has these impressions to counteract the horrors of the battlefield. He winds up by saying: "You can't think what I go through when I am out there . . . sometimes walking quite alone in the fields & no one to speak to & my heart goes out to my dear ones & I break my head how one could bring peace to the world & I find no answer . . ."[36]

Later in the war she had another message that Irène and her family were all well. 'It is always a bit depressing getting letters & news in this way,' Victoria commented, '& knowing nothing will ever be the same again, except our personal affection for our relations. You know how wholly English we are & yet can understand these other feelings . . .'[37]

That was in 1916. In the following year, and in 1918, the royal families of Europe were breaking up, losing their thrones, their titles and their lives. Although Louis's anguish went deep, he was in many ways fortunately placed in his adopted country. Within little more than a year, the Tsar and all his family would be dead, the Kaiser defeated and forced to abdicate and leave his country and the Emperor of Austria driven into exile – Romanoffs, Prussians, Habsburgs all gone . . .

The long drawn out agony of her two sisters and her other relations in Russia greatly concerned Victoria through 1917 and 1918. Although she had been an egalitarian from childhood, she was far from being a revolutionary socialist, believing in the natural and harmonious development of a socialist state through diminishing degrees of benevolent autocracy. She understood the problems of Tsardom better than most people in England, on the left or the right of the political spectrum.

Many years earlier, when Queen Victoria complained to her of Nicky's new severe restrictions in Russia, even before he was crowned, Victoria defended his step as 'not wholly unwise'. 'The great mass of the population in Russia,' she told her Queen, 'consists of peasants, who . . . are through want of education & isolation as yet very unfit to take a share in the government of the country or empire . . . So that I have the impression that on the whole Nicky is doing the right thing in suppressing the political aspirations of a numerically small class of his subjects, whilst apparently being resolved to introduce free education amongst the great bulk of the people.'[38]

But in later years she was to watch with apprehension Nicky's incapacity to govern and the growing influence of the powers of autocracy and evil in Russia. There was little she could do to influence her sister on her visits to Peterhof. These were all too brief family occasions, and Alicky's mysticism and obsession with her soul, with Rasputin, and with her health and the tragedy of her haemophilic son, made communication above the domestic level difficult between the two sisters. In Moscow Ella would always open her heart to Victoria, but she had no influence, and scarcely any communication at all with Alicky.

For the first two years of war, Victoria and Louis received fragments of news and even the occasional letter from Russia. Although the war news seemed to get worse and worse, and the popular anti-war and anti-Tsarist feeling grew stronger, life seemed to go on much as before in the royal palaces, the grandeur undiminished.

Dorothy Seymour, who was soon to return to England and call on Louis and Victoria, and later married General Sir Henry Jackson, noted this in her diary when the Germans were everywhere triumphant, and within a few days of the outbreak of the February 1917 Revolution in St Petersburg:

4th February 1917[39]

Went down to Tsarkoe Selo . . . to see the Empress. Met by gorgeous officials, footmen, horses all white and prancing – great state. At the Palace door two glorious footmen with huge orange and red ostrich plumes on their heads. Had luncheon with Baroness Sophie ('Isa') Buxhoeveden and Countess Heindrichoff in their sitting-room – both very young. Were then taken through miles of palace and a huge banqueting room . . . Door opened by huge negro . . . Empress quite lovely, wonderfully graceful, lovely eyes and colouring, very human and a sense of humour. Desperately sad eyes, very haunted. In gorgeous purple velvet, sables and huge amethysts . . . Is evidently a pacifist, and the War and its horrors on her nerves. Whole room a place heavy with tragedy. Can believe anything of Rasputin's influence there.

By chance Dorothy Seymour saw Victoria's other sister in Moscow two weeks later, and left this little sketch of her:

21st February 1917

The *Grand Duchess Serge* sent for me this morning. So I went down to the Martha and Mary Convent. After interview, she had me taken all over the Convent and Hospital and Schools by Madame Goidiffe.

The Grand Duchess lovely but frailer than I thought was possible to be. Fully realises hopelessness of present regime and her sister's want of comprehension of whole affair. Had been to Tsarkoe to try and help but was asked to leave. Told us that Rasputin once sprang at a photograph of her, and tore it up, jumped on it and spat on it, as he said she was a dangerous enemy.

Working every day in her garden at Kent House, in that cold spring of 1917, with Louis at her side, re-laying and cementing bricks of a forcing-bed, Victoria received news of Rasputin's reported death. She hoped that it was true, 'though poor Alix will probably fall ill at it. What harm he has done her! I fear that among the masses in Russia she is hated, chiefly due to that vile creature & a set of people who have always tried to injure her . . .'[40]

As revolution in Russia now appeared imminent, the Cabinet belatedly took action. A change of heart at court, new vigour instilled in the Army, could, in their view, still save the country and its capitulation to Germany. Earlier, Lord Kitchener had been sent to stiffen Russian resistance, but had been drowned *en route* in H.M.S. *Hampshire*, and for months nothing more was done. Sir George Buchanan had a long confidential talk with the Tsar early in January, but found him implacably opposed to making any concessions to the people.

On 16 January Arthur Balfour, Foreign Secretary, told the Prime Minister that 'there are persons of very sound judgement who think that the only chance is to send an emissary belonging to the royal caste, to whom the Emperor would be disposed to speak with more openness than to other folk, and who might convey to him a message from the King and explain how Allied Nations regarded Russian dissensions'.

Balfour went on to ask Lloyd George, 'What do you think of asking Prince Louis of Battenberg to go. He is a man of considerable ability, brother-in-law to the Tsar, and perfectly competent both to understand the British point of view and to explain it to his relative.'[41]

Lloyd George thought otherwise. Although Balfour argued that any disadvantage of Louis's German birth and earlier attacks on him would be 'far out-weighed by the qualification of general ability and diplomatic skill which Prince Louis undoubtedly possesses', Lord Milner was chosen instead to go on this important mission. The visit, as all the world was soon to learn, was a disaster.

Speculation seems fruitless on what would have been the outcome if Louis had been selected for this delicate mission to Russia. Perhaps by then things had gone too far; but he was the only man alive who might have delayed the catastrophic tide of events in Russia, for Nicky admired, respected and loved him deeply; and much can happen in even a brief period of delay.

So Louis continued his gardening, and his work indoors on his naval medals and his reminiscences, while revolution broke out in St Petersburg and Nicky was forced to abdicate.

'How awful about what has happened in Russia,' wrote Dickie from the Grand Fleet. 'I suppose Uncle Nicky is quite safe, though I can't understand why he has abdicated, if they're not going to form a republic, but become a constitutional monarchy ... It says [in the newspapers] Aunt Alix is under guard, so I suppose she is alright, also Aunt Ella & the cousins ...'[42] Dickie was thinking anxiously and lovingly of his sweet Marie, and those picnics and rides they had enjoyed together before the holocaust.

But Victoria was 'very grateful that Nicky has abdicated, for himself & the boy'. 'No one can tell how far the revolution may go & whether the Socialists & anarchists may not get the upper hand before long & then had Alix still been Empress they might have fallen on her ... I hope the rumour that they will be sent to the Crimea is true & that later on they can leave Russia.'

And now we hear the voice of the practical planner, the no-nonsense Victoria who used so to distress Queen Victoria. 'Once the great shock & pain of the people turning against them has been got over & they are in no further danger, they should not be unhappy for neither Nicky or Alix were happy in their high position.'[43]

Always tidy in her feelings, Victoria worried greatly about Ella, too, but seeking comfort, as always, by burying herself in physical work. Ella would 'find strength & comfort where we who are less good than she could not find it in the same degree ...'[44]

The weeks went by, and all the information from Russia appeared bad, and it was all based on rumour and surmise. On 19 April 1917 Dorothy Seymour came to Kent House for the night to report what little she could tell of Victoria's sisters. 'It's awful for her never getting a word of news,' she wrote of Victoria in her diary, 'not even knowing if [Ella] is alive, and when I saw her she looked so frail as if she couldn't stand much ...'

There seemed to be no end to these rumours. Some predicted that Alexis alone was dead, from the hardships of the Russian imperial family's confinement, others that all were alive, that they had been spirited away to a northern eerie. Victoria pursued the idea to ambassadorial level of appealing to Lenin's wife for news, and for mercy to be shown to her relatives; and persuaded her nephew the neutral King of Spain to announce publicly that he would offer safe refuge to Alicky and the five children for the duration of the war if the Bolsheviks would release them.

Not until 2 September 1918 did they know for sure – or as sure as the outside world would ever be – that all the family had gone. Princess Marie-Louise of Schleswig-Holstein, another of Queen Victoria's grandchildren, came to stay with Louis and Victoria in the Isle of Wight. Louis drove down to the ferry in Dickie's little car, which he used when on leave, to meet her. She gave him a letter from Buckingham Palace and told him to open it before they drove off. Louis read it in silence. 'Now at last we know,' he said, returned it to its heavy vellum envelope, and drove Marie-Louise to the house.

Before luncheon Louis found the opportunity to take Victoria aside and hand her the letter.

It was, Victoria wrote, 'a kind letter from George Rex with bad news from Russia'. It enclosed a copy of a letter from Milner to Stamfordham:

I think I ought to let you know at once for His Majesty's information that we have just received a very distressing telegram from the Intelligence Officer serving under General Poole at Murmansk to the effect that there is every probability that the Empress of Russia, her four daughters & the Czarevitch were all murdered at the same time as the late Czar. The information reached the Intelligence Officer from a source which he has no reason to doubt. I am much afraid, therefore, that the news is only too likely to prove true . . .[46]

Victoria, showing no sign of her desperate grief, went at once to her garden and worked as she had never worked before, all through those Autumn days, with Louis and Princess Marie-Louise working alongside. For once, she talked very little. She thought of that ill-omened visit to Ekatarinburg four years earlier, of that square, hostile house in the centre of the town. Later when she learned the details, her mind played on those mines, with their deep shafts, outside the evil town in the Urals. 'Though her loss is pain & grief to me, yet I am grateful that I can think of her as being at peace now. She, her dear husband & children removed for ever from further suffering.'[47]

In a curious way the continuing gnawing anxiety about Ella eased the suffering over the loss of the others. If there was still someone who might be saved, who might be given succour, or at least might be communicated with, there remained something to do. When she heard, later in September, that an American consular official, Mr Whittemore, was going to Russia, and that there might be a chance of his seeing Ella, she gave him a short loving note, and a longer verbal summary of the family news for him to pass to her if the opportunity occurred – how Georgie had married Countess Nada Torby, the daughter of the Grand Duke Michail Michailovitch, and already had a little baby, Tatiana; that Alice was in Switzerland with her family in exile; that she had news of some of their other Russian relatives . . .

But Victoria was despatching messages to a void. Ella had died on 18 July 1918 or soon after. It was not until 9 November that Lord Robert Cecil, just back from Russia, was able to tell her of the death of Ella, or Grand Duchess Serge of Russia, or Saint Elizabeth as she was often called: one more Hessian who had gone to Russia and given her life in the royal and noble cause.

'I telegraphed to Sir Charles Eliot & have now received a telegram from the consul at Ekatarinburg. The consul reports that he has learnt from the Russian Staff (I suppose of the relieving army) that the Grand Duchess was killed & that when Alapaevsk was taken by Russian troops on Sept. 29 they found her body sufficiently preserved to be recognized. The bodies were also found of Princes Ivan, Igor & Constantine as also of the Grand Duke Sergei Michailovitch & a lady-in-waiting . . .'

'If ever,' wrote Victoria, 'any one has met death without fear she will have, & her deep & pure faith will have upheld & supported & comforted her in all she has gone through so that the misery poor Alicky will have suffered will not have touched Ella's soul & may be had she lived, years of solitary suffering would have been her lot, for I have recently heard that all her work in Moscow has been destroyed . . .'[48]

Months passed before Victoria learned that Ella must indeed have needed all her faith and courage, such was the frightfulness of her end. Taken from the schoolhouse where she had been imprisoned with the others under the most severe conditions, she was put in a truck, driven to a disused mineshaft, and thrown down alive . . . When the last of her companions had fallen about her at the base of the mineshaft, the Bolsheviks had hurled down grenades.

Neither the fall nor the explosives had succeeded in killing them all. Ella was evidently one who had survived. And when their bodies were later recovered, it was seen that the young Princes had bandages, torn from Ella's Martha and Mary habit, bound professionally about their wounds. Only Ella, with her long nursing experience, had the skill to do that . . . and the faith and courage too.

Whether or not members of the Russian Imperial family, in the chaos of communications, combat and disputing revolutionary and loyalist and semi-loyalist groups, could ever have been saved, is as great an historic imponderable as the outcome of a mission to Russia by Louis six months earlier. It is doubtful if much could have been done. But what little chance remained in the summer of 1918, with Germany, too, tottering on the verge of revolution, was still-born. This was because Lloyd George was politically afraid of having anything to do with the Russian Imperial family who were regarded by trade unionists and the middle class alike as decadent traitors to the Allied cause. As for King George V, he felt his own position was too weak to fight Lloyd George.

As so often, before and since, that naughty old gossip Sir Henry 'Chips' Channon, probably dug out something nearer to the truth than anything else when he recorded twenty years later:

The Kaiser told Fritzi [his grandson] only last week that he is still haunted by the fate which befell the Czar and his family. He had sent the Czar a telegram offering him a free and protected passage through Germany, had he wished to escape by sea. (This was at the moment when the Czar had tried to get to England.) It was Lloyd George who spoilt and stopped everything, and the late King had been weak with him, not understanding the danger. Their responsibility in the matter has ever been a millstone to both Queen Mary and King George, and their failure to help their poor Russian relations in the hour of danger is the one blot on their lives. Of late, Fritzi tells me, Queen Mary has been sorely conscience stricken.[49]

Victoria's anger and bitterness towards all politicians, born many years before, had matured in the fierce heat of Louis's resignation enforced by Churchill and Asquith, and was now revived with new fire by the assassination of all whom she had loved in Russia.

With the arrival in England of news of further shootings of Russian Grand Dukes in St Petersburg in February 1919, she wrote privately and with unaccustomed savagery to Nona:

'Meanwhile Lloyd George & Wilson coquet with the Bolsheviks & think to reform them by moral suasion! The fools! I should like to present them with Le Notre's books on the French revolution ... There were criminal lunatics in France then, as there are in Russia now & as there are some here in waiting if they get a chance. You don't persuade such people except with cold steel, or leave them to devour each other, after they have slaughtered enough other people.

I don't hate them,' she concluded, 'because they are mad, but neither do I hate mad dogs . . .'[50]

The family never knew the violence of her feelings on the subject at the time.

As all the world learned, there was nothing left of the Russian royal family's bodies but a few fragments together with a few pathetic belongings. Nicky and Alicky and the four girls and little Alexis who had known so much pain in his life, have no grave. Ella's body, however, was recovered as if by a miracle. Two and a half years after her assassination, Louis and Victoria buried her, appropriately, in Jerusalem.

This is how it came about. In spite of the precautions they had taken, the Bolsheviks had not carried out their mass assassination unseen. Father Seraphim, a priest, had witnessed the outrage, and when the White Russian troops overran the town and drove out the Bolsheviks a few days later, he persuaded a party of them to lower him down the shaft. One by one the bodies were hoisted to the surface. Father Seraphim was a man of immense physical strength and some wealth, and he determined to see the woman he regarded as a saint, and her constant companion, Sister Barbara, buried safely in a Russian Orthodox chapel.

Louis, in a letter to his sister Marie from Jerusalem, told her what followed: 'He sealed them in lead coffins, and brought them gradually and with immense difficulty all the way from Siberia and Manchuria to Peking, to the Russian Chapel there. And then on December 1st he brought the two coffins (enclosed in beautifully made Chinese wooden coffins mounted with brass) with the help of two assistants, from Peking by train to Tientsin, from there by coastal steamer to Shanghai and thence by ocean steamer to Hong Kong, Colombo, and Bombay to Port Said.'

The bodies arrived in Port Said from the East two hours after the arrival of Louis and Victoria from the West. At Port Said they met Father Seraphim for the first time. 'This good priest, a Messianic looking man with long hair and a beard', had slept and lived by the coffins for 2½ years . . . 'A week ago today we brought our dear Ella here and laid her to rest on the Mount of Olives in the little Russian Church of Mary Magdalene . . . All the bearers wept and sobbed the whole way, and some fell to the ground. The priests of the orthodox Churches, who were dressed in black robes with silver embroidery and long veils falling from their tall hats, held the first service in the station itself, and again twice outside the Wall, the last time at the Virgin Mary's tomb . . .'[51]

When the war ended Louis was not invited to the formal surrender of the High Seas Fleet, that splendid and memorable occasion for the Royal Navy on 21 November 1918. Nor was that other architect of victory, Jacky Fisher – to the everlasting shame of the Board of Admiralty. The final insult was yet to come. On 9 December Louis received a formal and standard letter from the First Sea Lord, Wester Wemyss, one of Beresford's old cronies, telling him that he would not be employed again, and suggesting that he might wish to retire early from the service in order to make room for younger men.

He at once wrote to the Admiralty to accept their suggestion and asked to be placed on the retired list. George V, too, had to be informed, and Louis wrote also to Buckingham Palace:

10 December 1918[52]

My dear Stamfordham,

Would you kindly inform the King that in response to a letter from Admiral Wemyss I have just sent in my papers. As he did not appear to be aware of the reasons why I am still on the active list I informed him in reply that I had the promise of H.M. Government, when I resigned office, that I should hoist my flag directly the war was over.

Please don't trouble to reply, &
believe me,
Yours very sincerely,
Milford Haven

His younger son, Lord Louis, expressed the feelings of family and friends more briskly. He was now a lieutenant and, at eighteen, second-in-command of a fast little escort vessel, *P.31.* 'I see that they have accepted Papa's resignation,' he wrote to his mother. 'It would do you good to hear the remarks in the mess about it. They're all furious as they had hoped he'd get some big job now! I do think it is disgraceful myself . . .'[53]

Louis had lost all his investments in Russia and Victoria had never recovered any of her valuable jewels. They had Louis's pension, but little else, and Victoria had to resort to selling some land she owned to see them through. Later Louis sold Heiligenberg, but the money was almost all lost in the hysterical inflation in Germany at the time.

Louis had been only sixty-four when he had retired. A year later Victoria noticed that he was not as quick as he used to be and that his gardening hours were much reduced. 'I think he is beginning to show his age rather,' she wrote to Nona, who had married a nice safe, steady officer she had nursed during the war, Richard Crichton. 'He stoops a bit when he walks & does not care about walking fast . . .'

They went out to Greece to see Alice and her family after the long separation, and then settled down at Fishponds, a modest house in the grounds of Netley Castle, owned by Nona's husband.

In 1921 Arthur Lee, who had defended Louis in the Carlton Club and elsewhere, was appointed First Lord by Lloyd George. He was a benevolent, liberal-minded man quite lacking in the xenophobic venom of the Charlie Beresford clique, and deeply regretted the Cabinet's continuing hostility towards Louis when he was old and retired.

In May Louis was elected President of the Royal Navy Club of 1765 and 1785 for its annual dinner to celebrate the defeat of the Spanish Armada on 19 July 1588, and Lee was invited as guest of honour.

The invitations went out to members in the ordinary way, but the secretary was astonished to receive replies from three times the normal number. Old friends, retired admirals who had reached the top, others who were still serving or had retired as Captains or Commanders, came up from the country for the occasion.

At the end of the dinner after his own health was drunk as President, Lee offered the toast to Louis, deploring the stroke of fate which had befallen him seven years earlier, expressing his sympathy, thanking him for all he had done before the war for the service and wishing his family well. He remarked on the great numbers of fellow officers present – the greatest number who had ever attended the dinner. When Louis rose to make his own speech a great burst of cheering broke out. It was almost five minutes before he could make his voice heard.

The next day Louis took Louise to a Buckingham Palace garden party. It was a golden afternoon of sunshine, and between receiving his guests, King George V congratulated Louis on his reception.

It was not the last the King heard of that evening. Two weeks later, in a letter to Stamfordham for the King, Lee wrote of the 'most remarkable and significant ovation, repeated more than once during the evening, which made abundantly clear the anxiety and eagerness of his brother Officers to assure him of their sympathy and abiding confidence.'[54]

In the same letter Lee referred to 'the unmerited misfortune which fell upon [Louis] in October 1914 . . . I need not recall the details of the unhappy controversies of that moment, embittered as they were by the unchivalrous and vindictive conduct of "spy-hunters" who should have known better'. The main burden of this letter was to suggest that, for only the second time in history, George V might wish to honour an officer on the retired list with promotion to the rank of Admiral of the Fleet. The King agreed at once, referring to the manner in which Louis had 'bowed to his fate without murmur or complaint and with that dignity worthy of his generous nature'[55], and made him for the second time a G.C.B., this time of the military division.

There were other happy occasions for Louis during this summer. His first grandson had been born to Georgie's wife Nada two years earlier. Now he heard with special pleasure that Alice, who had so much wanted a boy, had been delivered of one at 'Mon Repos' in Corfu – and he was to be named Philip; like his own Dickie a late child and a handsome, fair and indulged child, too.

Dickie was much in the minds of Louis and Victoria that summer. His love affairs, if anything, surpassed in numbers and intensity even those of Louis himself fifty years earlier.

He was serving in the battle cruiser *Repulse*, and suggested to his Captain that, as a sort of celebration of his father's promotion to the rank of Admiral of the Fleet, he might invite him for a cruise. Father and son both experienced a sense of exaltation and celebration for great things accomplished on that last voyage into the northern waters where the Norse chieftains had once set the prows of their longboats towards the Scottish coasts, and more recently the Grand Fleet had kept tight shut the gates of blockade.

Nearly a decade had passed since Louis had felt a Dreadnought's decks vibrating beneath his feet, and had gazed forward over super-imposed gun turrets to the rise and fall of a great warship's bow cutting through the water. Since then the fleets he had helped bring into being and had once commanded had completed their duties through four years and more of war, and then had accepted the surrender of the mighty High Seas Fleet.

Dickie wrote to Victoria from Cromarty about the cruise. 'We had delightful weather coming round & I think Papa thoroughly enjoyed himself. I know the Ward Room here have thoroughly enjoyed having him. We arrived on Saturday morning & went ashore at Invergordon to a fete given in the grounds of the Castle ... Well Papa succeeded in catching rather a bad cold [when ashore] & getting a chill, anyway on Monday morning Dr Hunt took his temperature & found it was sub normal. At 5 p.m. he took it again & found it was 101 ... Then during the night Papa got lumbago ... Today he has been having his back massaged & he has remained in bed ...'⁵⁶

But in a day or two he seemed quite well again. He had planned next to go out to the Mediterranean to join Georgie, who was serving there in the cruiser *Cardiff*. He returned to London and met Victoria and Louise at the Naval and Military Club in Piccadilly. He told them of his cruise, and they talked family affairs – anxiously about Alice and Andrew because the Greek situation was, as usual, highly unstable; happily about Dickie; speculatively about Georgie. He would have fuller news of their elder son soon. Then he said he was not feeling too good, and Victoria made him go to bed in the suite they had booked in the club annexe in Half Moon Street.

Victoria was worried and called a doctor. The doctor did not seem very concerned but prescribed some medicine. Louise and she had tea together in his bedroom in the afternoon, then they went out to buy the medicine at a chemist's in St James's Street.

A few minutes after they had left the club, the maidservant knocked on Louis's door, intending to collect the tray. There was no answer. Thinking he must be asleep, she went in. He was indeed asleep, his eyes closed, his head lying back on the pillows. But there was something unnaturally peaceful about his appearance and she called the housekeeper. Suddenly they both realized that he was dead.

When Victoria and Louise returned to the club they were met by several weeping members of the staff ... 'Oh dear, the Admiral is dead, ma'am.'

Dickie had come from the *Repulse* to spend the week-end with the Duke and Duchess of Sutherland at Dunrobin Castle nearby. He had needed only one inducement to accept the invitation: a girl called Edwina Ashley would be there. But she would be only one of many, including the Prince of Wales, the Duke of York, the Archbishop of Canterbury, the Dudleys, Hélène Leveson-Gower and her sister Charlotte 'Baby' Demarest, the Duchess's sister and others. The telegram with the news arrived in the afternoon. Dickie rushed for the telephone to find out the time of the trains. But the one and only train of the day had already left, and it was out of the question to motor the whole six hundred miles to London.

The Archbishop suggested to his hostess that they might have a short service in Louis's memory before dinner. After cushions had been collected for the Prince of Wales and his brother, and the Duke, all of whom were in kilts, the Archbishop conducted the service in the drawing-room of the great castle. After a while the doors were flung open, and the butler marched triumphantly in carrying a cocktail shaker, followed by two footmen. He was not used to prayers at this time of the day.

It was an awkward moment, but there was a sort of rightness about it, for Louis would not have wished to spoil anyone's pleasure, and he was too fond of parties to wish one broken up for long on his account.

The obituaries were prominent and generous, but most of the responsible journals had said everything seven years before on his resignation and could now only repeat it. Fifty years later, he was still remembered clearly and with much affection among the handful of midshipmen who had served under him in the Mediterranean and the Atlantic Fleets. He was especially generous and kind with the snotties. He hated coarse or perjorative words, and never swore. His own harsh early days did much to shape his style of leadership in later days, and he would have no coarseness in the gunroom of his ships.

His courtliness extended even to his signalling. 'He was never known to send a rude message, which was unusual at that time,' one of his contemporaries recalled. 'I remember that I was sent aft with a message once. He called me back at the last minute, took the message from me, added "please", and sent me off again. He always was a very thoughtful man.'[57]

Those breakfasts with his midshipmen were prodigious feasts by present day standards. 'He breakfasted at 8.30 and took a full hour over it, during which he told the chief of staff of his requirements and programme for the day.'[58] 'Prince Louis was a big man,' wrote another of his contemporaries, 'and had a big appetite. At breakfast he began on porridge, then fish, then eggs and bacon or a meat dish, then a large plate of cold ham, then hot muffins or crumpets; and then a lot of toast and butter and jam, and finished on fruit. His meal would have fed an officers' mess.'[59] Yet he never grew stout.

In most books of memoirs and reminiscences, and in most naval biographies of this period, there are warm references to Louis. 'Prince Louis was a sea officer, and a Fleet Commander, second to none in our service,' wrote Roger Keyes. 'He had the gift of bringing out all that was best in his Captains, and gave them opportunities of handling his fleet when cruising and exercising, which were invaluable training for those who aspired to flag rank.'[60]

But for all that, it is as an administrator and staff-man that he will be best remembered and judged most valuable at a time when these assets were spread thin in the Admiralty. He was an exceptional chairman who was quick to recognize the heart of the matter and went straight to it. He brushed aside those who diverged from the point under discussion; and he was equally short with those who liked to reflect longer as well as those whose brains were less agile than his own. This made him a tough but highly effectual committee man. But even under the most trying circumstances, and surrounded by boneheads, he was always courteous and cool.

He was quick to adopt English parlance and mannerisms when he first came to England as a boy. He was for years nicknamed 'Old Soul' for his engagingly over-eager and over-frequent use of this term. But he never understood, through all his long service life with the English, why his peculiarly German manner of being right, and always right, of not being ashamed of showing he had brains, rubbed his fellow officers up the wrong way. 'These are the kind of administrative blunders which are never made in Germany,' he once wrote in anguish to Ponsonby. 'It is all a question of looking ahead and giving oneself time . . .'[61] True, no doubt, but not calculated to make friends.

Louis could no more cure this tendency than he could completely refine and anglicize his faint German accent, which ruffled feelings further when declaiming the excellent efficiency of German ways.

English feelings about the Germans were hard-set and inflexible and yet sensitive long before Prince Albert crossed the English Channel to marry Queen Victoria. It is possible to understand, but sometimes hard to forgive, the perverse and ungenerous way the English have treated their royal German immigrants. Prince Albert of Saxe-Coburg-Gotha, Prince Henry of Battenberg and Prince Louis of Battenberg all came to England to do their duty as they

335

saw it, and all died prematurely, having given much and received little in return.

Lord Charles Beresford killed Louis by stages from the day he first acquired senior responsibility, from about 1907 on, thrusting the lance into his quarry with the pack of gutter journalists and cruel and bigoted 'social' naval officers and their wives crying for blood behind him. Already in 1909 he was publicly calling him a German spy. Beresford was Louis's natural assassin. Louis represented everything that was antipathetic to Beresford's style and manner – his shameless pleasure in his work and in winning. The 'syndicate of discontent' was jealous of his relations with the court, suspicious of his relations with Germany and Russia, disapproving of his energy and popularity on the lower deck and in the gunroom.

Louis's spirit never really recovered from the blow of October 1914. Victoria knew this, and was thankful that at least his last year had been such a good one, and that he had died without premonition or pain, and with the salt air still in his lungs.

She told Queen Mary, in answer to her letter of condolence, 'It has all been so sudden that I can hardly quite realize it yet, but I am very very grateful that my dear Louis's life, a happy one as men's go, ended so quickly & quietly, without time for worry, anxiety or sorrow. He felt a very real affection for you & your children & quite especially for George, whom he had known so well in the old days in the Navy, & was always in the full sense of the words "at all your service".'[62]

15

'You have made my Dickie very happy . . .'

THE DOWAGER MARCHIONESS OF MILFORD
HAVEN *to Edwina Ashley*

VICTORIA MILFORD HAVEN was to live for nearly thirty years
more after the death of Louis on 11 September 1921. Born a Princess
fifty-eight years ago, she had from the age of fifteen willingly carried
the responsibilities of her rank, of motherhood, and of the wife of a
naval officer.

All these responsibilities had now ended. She was a bereaved
Princess of nowhere, without a seat, her children grown up, in a
world she no longer cared for.

'What a state the whole of Europe and America are in!' She
exclaimed shortly after the 1918 armistice. 'Once again, the immediate results of a great war are an outburst of all that is selfish, base &
ugly in mankind. "The old order changeth" – one can but pray
that it will give place to "a new" where people will be happier
again & that the "masses" may improve upon the mess made by
the "classes".'[1]

It was not in Victoria's nature to remain miserable for long,
either about Louis's death or the state of the world; nor, above all,
was she likely to remain without responsibilities for long. This
Princess, now a Dowager Marchioness who had given up her own
royal title, collected new duties and tasks as she had once mapped
the island of Malta, instructed her children in political history,
participated in Europe's royal matchmaking under the eye of Queen
Victoria, and conducted receptions for important people as the wife
of the First Sea Lord.

337

For the three decades left to her Victoria watched over and guided the destinies of her children and grandchildren, and became a central matriarchal figure in the lives of Europe's surviving royalty.

Like her famous and regal grandmother, for thirty years more her relations came to her for advice, or she gave it unasked: encouraged or discouraged and observed with shrewd and percipient eyes the matches they made; and passed comment on the world as she saw it.

With the sale of Kent House, her kingdom was a modest set of apartments in Kensington Palace, a grace-and-favour establishment, and the use of a small garden in the grounds.

Her authorized power was insignificant. But Victoria played a considerable part in royal events and public affairs. Her black, erect, rather disshevelled figure was always present, in spirit or in person, as royalty recovered their poise after the holocaust, and her children and grandchildren matured, some towards greatness, or suffered early death in the tragic Hessian tradition Victoria had known as a child and from time to time throughout her womanhood.

As soon after the war as she could she went to Germany to visit her surviving sister and brother. Irène was living quietly at Hemmelmark with Henry of Prussia. In one special way Irène felt most anguished of all the family about Alicky's death. These two younger sisters had always been close, and the sufferings they had shared with their haemophilic sons (Irène's died at four years) welded their affections more tightly.

It was a cheerless time in Germany, cold and without hope. The Imperial German Navy in which Irène's husband and both of her surviving sons had made their careers had endured the triple agony of mutiny, surrender and scuttling. But Waldemar ('Toddy') and Sigismund ('Bobby') had married in 1919, and this brought a ray of happiness into Irène's life.

Things could not, as Victoria had confided in Nona, ever be the same again between them, but the two sisters were pleased to see one another and their personal affection was undiminished.

Victoria hurried on to Darmstadt and greeted Ernie for the first time for more than five years. His heart had never been in the war, and he had been allowed to return home from the front. Then he and Onor had given themselves up to the care of the sick and war-wounded in Darmstadt as his mother had done when he had been only an infant.

It had been an exhausting and sometimes frightening time for the Grand Ducal couple. Hesse, ever liberal in its politics, had eagerly declared for the Socialist Republic in the revolution of November 1918, and the people demanded Ernie's abdication as Grand Duke. He refused, in the best Hessian tradition, as upheld by his cousin Sandro in Bulgaria, and there were hints of violence, from which they were saved by the Grand Ducal family's personal popularity.

Ernie was deposed all the same and deprived of his remaining powers, though left with his title and a few of his properties. The wonder and magic of Wolfsgarten were to live again, on a more muted level than before, but not for a while yet, not until the wounds of war had healed.

Victoria's immediate family affairs especially preoccupied her during the two years following Louis's death. Two of her children remained unmarried, and although Dickie's bachelorhood could happily (and eventfully) continue for years yet, Louise gave her much worry at this time. She was thirty-two when her father died, lanky, with a rather abrupt manner and, like her mother, with a tendency to be unfemininely dogmatic.

The family always agreed that they were clearly divided into two personality classes, Victoria, Louise and Dickie the extroverts, fearless and forthright in conversation, trusting their quick minds to seeing them through, while Alice and Georgie took after their father in being more contemplative and thoughtful and cautious before uttering.

Lord Mountbatten once made the distinction in these terms: 'My mother was very quick on the uptake, very talkative, very aggressive and argumentative. With her marvellous brain she sharpened people's wits, and of course especially my father's. Although my father had a good brain, it didn't have the pace and substance of my mother's. He would give careful thought before uttering, and never gave a rushed or unconsidered reply.'[2]

The brain power did not neatly follow the personality division. Louise was no cleverer than Alice, Dickie not as clever as Georgie. It was the nature of their brains that led to the clear personality division.

Louise, then, did not possess Victoria's keen brain, but she was immensely kind and humane and worried about things – about the world and its sufferings, and about herself. She lacked her mother's ability to analyse with her speed and precision. During those long and arduous years with the war wounded she had seen more of the awfulness of war than any of the rest of the family, even Alice. When it was over the gaiety of the balls and parties of the old peace had largely disappeared, along with most of her generation of young men. She felt out of things, alone with Victoria at Kensington Palace and with no part to play except as her mother's companion.

It was very different for Dickie. With his aptitude for filling his life with more enjoyment and activity than anyone else Victoria had ever known, he was a constant stimulus and delight to her, and only rarely an anxiety. He had hurled himself into the new peace with the power and speed of his beloved little *P.31*.

This humble little escort vessel, like his father's *Scout* thirty years earlier, was cherished like a glittering jewel and its tiny complement of some fifty petty officers and men had to be the smartest in the service, even though Dickie was only second-in-command.

'Dickie turned up yesterday,' wrote Victoria from London, 'when P.31 came up the river & anchored opposite Whitehall steps. He is delightfully excited about tomorrow, the King coming on board about 11 a.m. The whole ship has been "enamelled" at Sheerness & Dickie is in agonies at every scratch she gets by passing boats etc.'

The Press were, of course, already there, as they were always to cluster about this nineteen-year-old glamorous naval officer wherever he went. 'Newspaper interviewers are assailing her already & the "Mirror" representative has been busy with his camera . . .'[3]

That *P.31* was in commission at all at this time was thanks only to Dickie's devious ingenuity. All but four of her class were ordered to pay off. At Portland she lay alongside others of her kind which were already in care and maintenance ('c and m') and without a crew, their work finished. *P.31*, too, was ordered to terminate her commission. Her captain rushed up to the Admiralty to appeal for a stay of execution, while Dickie assumed temporary command.

His duties included receiving the Admiral in command at Portland when he announced he would be coming on board to inspect the ship and see how far her paying off had proceeded. Below decks all was quiet, and all shipshape. There was even a notice hanging on a boiler-room door – WET PAINT!

'So your ship is in "c & m" is it?' the Admiral demanded, having been politely obstructed from coming on board.

'She's next door to it, sir,' Dickie answered, bending the truth only slightly.

As soon as the Admiral was well clear, Dickie went below to release the crew from their temporary, and confined, boiler-room quarters. In this way was the *P.31*'s commission further extended, so that later she took part in the Baltic operations.

But by then Dickie had gone up to Cambridge. In the tumult of demobilization and the immense reduction in personnel in the fleet, all the so-called 'war babies' who had been sent to sea at about sixteen were appointed for special courses at one or other of the Cambridge colleges.

Dickie went to Christ's. 'I do understand the horrible wrench it will be to give up your beloved P.31,' Victoria wrote to him, 'but I think you will find it easier going from her to Cambridge than if you had to join some big ship as a mere "Sub".'[4]

Later she heard from him about his lively Cambridge life. In his first term he joined the Union and in his second term led the debate against Oxford on the subject: 'The time is ripe for a Labour government'.

As leader it was his privilege to invite an outside guest. Victoria learned with amusement that he had at once telephoned Winston Churchill, now back in power as War Minister, who accepted the invitation with alacrity.

And how typical of the boy, she thought, that he should open his reply: 'Sir, in my humble opinion everything that has been said so far by the speakers on both sides is tripe . . .'

Some of his listeners might have wondered about the 'humble' part. Surely here was a uniquely arrogant young man to be condemning out of hand the words of wisdom spoken by the leading 'brains' at the universities of Oxford and Cambridge – and in his second term at that!

Lord Mountbatten tends to explain the situation in this way: 'Part of the success I have enjoyed in life can be traced back to my upbringing. I was brought up in an exceptional family. When I was a boy I thought that the intelligence of all those about me was normal in life. It came as a great shock to me when I went out into the world and discovered that this was not true at all. This led me from quite an early age to feel a lack of reverence towards, say, great politicians with their supposedly great brains. This made it much easier for me to feel at least their equal when I was in their company.'[5]

At this time, at the beginning of 1920, Victoria was wondering more about her younger son's love life than his debating powers. Every weekend he was in London at parties and balls, or at great country houses. He was among the first two or three most eligible bachelors in the country, he was invited everywhere, and, like his father, everywhere the loveliest girls fell in love with him.

Victoria helped him keep his head. He was due to come home soon. 'You can then enjoy seeing Poppy Baring again & feeling "in love",' she writes. 'It does not matter how often you are in that state as long as somewhere in your heart you keep the knowledge of the difference of a love that is merely based upon strong attraction, & that other love which I hope may come to you only later on & which is one of head & heart together for a girl you will want to make your wife. I think the test will be when you feel that your love is so strong that you will be willing to wait any time for a girl to become yours without a fear that your mind will change . . .'[6]

This happened earlier than she had expected or wanted. Dickie's love affair with Edwina Ashley had continued as ardently as ever after Louis's funeral. Louis briefly met Edwina before he died and at once fell under the charm of this slight, lovely, sharp-witted girl. This gave Dickie both encouragement and great pleasure.

Victoria, too, took to Edwina from the beginning. At the same time she ruled out of her mind any consideration of marriage for her boy. Edwina was an heiress, her son a too young naval officer of modest means and with few expectations. It just would not work.

Like Victoria, Edwina had experienced a troubled childhood and had lost her mother early in life. Her father, Wilfrid Ashley, had married again and Edwina was quite unable to reconcile herself to her stepmother. She had been brought up mainly by governesses and servants, and more remotely by her fabulously rich grandfather, the international banker Sir Ernest Cassel.

After a turbulent time at boarding school and a domestic science college, and a more satisfying and rewarding grand tour of Italy, she was invited by her grandfather to live with him and act as his hostess at his vast London home, Brook House in Park Lane. Here he died a few days after Louis.

The poor little rich girl with the vividly extravagant personality, now momentarily subdued and lost without her grandfather, and the jaunty, self-confident naval lieutenant, became closer than ever to one another in the aftermath of their tragedies.

Could their relationship survive not only the disparity of their wealth, but also a long separation? This was soon to be tested.

Dickie had already made one long royal tour with David, the Prince of Wales and future King Edward VIII and Duke of Windsor. Like their fathers, they were firm naval friends, and Lord Louis, just down from Cambridge, had accompanied him in the battle cruiser *Renown* on an imperial tour of Australia, New Zealand, the Pacific and the Caribbean colonies as A.D.C.

Now the Prince of Wales was to undertake another official tour, this time of India and Japan, and he decided that he could only suffer the strain of receptions and banquets and formal speech-making if he had his lively cousin with him as light relief – 'at twenty-one, a vigorous and high-spirited young man,' as the Duke of Windsor later described Dickie, 'who became the instigator of many an unexpected diversion outside the official programme'.

The trip would take eight months. But Edwina devised a plot which would lead to their meeting briefly during the tour. So he said goodbye to Victoria and sailed from Portsmouth with his customary light heart.

The auguries and precedents were right, and these were important considerations all through Dickie's professional career, which, more than ever since his father's death, was to be patterned on his father's life. It was right and proper that he should be touring India with the Prince of Wales at the same age and with the same junior rank as his father 45 years earlier. A second satisfaction was that the *Renown*'s commander, Captain the Hon. Herbert Meade, was the son of the Earl of Clanwilliam who had commanded the Flying Squadron in 1880 when the friendship between the Prince of Wales's father and his own father had been so firmly cemented.

Edwina turned up as she had said she would, her journey beset by the greatest difficulties, amidst the hurly-burly of Delhi where there was scarcely any privacy.

But Dickie found the time, and the place – a room in the temporary Viceregal Lodge overlooking the gardens – and proposed, and was at once accepted.

The Prince of Wales was the first to learn the news, which delighted him. Within a few hours Victoria knew, too. It was, she later told him, no surprise. 'Indeed dear I had been expecting the news & am really & truly happy at it as I think you both know your own minds now. May much happiness be in store for you.'[7]

The engagement confirmed the promise of a warm and intimate relationship between Edwina and Victoria. Their minds matched, they shared an unquenchable curiosity, they were impatient to learn and exchange ideas, they were both lifelong socialists at heart, and Victoria soon replaced the real mother Edwina had lost as a child.

343

At first Victoria remained anxious about what the new wealth would do to her son, and how it would affect the style of the marriage for which they were otherwise so well suited. She was worried that her son, now that he would no longer have to work for his living, might be tempted to slacken off the pressure in his naval career, or even give it up altogether. (She need not have worried!)

'You have made my Dickie very happy by accepting him,' Victoria wrote to Edwina, 'for he loves you dearly & that you should love him too brings you near to my heart . . . It is not always easy being the wife of a naval man & the many separations hit one hard. Yet I & Dickie's father were very happy in spite of them & I hope you will be able to take much pride & interest in his career for that helps one a lot & to my mind a man without a profession leads a poor sort of life & when one cares for a man one does not want him to be a slacker or stand in the way of his work, or make him feel that one grudges him the place it must take in his life and feelings . . .'8

The wedding, on 18 July 1922, was on the scale of a royal ceremony. King George V and Queen Mary were there, of course, and – whether or not they had lost their thrones, their titles, their power, their wealth or their land – so, too, were Grand Dukes and Grand Duchesses, Princes and Princesses from all over Europe, and half of Britain's *Debrett* from Dukes to Baronets.

As a reminder that monarchy was not dead after all, and that war and revolution had not entirely destroyed royal dynastic continuity, Uncle Bertie's Queen Alexandra and Tsar Alexander III's Dowager Tsarina, Aunt Minnie (who had escaped the holocaust), were in St Margaret's, Westminster, on that summer day.

As a talisman of royal survival of future wars and revolutions, a pretty one-year-old tow-headed boy, Prince Philip of Greece, waved to his mother and father as they left for the church. His sisters, the Princesses Margarita, Theodora, Cecile and Sophie, were among the bridesmaids, all in delphinium blue dresses; and the Prince of Wales acted as Lord Louis's best man.

There were more spectators lining the streets of Westminster than ever Darmstadt could muster, and when they caught a glimpse of Edwina, a shining white pearl of loveliness, they cheered as if she were a Queen.

Even in the church, according to *The Times*, 'A discreet murmur of admiration rose from the congregation as the bride entered on the arm of her father . . .'

The same newspaper was driven into uncharacteristic lyrical mood by the sheer beauty of the occasion, and offered its readers a detailed description of 'the bride's gown' which was 'conspicuous by its combination of simplicity and richness. Of dull silver tissue cut on long, straight lines, with a waistless bodice, mitten sleeves and round neck, its effect was of subdued splendour. Narrow stole panels, of unequal length, embroidered with crystal and diamanté, hung from either hip. The train, four yards in length, was of fifteenth century point lace mounted on cloth of silver and edged with a heavier border of Spanish point-lace, forming a stole drapery across the shoulders. The tissue foundation was turned back at the edge over the lace, so as to form, as it were, a frame for it.'[9]

Here, surely, was the very apotheosis of romantic love and a gilded made-in-heaven wedding. Their five-months-long honeymoon began at Broadlands, where the young couple spent a few days before travelling to the Continent and then to America.

Awaiting them at Broadlands was a touching note written by Victoria before the wedding – 'just a few lines' to 'give you and Edwina my love. To you my very dear son & to your wife, whom I welcome with all my heart as a daughter & who I hope will by & by be able to feel that the "in-law" has become an "in reality". Please don't answer these lines,' she added. 'I know that they are not necessary. I write them merely because you are so much in my thoughts. I am sure Papa's blessing rests on you as does mine...'[10]

Victoria experienced a feeling of relief as well as happiness at Louise's wedding the following year. Crown Prince Gustafus Adolphus ('Gustaf') of Sweden, eldest son of King Gustafus V, had married in 1905 Margaret, Princess of Connaught, the elder daughter of Queen Victoria's third son, Prince Arthur, Duke of Connaught. She had died in 1920, leaving five motherless children, and a very lonely widower.

In June 1923 the Crown Prince paid a visit to England with two of his sons for the season. He had met the Battenberg children often before the war, and the last time he had seen Louise was during that hectic time in 1914 when she and Victoria were trying to get home from Russia. Now in London, it was observed that he was paying special attention to Louise. They met many times that summer at the home of Georgie and Nada, the new Marquess and Marchioness of

Milford Haven; and it became increasingly clear to Louise that the Crown Prince of Sweden was going to propose to her.

Louise was nervous and uncertain. Victoria urged her to accept. She was fond of Gustaf and he would offer her a home and ready-made family life in a safe and pleasant country. It was all very well for you, comfortable in your London, Louise told her mother. 'Think about me, faced with leaving England, and settling down in a strange country!'[11] But she took her mother's advice all the same.

'There was nothing of the blushing bride about Aunt Louise, when she told us she was going to get married,' one of her Greek nieces recalled. 'She seemed embarrassed, almost annoyed with herself, and with her typical inclination to understatement, especially on her own account, she explained that she thought she was much too old and thin to be a bride. And what was her bridal gown to be like? She was certainly not going to wear white!'[12]

King George V arranged the wedding, and it took place on 3 November 1923 in the Chapel Royal with almost as much glitter and as many royalty and ex-royalty present as the previous year. The bride did wear white after all – a beautiful long dress made from silk sari material sent to her from Darmstadt by her Uncle Ernie, and she was given away by her elder brother.

Victoria saw the couple off on their honeymoon to Italy, and returned well satisfied to Kensington Palace. And now she was really alone for the first time in her life, and would be for twenty-seven more years.

The Greek taste for revolution and change of regime has developed so strongly over the centuries that it is as deeply embedded in their way of life as parliamentarianism is in Britain or terrorism in Russia. It is a style of living that obviously suits the Greek temperament or they would not have accepted it for so long. But it has also been unsettling for the Greek royal family, and for most of Princess Alice's long life (she died in 1969 at the age of eighty-four) her husband and his family were in and out of favour and power with bewildering frequency.

Alice's four girls were nine, eight, three, and a few weeks old at the outbreak of the First World War. Andrew's eldest brother Constantine, Duke of Sparta ('Tino'), had become King of the Hellenes on the assassination of his father in 1913. Inevitably, his reign was uneasy and over-eventful, and he contributed to its controversial element by frustrating his prime minister, Eleutherios Venizelos, who wanted to end the country's strict neutrality and bring Greece in on the side of Britain and France. In 1917 Allied warships appeared in the Piraeus to add their weight of influence to Venizelos's cause.

One French warship actually opened fire on the royal palace. Alice rushed protectively to the nursery wing just after a shell had burst outside the window. No one was hurt, the shelling soon ceased, but the King had to go after this and Andrew found himself sacked from the Army. If that was not enough, the British and French told Andrew that he must now leave the country, and he packed up his belongings and left with Alice and the children for Switzerland.

The moment the war was over, and he could get leave, Dickie raced to Lausanne, where his sister and her family were living, to get a first-hand report on them all for Victoria.

'He made the greatest of friends with the children,' Victoria reported, 'after his first shyness at finding his nieces so big had gone. Dolla [13] is only an inch shorter than Alice & both girls are full of learning & have lots of lessons. Cecile [8] is still Andrea's pet & the prettiest, 'Tiny' [4] is delightful and converses like a child of six . . .'13

The Greek family was also (and not for the first nor for the last time) feeling rather poor. Victoria sold some Burmah Oil shares and divided the proceeds between her four children, expecting the two boys and Louise to invest the money. 'Alice, poor girl,' she wrote, 'will probably need it for immediate use, but it will be an unexpected windfall & I am only sorry I can't see her face when she gets my letter.'14

In November 1920 Greece held a tempestuous election, which resulted in Venizelos's fall from power and the return to his precarious throne of King Constantine. Andrew returned with his brother Christopher. 'They were accorded an enthusiastic reception,' wrote Alice proudly, 'and were dragged from their car and borne on the shoulders of the populace, frenzied with joy, the whole way from Phalerum Bay to Athens, and he [Andrew] was forced to make a speech from the balcony of the Palace to the vast crowds gathered below.'15

As usual the Greeks were at war in Asia Minor, and the campaign was stepped up under the new regime. Andrew, who must surely be numbered among the most enthusiastic and most frustrated generals of this century, managed to get command of a division after three months' effort, and did so well that he was promoted to Lieutenant-General and given the 2nd Army Corps. It was with this rank, and with the distinction of recent military victory, that he accompanied Alice and the children to his brother-in-law's glamorous wedding in July 1922.

Soon after Prince Andrew returned to Greece, King Constantine was deposed and exiled again. It was a confusing time but Andrew for the present was allowed to stay so long as he and his family confined themselves to 'Mon Repos'.

Andrew's sentence was only deferred. A military junta took over power in Athens and Andrew was summoned as a witness at the court of the Revolutionary Committee. This was just a trick. He was seized on landing, thrown into prison, and himself charged with treason.

Alice, in a paroxysm of anxiety, cabled her mother in London, the Pope, and others who might use their influence, and herself fought for his life from Athens.

Victoria immediately got into touch with George V, who acted with unusual decisiveness. The King was only too aware of the weak manner in which he had allowed Lloyd George to overrule his wish to help the Russian Imperial family to leave Russia. He was determined not to have what he regarded as the blood of another cousin on his hands. For the first and last time in his reign he exercised the royal prerogative.

The King telephoned the Admiralty and said that he wanted the Royal Navy to save his cousin, Prince Andrew of Greece, emphasizing that they must act at once to release him from prison.

The power of royalty, the despatch of a gunboat, could still influence events in foreign lands in 1922. The Admiralty, and Lord Curzon at the Foreign Office, acted swiftly. Commander Gerald Talbot R.N., who had once been a naval attaché in Athens and knew more of the tortuous channels of Greek politics than most Greek politicians, was sent out from Switzerland where he was serving to begin negotiations with the Greek revolutionary leader, General Pangalos. The 6-inch-gunned cruiser, H.M.S. *Calypso*, was sent to the Piraeus.

By the time both arrived, the officer surreptitiously, the cruiser later and ostentatiously, Andrew lay in prison under sentence of death – and this was no bluff because six others who were tried at the same time *were* shot almost immediately.

Talbot got an interview with Pangalos, whom he knew well, but received only a dusty answer from the soldier. 'You are wasting your time,' Talbot was told. 'I cannot intervene, it is the decision of the court.'

Talbot repeated his demand, this time 'in the name of the King of England.' That made no difference, Pangalos repeated, it was not his decision.

At that moment, with timing that a spy story writer would not dare to expect his readers to credit, a messenger arrived, somewhat pale and breathless, to inform the General that a British cruiser was steaming into Phaleron Bay, cleared for action, guns trained on the city. (The last part was not true but the sight of a hostile warship not only concentrates the mind wonderfully but convinces the beholder that it *must* be cleared for action.)

The tone of the conversation went sharply into reverse, and that evening, under cover of darkness, Princess Alice and Commander Talbot R.N. were escorted to Prince Andrew's cell by General Pangalos personally. There was a brief, tearful reunion; then the three were put into a car by the General who accompanied them speedily to a quayside where a Royal Navy cutter awaited them.

The *Calypso* headed for Corfu where she embarked four Princesses, an infant Prince, a nursemaid, a governess and a lady-in-waiting, and took the whole family to Brindisi and put them ashore on 5 December. 'The Prince is so delightful, and so English,' remarked the cruiser's captain, 'and I am quite in love with the youngest daughter aged 8. They were rather amusing about being exiled, for they so frequently are . . .'[16]

On Talbot's arrival in London, the King sent him along to Kensington Palace to recount to Victoria and the rest of the family the cloak-and-dagger events which had secured the release of her son-in-law. Before he could begin his recital of events, Victoria said:

'I understand the King got the Admiralty to send you out to Athens to rescue my son-in-law from the firing squad and I believe he promised to send a cruiser. I imagine you went overland ahead and managed to get into Greece.'

Warming to her narrative she continued before he could interrupt, 'Since you were chosen you must have known Greece well and no doubt knew General Pangalos and so were able to confront him, but at first without success . . .' And so she continued, reciting her idea of the whole sequence of events and scarcely pausing for breath.

When she had at last finished she had flattened out all but her younger son Dickie. 'And now that you have told Commander Talbot what you imagine happened,' he told her, 'suppose you give him the chance to tell us what really happened.'

Victoria was at once contrite and full of apologies. But Talbot smiled and said, 'You have got the whole story absolutely correct, ma'm. I have nothing to add. Perhaps I may now take my leave?'

He was not, of course, permitted to do so and was taken into lunch.

The incident had staggered his daughters-in-law but not her own children who realized how intently their mother had been thinking about the matter and how her clear, logical mind had worked out, step by step, what must happen if Prince Andrew was to be saved from the shooting squad.

Alice and Andrew settled at St Cloud outside Paris. Andrew's brothers tended to make more prosperous marriages than his own. His brother George had married Marie Bonaparte and they lived in a large house in the park at St Cloud. They owned several other houses too and they gave one near to their own to their banished and impoverished relatives.

Victoria often visited them at St Cloud and they all made the regular pilgrimages – to Darmstadt and Wolfsgarten and Sweden and to Rumania to stay with Queen Helen and her son Michael, the future King.

The visits, and the number and the power and the grandness of their relatives were all diminished now, the palaces and residences less regally splendid. It was a little grey compared with those glittering years before 1914.

But if there was among the grown-ups an inevitable regret for lost power and wealth, and for lost relatives, the children played as merrily together as ever, in Kensington Gardens or in poor little Elizabeth of Hesse's half-size house of magic at Wolfsgarten, at Holkham and Blakeney in Norfolk, in the palace grounds at Ulriksdal, or on the sands of the Black Sea coast in Rumania.

At St Cloud Andrew played with his children and helped with their lessons. He adored his little boy, and Prince Philip's sisters can remember today their happy laughter when they played together, usually rather boisterously. But there was really not enough for Andrew to do. So he took to writing a book about his experiences.

His memoirs could well have been fascinating for he had campaigned so often and so successfully and usually under somewhat bizarre circumstances, and he was a good soldier, skilful and courageous. But by now Andrew was bitter at his dismissal, at his corrupt court martial and banishments, and was determined to refute publicly the accusations of bad generalship and cowardice which had been hurled at him after the last campaign. His book turned out to be a rather shrill defence of all that he had accomplished in his last operational command. It was aptly titled *Towards Disaster*. It was a pity because Prince Andrew's record spoke for itself.

Princess Alice had increasingly shown signs of the deeply intro-spective religious characteristics of her Aunt Ella, and the same need to give up her time and energies to the care of the sick and unfortunate that her grandmother and namesake had felt. She opened up a shop in St Cloud – something that outraged many of the older relations but not her broadminded mother – and it did quite well because people liked to be served by a lovely royal Princess. Her profits contributed to her special charities and were used for the support of Greek refugees.

In these, Prince Philip's early years, his mother gave him a lot of attention and she spent much time with him and they travelled about together. She loved showing him things and watching his alert intelligence growing. In the autumn of 1924, when Philip was three-and-a-half, Alice was staying with Victoria at Kensington Palace. The nurse brought Philip over from Paris to join her. Alice went to Victoria Station to meet her boy. It was his third visit to London (Louis's funeral and Dickie's marriage had been earlier occasions) but the first one of which he was later to recollect anything.

At their meeting he was 'very excited & pleased', Alice reported, and he 'discovered the first policeman by himself & pointed him out to me. Also the buses were his joy, & I had to take him in one this afternoon. Of course he made straight for the top, but it was too windy and showery to go there, but he was reasonable & went inside . . .'[17]

Philip was already at school, an exclusive infants' school at St Cloud called 'The Elms', full of tiny children of American million-aires and exiled royalty. Andrew's brother Christopher paid the fees. Philip was nearly five when Victoria came on one of her visits. It was her sixty-third birthday, and the special celebration of birth-days was something she had inherited from her own mother and from Queen Victoria.

Alice and the children rose to the occasion and gave her a lovely time and suitable, but very modest, presents. 'Philip is a delightful boy,' Victoria wrote back to England, '& the others are very dear girls & fuss almost too much over me and my health.'[18]

But at this time it was Alice's health that was giving more anxiety than Victoria's. The strain of those years in alternating exile and favour, of worry over Andrew, and worry over the sufferings of the Greek people in their wars and famines, was now beginning to take its toll.

Five years earlier, when Andrew had gone off to fight yet again with an ill-equipped and mainly demoralized army, and on the very day before Philip had been born, Victoria had written, 'This is the ninth year he & Alice are passing in an atmosphere of war and sore trial.'[19] Twelve years earlier still there is a hint in Victoria's letters of how tense and unpredictable her eldest daughter's life had been: 'Matters are still so uncertain,' she wrote, '& the whole situation of the King and his family so precarious in Greece.'[20]

Alice and Andrew may have given the impression to the *Calypso*'s captain that they treated exile lightly. But this most recent experience has strained Alice's nerves near to breaking point. Now, and for some twelve more years Alice spent much of her time having treatment and living in sanatoria in Germany and Switzerland.

With the temporary loss of their mother the girls were looked after by their governess and by friends and relatives, with distant control in the hands of Victoria. Philip's life for a time was under Victoria's more local and direct control, and his arrangements occupied a great deal of her time.

'Philip goes to Adsdean [Dickie's and Edwina's country home] where they can keep him till the autumn if desired,' we find her writing in June 1926, 'only for Goodwood week his room will be needed for guests, so if you [Nona] still would like & could have him . . . that would be the time for his visit to you.'[21]

Before Goodwood he went to Fishponds where Nona always loved to have Alice's last fair-haired, boisterous and totally fascinating boy. Nona's affection was warmly reciprocated. Victoria told her later that 'Philip still speaks of what he did at Fishponds with "Mrs Good" as he persists in calling you, "because she is good & that is the right name".'[22]

Then, for Philip, it was a holiday in Norfolk at a small private hotel with his sisters, where there was much sailing and playing in the sand and walks on the salt marshes.

There was also, as usual, a good deal of 'squashing' of Philip by his sisters, who disapproved of his upbringing, which they thought was too soft. They tried to redress the balance by being rather severe with him, and firmly discouraged antics like standing on his head when people came into the room. In fact he was rarely bumptious or rude as a little boy, just extremely high-spirited.

There was one memorable (and dreadful) occasion when he was especially reluctant to go to bed while staying with his Uncle Dickie at Adsdean. After a number of unsuccessful efforts his grandmother caught sight of him in his pyjamas peering down at the hall through the banisters at the top of the stairs. He answered her repeated peremptory order by putting out his tongue.

What exactly followed is lost in the darkest annals of the family. But Philip went to bed when he was told in future. A light application of discipline usually did the trick at once.

The late summer of 1926 marked a turning point in the young Greek children's upbringing. They went from Blakeney a few miles along the coast to stay with the Leicesters at Holkham. Then the girls went back to St Cloud on 10 September, under the control of aunts and uncles, and their governess, and the usual distant supervision of Victoria.

Philip stayed in England a little longer. Prince Andrew had decided to place him under the direct supervision of his mother-in-law and her two sons.

Victoria gladly took on the responsibility of mother, while Georgie Milford Haven and Dickie Mountbatten, assisted by their wives, shared the role of father.

From this summer Philip became more and more conditioned to life in England, sometimes at Kensington Palace, sometimes in the charge of his Uncle Georgie and Aunt Nada at Lynden Manor, or Uncle Dickie and Aunt Edwina at Brook House or Adsdean, or another family with whom he became very close, the Wernhers.

Harold Wernher, an astute businessman and millionaire, had married Lady Anatasia 'Zia' Michaelovna Torby, the daughter of Grand Duke Michael of Russia and the Countess de Torby. She was also the sister of Georgie's Nada.

Philip saw little of his father from this time, other father figures – Uncles Dickie and Georgie and Harold – took Andrew's place in his life.

Philip had to get used to always being on the move. He did not seem to mind. Although he saw little of his parents after the age of five, Victoria, watching over him with a practised eye, saw only a questing, energetic and waggishly humorous boy, full of promise.

Victoria loved her youngest grandson deeply and enjoyed guiding and advising him, arranging his life and observing his development. After she had accepted regretfully the boy's temporary loss of his mother, she arranged her life accordingly and dealt with the supervision of his upbringing with the same enthusiasm she had exercised on her own sons.

Philip's arrival at Kensington Palace, or Brook House, was always looked forward to happily by the servants. Life for them was never dull when he was around. Dickie's footman, Charles Smith, remembers the brightness he brought to Brook House and Adsdean.

It would sometimes be Smith's task to escort Philip to the cinema from Kensington Palace. Victoria would give him six shillings, and this included the tea and bus ride – on the top deck of course.

Once it was 'Treasure Island' at the Victoria Metropole, a cinema from which Philip succeeded in purloining a pile of 'Reserved' labels. Smith noticed nothing unusual until they were half way back to Kensington when he saw puzzled fellow travellers trying to find an unreserved seat. The next morning the same stickers were on every lavatory door throughout Kensington Palace.

When Philip began at Cheam Preparatory School in 1929 Victoria often saw him during the term, and he spent half terms with her at Kensington Palace. Later when he went to Salem in Germany and then to Gordonstoun in Scotland, she normally saw him only in the holidays when he would return to her apartments to reorganize himself before going off to stay with Uncle Georgie and Aunt Nada, or Uncle Dickie and Aunt Edwina, or to Wolfsgarten or, once or twice, to Monte Carlo where his father had gone to live after he left St Cloud.

'Kensington Palace was a sort of base where I kept things,' recalls Prince Philip today. 'I liked my grandmother very much and she was very helpful. She was very good with children. Like my own mother she took the practical approach to them. She treated them in the right way – the right combination of the rational and the emotional.'[23]

Nona Crichton, still nominally Victoria's lady-in-waiting though she no longer lived with her or saw her as often as before her marriage, acted the part of Chief of Staff to Victoria as C.-in-C. of 'arrangements'.

'Would you arrange direct with Nada about Philip's going to you. Thank you for being willing to have him for part of his holidays ...'[24] is the sort of instruction that was constantly passing from Victoria

354

to Nona during the period from 1927 until Prince Philip entered the Royal Naval College, Dartmouth, in 1938. 'I hope it won't be too much trouble having Philip for so long,' she writes a few weeks later. 'As he is one of those lucky people who can take an interest in any job & you have a talent to occupy children, I am sure he will be quite happy at Fishponds.'[25]

Visits to relations, visits to the dentist, visits to the tailors for special clothes ... 'I have to see Philip's Headmaster on the forenoon of the 8th when he comes through London ...' 'I shall be able to overhaul Philip's clothes before he goes back to Cheam ...'

No trouble was too great for her. The muscles of responsibility for others, developed in her own early childhood and exercised constantly since 1878, were as powerful as ever in the 1920s and 1930s. 'You might spend the few days after leaving Gordonstoun & starting for abroad with me at Kens. Pal.,' she writes to Philip in the summer of 1935. 'Write me a line in time to let me know when you will arrive at K.P. & when you will leave.'

Arrangements, always arrangements! 'If you cross as usual via the Hook, there is a through-going carriage all the way ...' 'I enclose three one pound notes for journey to London & etc...' 'I will find out your best route from here to Salem ...' And guidance, too, for the thirteen-year-old Prince:

KENS. PAL.
Feb. 6 1935

My dear Philip,
Dolla has sent me the photos of you, which I asked for. Send one soon to the kind man who gave you dinner in the train & the wrist watch. This is his address:

[and it follows]
I think it will be enough if you write on the back of the card:

To _____

in kind recollection
from Philip, Prince of Greece, & the date.

I think the one with your hands in your pockets is the most suitable, but that is for you to decide.
Don't forget to let Georgie know in time when your easter holidays start. You can come round here to repack. The things you left with Tiny have arrived here, she sent them off at once.

Much love from
Your devoted Grandmama

355

Sometimes arrangements in the restless round during school holidays broke down or had to be rescheduled, and this could have led to difficulties and, to a less privileged, less cherished and less self-confident boy, to a feeling of being unwanted.

'I have just heard from Dolla,' Victoria writes to him at Gordonstoun in the Spring of 1938, 'that Papa has written to her to say that as your cousin George is having guests at the Palace at Athens over Easter there is no room for you with him & as Palo's house is not ready & they are only in a flat, they can't put you up either.'[26]

New arrangements were made on this occasion, and on others, too.

Sometimes there had to be an admonitory touch, as when he left his passport behind on one of his highly involved journeys – he had two, a Greek and a Danish passport, which further complicated things – or when he failed to write important letters, though Victoria admitted to Dickie that she suffered from 'this Schreibfaulheit' too, 'a fault which I have passed on to you.' And to her grandson.

School reports are not always satisfactory, and it is Victoria's duty to draw Philip's attention to any failings. 'I enclose your school report, which you will like to read & I think you should think over what the Headmaster [Kurt Hahn] writes, for it is always useful to know what other people, if they are sensible ones, think of us.'[27] And she follows with the leading-the-horse-to-water proverb.

Once he failed to let his host know in time that he was coming to stay, and Victoria took him warmly to task: 'I think if you are old enough to travel by yourself,' she tells him, 'you should also assume the responsibility of letting people know when you propose arriving anywhere.'[28]

Cheam, Salem, Gordonstoun, and every holiday the descent on K.P., and every time the fair-haired boy with so much of her own late husband's good looks, was taller and stronger and more self-reliant, his voice deeper, a real talker, like herself. Victoria looked forward to these noisy arrivals, probably more eagerly than she was prepared to show him, or anyone else for that matter. A few days of reorganization, then the re-packing, the arrangements, and off he would go again . . .

Before he disappeared to his Uncles Georgie or Dickie, or to Germany, Greece, Switzerland, Monte Carlo or Stockholm, there might have to be visits to the dentist, or to the doctor's surgery. By chance a young student doctor working in a hospital in Golden Square in London in the Spring of 1936 recently recalled the arrival of an elderly, black-clad grandmother accompanied by 'a young good-looking teenager with strikingly blond hair' who was to be admitted for a tonsilectomy. There was, it seems, a good deal of anxious talk with the surgeon about the risks of haemophilia, with the grandmother justifying her seemingly eccentric anxiety because there had been so much of it in her family. It was Prince Philip's first operation and Victoria's fears were deep-rooted and went far back in time to that terrible day in Darmstadt when her little haemophilic brother had tumbled from the window.

This fear remained with her all her life. She did not attempt to hide it. If she was going to have a fear of something, she was not the sort of person to be ashamed of the fact. She was fearful that Louise might be a haemophilic carrier because her health in childhood was not very good. She grieved, all the same, when Louise's only child was stillborn.

In the autumn of 1935 Andrew came to stay with his mother-in-law in London for 'a sort of [Greek royal] family meeting'. The situation in Greece was boiling up yet again. Andrew's nephew, George II, had been invited back onto his throne. Andrew was to follow him to Athens 'to show himself & to be received well, to wipe out the shameful departure after the mock court-martial'.[29]

Andrew took the opportunity to discuss his son's future. He said he wanted him to go into the Royal Navy. Victoria was as delighted as her own mother had been when she heard that Prince Louis was to enter the senior British service. Nothing gave her greater pleasure than to see her family following in the footsteps of her beloved husband: first Georgie, then Dickie, Georgie's son David, already at Dartmouth, and now Philip.

But they had all been British when they had entered the service, and Victoria felt compelled to ask: 'Why not the Greek Navy? After all, he is Greek, not English. He would have to be naturalized.'

'Never the Greek Navy!' exclaimed Andrew with some vehemence. 'In the Greek Navy after a bit they would throw him out – that's what they did to me, not once, as you know, or twice, but three times!'

A few days after this Victoria wrote to Dickie out in Malta: 'Andrea has decided that Philip is to finish his schooling at Gordonstoun & hopes it can be arranged after that for him to pass the public school exam. for entrance in our navy & be allowed to serve for a few years ... It will be the best training for the boy & Philip is quite keen about it. The naval officer who is sportsmaster etc. at the school will work him up.'[30]

Philip's 'Uncle Dickie' was as pleased as Victoria had been at this turn of events – which, in fact, was not completely unexpected.

Louise was in London, too, at that time. Crown Prince Gustaf Adolf was an enthusiastic patron of the arts, like Louise's Uncle Ernie, and had come to London to help arrange the Chinese exhibition at Burlington House, and they both stayed with Victoria.

Princess Louise had led a happy and unspectacular life in Sweden since her marriage. Both she and her husband were ardent democrats and the enlightened attitude of the Swedish people towards class, the equalising of the nation's wealth and the emancipation of women, matched her personality and the opinions she had inherited from her mother.

The Swedish couple lived without grandeur, yet contrived to keep up a wide range of residences for the various seasons – Ulriksdal Palace just outside Stockholm, their spring and autumn home; a wing of the royal palace in the capital; Drottingholm, belonging to the Crown Prince's parents, for Christmas; and Sofiero in the south down by the water, where they both gardened with much enthusiasm during the late summer.

They loved skiing and skating, and were a thoroughly happy couple together who were often seen, in the best Scandinavian tradition, bicycling on the streets of Stockholm.

Louise loved her step-children, the more so when she failed to have any children of her own after the sad still-birth. The couple travelled widely, once to America and the Far East early in their marriage, and often to England and Germany to see their relatives.

Like all Battenbergs, Louise was never bored. She filled her life with interests and charitable work, and her duties (which increased heavily with the death of the Queen of Sweden in 1930) took up much of her time.

In 1934 Louise and Gustaf arrived in London for the wedding between George V's handsome youngest son, George, Duke of Kent, and that most lovely of princesses, Marina of Greece and Denmark, the youngest daughter of Andrew's brother Nicholas and the Romanoff Grand Duchess Helen Nicolaevna of Russia.

The Marina wedding, as it came to be known, was the most notable, glamorous and popular royal wedding since the war; a reminder, in days of economic depression and increasing anxiety about the future peace of Europe, of those great weddings at Potsdam and Darmstadt, Coburg and Peterhof, when Princes and Princesses went to the altar to help bind tight together Europe's royal dynasties.

For the first time for years, Victoria had all her family with her (except, alas, for Alice and Dickie), Louise and Gustaf and Andrew and the four girls and Philip all crammed into her apartments.

Georgie had decided to end his naval career two years earlier, in 1932. To retire from the Royal Navy was a hard decision for him to make. He loved the sea and service life. For some time both he and his younger brother served together in the Mediterranean. Edwina got on marvellously with Nada, and they shared Casa Medina, the big villa they had rented in Malta, while their husbands were serving in the fleet. For Victoria it was just like the old days at Malta when she and Marie Edinburgh used to play with their children when the fleet was away.

Like Louis, the Marchioness of Milford Haven had lost her fortune in Russia, and if only for the sake of his two children, Georgie knew he had to make some money himself before he grew too old. He had reached the rank of Commander and had been advanced to the Knight Grand Cross of the Royal Victorian Order. His naval career had been brilliant. He was a born leader, like his father, and possessed enormous charm. The men loved him, and unlike his father and his younger brother, who had their difficulties, he got on immediately and very well with his fellow officers and superiors.

'Georgie's brain power was astonishing,' Lord Mountbatten recalls. 'Without trying at all – and his brain was lazy as well as brilliant – he would come in first or second in his exams. If he tried at all he always came out top. I was a late developer and had to work hard to do well, entering the Royal Naval College 42 out of 84, passing out of Dartmouth 18th, and finally, on a special course at the R.N.C. Keyham, top, after very hard work.

George Milford Haven's brain was essentially a mathematical one. He read books on higher calculus casually in trains, or in the evenings with people talking all round him, as other people might read detective stories. He could work out the most complicated gunnery problems in his head, which astonished his fellow officers.

Outside mathematics and service technicalities he never went into things very deeply, and in the hurly-burly of talk and cross talk, usually in several languages, which remained a characteristic of

Hessian meals, Georgie would lag behind the conversation. His mind was on other things.

His technical and mathematical skills were recognized by the British Sperry Gyroscope Company which made him such an attractive offer that he could not afford to refuse it. He very soon became managing director and chairman, and was earning ten times as much as his naval pay.

The old Works Manager still tells the story that when he was a young workman he noticed 'the Marquess' go quickly up to the man on the best lathe and say 'You've got your setting wrong.' The man replied in a huff, 'Are you trying to tell me how to do my job?' 'The Marquess' said 'yes', took over the lathe, corrected the settings and did a perfect job.

But it is for his kindness and charm that people remember Georgie Milford Haven today. Many people who knew him in the 1930s can recall some act of special kindness which he did for them, or some proof of his charm. Among these is the present Queen who remembers him clearly when, as Princess Elizabeth and at the age of eight years, she was a bridesmaid at the Marina wedding.

'I only once talked to him for any length of time,' she recalls, 'and that was when he – poor man – found himself next to me at the wedding breakfast. But I don't think I have ever enjoyed a meal so much. He was one of the most intelligent and brilliant of people. He spoke to children just as if they were grown up.'[31]

16

ALL Princess Andrew of Greece's four daughters got married in a
nine-months-long rush between November 1930 and August 1931.

Tiny, Princess Sophie, was still only sixteen when she married
Vicky's grandson, Christopher, Prince of Hesse. Then in February
1931 the prettiest of them all, Princess Cecile, nineteen, married
Ernie's elder son, George Donatus, hereditary Grand Duke of
Hesse and the Rhine, who was her mother's first cousin. Two
month's later Princess Margarita, the eldest at twenty-five, married
her mother's second cousin, Affie's grandson Godfrey, hereditary
Prince of Hohenlöhe-Langenburg. And finally in August Dolla,
Princess Theodora, twenty-four, married Berthold, Prince and
Margrave of Baden, a more distant cousin.

For Victoria and her brother it was particularly satisfactory that
with Cecile's marriage to the hereditary Grand Duke the Greeks
had made the natural return to the very heart of Hesse.

The recurrent tragedies of the Grand Duchy seemed at last to
have ended. Every year Victoria spent some of her time with her
brother at Darmstadt or Wolfsgarten where life remained cultural
and comfortable in spite of the economic and political storms raging
outside. It was also satisfactory that the marriage of the Grand Duke
and Grand Duchess remained a blissfully happy one. Ernie and
Onor strongly sustained the Hessian tradition of supporting charitable works and the arts. The theatre and the opera flourished and
Darmstadt, now a great city, was still considered a leading European
cultural centre.

361

To many enlightened people in Germany the advent of Nazism in 1933 at first appeared to be a blessing and an augury of recovery from the aftermath of the war. With its long democratic tradition, Hesse welcomed the arrival of the deceptively named National Socialists.

'The coup d'état is very popular here,' wrote Victoria from Darmstadt in the Spring of 1933. 'There was an enormous torch-light procession last night, which passed without any disturbances & now normal life has returned, after a week's holidaying, when all the town was out on the streets. The fine dry weather & warm sun increases the holiday feeling.'[1]

It all sounds so joyous like this. How could Victoria know that in six years time this 'popular coup d'état' was to lead to another tragic split in the family – 'brother against brother, friend against friend' – and to lead Alice to regret that all her daughters had married Germans?

Six years after Ernie's elder son had married Cecile, his younger son Prince Louis of Hesse ('Lu') became engaged to the Hon. Margaret ('Peg') Geddes, the daughter of Lord and Lady Geddes. Once again a Hessian Prince was taking an English bride.

Lu worked as an honorary cultural attaché at the German Embassy in London under the Ambassador, Joachim von Ribbentrop, who was later executed in 1946 after the Nüremberg Trial. The Nazis never understood the Hessians, nor the special relationship between Hesse and the British royal family. Their puzzlement was revealed time and again, but never more absurdly than when Dickie and Edwina asked King George VI and Queen Elizabeth to a dinner party at Brook House which was intended to welcome Lu to London. Their Majesties duly came, but von Ribbentrop – presumably on orders from Berlin – at the last moment forbade Lu to attend. Who this 'slap in the face' was intended for no one will ever know.

Lu had met Peg on a skiing holiday in Bavaria. The couple planned to marry in London on 23 October 1937.

As the time approached it became increasingly doubtful whether the Grand Duke would live to see his second son married. Ernie's health had begun to fail at the beginning of the year. Victoria helped to nurse him in the summer, and other members of the family arrived to offer their sympathy and comfort.

It was, noted Victoria, the 100th anniversary of their father's birth, 'which makes me feel more venerable than ever'.

Dickie and Edwina came for a week with their elder daughter

Patricia. Prince Philip, now sixteen, stayed for three days. He was accompanied by his father 'who is getting very grey and rather deaf',[2] Victoria observed.

A month later the Grand Duke who had lost two sisters by assassination, his little daughter when she was only eight, and fifty-nine years ago his mother and another sister and had asked 'Why cannot we all die together?', himself died alone on 9 October 1937.

Ernie had asked that his son's wedding should go ahead as planned. This was not possible but it was postponed for only a month, until 20 November. The hereditary Grand Duke and his family were due to arrive in London by air four days earlier.

Just as Europe's royalty had been among the first and most enthusiastic users of the railways and the first to buy motor cars, so they took to the air as soon as regular routes opened up. Prince Philip often flew about Europe long before rigid safety regulations applied. As early as 1935, after her grandson had recently experienced an unpleasant knocking about on one journey, Victoria wrote to him: 'This time I really think you had better not fly across, as it is such a stormy time of the year.'[3]

The Hessian Grand Ducal family took off from Frankfurt aerodrome on the afternoon of 16 November. Besides the hereditary Grand Duke George Donatus and his wife, who was expecting another child, the Junkers tri-motor aircraft of Sabena Airlines had on board Ernie's widow, Onor, Don's two boys Louis and Alexander, the best man, and the boys' nursemaid. The only one left behind was the infant daughter Johanna.

It was a clear, bright day and the Junkers descended over Ostend to make its only stop before Croydon, London. A mist had come in from the sea, reducing visibility. But the pilot, a man of great experience, knew the aerodrome well, or so he believed . . .

Onor was due to stay at Kensington Palace with Victoria and the rest of the party with the Mountbattens at Brook House. Dickie had arranged for two cars to meet the 'plane at Croydon, and the betrothed pair drove there to greet the Hessian family.

At 5.30 p.m. Lu made anxious enquiries at the Sabena office and was told there was some delay. A few minutes passed. An Imperial Airways airliner took off, and Lu and Peg watched it rise into the dusk.

An official tapped Lu on the shoulder and asked him to come inside the Sabena office. There he was told what had happened.

Although visibility was down to twenty feet when the Junkers began its approach run, the pilot insisted on landing. At 150 feet, flying blind, a wing caught the top of a brick chimney. Wing and engine were severed and the rest of the 'plane crashed and burst into flames. No one survived.

The families were hastily summoned to the house of Lord Geddes, and it was at this meeting that Victoria proposed that the wedding should not only go ahead, but that it should take place the very next morning, quietly and privately, while they were all still in a state of shock.

Everyone agreed. It was obviously the wisest thing to do. Yet there was a bizarre as well as a deeply tragic element in the ceremony at St Peter's, Eaton Square, between the man who could now claim to be the new Grand Duke of Hesse and the young woman who had suddenly become a Princess and now stood at the altar in black coat and skirt and black veil, while Dickie stepped in as best man. Two hours later they left London for Ostend and the scene of the disaster, and then went on to Darmstadt with the coffins on their train. At the funeral these coffins were borne in a mournful but ceremonial procession, watched by the shocked and bereaved citizens of Darmstadt. And five more members of the Hessian royal family joined Ernie and his Elizabeth, Frittie and May and Queen Victoria's Alice in the Rosenhöhe. Ernie's wish that 'we all die together' had after all come close to fulfilment.

The epilogue to this tragic drama was completed eighteen months later when the little Princess Johanna, the only survivor of the family, died, just as if the hand of Hessian fate had signed the cancellation of her reprieve. Then the young Prince and Princess Louis failed to have children of their own – and it seemed that the timeless Hessian Darmstadt dynasty was now threatened with extinction . . .

'As you say,' Victoria wrote to Philip at Gordonstoun in reply to his letter of sympathy on her brother's death, 'it is no good dwelling on what one feels, but it is a comfort to me that you understand & join in my sense of loss.'[4]

Victoria's resilience was tested to the full when Ernie's death had been followed by the holocaust at Ostend.

The blows of fate were unremitting at that time. Alice had recovered her good health and stability at the time of Ernie's death. Victoria was able to tell Philip that 'she was quite her old self again, like before she fell ill, and it is a great joy.'[5]

But within weeks Alice was at death's door with inflammation of the lungs following 'flu. Her girls gathered about her in hospital in

Cologne. She recovered at last, but her recovery was followed by a curious and ominous accident to her brother Georgie, who fell down for no special reason and broke his leg. It refused to knit together again properly, and he was in great pain for many weeks.

'It is a mystery how a hitherto so healthy man & one in whose ancestors & relations there has been nothing of the kind,' wrote Victoria sadly, 'can have developed this.'[6]

It was cancer of the bone, and all that could be done was to relieve his sufferings as far as possible. Victoria felt every stab of pain Georgie suffered as she spent hours at his bedside all through that winter of 1937–8. 'He has been moved to a nicer nursing home,' she told Philip in February, 'where he can have treatment. Such a lot of worries all on top of each other.'[7]

On 8 April 1938 the Second Marquess of Milford Haven died in London. Victoria's anguish was perhaps more acute than she had suffered even at the death of her husband for his had been a merciful sudden death. At this time one of her grandchildren entering her room to say goodnight, saw her at her desk attempting to write letters. There were tears pouring down her lined cheeks. It was the first time this girl, or anyone else for that matter, had ever seen her cry, and it left a lasting impression on the thirteen-year-old.[8]

The brief, love-torn reign of Edward VIII was of course a national problem and a national crisis. But Victoria, with her connections with the royal family, followed the progress of events closely and felt the repercussions.

At first she knew more of what was going on than her Dickie, who was serving in the Mediterranean. At the time of the Silver Jubilee celebrations in 1935, and the Naval Review which she had attended on board the Royal Yacht, Victoria learned of the anxieties of the royal family about the affair when she went for afternoon tea with George V and Queen Mary.

Afterwards she told her son, 'The P. of W. is still, I hear, quite under the sway of his inamorata, who likes to show this publicly & keeps him hard in hand. Nobody who does not bow to this situation is acceptable – let us hope it will not last long.'

The situation for Victoria was complicated by her knowledge that Dickie was a close and lifelong friend of the Prince of Wales, and, willy-nilly, was involved in his love affair with the American divorcée

Mrs Ernest Simpson. The world was soon to learn of the tragic outcome.

Victoria viewed with her far-seeing eye the imminence of general war as soon as she understood the full meaning of Nazism, and long before most people. She feared its onset with the dread of one who has known too much of its evil, pain, destruction and unhappiness. For her, too, once again there was the renewed agony of separation from those she loved, and of her closest relatives being lined up on opposite sides. Her German grandsons-in-law were all to serve in the army or to fly with the Luftwaffe.

When war came again in 1939 and her men went away to fight, Victoria recognized the parallel between Edwina's relationship with Dickie and her own with Louis a quarter of a century earlier.

'You have so much of Papa's nature in you,' she wrote to her son on board his new destroyer H.M.S. *Kelly*, 'so much of his sensitiveness, so that I through this trait of his know how much you suffer, & perhaps it is well for you as he used to say of himself, that a certain hardness in one's wife is a help against this sensitiveness torturing one uselessly.'

'He knew I loved him,' she went on, 'as I do you my dear boy, & I understand you even if my harder nature denies the expression of sympathy that perhaps your heart craves for. He understood & trusted my love inspite of this difference in our characters, & I feel you do so too.'9

Mother and son were both fond of poetry, and when he asked for a selection of poems to take to sea and to war, she copied out some for him. She had done the same for Louis. Yet in doing this, she now felt she was not in tune with popular feeling. 'It is strange,' she wrote in the letter accompanying the poems, 'comparing this war with the last how terribly matter-of-fact this age is. Not one paper I have seen has a poem that has moved me, & they contain very few.'

She saw 1939 as a much cooler time than 1914, lacking the passions and hatreds that had destroyed her husband but had also brought fervour and sentiment into the hearts of the fighting men. '"Let us get through with this distasteful business at all costs, so that we shall not soon be disturbed again" is everyone's sentiment I think. Twenty-five years of peace have utterly shattered the dreams & hopes that inspired people in the last war.'10

The outbreak of the Second World War signalled a complete

change in Victoria's way of life. She remained as dearly loved by her family and relations as ever, but she no longer could enjoy the satisfaction of responsibility, for they had either grown up or were no longer accessible. Suddenly the need for 'arrangements' ceased, suddenly she was cut off from the children in Germany, and from her two daughters. Because she was never heard to complain, it is hard to say which she regretted more, the fact that she was now less needed or that travel had become impossible.

In 1938 Alice had gone to live in Athens. She had embraced the Greek Orthodox Church ten years earlier, and like her Aunt Ella had now given up all her life to the poor and the sick. Her husband lived quietly in Monte Carlo, and until the war visited his daughters in Germany and saw his son there from time to time.

Until the summer of 1940 it was possible to keep in touch with Louise in Sweden, and with Alice, too. And then the Germans overwhelmed Greece in 1941. Otherwise Victoria was dependent on scraps of information which she collected hungrily and passed on to other members of the family.

As in the First World War, the fact that she had close relatives on both sides only compounded the pain she suffered. For others there was comfort in success in battle for one side. For Victoria there was never any relief. Even as France fell, she heard through devious channels that Dolla's Berthold had been terribly wounded after taking a French machine-gun post and capturing twenty men on 7 June 1940.

Georgie's son David was at sea in the *Kandahar*, one of Dickie's Fifth Destroyer Flotilla. Philip was at Dartmouth shortly before the outbreak of war, just as Dickie had been at his naval college in 1914.

On the other side, Lu was in the German Army on the Polish front, and Tiny's husband was in the Luftwaffe. Later she heard that he had been killed flying in Sicily, and was told that it was believed the Nazis had put a time bomb in his aircraft as he was known to have turned against Hitler.

As for Victoria's Dickie, he was of course in the heat of action almost from the beginning. In his case she worked out in her logical mind that the fear for his life would be tolerable only if she formulated a ruthless and fatalistic policy for her own comfort. She therefore convinced herself that he could not possibly survive. Each time she saw him alive she regarded as a God-given gift for which she was profoundly grateful, yet certain in her mind that each time must be the last.

367

It would have been understandable if she had become bored and irritable, as well as frightened sometimes for her own safety during those long years of war. Her inner resources, her clarity of mind and her self-discipline, prevented this from happening. Considering the passage of time and the shattering upheavals that had occurred about her, those who were close to her before the war saw her little changed at the end of it.

When Victoria's German grandchildren were preparing to visit her in England for the first time after the end of the war, they asked their Uncle Dickie if they would see many changes in her. He answered, 'No, none whatever. She is just the same. Except that she now talks and coughs *at the same time*.'[11]

The whole family, and all her friends, regarded Victoria's two excesses, of smoking and talking, with tolerant affection. They were the first characteristics that any stranger must recognize. Talking for her was like breathing for other people. Probably her only long period of silence was those dreadful weeks after she learned of the Russian assassinations, when she had gardened with such ferocious concentration at Kent House.

Victoria's restless mind demanded constant expression when she was with other people. Few could compete with or stem the tide – and the competition was often severe. In all her life only three people could silence her. Besides Queen Victoria, her husband had been known to quell her with a sudden and shocking 'My dear child, will you kindly SHUT UP!' And Lord Mountbatten will claim today that he sometimes won by persistence.

Meals with her closest family about her were sometimes utter conversational chaos in several languages. 'Pealing arguments would be worked up,' as one participant has recounted. Victoria would concentrate on the subject and hold on tenaciously. She listened simultaneously even when in full spate herself. She paused only to cough, and for a time this gave the others an opening; but with experience, as Dickie had observed, she learned to talk through her coughing.

Always the arguments were passionate, very occasionally they were angry. Then Victoria would turn on her son and say, 'You ought to have more sense than to argue with an angry woman, Dickie.'

People who remember her at Kensington Palace in her later years, when she was also becoming a little absent-minded, describe how she might remember something she needed upstairs while she was talking, and would continue to talk unceasingly as she left the room, the sound of her voice fading with the distance. Then it would again become audible as she returned to the room.

It is true that she was never discovered talking to herself. But her audience was an incidental factor, and she could also be talking when her audience left the room to talk on the telephone and be found still talking on their return.

One of her grandchildren remembers how Victoria ignited one of those vertical boxes of matches secured into an ashtray, spilling them over the table at the same time in her excitement at her theme. Not for one second did her flow hesitate as she extinguished them – pat, pat, pat! – in turn.

She did not care for the wireless because she could not talk effectively to it, or worse still correct it. During the war when it was all fighting news she became furious at the way the announcers made what she regarded as terrible mistakes, especially in the pronunciation of Russian towns after the German invasion. She would correct the newsreader angrily and then, in exasperation, switch off the wireless. She would get on with a good talk instead, giving her own interpretation of the news, which more often than not was as good as anything the B.B.C. might contribute.

She had the same enthusiasm for answering the telephone as an ambitious businessman. Even in her late seventies, she would always run for it in terror that it might cease to ring before she got to it, depriving her of some priceless knowledge.

For some reason no one understood, the telephone was kept in an obscure corner at the end of a passage at the Palace, and this, according to her friends, was one reason why she kept so fit. But she was always brief on the telephone and never wasted words. She thought needless expenditure bad form and reprehensible in a world where there was so much poverty. She always took her children and grandchildren to the museums, their standard outing, by bus, and was very angry when later they all clubbed together and gave her a car. Quite unlike her two sons, and Louis, she regarded a car as a superfluous luxury until she was an old lady.

As for her smoking, this became an increasingly elaborate ritual in her days of widowhood. Prince Philip as a boy used to watch it being played out with fascinated attention. Among her black petticoats beneath her uniform black dress, there was one with a special pocket, a smoking pocket.

In this pocket, which took a good deal of hitching and heaving to find, there rested a silver Fabergé cigarette case with an elaborately engraved 'Victoria' in enamel on it designed by her brother, a red morocco case containing several glass tubes which her maid had stuffed with cotton wool and a box of matches. Without pausing in her talk – almost as a reflex action – these were drawn out one by one. Amidst a good deal of coughing, but still talking, Victoria succeeded in lighting the cigarette and then returning all the equipment to its home.

After a certain number of cigarettes had been smoked the nicotine-soaked cotton wool was extracted and tossed, hissing, into the fire.

When her doctor ordered her to cut her smoking during the war to ease her cough, she took him at his word and cut her cigarettes in half, with no evident reduction in the total number she smoked.

Her hairstyle could be described as conservative and unenter-prising. It was pulled back into a bun with a little curly fringe at the front, and had been since time immemorial. When her hair began to recede she bought a wig, which she called her 'transformation', in a replica of her fringe. She used to push her pencil through it when doing crossword puzzles, or when especially animated, so that it was often askew.

Clothes had bored her as a young married woman. They bored her all the more in old age. Like the famous Model T Ford motor car, she was *always* black. Grey depressed her, and so her hats were black too. The only colour might be in a priceless necklace which she would wear as carelessly as if it were junk jewellery. There was an especially lovely one remembered by a grandchild, a long gold chain with coloured enamel flowers at intervals, also no doubt designed by her brother Ernie.

Victoria never wore make-up. Once one of her granddaughters found, to her surprise, a bottle of Elizabeth Arden skin lotion on her dressing table. 'My skin is a disgrace to the family,' she explained crossly. 'I am doing something about it.'[12]

Although she was fascinated by all medical talk her own health bored her. She kept fit by instinct. Not only did she run to answer the telephone, she also walked for up to four hours a day, when circumstances allowed and while she was able to. She always walked in flat-heeled shoes with thin leather soles so that at the end of her life she still had perfect feet.

During the worst of the flying bomb period in 1944, she was persuaded by George VI and Queen Elizabeth to leave Kensington Palace and stay at Windsor Castle. She arrived looking grey and tired from lack of sleep, but at once insisted on her daily constitutional.

Princess Elizabeth and Princess Margaret were asked by the Queen to accompany her because she was afraid that she might overtire herself and need assistance. 'Walking from Windsor is all very well, you go off downhill and it is very nice. But it is more difficult to get back again when you are rather old. And at this time, in 1944, she was beginning to get arthritic,' Queen Elizabeth II recalls today. But her stride, these sisters noted, was firm and masculine (as it had been all her life), and they never had any difficulty with her returning uphill to the castle. And the two young people learned a great deal from her ceaseless torrent of words during these swift expeditions.

On the rare occasions when she was ill Victoria did not care for anyone to notice. Nor did she want anyone to call the doctor, who would be busy with more serious cases. If pressed she might reluctantly say as the illness ran its course, 'I am well enough to see the doctor now if you really wish to send for him.'

She possessed what is sometimes called 'an iron constitution', and was proud of it. Until the arthritis of old age, her only weakness remained circulatory. She suffered greatly but uncomplainingly from chilblains on her fingers and toes, and this made her cross because it restricted her gardening.

To children Victoria might at first appear formidable. But not for long. And most young people accepted her style of relationship. This was considerate and affectionate towards them and, as one of her grandchildren recalls, 'She had a knack of making people feel special. She was a very calm and soothing person to be with as a child. There was never any question as far as I was concerned of not doing as she wanted. She was not that sort of person. She never gave commands because somehow, without saying anything, she made it known to you what was the right thing to do.'[13]

Just as Louis had had a calming influence on any contentious situation, so Victoria – in contrast with her abrasive, argumentative style with grown-ups – soothed away childhood cares in a most restful manner. When she played with children she became utterly absorbed in whatever activity they took up together, whether it was doing a jigsaw puzzle, going round a museum, drawing, or discussing some personal problem.

'When I was a child, she would do marvellous things with her hands,' recalls Lord Mountbatten's elder daughter, Lady Brabourne.

'She would make a complete tea service out of acorn cups with a penknife. First we would collect the acorns together, and then she would work away with her penknife, talking all the time. She would carve out not only the cups but the teapot and everything else. She would throw herself completely into everything we did together as if it was the most important thing in the world.'[14]

For all her excessive smoking and excessive talking, she maintained a serene dignity through old age. She was often lonely and could have been forgiven for resenting that people did not come to see her as often as she would have liked. But, no doubt remembering her own full life when she had been younger, she would patiently await a visit.

'When you went to see her as an old lady at K.P. she would be sitting in front of the fire doing a crossword or jigsaw puzzle, or more likely reading. If she was reading she would mark the place in her book carefully when you came in before getting up to greet you. Once it was Agatha Christie's *Death in the Clouds*, another time I can remember it was a thick book on German philosophy.

'"How lovely to see you!" she would say, always as if you had given her a treat.'

Victoria's family have often speculated on the likely outcome if she, rather than her youngest sister, had married Tsar Nicholas II. 'She would have made the right wife for a great King,' Princess Margaret of Hesse claims. 'She had a remarkable brain. She never forgot anything, and after the terrible air crash she looked after us entirely. Although she had a warm heart she did not like to show it, and she did give offence sometimes with her abrupt manner.'

For many years at Kensington Palace Victoria's neighbours were her aunt and sister-in-law, Beatrice, who lived until 1944 and worked almost to the end on censoring her mother's journal, and her cousin Princess Alice Countess of Athlone. Princess Alice found her lacking in charm but full of fascination all the same, and possessing what she calls 'a master mind'.

'She was remarkably well informed, and a genius. She had a natural talent for passing on knowledge and for drawing people out in conversation.' Of her appearance she says, 'She looked like a rag-bag, just scraping her hair back anyhow. But she was handsome all the same with very bright clever eyes, and she always held herself well. Her heavy smoking gave her a very hoarse rough voice.'

Another of Victoria's grandchildren, Lady Pamela Hicks, remembers how upset she felt if for any reason she thought that she had displeased her grandmother. 'This stemmed from the immense respect I felt for her. I always found her formidable, but never intimidating. In a way she had an agelessness about her which I found a comfort. Her mind was almost entirely masculine. She was also a supremely honest woman, full of commonsense and modesty. At the age of seventy-eight she once leapt from a dog cart she was driving when the pony began to rear and plunge and ran to the pony's head and held it and calmed the animal. She made no fuss at all about it.

'Like her grandmother, love affairs bored her. She never gossiped and she never discussed love affairs. Either you were married, or not married, and anything in between was a bore.'[15]

Victoria's direct control over her grandson Philip's affairs more or less ceased when he left Gordonstoun and went to Dartmouth. But before he left boarding school Prince Philip was able to pass on some news to her which she found pleasing because any acknowledgement of her husband's achievements was gratifying.

She replied to his letter: 'I am very pleased that the School Ship, which you have given me so clear a description of & found so seaworthy, is now to be rechristened the "Prince Louis" after Grandpapa.'

Kensington Palace remained Prince Philip's firm base in London, the one place where he could leave and collect his gear and be sure of a welcome. At the beginning of September 1939, when war broke out, Philip, still a Greek national, was in Greece with his father who was visiting his mother. It was the last time the three were together, the last time he was ever to see his father.

Greece was for the present neutral and Prince Philip presumed that he would remain in his own country as he would be nothing but an embarrassment in England. King George of Greece thought otherwise and decided that he should complete his naval training at Dartmouth where he had been doing well – he had been awarded the Eardley-Howard-Crochett prize as best cadet of the year.

Three weeks after war was declared Victoria who was staying with Nada in the country was surprised to hear that her grandson had turned up at Kensington Palace, and that he was going to remain in England in spite of his neutral status.

'I still think it would have been better if he had stayed in Greece where he belongs,' she wrote to Dickie. One son and a grandson in danger at sea was a sufficient contribution for the present and from one family, she considered.

Later, she heard from George VI that Philip 'is to be appointed to the [battleship] *Ramillies* – when? he did not say – she I gather will be doing escort work in the Mediterranean & eastward. Later on he may be appointed to a ship of the Mediterranean Fleet. I think,' Victoria continued to Dickie, 'this is a satisfactory arrangement on the whole & trust no pocket-battleship may cross her path.'[16]

Over the following months Victoria heard from Philip in Australia and East Africa, and then, to her surprise, from Athens. He had gone on leave to see his mother from his ship refitting in Alexandria.

Greece had been invaded in October 1940. Her grandson was no longer a neutral. He was now a belligerent serving in the hottest of all war zones, along with his uncle Dickie in the *Kelly*, and his cousin David Milford Haven in the *Kandahar*. The *Kelly* sank with heavy loss of life on 23 May 1941, the *Kandahar* on 19 December. In the great night action off Matapan, Philip was in the battleship *Valiant*. The lieutenant in charge of searchlight control was on the sick list. Philip, still only a midshipman, controlled the searchlights so well that he was mentioned in despatches by Admiral Cunningham.

From then until the summer of 1945 the war was a time of unremitting worry for 'my men', broken by sudden and usually unexpected descents by one or the other of them.

With Philip, as in the old days, there might be an indirect warning of arrival. 'Some great heavy cases have been sent round here,' she writes in November 1943, 'so I suppose he will be coming to London on longer leave or changing ship . . .'

Then the uniformed figure would appear at Kensington Palace, at any hour of the day or night, full of concern for her welfare, full of laconic tales of war and perhaps some inside story of new plans or new successes at sea.

In the early days of war, Victoria was persuaded to leave London, which everyone expected to be the first target of the Luftwaffe. She then returned to K.P. and for some time lived either there or at Broadlands, the beautiful Hampshire family home Edwina had inherited on the death of her father in 1939. Here Victoria kept her granddaughters, Patricia and Pamela, company during the school holidays.

With the fall of France in the summer of 1940 these girls were packed off in one of the government-sponsored children's trips to stay with friends in America. It was essential that they should leave. Dickie knew that, with a Jewish great-grandfather (Sir Ernest Cassel) his daughters would have been amongst the first to go to the gas oven if the Germans landed. Now Victoria was more alone than ever. Her dear friend and another neighbour at the Palace, Louise, Duchess of Argyll, had died in December 1939. 'When I pass Aunt Louise's door without going in,' she wrote, 'I feel I miss her affectionate pleasure at seeing me very much.'[17]

Broadlands was half military encampment, half hospital. Kensington Palace was packed round with sandbags, the skylights painted black. Outside in Kensington Gardens and Hyde Park the grass was criss-crossed with slit trenches and there were air raid shelters and emplacements for the anti-aircraft guns that thundered at night, and searchlight and balloon barrage stations. It was total, inescapable war, and in winter the nights seemed endless and the days grey and brief.

When the very bad bombing started Victoria returned to Broadlands with 'the Pye-crust', the indefatigable and devoted maid Miss Pye who had been with her since time immemorial, and was the only person Victoria could bear to do her hair.

Victoria's spirits remained remarkably buoyant during these lonely years and she always wrote cheerfully to her son and grandsons.

'You know how quietly & out of the world my life here is spent,' she wrote to Dickie from Broadlands in May 1941 six days before his *Kelly* was sunk, '& that I have little of interest therefore to tell you. I love being here & am in very good health. I read much for pleasure . . .'[18] (In that month thirteen books including *History of Socialism* by Thomas Kirkup, *London Fabric* by James Pope-Hennessy, *European Spring* by Clare Boothe, three detective novels and *The Spanish Pioneers and the California Missions* by C. F. Summis.)

Later, in answer to the pleas of Dickie and Edwina to look after herself, she told her son not to worry. 'I am determined not to cause you any. My days of actual usefulness are over & the only duty I feel incumbent on me is the passive one of not being a burden to those I love, though I can't be so passive as not to use my own judgement in this matter.'[19]

It was not true that her usefulness was exhausted. She had much to offer in advice and wisdom to her children and the rest of her family, and she was able to carry out some limited duties during the war. In December 1942 the Admiralty invited her to come to Glasgow to launch a new aircraft carrier, the *Indefatigable*.

It was quite a family affair, with Edwina and Patricia as well as

Dickie, and Victoria thoroughly enjoyed herself sending the great ship down its slip and making a little speech. The shipbuilders gave her a casket, and there was a formal luncheon, and for one day in this dark war it was quite like old times.

Her eightieth birthday six months later was another golden day for her. Afterwards she wrote to 'My dear faithful Nona' about it, telling her how in the midst of total war many of her family had contrived to gather together to wish her many happy returns. 'Dickie and Edwina have given me a silver shallow bowl, about the size of a porridge dish.'[20] It had facsimile signatures of all her family engraved on it.

When the flying bombs started to come over London after D-Day in 1944, Victoria felt like a veteran and decided she preferred 'these new-fangled machines' to piloted bombers, although at times the noise of guns and exploding bombs was cacophonous, and glass smashed and K.P. shook as if in an earthquake.

She did her best to calm the nerves of Miss Pye and her cook, convincing herself that she was past worry on her own account. But the sleepless nights and noisy days were taking their toll on her nerves. This was unnoticed by herself but observed by the King and Queen when they visited her towards the end of June 1944. It was at this time that they persuaded her to move down to Windsor, where they too spent the weekends.

Although she felt rather ashamed of being 'a refugee', she enjoyed herself with them and found it a moving experience which brought back so many memories of her childhood and of long visits to Windsor to stay with Queen Victoria.

She wrote to Nona Crichton:

'I am living in rooms next to the "Tapestry Room" overlooking the Long Walk [where she had been born]. So much reminds one of old days here. We take our meals together otherwise I am free to do what I like. Princess Elizabeth does host at meals when her parents are away. These young girls [Princesses Elizabeth and Margaret] are charmingly brought up, not shy and quite natural. The younger does not come to dinner yet. They make a pair much like Patricia and Pamela . . .'[21]

Besides those walks from the Castle with Victoria, today the Queen remembers the luncheons, over which she presided except at weekends, and the rather curiously mixed household that was living at Windsor at that time – Sir Gerald Kelly, the resident painter, an officer from the Privy Purse office, the censor from the Lord Chamberlain's office, and one or two others besides her sister and Victoria.

The most lasting impression that Victoria made on both Princess Elizabeth and her mother Queen Elizabeth was the sudden acceleration in pace and increase in volume of the conversation. 'It used to rattle along when she was at the table.'[22]

Victoria got on splendidly with George VI whom she had seen only occasionally since Louis had died, and they had a fine time talking geneaology and family history, the Navy and about the old days with Louis.

The King and Queen were working especially hard just then, immediately after D-Day, and it was early bed for everyone. It was all very quiet and domestic compared with the last time Victoria had stayed at Windsor for more than a night or two, back in 1894. Then there had been Nicky and his suite, and dear Alicky so excited about her engagement, and the present King's elder brother David had been born and Nicky had stood as godfather ... What a long time ago it seemed, and how times had changed!

Through all those war years it was her beloved Dickie who was Victoria's first concern. Once she had rationalized her gnawing anxiety for his safety, she followed his comet-like career with fascinated interest and pride.

She had long since recognized in her younger son the abiding ambition to emulate his father and to right the wrong which had destroyed him at the summit of his career.

From his earliest days in the Navy she had seen him suffer the same difficulties and obstructions which had beset Louis's own naval career. He did not need to tell her of them, she knew them too well. She understood about the suspicion and latent hostility that met him in the wardroom when he joined a new ship, how patiently he had to break down this attitude, what a long time it could take, and then, at the next new appointment, how he would have to start all over again. She knew it all.

Victoria had seen her son through the difficult years between the wars when he and Edwina had been regarded by many only as the golden leaders of the 'bright young things', hobnobbing with royalty, society and the stars of stage and screen. At that time the more serious and professional side of her Dickie's life had been obscured beneath the glitter of the playboy image.

Victoria had also recognized the sharp edge of the sword, the

377

cutting edge of his will to succeed. It touched and amused her to see, especially when she was staying with him in Malta while he was serving in the Mediterranean Fleet, the same qualities producing the same successes as her Louis had achieved some forty years earlier.

First there was the outstanding efficiency he produced in the wireless communications between ships for which he was responsible. Then came his first commands, the destroyers *Daring* and *Wishart*, which achieved the same outstanding smartness, efficiency and happiness which Louis had produced in his first commands, the *Scout* and the *Cambrian*. They won the largest number of trophies for gunnery, regattas and sports.

Dickie even thought up inventions, of which the most important, 'The Mountbatten Station Keeping Equipment' paralleled his father's 'Battenberg Course Indicator'. There were also the 'Sub-Focal Signalling Shutter', and a little semaphore machine that worked on a typewriter board and was capable of an unprecedented 45 words per minute.

Dickie possessed that same special knack of getting on with the lower deck, and, sometimes, getting on with them more successfully than with his fellow officers. Just as his father had his 'bolshie' worshippers, so did Dickie – in one special case, a real Bolshevik.

One of the ringleaders of the notorious Invergordon Mutiny in 1931, who later emigrated to Russia and became a naturalized Soviet citizen, stated that the mutiny would never have taken place if Lord Louis Mountbatten had been in command of events at the time. Victoria derived greater satisfaction from this human quality in her son, which was so reminiscent of Louis, than from his more public and spectacular later achievements.

In spite of the contrast in their personalities, the similarity between father and son was sometimes uncanny. Victoria observed how they both reacted to tiredness in the same way – by turning to other voluntary tasks and working as hard as ever, and thus sometimes achieving a remarkable daily output of work. It was an ability that was to stand him in good stead in the future.

For example, when things in India were at their worst and the pressure on him was most severe, Victoria learned that he had (for relaxation, he said) worked on an immensely complicated genealogical volume which she had helped him to start and which he later printed for private circulation under the title *Relationship Tables*.

In 1939 with her son as a captain of under forty years and com-

manding a flotilla of eight new destroyers, Victoria never had a
glimmer of doubt about his success. She was gratified by his award
of the D.S.O. for bringing the savagely damaged *Kelly* back safely
to port in the face of four days of air attack.

But, ever the realist, ever on the alert, she recognized the dangers
for him of what might be a suspect award for bravery in the eyes of
those who were jealous. 'On the whole,' she wrote at the time, 'it is a
good thing he did not get it till after everybody had heard or read the
details . . . Now no one can in fairness say that he has not fully
earned it.'[23]

Victoria was immensely relieved when Dickie returned safely
from the holocaust of the eastern Mediterranean in May 1941,
leaving behind the shattered remains of the *Kelly* at the bottom of
the sea. But it was a short period of relief for her. His new appointment was a fighting one again, and command of the aircraft carrier
Illustrious was likely to be at least as dangerous as that of the destroyer
Kelly.

Then Churchill suddenly took him away and put him in charge of
'Combined Operations', and Victoria's relief was as great as
Dickie's fury. She knew he would certainly be in dangerous situations until the war was over and that the huge responsibilities he
now bore as a member of the Chiefs of Staff Committee would be
very wearing. But at least the immediate day to day risk element
was greatly reduced, and she shared with Edwina a profound thankfulness for that.

Victoria's concern now was first for the success with which Dickie
handled these new chief of staff responsibilities, and second for his
avoidance of what she regarded as the disreputable snares of politics.
But this time Lord Beaverbrook and the *Daily Express* had in her
eyes become for her son what Horatio Bottomley and *John Bull*
had been to Louis in the First World War, sniffing and sniping at
the patriotic leader serving his country.

When the *Daily Express* attacked her son's replacement of seventy-
year-old Roger Keyes, the previous chief of Combined Operations,
Victoria wrote to him to offer reassurance, as she always did when
he was under attack. 'Luckily the general public is not much per-
turbed by the Daily Express's outcries & scandal-sniffing,'[24] she
told him.

Victoria may have considered that her own war aim was to make
herself as little of a nuisance as possible, but for once she was wrong.
The wise counsel and the love that were always there for her son

through these tumultuous years never failed to renew his strength and resolve, and never failed to touch his heart.

'Are we not as our motto says "in honour bound"?' she once asked him, '& so I will not grudge the sacrifices of personal affection our separation will entail upon us, but gratefully remember how you have come safely through the perils of your sea-going experiences & the joy of seeing you often during your period at home.'[25]

By the middle of 1943 Victoria knew that Dickie was pining for action again. He had done all he could (and a great deal more than has so far been acknowledged) to prepare and plan for the successful invasion of Europe the following year, and now – like his father before him – he longed for the sharp tang of sea air.

Dickie's wish was fulfilled, but only briefly and not in the manner he had hoped for. On 4 August 1943, Lord Louis Mountbatten, now an Acting Vice-Admiral, sailed down the Clyde in the *Queen Mary*, bound for Canada and the Quebec conference.

On board the liner with him were all the men who provided the fighting heart of beleaguered Britain at war: Winston Churchill and the other three Chiefs of Staff, Alan Brooke, Peter Portal and Dudley Pound, as well as younger men who had already fought the good fight, or were soon to do so – Orde Wingate and Guy Gibson VC, DSO and bar, DFC and bar.

Dickie spent part of the voyage cultivating the First Sea Lord, Pound, whenever he visited the bridge, emphasising that he had completed the job of preparing for the invasion of Europe, and wasn't it time he went back to sea? 'I would very much like to go back to the *Illustrious*, sir.'

The First Sea Lord was very evasive. A few days after they arrived at Quebec, Dickie discovered why. When he later returned to England he recounted this curious and historic conversation to Victoria at Broadlands.

Churchill and he were walking up and down the battlements overlooking the Heights of Abraham in Quebec:

w.s.c.: How is your health?

l.l.: Pretty good now, sir. (He had been working 16 hours a day for so long he had recently, and almost literally, killed himself with overwork.)

w.s.c.: Do you feel up to anything?

l.l.: Yes, anything.

w.s.c.: What do you think of the situation in South East Asia?

L.L.: It's a pretty good mess, isn't it.

W.S.C.: Yes, I think it is. Do you think you could put it right?

L.L.: (Thinking he meant to do a paper assessment for the Chiefs of Staff.) Well, I don't know, sir, isn't that a thing for Pug Ismay to do?

W.S.C.: Pug Ismay? You don't understand what I am offering you. I am offering you to go out there and do the job!

L.L.: On a trip out there?

W.S.C.: A trip! I'm offering you the job of Supreme Allied Commander of South East Asia. (Pause.) What do you think of that?

L.L.: May I have 24 hours to think it over?

W.S.C.: Why? Are you afraid you can't do the job?

L.L.: Not at all. I have a congenital weakness for feeling certain I can do anything, but I do want to ask the British and U.S. Chiefs of Staff to satisfy myself that they agree with your choice wholeheartedly and will back me to the full.

It was almost twenty-nine years since Churchill had accepted Prince Louis's resignation as professional head of the Royal Navy. Now this same war leader was asking his son to take on a responsibility quite as great as his father had had to surrender. Now in Dickie's eyes at last justice had been appropriately upheld and a great wrong to the family righted in the name of the first Mountbatten.

Churchill agreed to Dickie's condition, and Prince Louis's son was gratified and astonished at the complete backing all these six men in charge of the military side of the war gave him. And so he accepted.

Dickie sent a preliminary account of the affairs in Quebec, including the news of his appointment, to Victoria. 'I am so thrilled by & proud of you and your news,' she replied. 'Undoubtedly it is a good thing that it should be a naval man who should hold the new command & I think you are a good choice for it. But it is a colossal job.

'It is perhaps motherly pride that makes me think you are the right man for it, with the gifts of energy needed to make a success of it. May you be granted the health & luck to carry out the great task laid upon you. You are always in my thoughts & no matter what the result may be I shall not alter my opinion about your fitness nor your whole-hearted devotion to the work. From the fulness of my heart I can & do pray God bless you my own dear boy & strengthen & help your spirit to do what is right according to your lights without worry or fear of consequences.'[26]

Add to this Edwina's unstinting spiritual and practical support through the difficult and dangerous months that lay ahead, and it can truly be said that no commander has gone into battle with more deeply felt support from the women who loved him than did Lord Louis Mountbatten in 1943.

The year 1944 was a full one for Victoria. This was the year when, worn out by flying bombs, she had been taken to Windsor Castle and when she had re-established contact with Alice in Athens after the German withdrawal.

Only brief and sometimes harrowing messages had filtered out from Athens during the German occupation. But the see-saw of war then allowed Alice to re-establish contact with her daughters in Germany. They managed to despatch some food parcels to their mother when people were dying of starvation in hundreds in Athens. Alice gave them at once to her patients and to those she regarded as the really needy.

On 30 October 1944, two weeks after the German withdrawal, Alice managed to get a brief note to her mother by air. She was thankful to be in touch with England again but, conversely, 'worried to be quite cut off from her girls now',[27] and sad that her son Philip was serving so far from her in the Far East under his Uncle Dickie.

Another matter of greater importance bearing on Prince Philip's future was being clarified during 1944. Although she had no evidence, nor of course did she seek any nor discuss the matter, Victoria had become increasingly aware that there was growing affection between the young cousin who had presided at table at Windsor in the summer, and whom she liked so much, and her grandson Philip, now a bearded, war-experienced naval lieutenant.

No mention was made of the matter, nor anything decided for some time to come, but a marriage that had been an unspoken consideration in the minds of Prince Philip's relations for several years was believed by Victoria to be closer.

As future plans for her family gently matured in 1944, so connections with the distant past were severed. Princess Beatrice, who used to join in those rumbustious games at Windsor and Buckingham Palace so long ago in the 1870s and had lived in adjoining apartments to Victoria's at Kensington Palace between the wars, died at last after a long and painful illness.

Victoria wrote of her death to her granddaughter Pamela in reply to the girl's letter of commiseration:

'She was only 6 years older than I & we had many recollections of our youth in common. Though she became my sister-in-law, as she married a younger brother of your grandfather's & later than we married, I always thought of her as my Aunt.'[28]

A tightly-knit, loyal and loving family life was the cornerstone of Victoria's philosophy. Once again, as in 1919, the moment the war was over and communications allowed, she invited to Kensington Palace her children and grandchildren from Germany, Greece and Sweden, or went to stay with them.

The tottering remains of the royal dynastic structure of Europe had suffered more crippling blows during the past six years. King George of Greece had been prevented from returning to Athens, ex-King Carol of Rumania had no intention of returning to Bucharest where his son had been King since 1940 but was forced to abdicate by the communist government in 1947. The monarchy had been abolished in Italy and there was no sign of its return to Spain, France or Germany.

Darmstadt, which had seen so many royal births, weddings and funerals, which had for so many centuries been the fountainhead of that enriching Hessian blood, had been torn apart by bombs. Prince Louis of Hesse never attempted to take his father's title of Grand Duke, but it had been a difficult time for him, and for Princess Margaret, during the war and immediately after Germany's capitulation.

By remarkable good fortune there had been no casualities amongst the closest members of Victoria's family, except Prince Christopher and her son-in-law Andrew. Prince Andrew had lived in Monte Carlo without interference from either side until he had died of a heart attack there in 1944 at the age of sixty-two.

But all Victoria's children and grand-children had survived the last two years of war. Louise had suffered little in Sweden except from anxiety about her less fortunate relations. Philip was safe, and so were his three surviving sisters in Germany. Alice had once again showed her remarkable powers of surviving war, pestilence and famine, and emerged emaciated from starvation but cheerfully enough in Athens.

Victoria reserved her deepest-felt thanks for the safe return of her Dickie. He had faced the greatest dangers and had risen to the loftiest heights of command. With the explosion over Hiroshima in September 1945 Victoria could at last dispense with that much-dented protective shield of fatalism. Dickie had come through it all uninjured and was now hailed as once of the great architects of victory.

In the closing years of Victoria's life Dickie and his family – Edwina, Patricia and Pamela – gave her special pride, satisfaction and pleasure. On Dickie's and Edwina's Silver Wedding anniversary celebrated in India she opened her heart to them.

'In these 25 years,' she wrote, 'I have not only never lost the love of my son, but have freely been given the love of a daughter, very dear to me, too. I thank you from my heart for the many proofs you have given me of this. Your dear girls have been the truest link between you & you can be proud of them who are so devoted to you & whose love I hope & feel will never fail you. I can say from experience "blessed are they who have good children", they are the reward for all one has done for their sakes.'[29]

She was thankful that never for one moment during those 25 years had Edwina done anything to disturb the special love Victoria felt for her son. Victoria quoted to Dickie the old mother's saying, 'My son is my son till he gets me a wife, my daughter's a daughter all her life', and then joyfully added, 'I can never be grateful enough that in your case, dear boy, it has not proved true, for you have always remained the same to me.'[30]

Victoria changed no more in those last years after the war than she had during it. The pain she suffered from her chilblains and arthritis sometimes made her shorter tempered than she used to be, and she found herself rather more frequently having to write letters of apology after a sudden outburst. The only person who worried about them was herself. Her greatest outburst was in December 1946 when Dickie visited her at Kensington Palace with some extremely unwelcome news.

With the surrender of Japan his war duties as 'Supremo' in South-East Asia had come to an end. But he could not yet return home. From Supreme Allied Commander of a great armed force, he became the unwilling Military Governor over 128 million people, many of them diseased, starving and homeless. Above all they were engaged in a struggle against their colonial masters, British, French or Dutch, almost as threatening to the future of South-East Asia as the Japanese armies had been so recently.

Lord Louis had remained at his post until June 1946. When he returned to England it was for only a short time. His eagerness to return to sea was as keen as his father's had been after long and gruelling administrative work ashore. In emulation of his father when he had asked for a post-war appointment in 1915 after his resignation, Dickie wanted command of a sea-going squadron, and hoped it would be a squadron in the Mediterranean.

But not yet. There was another job of work to be done before he would be allowed to take up a seagoing command again.

Against his strongest wishes, and only on condition that he was granted unprecedented powers, he was persuaded to accept the appointment of Viceroy of India in order to organize the handing over of responsibility to the Indians themselves.

As soon as he knew that he was going, Dickie steeled himself to tell his mother. He knew that she would not be pleased. But even he was amazed at the violence of the outburst of anguish and fury that exploded over him when she heard the news.

Since that time more than thirty years ago, when she had seen Louis's career destroyed by slow degrees, her suspicion of politicians had become deeply embedded in her soul.

In the government's invitation to her son to organize the handing over of power in the great subcontinent Victoria saw him being used as a scapegoat for its own timorousness. It would, she believed, be the end of Dickie's career, just as 1914 had marked the end of her husband's. It was more than she could bear to see it all happen again!

And now here he was, or so she believed, laying himself open to the duplicity and manoeuvrings of wily and dishonourable politicians! For once she did not know what to say or do and for the first time in her life she began to swear. It was her only answer to unaccustomed incoherence. 'Damn! Damn! Damn! Damn! Damn! . . .' five times.

Then Victoria ordered up her arguments in proper formation and went into battle.

The results, she said, would be fatal to his career. He would be double-crossed by the politicians – 'Politicians are incorrigible!' as her Louis had told him more than thirty years earlier. He was

playing with something he did not understand and it was dangerously arrogant of him to think that he did. He was playing with
fire! 'Damn! Damn!'

Dickie counter-attacked and attempted to soothe her passions at
the same time.

'Well, Mama, at least I think I shan't be away for more than a
year.'

'What on earth do you mean?' Victoria demanded.

Dickie repeated, 'I have explained, I don't think . . .'

He was not allowed to finish. Again, and more vehemently than
ever, she returned to the attack.

Dickie was at last reduced to saying, 'Look, Mama, I am sorry . . .'
And made hurriedly for the door.

He did not get far. She called him back. 'Dickie, come here. If
my own son has to *apologize* to me . . .' And now she was really
furious, not just frightened for him. For the first time the heat and
worry had brought the row into a new dimension.[31]

When at last he left her he had done his best to put things right.
But she was still upset, frightened and angry all at once. And he was
sad for her, disappointed that he had failed to placate or to convince
her that he could not refuse and was still utterly confident that he
could see through to the end this most difficult and delicate of duties.

It is not this biographer's task to make any judgement on Lord
Mountbatten's work in India in 1947 and 1948, nor even to re-
capitulate it and the events that followed. The full story, drawn
from the last Viceroy's own record, has been told in *The Great
Divide*. What is relevant to this story is the fact that, once having
made her protest, Victoria stood loyally by her son, commiserating
with his difficulties, sharing his distress, proud of his triumphs,
hostile to his enemies.

With his two tasks completed, those of last Viceroy and then, at
the Indians' own request, as constitutional first Governor-General,
Lord Mountbatten returned to England in June 1948.

By this time he had been granted an Earldom and created a
Knight of the Garter, had been made a member of the Privy Council
like his father, and, on his last day of service, of the Order of Merit.
He had four Grand Crosses of the Bath, Star of India, Order of the
Indian Empire and Royal Victorian Order.

None of this much impressed Victoria, referring to what she
called 'the ups & downs in titles etc. which our Battenberg family

has been subject to'. 'What will live in history,' she told her son, 'is the good work done by the individual & that has nothing to do with rank or title.'[32]

But she was pleased at 'the good work done' all the same by her now world famous son. 'Well,' she once pronounced crisply to him, 'I'm very glad you're doing so well. I never thought I would be known only as your mother. You're so well known now and no one knows about me, and I don't want them to.'

Victoria was never to see her Dickie fill the office of First Sea Lord which her Louis had vacated forty-one years earlier, nor to see him rise higher still to become head of all the services as Chief of Defence Staff and carry through inter-service reforms far more radical and dramatic than those engineered by Louis and the other great reformers in the Navy before the First World War.

But before she died Victoria knew that the momentum which she had first seen in the Midshipman of 1916 was by no means spent in 1950. He, above all the dutiful Battenbergs she had known, was least likely to leave responsibilities uncompleted. The correction of past wrongs was in the best of hands.

The greatest joy of Victoria's last years was the marriage of Princess Elizabeth and Prince Philip.

She had seen her grandson return from the war with all the characteristics she had earlier recognized now fully matured. As for the bride, 'I have a great liking for her,' she told her son later, '& admire her unselfish character & sense of duty.'[33]

Victoria had long believed that this would be an ideal match. It was historically tidy and firmly in the traditions of her family. Like her own mother, she strongly encouraged the strengthening of ties between the two families. For Victoria, what could be a more satisfactory fulfilment to a long, dutiful and arduous life than this marriage of her grandson to her young cousin and Heir Presumptive to the British throne?

For the last time in her life she witnessed the gathering of the survivors of Europe's royalty in London in November 1947.

For the arrival of her two daughters, Louise from Sweden and Alice from Athens, 'I have had my rooms painted,' she noted with satisfaction. Dickie and Edwina returned briefly from the worries of India. It was the first full-scale royal wedding in London since the

Marina wedding of 1934, and the capital had seen nothing like it since the coronation in 1937.

In spite of the strain it imposed on her at the age of eighty-four Victoria loved every moment of the occasion. It brought together so many of her friends and relations. And in spite of her socialist theories and her doubts about the future of monarchy in the modern world, she had always loved the colour, the pageantry, the elaborate ceremonial and the happiness of a wedding. And, contrary to some people's judgements, she believed that with the right sovereign, constitutional monarchy still had a great deal to offer.

There was no one else alive in 1947 who had seen as many royal weddings as she had – in Moscow, St Petersburg, Berlin, Coburg, Whippingham, London and Darmstadt – and now this union of two great families in Westminster Abbey.

Victoria's last years were full of arthritic pain and she would tell her friends without a note of complaint in her voice that her brain was outliving her useless old body. Her mind remained as nimble and shrewd as it had always been, and for her friends and relations it was never a chore to visit her because there was never a dull moment in her company.

Except on foggy dark days she read as rapidly and with as much enjoyment as when she was a girl – the new Nigel Balchin one day, and on another (as Prince Philip recalls) she was re-reading Gustav le Bon's *Psychologie des Foules*.

Victoria had the satisfaction of seeing a boy born to Princess Elizabeth and Prince Philip on 14 November 1948, and of knowing that her great-grandson Charles would be the next Prince of Wales, heir to the throne.

Her health was already beginning to fail when Princess Anne was born on 15 August 1950. She viewed her own imminent death without apparent fear and with characteristic good sense.

'I realize more than ever,' she wrote to her son ten months before the end came, 'that old age & its consequences are a burden one will exchange without murmuring when the time comes for it all to end. Remember this when I am laid to my last long rest.'34

She was staying at Broadlands in the late summer of 1950 when she was taken ill. 'I shan't be coming back here,' she told everyone briskly, including her anxious son Dickie who was back in England with a shore appointment. 'I am going home to London. It is better to die at home.'

She worked out the timetable of her last days and waved away doctors and nurses who might dictate to her. Instead she allowed some nuns to come and help.

She had arranged to be buried at Whippingham Church alongside Louis. It would be cold on the steamer to the Isle of Wight. It always was cold. 'Do not forget to wear your woolly boots for the crossing,' she sternly instructed her lifelong friend Baroness Buxhoeveden, her sister Alicky's last surviving lady-in-waiting.

When she heard that Princess Elizabeth and Prince Philip had postponed their departure on an important visit because of her critical illness she was not pleased. In her judgement, the act of dying was not an important enough business, either for her or for others, to cause the upset of people's plans.

People came to see her for the last time. But she did not die as quickly as she hoped she would, an untidy and unforgivable lapse on her part which made her cross, especially when her grandchildren had to come to see her for a second time. Arrangements, she had always believed, were made to be conformed to. That was one of the basic tenets of her way of life, and it must be upheld in the leaving of it.

On these last mornings she would wake up and open her eyes and find the world a distasteful place.

'Am I still here? I'm not supposed to be here,' she would complain as if she had mis-arranged some appointment.

She died quietly at last, and without pain, on 24 September 1950.

Victoria's life had been a mainly private one. In her 87 years she had known the great artists and scientists, politicians and royalty, musicians from Madame Patti to Malcolm Sargent. Still alive in the second half of the twentieth century, with the world reshaped to its new power structure and adjusting itself to meet new fears and threats, she had also been alive at the same time as men like Wellington and Bismarck who had shaped the two halves of the nineteenth century.

She had known Queen Victoria as a middle-aged woman with young children, the last of the Tsars as an enchanting little boy. She had seen Russia brought twice to her knees and become a super-power, the United States develop into the greatest power of all.

She had witnessed the extreme fluctuations in strength and status of Germany and Japan, France and Britain, and had experienced three crippling European wars, in all of which her family had fought and died.

Victoria Milford Haven had seen the monarchical system at its most flourishing, and at first hand, and had watched its convulsive decline and death almost everywhere except in the country she had adopted and loved most.

She was a mine of knowledge and information in several languages, and when she was an old lady, if there was doubt or argument among her grandchildren they would find themselves saying, 'Let's ask Grandmama.' They did, and she always knew.

Victoria was little known by the general public, wielded little direct power, and will figure in few history books. But her influence was profound and lasting, and the clever, well-ordered mind beneath the untidy façade brought about great changes in public lives and public affairs.

In this age of too many doubts, she will be remembered as a woman who debated furiously in her own mind and with others in order to reach the truth. Once there she held her position tenaciously and unquestioningly. Her example, and the richness and strength of her mind, are remembered more than twenty years later by all who knew her.

Indiscreet and garrulous she certainly was, and to many she appeared as a *dame formidable*. But her loyalties were always beyond question. Her love for Louis was the greatest force in her life, his death the cruellest blow she suffered.

Since she was a child in Darmstadt, she enjoyed writing as well as reading verse. After Louis died she composed a brief epitaph which served equally well for herself twenty-nine years later:

> Then come what will and come what may!
> As long as thou dost live, 'tis day.
> And if the world through we must roam,
> Where ere thou art, there is my home.
> I see thy face so dear to me,
> Shades of the future I do not see.

Reference Notes

ABBREVIATIONS

BA	Broadlands Archives
BM	British Museum
GMH	George Milford Haven ('Georgie'), 2nd Marquess
IWM	Imperial War Museum
JAF	Admiral of the Fleet Lord Fisher of Kilverstone ('Jacky')
Journal	Queen Victoria's Journal, Royal Archives, Windsor
MB	Admiral of the Fleet the Earl Mountbatten of Burma ('Dickie')
NMM	National Maritime Museum, Greenwich
NK	Miss Nona Kerr, later Mrs Richard Crichton
PL	Admiral of the Fleet the Marquess of Milford Haven, formerly Prince Louis of Battenberg
PRO	Public Record Office
QV	Queen Victoria
RA	Royal Archives, Windsor
VMH	Marchioness of Milford Haven, formerly Princess Louis of Battenberg, formerly Princess Victoria of Hesse ('Victoria')
WSC	Winston Churchill

CHAPTER 1 (*pp. 1–26*)

1. Count Egon Corti, *The Downfall of Three Dynasties* (London 1934) 37
2. Princess Marie zu Erbach-Schönberg, *Reminiscences* (London 1925) 4
3. *ibid.*
4. BA, PL to Prince Alexander 2 August 1864
5. *Alice, Grand Duchess of Hesse: Biographical Sketch and Letters* (London 1884) 40
6. *Cited* F. H. Cookridge, *From Battenberg to Mountbatten* (London 1966) 59
7. *Cited* David Duff, *Hessian Tapestry* (London 1967) 102
8. RA Journal 28 April 1863
9. M. Buchanan, *Queen Victoria's Relations* (London 1954) 49
10. *Alice* 75
11. Marie *Reminiscences* 25
12. *Alice* 126
13. Marie *Reminiscences* 53

CHAPTER 2 (*pp. 27–57*)

1. BA, VMH, *Recollections* (1942 unpublished) 1
2. RA Journal 5 April 1863
3. *Alice* 168
4. RA Journal 27 April 1863
5. *Alice* 168
6. VMH, *Recollections* 31–2
7. *Alice* 186
8. VMH, *Recollections* 5
9. *Alice* 240
10. VMH, *Recollections* 3
11. *ibid.* 4
12. *Alice* 219
13. *ibid.* 220
14. *ibid.* 247–8
15. *ibid.* 256
16. *ibid.* 298
17. *ibid.* 305
18. *ibid.* 327
19. *ibid.* 342
20. *ibid.* 348
21. VMH, *Recollections* 30
22. *ibid.* 31
23. *ibid.* 43
24. *ibid.* 39
25. *ibid.* 36
26. *ibid.* 26
27. RA Journal 14 December 1878
28. BA
29. VMH, *Recollections* 50
30. *ibid.* 52
31. BA
32. VMH, *Recollections* 51
33. BA, QV to VMH 3 March 1879
34. *ibid.* 2 April 1879
35. *ibid.* 29 May 1879
36. *ibid.* 4 April 1880
37. *ibid.* 4 November 1879
38. *ibid.* 27 February 1880
39. RA Journal 31 April 1880
40. BA, QV to VMH 7 March 1883
41. VMH, *Recollections* 65

CHAPTER 3 *(pp. 58–81)*

1. BA, PL to Prince Alexander 4 November 1868
2. BA, PL to Pcss Alexander 13 March 1869
3. W. H. Russell, *A Diary in the East* (London 1869)
4. BA, Prince Louis of Battenberg, *Recollections* (Unpublished, undated) 41
5. *ibid.* 40

6. *ibid.* 53
7. BA, PL to Prince Alexander 19 May 1870
8. BA, PL to Pcss Marie of Erbach-Schönberg 23 April 1873
9. *ibid.*
10. *ibid.*
11. BA
12. PL, *Recollections* 90

CHAPTER 4 *(pp. 82–111)*

1. RA, F49/33
2. *Cited* Elizabeth Longford, *Victoria R.I.* (London 1964) 386
3. *The Times* 1 August 1900 8
4. Corti, *Three Dynasties* 241
5. *ibid.*
6. PL, *Recollections* (Unpublished) BA 113–4
7. Corti, *Three Dynasties* 242
8. BA, PL to Pcss Alexander 8 January 1878
9. BA, Prince Alexander to PL 11 April 1877
10. RA, E 53/61, QV to W. H. Smith 10 April 1878
11. PL, *Recollections* 116
12. Corti, *Three Dynasties* 243
13. *Cited ibid.* 251
14. RA Journal 6 & 7 June 1879
15. *ibid.*
16. *Cited* Corti, *Three Dynasties* 257
17. RA Journal 8 June 1879
18. PL, *Recollections* 120
19. *Chips, the Diaries of Sir Henry Channon* (London 1967) 241

20. PL, *Recollections* 126–7
21. *ibid.* 138
22. *The Naval Review* (1935) 384
23. G. Loomis, *Fabulous Admirals* (London 1957) 166
24. *The Naval Review* (1935) 386
25. RA, T8/81, PL to Prince of Wales 13 September 1882
26. BA, QV to VMH 5 July 1880
27. BA
28. BA, QV to VMH 21 August 1885
29. *ibid.* 4 August 1880
30. *ibid.* 23 February 1881
31. *ibid.* 2 April 1882
32. *ibid.* 5 September 1882
33. *ibid.* 23 September 1879
34. *ibid.* 8 December 1880
35. *ibid.* 19 June 1883
36. *ibid.* 22 August 1883
37. RA, Add. U32, QV to Crown Pcss of Prussia 25 June 1883
38. RA, GV AA 43/10

CHAPTER 5 *(pp. 112–134)*

1. BA, QV to VMH 21 September 1883
2. *ibid.* 21 October 1883
3. *ibid.* 25 January 1883
4. *ibid.* 29 July 1883

5. *ibid.* 22 August 1883
6. *ibid.* 1 January 1883
7. RA Journal 15 April 1884
8. *ibid.* 17 April 1884
9. *ibid.* 30 April 1884

393

10. Arthur Ponsonby, *Henry Ponsonby: Queen Victoria's Private Secretary* (London 1942) 301

11. BA, QV to VMH 26 April 1884
12. *ibid.*
13. RA Journal 30 April 1884
14. *Henry Ponsonby* 301
15. *ibid.* 302
16. *ibid.*
17. BA, PL to Prince and Princess Alexander 1 May 1884
18. BA, QV to VMH 20 May 1884
19. *ibid.* 27 June 1884
20. BA, VMH to QV 18 June 1884
21. Baroness Sophie Buxhoeveden, *The Life & Tragedy of Alexandra Feodorovna Empress of Russia* (London 1928) 19

22. BA, VMH to QV 29 June 1884
23. *ibid.* 18 June 1884
24. *ibid.*
25. BA, PL to Prince Alexander 3 July 1884
26. BA, QV to VMH 14 November 1884
27. RA Journal 25 February 1885
28. *Cited* Longford 479
29. BA, QV to VMH 11 July 1885
30. *Vanity Fair* 1 August 1885 65
31. BA, QV to VMH 21 August 1885

CHAPTER 6 (*pp. 135–157*)

1. BA, QV to VMH 1 September 1885
2. *Cited* Virginia Cowles, *The Russian Dagger* (London 1969) 175
3. BA, QV to VMH 9 December 1885
4. BA, Prince Francis Joseph of Battenberg to PL 1 December 1885
5. RA, H30/111–112, PL to QV 30 August 1886
6. BA, QV to VMH 3 September 1886
7. RA (as 5)
8. BA, VMH to QV 16 May 1888
9. BA, QV to VMH 31 March 1889
10. RA, H36/136, PL to QV 1 January 1894
11. BA
12. BA, QV to VMH 4 July 1888
13. BA, VMH to QV 29 September 1888
14. BA, QV to VMH 2 October 1888
15. BA, QV to PL 27 September 1895
16. BA, QV to VMH 30 October 1889
17. *Cited* Longford 542
18. BA, QV to VMH 8 December 1895
19. *ibid.* 2 February 1887
20. E. C. Corti, *The English Empress* (London 1957) 378
21. BA, QV to VMH 15 February 1887
22. *ibid.* 2 March 1887
23. *ibid.*
24. QV to Pcss Frederick of Prussia. *Cited* Longford 512
25. BA, QV to VMH 31 March 1889 (?)
26. *ibid.*
27. *ibid.* 15 July 1890
28. *ibid.* 15 October 1890
29. *ibid.* 15 February 1894
30. *ibid.* 25 May 1894
31. *ibid.*
32. VMH, *Recollections* 155
33. *The Letters of Czar Nicholas and Empress Marie* (London 1937) 82
34. VMH, *Recollections* 152
35. *The Lady* 5 July 1894
36. Author's interview 7 January 1972
37. *ibid.*
38. BA, QV to VMH 22 October 1891
39. Darmstadt Archives, VMH to Grand Duke of Hesse 29 March 1893
40. BA, QV to VMH 24 September 1893
41. *ibid.* 31 March 1895
42. *ibid.*

CHAPTER 7 (*pp. 158–179*)

1. Mark Kerr, *Prince Louis of Battenberg* (London 1934) 109
2. BA, VMH to QV 17 June 1887
3. BA, QV to VMH 10 June 1887
4. *The Broad Arrow & Naval & Military Gazette* 6 August 1887 173
5. *Cited* Kerr, *Battenberg* 111
6. BA, QV to VMH 26 August 1887
7. VMH, *Recollections* 100
8. C. C. Penrose Fitzgerald, *From Sail to Steam* (London 1916) 183
9. *ibid.* 185.
10. *ibid.* 184
11. BA, QV to VMH 22 July 1883
12. RA, E56/111, PL to QV
13. L. King-Hall (Ed.), *Sea Saga:*
Being the Naval Diaries of Four Generations of the King-Hall Family (London 1935) 294
14. RA, E5 6/45, QV to Lord George Hamilton 5 September 1891
15. King-Hall 294
16. *ibid.* 295
17. *ibid.* 294
18. *Cited* Kerr, *Battenberg* 128
19. BA, QV to VMH 15 November 1892
20. BA, VMH to QV 9 March 1889
21. *Cited* Jonathan Steinberg, *Yesterday's Deterrent* (London 1965) 66
22. *Cited Fear God* i 293

CHAPTER 8 (*pp. 180–198*)

1. Bodleian Library. Selborne MSS. 28 January 1905
2. VMH, *Recollections* 168
3. VMH, *Recollections* 171–2
4. BA
5. RA Journal 25 June 1896
6. RA, W56/120, 16 May 1904
7. PL to Selborne 7 June 1904. Selborne MSS.
8. RA, 25/26 W44/198 (PL report to Arthur Balfour 28 August 1904)
9. *ibid.*
10. BA, Edward VII to VMH 3 September & 31 October 1904
11. BA, Edward VII to PL 15 April 1905
12. PRO, Landsdowne MSS. F.O. 800/130
13. BA, Edward VII to PL 15 April 1905
14. Kilverstone MSS.
15. PRO, Cab 37/72 131 2 October 1904
16. Selborne MSS 248 3 October 1904
17. JAF to Beresford 27 October 1902 *Cited Fear God & Dread Nought: The Correspondence of ... Fisher of Kilverstone* ed A. J. Marder (London 1952–9 3 vols) i, 232
18. NMM, Cyprian Bridge MSS Prince Louis to Bridge 11 October 1903
19. JAF to Esher 17 January 1904 *Cited Fear God* ... i, 298
20. Bridge MSS. PL to Bridge 11 October 1903
21. Selborne MSS. Hon. H. Lamb to Selborne 28 January 1905
22. *ibid.* PL to Selborne 12 June 1904
23. BA (undated)
24. JAF to Esher 30 April 1904. *Cited Fear God* ... i 313–4
25. Col. Lord Sydenham of Combe, *My Working Life* (London 1927) 207
26. Prince of Wales to JAF 23 August 1904. *Cited Fear God* ... i 326
27. JAF to Balfour 5 January 1904. *Cited Fear God* ... i 293

28. RA, W57/109, JAF to Edward VIII 15 December 1905
29. Lennoxlove MSS. PL to JAF 17 July 1904
30. BA, Edward VII to PL 15 July 1905
31. *Cited* R. Mackay, *Fisher of Kilverstone* (London 1974) 350

CHAPTER 9 (*pp. 199–221*)

1. RA, Journal 17 July 1900
2. BA, VMH to QV 27 July 1893
3. *See* Sir Frederick ('Fritz') Ponsonby, *Recollections of Three Reigns* (London 1951) 14–15
4. VMH, *Recollections* 205
5. BA. Captain Arthur Barrow RN, then Captain of Whale Island, in an undated memo to Lord Mountbatten
6. *Recollections 3 Reigns* 89–90
7. BA, VMH to NK 25 May 1897
8. *ibid.*
9. *ibid.* 11 October 1901
10. *ibid.* 6 July 1902
11. *ibid.* 19 August 1900
12. VMH, *Recollections* 221–2
13. *ibid.* 224
14. Kerr, *Battenberg* 170–1
15. *ibid.* 171–2
16. Darmstadt Archives, Grand Duke of Hesse – VMH 10 November 1901
17. VMH to NK 23 November 1903
18. VMH, *Recollections* 235
19. *Letters Czar Nicholas* 213
20. VMH, *Recollections*, 249–50
21. BA, VMH to NK 20 January 1907
22. VMH, *Recollections* 277
23. *ibid.* 285
24. BA, GMH to VMH 5 May 1912
25. BA, VMH to NK 20 October 1912
26. *ibid.* 14 February 1913
27. BA, GMH to VMH 20 October 1912
28. J. M. Kenworthy, *Sailors, Statesmen & Others* (London 1933) 39
29. BA, MB to VMH 2 July 1909
30. BA, VMH to MB 16 June 1910
31. *ibid.* 21 June 1910
32. *ibid.* 3 July 1910
33. *ibid.* 8 May 1911
34. *ibid.* 11 July 1911
35. BA, MB to VMH 10 May 1913
36. *ibid.* 24 May 1913

CHAPTER 10 (*pp. 222–239*)

1. Brassey, *Naval Annual,* 1903
2. Admiral Sir S. Fremantle, *My Naval Career* (London 1949) 94
3. IWM, PLB 1/3, President Theodore Roosevelt to PL 14 September 1906
4. J. A. Minter, *The Cruise of the Drake* (London 1907) 4
5. Gerald Sowerby to Lady Mabel Sowerby. *Cited* Kerr, *Battenberg* 186
6. Minter, 141
7. New York *Times* 15 November 1905
8. *ibid.* 21 November 1905
9. BA, PL to NK 23 September 1905
10. Admiral of the Fleet Lord Chatfield, *The Navy & Defence* (London 1942–47 2 vols) i 36
11. Minter, 176–7
12. Chief Yeoman of Signals S. Hills in Memo to MB 1973
13. Commander David Joel RN. Fragment of unpublished Memoirs
14. Vice-Admiral H. T. Baillie-Grohman. Interview with author 13 June 1972
15. Chatfield i 88
16. Vice-Admiral C. V. Usborne, *Blast and Counterblast, cited* P. Padfield, *Aim Straight* (London 1966) 151

17. *ibid.* 85–6

18. Chatfield i 86–7

19. Recollection of J. O. Moon, the driver's grandson. Letter to MB 15 September 1973

20. *Recollections 3 Reigns* 133

21. *Cited* Kerr, *Battenberg* 221

22. Winston Churchill, *World Crisis* (London 1923–9, 4 vols in 5) i 74–5

23. *Cited* Kerr, *Battenberg* 189

24. RA, W51/95, PL to Edward VII 5 September 1906

25. *Recollections 3 Reigns* 132

26. RA, W59/16, JAF to Edward VII 26 March 1908

27. PL to McKenna 1 February 1910. *Cited Fear God* ii 302

CHAPTER 11 (*pp. 240–260*)

1. VMH, *Recollections* 284

2. *Cited Fear God* ii 398

3. RA, Geo V 02580, PL to George V 23 May 1911

4. *ibid.*

5. *ibid.* WSC to Lord Knollys 24 May 1911

6. BA, PL to Asquith 28 June 1912

7. *Cited* Arthur J. Marder, *From the Dreadnought to Scapa Flow* (London 1961–70 5 vols) i 244

8. Selborne to WSC 29 November 1911. *Cited* R. S. Churchill, *Winston S. Churchill* (London 1966–? ? vols. Vols. 1 and 2 by R. S. Churchill, subsequent vols by Martin Gilbert). Companion vols published subsequently. Companion ii Part 2 1346–7. Hereafter cited as *Churchill*

9. *World Crisis* i 67

10. JAF to WSC 25 October 1911. *Cited Fear God* ii 397

11. Dudley Somer, *Haldane of Cloan* (London 1960) 247

12. BM, Jellicoe MSS. 489 90/21 Memo. Jellicoe to McKenna 24 January 1909

13. *John Bull* 2 November 1911

14. JAF to WSC 28–30 October 1911. *Cited Churchill* Companion ii Part 2 1301

15. BA, JAF to PL 13 December 1911

16. Selborne to WSC 29 November 1911. *Cited Churchill* Companion ii Part 2 1346

17. BA, VMH to MB 30 November 1911

18. *See* Admiral Sir P. Gretton, *Former Naval Person* (London 1968)

19. BA document

20. PRO, Cab 37/109 1 January 1912

21. R. B. Haldane, *An Autobiography* (London 1929) 232

22. Gretton 79

23. BA, WSC to PL 21 May 1913

24. *ibid.* 10 November 1911

25. BA, Marshal Memo R.A.F. Sir John Slessor in conversation with MB

26. BM, Balfour MSS. J. S. Sandars to Balfour 10 October 1912

27. *ibid.*

28. RA, GV G286/2

29. RA, WSC 1536 28 March 1912

30. PL to WSC 1 July 1912. *Cited Churchill* Companion ii Part 3 1584

31. V. Bonham-Carter, *Winston Churchill as I Knew Him* (London 1965) 261

32. *ibid.* 253

33. Rear-Admiral W. S. Chalmers, *The Life & Letters of David Earl Beatty* (London 1951) 114

34. JAF to WSC 28–30 October 1911. *Cited Churchill* Companion ii Part 2 1300–1303

35. S. Reynolds, *The Lower Deck* (London 1912) 24

36. *ibid.* 6

37. Commander Harry Pursey RN (Retd). Interview with author 4 January 1972

38. Lt.-Commander H. D. Capper, *Aft – from the Hawsehole* (London 1927) 193-4

39. Rear-Admiral Sir T. J. Spence Lyne, *Something About a Sailor* (London 1940)

40. BA, VMH to NK 14 November 1912

41. BA, Bridgeman to PL 28 April 1912

42. *ibid.* 14 September 1912

43. RA, WSC to George V 29 November 1912. *Cited Churchill* ii 631

44. BA, Bridgeman to PL 3 December 1912

45. *Cited Churchill* Companion ii Part 3 1678

46. *ibid.* 1679

47. PRO, Cab 37/113, Bridgeman to PL 14 December 1912

48. BA, VMH to NK 15 December 1912

49. RA, GV M5 20A/1

50. BA, Quoted in VMH to NK 9 December 1912

CHAPTER 12 (*pp. 261–286*)

1. VMH, *Recollections* 288

2. Buxhoeveden 144

3. BA, Empress of Russia to Pcss. Bariatinsky 28 October 1910

4. *ibid.* 29 December 1911

5. Pcss. Marie Louise, *My Memories of Six Reigns* (London 1956) 1961

6. BA, Empress of Russia to Pcss. Bariatinsky 11 December 1912

7. *Letters Czar Nicholas* 265–6

8. BA, Grand Duke of Hesse to VMH 12 March 1912

9. *ibid.* 3 April 1912

10. MB Interview with author 2 November 1972

11. *Dreadnought Scapa Flow* i 255

12. *ibid.* 254

13. BA, Poore to PL 5 November 1913

14. See *Dreadnought Scapa Flow* i 260-1

15. IWM, PL to Samson 28 August 1911

16. *ibid.* 29 October 1911

17. PRO, Cab 37/115 35

18. PRO, CID Meeting 6 December 1912

19. IWM, Samson to PL 19 September 1911

20. BA, PL to WSC 12 November 1913

21. C. Ernest Frayle, *Seaborne Trade* (London 1920–4 3 vols) i 45

22. PRO, CID Meeting 21 May 1914

23. JAF to Jellicoe 25 May 1914. *Cited Fear God* ii 506

24. JAF, *Records* (London 1919) 184

25. *World Crisis* ii 280

26. PRO, Cab 37/118

27. Beaverbrook Library Lloyd George MSS. C. P. Scott to Lloyd George 29 February 1914

28. *See Churchill* ii 668

29. BA, WSC to PL 13 February 1914

30. RA, GV M520A/1, PL to George V 5 December 1912

31. BA, WSC to PL 5 June 1913

32. *World Crisis* i 197

33. BA, MB to VMH 22 July 1914

34. *World Crisis* i 197

35. *ibid.* 198

36. BA, Based on PL's conversations with VMH, MB and Pcss. Louise of Battenberg, later Queen Louise of Sweden

37. *World Crisis* i 433

38. *ibid.* 212

39. *ibid.*

40. Fremantle 171

CHAPTER 13 (pp. 287–299)

1. VMH, *Recollections* 303
2. NMM, Milne MSS. PL to Milne 27 August 1914
3. 'A Gentleman with a Duster' (Harold Begbie), *The Mirrors of Downing Street* (London 2nd Ed. 1920) 122
4. *World Crisis* i 239–41
5. *Winston Churchill as I Knew Him* 219
6. (Southborough Papers) Stamfordham to Hopwood 6 October 1914. *Cited Churchill* Companion iii Part 1 175
7. IWM, PL Naval Papers. Recollections of Admiral C. S. Townsend

(then Captain Townsend), Duty Captain at the time, who overheard the conversation.
8. (Montague Papers) Asquith to Venetia Stanley 6 October 1914. *Cited Churchill* Companion iii Part 1 173
9. BM, Jellicoe MSS. 48990/149 1 August 1914
10. MB Interview with author 29 November 1972
11. *See* Captain G. Bennett RN, *Coronel & the Falklands* (London 1962) 79

CHAPTER 14 (pp. 300–336)

1. BA, MB to VMH September 1914
2. BA, Violet Bonham-Carter to MB 10 January 1968
3. *Something About a Sailor*
4. (Montagu Papers) Asquith to Venetia Stanley 20 October 1914. *Cited Churchill* Companion iii Part 1 206
5. BA, MB to VMH 18 October 1914
6. *World Crisis* i 395
7. (Montagu Papers) Asquith to Venetia Stanley 27 October 1914. *Cited Churchill* Companion iii Part 1 220
8. BA, Violet Bonham-Carter to MB 10 January 1968
9. RA, Add U32 28 October 1914
10. (Montagu Papers) Asquith to Venetia Stanley 28 October 1914. *Cited Churchill* Companion iii Part 1 223
11. *World Crisis* i 400
12. BA, WSC to PL 28 October 1914
13. The Duke of Windsor, *A King's Story* (London 1951) 108
14. *World Crisis* i fn 400–1
15. PL to WSC 28 October 1914. *Cited Churchill* Companion iii Part 1 226–7
16. RA, GV AA 43/249

17. BA, VMH to NK 25 October 1914
18. BA
19. BM, Balfour MSS. 49694 WSC to Balfour 17 September 1915
20. BA, MB to VMH 19 May 1915
21. Princess Alice, Countess of Athlone. Interview with author 7 January 1972
22. Kilverstone MSS. JAF to WSC 9 November 1911
23 BA, PL to NK 20 November 1914
24. *ibid.*
25. BA 3 September 1915
26. BA, VMH to NK 25 May 1915
27. BA, PL to Admiral Sir Frederic Hamilton 2 April 1916
28. MB to G. N. Pocock 27 May 1917. Pocock Papers
29. BA, PL to Admiral Sir Frederic Hamilton 2 April 1916
30. BA
31. BA
32. BA, VMH to NK 7 June 1917
33. *ibid.* 11 June 1917
34. *ibid.* 22 August 1916
35. *ibid.*
36. *ibid.* 12 May 1915
37. *ibid.* 22 August 1916

38. BA, VMH to QV 4 March 1895
39. BA, Diary extracts enclosed with letter from General Sir Henry Jackson to MB 15 December 1959
40. BA, VMH to NK 3 January 1917
41. PRO, Cab. Balfour to Lloyd George 16 January 1917
42. BA, MB to VMH 16 March 1917
43. BA, VMH to NK 18 March 1917
44. *ibid.*
45. BA, Dorothy Seymour diary extracts (*See* 39 *above*)
46. BA, VMH to NK 3 September 1918, enclosure
47. BA, VMH to Whittemore 14 September 1918
48. BA, VMH to NK 10 November 1918
49. Channon, *Diaries*, 175
50. BA, VMH to NK 6 February 1919
51. BA, PL to Princess of Erbach-Schönberg 4 February 1921
52. RA, KGV Q711/3
53. BA, MB to VMH 1 January 1919
54. BA, Lee to Stamfordham 8 August 1921
55. BA, Stamfordham to Lee 9 August 1921
56. BA, MB to VMH 6 September 1921
57. Admiral Baillie-Grohman. Interview with author 13 June 1972
58. Admiral Sir William James, *A Great Seaman: the Life of Admiral of the Fleet Sir H. Oliver* (London 1956) 118–9
59. (Esher MSS) Admiral Sir Charles Ottley to Lord Esher 25 October 1911. *Cited Dreadnought Scapa Flow* i 407 fn.
60. Admiral of the Fleet Sir R. Keyes, *Naval Memoirs*, 1910–15 (London 1934) 128
61. RA, XV/34, PL to Ponsonby 15 May 1907
62. RA, GV CC45/602, VMH to Queen Mary 15 September 1921

CHAPTER 15 (*pp. 337–360*)

1. BA, VMH to NK 6 February 1920
2. Interview MB 2 November 1972
3. BA, VMH to NK 3 August 1919
4. BA, VMH to MB 1 September 1919
5. Interview MB 29 November 1973
6. BA, VMH to MB 1 September 1919
7. *ibid.* 23 February 1922
8. BA, VMH to Edwina Ashley 27 March 1922
9. *The Times* 19 July 1922
10. BA, VMH to MB 18 July 1922
11. Margit Fjellman, *Louise Mountbatten, Queen of Sweden* (London 1968) 98
12. *Cited ibid.* 99
13. BA, VMH to NK 16 February 1919
14. *ibid.* 3 November 1919
15. Prince Andrew of Greece, *Towards Disaster* (London 1930). From the Introduction by Princess Andrew of Greece
16. *Cited* B. Boothroyd, *Philip* (London 1971) 81
17. BA, Pcss Andrew of Greece to NK 30 October 1924
18. BA, VMH to NK 7 April 1926
19. *ibid.* 14 June 1921
20. *ibid.* 10 September 1909
21. *ibid.* 20 June 1926
22. *ibid.* 21 August 1926
23. Interview H.R.H. Prince Philip 12 April 1972
24. BA, VMH to NK 14 March 1933

25. *ibid.* 6 April 1933
26. Prince Philip Pprs. VMH to Prince Philip 31 March 1938
27. *ibid.* 30 December 1934
28. *ibid.* ? 1936 (undated)

29. BA, VMH to MB 5 November 1935
30. *ibid.*
31. Interview H.M. Queen Elizabeth II 11 July 1972

CHAPTER 16 (*pp. 361–390*)

1. BA, VMH to NK 14 March 1933
2. *ibid.* 12 September 1937
3. Prince Philip Pprs. VMH to Prince Philip 16 December 1935
4. *ibid.* 29 October 1937
5. *ibid.*
6. BA, VMH to NK 30 January 1938
7. Prince Philip Pprs. VMH to Prince Philip 3 February 1938
8. Interview Lady Brabourne 23 October 1972
9. BA, VMH to MB 26 September 1939
10. *ibid.* 28 September 1939
11. Interview Princess George of Hanover 21 November 1972
12. Interview Princess Margarita of Hohenlohe-Langenburg 21 November 1972
13. Interview Lady Brabourne 23 October 1972
14. *ibid.*
15. Interview Lady Pamela Hicks 2 October 1973
16. BA, VMH to MB 14 December 1939
17. *ibid.*
18. *ibid.* 17 May 1941

19. *ibid.* 9 January 1944
20. BA, VMH to NK 6 April 1943
21. *ibid.* ? June 1944
22. Interview H.M. Queen Elizabeth the Queen Mother 3 February 1972
23. BA, VMH to NK 7 January 1941
24. BA, VMH to MB 16 November 1941
25. *ibid.* 25 August 1943
26. BA, VMH to MB 25 August 1943
27. BA, VMH to NK 5 November 1944
28. Lady Pamela Hicks Pprs. VMH to Lady Pamela Hicks 6 November 1944
29. BA, VMH to MB and Lady Mountbatten 13 July 1947
30. BA, VMH to MB 8 January 1950
31. Recollection of Lady Brabourne. Interview 23 October 1973
32. BA, VMH to MB 23 August 1947
33. BA, VMH to MB 8 January 1950
34. *ibid.* 28 December 1949

Index

Compiled by Philip Guy, member of the Society of Indexers

BATTENBERG – *contd.*

Louis, Princess of (Princess Victoria of Hesse). *See* Milford Haven, Marchioness of

Louis ('Dickie'), Prince of. *See* Mountbatten of Burma, Earl

Louise, Princess of. *See* Sweden, Queen of

Marie, Princess of. *See* Erbach-Schönberg, Princess Gustavus of

Maurice, Prince of, 284, 307

Bay of Biscay, 66

Beaconsfield, Lord, 103, 203

Beamish, Rear-Admiral Tufton, 234, 301

Beatrice, Princess, carrier of haemophilia, 37; *not* to marry, according to Queen Victoria, 55; forbidden to talk to Prince Louis, 74; in love with Prince Henry of Battenberg, 121, 129; 1885 – marriage of, 132; Prince Henry's death, 145; at Grand Duke Ernest Louis's wedding, 157; mentioned, 17, 372

Beatty, Admiral Sir David, 65, 254, 291–292, 310

Beaverbrook, Lord, attack on Lord Louis Mountbatten, 379

Belgians, King Leopold of the, 41, 284

Benares, 78

Bender, Hof Prediger, 28

Berehaven, 236

Beresford, Lord Charles, 81, 104, 190, 193, 196, 197, 302, 336

Berlin, Irving, 229

Bermuda, 68

Bernhardt, Sarah, 97

Besika Bay, 85

Besserabia, 139

Bismarck, Prince, 22, 94

Blakeney, Norfolk, 350, 353

Blankenberge, 44

Blèriot, L, 215

Blücher, Countess, 16

Borissoglebosky 17th Lancers, Prince Alexander made Colonel-in-Chief of, 4

Bottomley, Horatio, 246, 302, 304, 306

Brabourne, Lady, 371

Breslau, 292

Bridge, Admiral Sir Cyprian, 192

Bridgeman, Admiral Sir Francis, 247, 257, 260

Bridport, Lord, 115

Brindisi, 33, 65, 166, 349

Bristol, training ship, 61

Britannia, 61

Britten, Commander Richard F., 87

Broadlands, Hampshire, 234, 345, 374–375, 388

Brooke House, London, 342, 354

Brooke, General Sir Alan, 380

Brown, John, 49, 84, 114

Buccleuch, Duchess of, 159

Buccleuch, Duke of, 100, 115

Buchanan, Sir George, 287, 324

Buckingham Palace, 42, 56, 75–76, 145, 159, 177, 207, 253, 286, 331

BULGARIA:

Alexander, Prince of. *See* Battenberg, Prince Alexander of

Ferdinand, Prince of, 182

Bullers, General Sir Redvers, 178

Burke's Peerage, 319

Burlington House, 358

Burney, Dr., 59

Buxhoeveden, Baroness Sophie, 287, 323, 389

Calcutta, 78

Callaghan, Admiral, Sir George, 296

Calypso, H.M.S., 348

Cambrian, 172, 174

Cannes, 52

Capper, Henry D., 256

Carlton Club, London, 302

Carlyle, 45

Carmen, S.M.S., 217

Casa Medina, 359

Cassel, Sir Ernest, 342, 375

Cecil, Lord Robert, 327

Challenger, H.M.S., 72

Chalturin, Stephen, 95

Channel Fleet, 69, 174, 190

Channon, Sir Henry, 98, 328

Charles, Prince of Wales, 388

Charlottenburg Palace, 147

Chatfield, Admiral of the Fleet Lord, 234

405

Martha and Mary Convent, 323

Mary, Queen, engagement to Prince Albert Victor, 149; marriage to Prince George, 149; 1911 – coronation of, 241; letter of condolence to Princess Victoria, 336; 1922 – at Lord Louis Mountbatten's wedding, 344

Matapan, Battle of, 374

Maud, Princess. *See* Norway, Queen Maud of

May, Admiral Sir William, 101

Mayfly, 270

Meade, Captain the Hon. Herbert, 343

Mediterranean Fleet, 81, 85, 162, 238, 311–2

Melbourne, Lord, 37

Men-of-War Names, 174

Messina, 85

Michailovna, Grand Duchess Catherine, 5

MILFORD HAVEN:

David, 3rd Marquess of, 367

George, 2nd Marquess of, 1892 – birth of, 175; at Mr. Moreton's school at Cliveden Place, 201; a naval cadet, 212; enthusiastic supporter of naval flying, 215; serving on board the *Colossus*, 216; reunion with his father at Gibraltar, 232; appointed senior midshipman of the *Cochrane*, 240; lieutenant in the battle cruiser *New Zealand*, 273; with the Fleet at the outbreak of war, 287; eventful and dangerous life in battle cruisers, 315; 1916 – the Battle of Jutland, 317; marriage of, 327; the second Marquess of Milford Haven, 345; 1932 – retirement from the Royal Navy, 359; the Queen's memories of his kindness, 360; a mathematical brain, 359; broken leg and cancer of the bone, 365; 1938 – death of, 365

Louis, 1st Marquess of (Admiral Prince Louis of Battenberg), 1854 – birth of, 11; appearance, 14, 24,

73, 168; responsibility for his three younger brothers, 15; playing at Heiligenberg, 24; interest in the sea, 25; wish to join the Royal Navy, 26; 1868 – preparations to join the Royal Navy, 58–59; oath of allegiance to the Queen, 60; joining the Royal Navy on passing his examinations, 61; 1869 – Christmas at Heiligenberg, 61; the glamorous figure in his smart British naval uniform, 45; life as a midshipman aboard *Ariadne*, 62; 1869 – arrival at Alexandria, 63; hunting on the Nile, 63; Medjidieh, Fourth Class, 64; 'Into the, Valley of Death', 65; Osmanieh, Fourth Class, 65; his first cigarette from the King of Greece, 65; gunroom cruelty, 65; unable to endure the Royal Navy, and the Prince of Wales' advice, 66; 1869 – appointment to the flagship *Royal Alfred*, 67; 1870 – homecoming for his confirmation, 56, 72; gaining a reputation as a Lothario, 70; visit to New York, 70–71; his sobriety, 71; 1872 – meeting with his cousin Alexei, 71; letters to his relatives, 72; 1873 – homesickness, 72; temptations of the social scene, 74; Princess Beatrice forbidden to talk to him, 74; 1874 – at the Royal Naval College, Greenwich, 75; wearing Ludwig order over the wrong shoulder, 75; passing out first at seamanship, 76; 1875 – at Marlborough House, 76; invitation to accompany the Prince of Wales to India, 78; memorandum from Queen Victoria's secretary supporting his integrity and loyalty, 82; appointment to the battleship *Sultan*, 85; at the centre of a political storm, 88; desperately worried about Prince Alexander ("Sandro"), 88; 1878 – the defence of Constantinople, 88; visit of Prince Alexander to the *Sultan*,

MILFORD HAVEN, Louis 1st – *contd.*
medals, 315; invitations to carry
out public tasks and sit on committees, 318; informed that he
must change his name, 319; 1917 –
suggestion that he be sent as an
emissary to the Tsar, 324; Grand
Duchess Elizabeth's burial in Jerusalem, 329; meeting with Father
Seraphim, 329; request to George
V to be placed on the retired list,
330; the sale of Heiligenberg, 330;
visit to Princess Alice in Greece,
331; 1921 – invitation to take the
chair at a Royal Navy Club
dinner, 331; made Admiral of the
Fleet, 332; cruise with his son in
Repulse, 332; sudden death of, 333
Nada, Marchioness of, 327
Victoria, Marchioness of (Princess
Victoria of Hesse, Princess Louis of
Battenberg), 1863 – birth of, 28;
nurses and governesses, 29–30;
passion for reading, 30; sharing her
joys, sorrows and secrets with
Princess Elizabeth, 30; 1867 – first
visit to England and a review at
Spithead, 31; memories of the
Franco-Prussian War, 33; helping
the wounded, 34; 1871 – celebrations at the declaration of peace,
35; memories of Prince Frederick's
death, 39; appearance, 40, 53, 168,
370; thriving on controversy, 40;
journeys around Europe, 41; improving visits to national institutions in London, 41; passion for
dare-devilry and animals, 43;
development of her tastes and
intellectual enthusiasm, 45; strict
regularity at New Palace and the
'awful' food of England, 46; 1878
– outbreak of diphtheria at Darmstadt, 46; letters from Queen
Victoria, 49, 107, 109, 135, 137,
147–52, 155, 157, 167; memories
of Prince Leopold, 51; a confirmed
smoker at sixteen, 53; 1880 – confirmation at Darmstadt and the visit

of Queen Victoria, 54; visit to
Eastbourne, 56; 1882 – engagement of, 57; her family's disapproval of the match with Prince
Louis, 106; turning to Queen
Victoria for guidance, 107–109;
plans for the wedding and Queen
Victoria's ripening affection for
her, 112; breaking the news to
Queen Victoria of her father's
intention to marry Madame de
Kolemine, 117; 1884 – marriage
of, 118–119; honeymoon, 122–123;
arrival at St. Petersburg for Princess Elizabeth's wedding, 125;
1885 – birth of Princess Alice, 130;
news of her brothers-in-laws' abduction from Sofia, 138; supervision of Princess Alix's programme before her marriage, 151;
accompanying her to Harrogate,
152; the house at Walton-on-
Thames, 152; her fear of haemophilia, 156, 357; 1887 – typhoid,
158; impressions of Malta, 164;
visit to Prince Henry and Princess
Irène in Kiel, 167; 1889 – birth of
Princess Louise, 167; love of
galleries, museums, archaeology
and gardening, 168–169; long
drives with Queen Victoria at
Nice, 172; 1892 – birth of Prince
George, 175; discovery of Princess
Alice's deafness and the worry of it,
175–176; a house in Eccleston
Square, 176; instilling in her
children a sense of pleasure in
knowledge and inquiry, 177; 1896
– at the coronation of Tsar Nicholas and the Tsarina, 180; 1900 –
birth of Prince Louis ('Dickie'),
200; 1901 – summoned to Osborne
for Queen Victoria's last days, 201;
1897 – decision to have a permanent lady-in-waiting, 204; recognition of Grand Duke Ernest
Louis's impossible marriage, 209;
comforting Ernest Louis on the
death of his daughter, 210;